IN THE NATION'S SERVICE

IN
THE NATION'S
SERVICE

*The Life
and Times
of
George P. Shultz*

PHILIP TAUBMAN

STANFORD UNIVERSITY PRESS
Stanford, California

Stanford University Press
Stanford, California

Printed in Canada on acid-free, archival-quality paper

Library of Congress Cataloging-in-Publication Data

Names: Taubman, Philip, author.
Title: In the nation's service : the life and times of George P. Shultz / Philip Taubman.
Description: Stanford, California : Stanford University Press, [2023] | Includes bibliographical references and index.
Identifiers: LCCN 2022012995 (print) | LCCN 2022012996 (ebook) | ISBN 9781503631120 (cloth) | ISBN 9781503633667 (ebook)
Subjects: LCSH: Shultz, George P., 1920–2021. | Statesmen—United States—Biography. | Cabinet officers—United States—Biography. | United States—Foreign relations—1981–1989. | United States—Politics and government—1945–1989. | LCGFT: Biographies.
Classification: LCC E840.8.S535 T38 2023 (print) | LCC E840.8.S535 (ebook) | DDC 327.2092 [B]—dc23/eng/20220615
LC record available at https://lccn.loc.gov/2022012995
LC ebook record available at https://lccn.loc.gov/2022012996

Cover design: George Kirkpatrick
Cover photograph: George Pratt Shultz. George Pratt Shultz papers, Box 2456, Folder 13, Hoover Institution Library & Archives.
Text design: Rob Ehle

To Felicity, and for our grandchildren, Sophia and Avery

CONTENTS

Contents

photo sections follow pages 122 and 314

PREFACE

*Without Reagan the cold war would not have ended, but without
Shultz, Reagan would not have ended the cold war.*
—MIKHAIL GORBACHEV[1]

DEFTLY SOLVING CRITICAL BUT intractable national and global problems
was the leitmotif of George Pratt Shultz's life. No one at the highest levels
of the US government did it better or with greater consequence in the last
half of the twentieth century, often against withering resistance. His quiet,
effective leadership altered the arc of history.

The Shultz model of public service seems almost quaint today, relying as
it did on common sense, trust, a human touch, openness to new ideas and
the muting of ideology, partisanship and histrionics. But it is actually quite
relevant in our discordant day. While political, social and cultural dynamics
have changed profoundly since Shultz served at the commanding heights of
American power in the 1970s and 1980s, his legacy and the lessons of his
career have enduring meaning as the nation and world seek to heal divisions
and subdue the ruinous polarization of recent years. The example of George
Shultz's effective leadership can serve as a guide to creating a more temperate time, a return, if one is possible, to an era when patriotism is defined by
what Americans can do together and individually to lift their country rather
than demolish their opponents and silence opposing points of view.

Shultz represented a form of conservatism that has been all but erased in
recent years by Trumpism and its acolytes in the Republican Party. The roots
of Shultz's conservatism can be found in Edmund Burke, Milton Friedman

and the leadership of people such as Dwight Eisenhower, General George Marshall and Ronald Reagan, not the conspiracy theories of QAnon or the unruly passions of the mob that stormed the Capitol on January 6, 2021. Shultz developed a knack for solving the most difficult problems as a labor economist and business school dean and applied it successfully across two Republican presidencies. Tackling knotty problems in Washington is hard work. The capital runs on high-octane partisanship and one-upmanship. More so now than ever, but Washington was hardly a kumbaya town during the Nixon and Reagan administrations. Open-minded, even-handed pragmatists with a gentle touch rarely thrive or last long.

Shultz survived this tumult, joining an elite club as one of only two people in American history to hold four cabinet posts.[2] Despite the inhospitable Washington environment, he recorded historic achievements during the Nixon administration as labor secretary, budget director and treasury secretary. Applying his problem-solving acumen, he helped turn the unfulfilled promise of the landmark 1954 Supreme Court ruling, *Brown v. Board of Education*, toward reality by coaxing Southern states to desegregate public schools. He accelerated integration of the building trades and other unionized industries. Based on a Shultz design, Washington engineered changes in international monetary practices, scrapping the fixed exchange rate system between foreign currencies and the dollar that was codified in the 1944 Bretton Woods Agreement. Under the Shultz plan, foreign currencies were delinked from the value of the dollar and price of American gold reserves, in effect, establishing floating exchange rates, a system that continues to this day.

Shultz's approach nearly fizzled during the Reagan presidency. He came to town in 1982 as secretary of state with a vision of easing cold war tensions and ran into a buzz saw of opposition among anti-Soviet ideologues in Reagan's inner circle and the neglect of an inattentive president. For several years, he was adroitly outmaneuvered by rivals and bewildered by the disarray in the Reagan national security team. But he persisted. With a combination of determination, resilience, competitiveness, multiple resignation threats and an abiding faith that anything is possible when people come to trust one another, he slowly forged a remarkable partnership with President Reagan. Together they played a pivotal role in solving the biggest global problem of the second half of the twentieth century, the cold war.

They did so in concert with two other men prepared to think outside cold war doctrinal boundaries, Mikhail Gorbachev, the Soviet leader, and his foreign minister, Eduard Shevardnadze.

In chronicling the end of the cold war, scholars and journalists have understandably concentrated on Reagan and Gorbachev and the critical, constructive endgame roles played by President George H. W. Bush and his secretary of state, James A. Baker III. Shultz received less credit and attention, partly because of his circumspection and his conviction that his role was primarily in service to Ronald Reagan. His modesty was admirable, if a tad feigned. It was also misleading. He deserves a great deal of credit. Once he gained Reagan's trust with a vital assist from Nancy Reagan, Shultz helped Reagan act on his own genuine but muffled desire to improve relations with Moscow and reduce the danger of nuclear war. Shultz translated Reagan's better instincts into practical policies and a productive diplomatic agenda with the Kremlin. In essence, he made it possible for Reagan to break free of the ideological warriors who surrounded him and his own belligerent anti-Soviet rhetoric. "I have always thought that letting Reagan be Reagan means a self-confident and positive approach," Shultz said.[3] In Gorbachev and Shevardnadze, Reagan and Shultz found negotiating partners motivated by a faltering Soviet economy, unsustainable defense spending and their own wish to wind down the cold war.

Shultz's decisive role belies the proposition that Reagan came to power with a coherent vision of how to handle the Soviet Union and then brilliantly executed it. In this view, he skillfully combined combative rhetoric, muscular policies and large defense investments to coerce the Kremlin to the negotiating table and make concessions. Indeed, there were plenty of bombastic declarations, unyielding policies and a huge military buildup, all of which put pressure on the Kremlin. But by the fourth year of the Reagan presidency, there was little productive diplomacy in motion to capitalize on Reagan's hard-line tactics. If Reagan had a clear vision in mind from the outset, he seemed incapable of moving beyond the intimidation phase until Shultz settled into his job, developed a diplomatic strategy and became America's chief negotiator with the Kremlin.

National security documents, including detailed records of Shultz's numerous negotiating sessions with Gorbachev and Shevardnadze, make clear how indispensable Shultz was. During hundreds of hours of talks with Shevardnadze and dozens of hours with Gorbachev from 1985 to 1989, Shultz dexterously guided the United States and Soviet Union toward agreements and understandings that resolved or eased many cold war conflicts. Reagan and Gorbachev operated in the limelight and got most of the credit, but Shultz and Shevardnadze made the progress possible through their tireless, patient work in the diplomatic trenches.

I first met George Shultz aboard a US Air Force plane in June 1983 on the opening leg of a flight from Washington to Manila. Not quite a year after becoming secretary of state, he was heading to a meeting of the Association of Southeast Asian Nations. I was in my fourth year as a Washington reporter for the *New York Times*, assigned to cover the Shultz trip after the newspaper's chief diplomatic correspondent, Bernard Gwertzman, demurred to focus on other matters in the capital.

Shultz invited me to join him briefly in the secretary's quarters at the front of the cabin as the plane cruised toward a refueling stop in Anchorage. He welcomed me aboard, exchanged pleasantries and introduced me to the small group of senior government officials traveling with him. Later in the flight, I joined half a dozen fellow reporters from the *Washington Post*, ABC News and other organizations for a thirty-minute airborne press conference with Shultz. I quickly discovered, as the veteran reporters aboard the plane had foreshadowed, that Shultz rarely made news in his interactions with journalists. Over the next week, I accompanied Shultz to the Philippines, Thailand, India and Pakistan. In a change of plans, he announced that instead of heading home for the Fourth of July, we were adding stops in Saudi Arabia, Lebanon, Syria, Israel and Egypt.

Over the next few years I intermittently covered Shultz while focusing my attention on American military and intelligence operations in Central America. On a multistop trip with him to Latin America in early 1984, he suggested I bring along my tennis racquet, and we spent a few hours playing singles one afternoon in Rio. His steady, unflashy tennis game was like the man himself. I could see that he was an embattled figure in the Reagan administration, often at odds with Caspar Weinberger, the secretary of defense; William Casey, the director of Central Intelligence; William Clark, the national security adviser; and a host of other officials who considered Shultz dangerously eager to temper Washington's stormy relationship with Moscow.

In 1985, I relocated to the *Times'* Moscow bureau, a spectacular vantage point to observe the twilight of the cold war, improbably engineered by none other than Ronald Reagan, working with Gorbachev. The two unlikely peacemakers were constantly attended and aided by their respective foreign ministers, Shultz and Shevardnadze. I chronicled the rapidly unfolding developments from Moscow, with side trips to European capitals and Washington, encountering Shultz at various places where he intersected with Gorbachev or Shevardnadze, including summit meetings in Iceland, Washington and Moscow. In January 1989, Reagan and Shultz exited government, and the cold war rapidly defrosted. Like others who covered the Reagan presidency, I was curious to understand why and how Ronald Reagan had flipped from anti-Communist crusader to diplomatic dealmaker with the Kremlin and what role Shultz played in that transformation.

So I was intrigued when Shultz inquired one day in 2010, when we were both based at Stanford, if I might be interested in writing his biography. As an inducement, he offered exclusive access to his papers, housed in a sealed archive at the Hoover Institution, where Shultz had set up shop when the Reagan presidency ended. After retiring from the *Times* in 2008, I had relocated to Stanford's Center for International Security and Cooperation and was just starting work on a book about the joint effort of Shultz and four other cold war figures to abolish nuclear weapons. As I neared completion of the book a few years later, I agreed to tackle the Shultz biography.

By then, with some initial access granted by Shultz, I had discovered in the archive materials an insider account of Shultz's first years as secretary of state. The voluminous diary, chronicled by Shultz's first executive assistant, offered an unvarnished look at Shultz's protracted struggle to overcome his opponents, a brutal brawl that matched, and at times exceeded, other postwar White House power struggles. The journal also described the hidden hand of Nancy Reagan as she reached out to assist Shultz in his tortuous effort to build a trusting relationship with an aloof Ronald Reagan. When I told Shultz I was ready to begin work, he instantly accepted my proviso about editorial independence: "It's your life but my book." He honored that understanding, never pressing me to bend the book to his liking.

By the time Shultz died on February 6, 2021, just weeks after he celebrated his centennial birthday, I had learned a great deal about him that I failed to divine in our early encounters nearly forty years earlier. The multidimensional Shultz I came to know was a protean figure who left an enduring mark on American and world history. A longtime Republican and vigorous free-market advocate, Shultz was exceptionally open-minded and guided by an uncommon degree of common sense. He was even-tempered and patient, sometimes to a fault. He shunned the limelight, listened intently to all comers and rarely rushed to judgment. His early background as a faculty member at the Massachusetts Institute of Technology and professor and dean at the University of Chicago were apparent in the careful way he weighed issues and time he devoted to reading history.

He could be prescient about the economic, social and political impact of new technologies and the long-term effects of changing demographics. Long before most national leaders understood that new information technologies were destined to alter their societies in fundamental ways, Shultz gave Gorbachev two unsolicited tutorials on the advent of a new information age and the threat it posed to insular governments. He recognized the coming of climate change and called for radical steps to combat it. In his last years, he frequently drew attention to the aging populations of Japan and China and explosive population growth in Africa as factors likely to alter the global economy in coming decades. In 2014, in words that foreshadowed the 2022 Russian invasion of Ukraine, Shultz seconded the analysis of a former State Department colleague who warned that Russian president Vladimir Putin was intent on dominating the newly independent states on Russia's border that had once been part of the Soviet Union. To contend with Putin's expansionist ambitions, Shultz said, "Americans will have to rise to the occasion by building a consensus, hard as that may be, around our own goals in a world awash in change."[4]

Shultz had a gift for forging trusting relationships with people and then harnessing the rapport to address national and international challenges. "Trust is the coin of the realm," he would often say. He tended meticulously to his working relationships with domestic and foreign leaders, dealing with small problems before they escalated into big problems, and maintained a constant stream of correspondence and gracious courtesy notes. He called it "diplomatic gardening." As he said, "If you plant a garden and ignore it for six months, it's taken over by weeds. But if you keep at it, month after month, then it grows. In diplomacy, the same thing is true."[5]

All these traits formed the foundation for his problem-solving efforts. He added to the groundwork a simple but highly effective formula he developed: "As long as people are arguing about principle, you can't get anywhere," he liked to say. "If you can translate the disagreements into problems, people are pretty good at solving problems." He managed large organizations inclusively and humanely, a rare practice in Washington. James Goodby, a veteran American ambassador, has never forgotten the day that he and Shultz stepped into the Oval Office to meet with President Reagan. In a show of respect to Goodby, Shultz guided him to the wingback chair next to the president, usually reserved for the most important guest.

After leaving government service in 1989, Shultz refocused his interest on nuclear threats, leading an inspiring campaign to abolish nuclear weapons and draw attention to nuclear dangers. It ultimately failed to make much headway toward eliminating the weapons. He also addressed climate change, sustainability, health care, federal entitlement programs and an array of other vital issues, tirelessly working these problems in a nonpartisan way right up to his death.

Donald Trump's 2016 presidential campaign unsettled Shultz, but he wavered over whether to speak out. He eventually settled for a joint statement with Henry Kissinger in which the two former Republican secretaries of state said they would not endorse Trump or Hillary Clinton but would work to foster a bipartisan foreign policy. The written statement was unveiled in 2016 on the Friday before Labor Day weekend, guaranteeing it would receive scant media coverage.

Shultz grew increasingly alarmed as the Trump presidency unfolded but generally refrained from publicly rebuking Trump and a nativist Republican Party that was barely recognizable to him. The few exceptions were notable. In a February 2017 appearance at the Olympic Club in San Francisco, Shultz lamented Trump's anti-immigration policies and quoted at length a Reagan speech celebrating the history of immigration in America. After Trump inexplicably defended and deferred to Vladimir Putin at a joint news conference with the Russian leader following their July 2018 meeting in Helsinki, Shultz sent word to journalists that he fully agreed with John McCain's comment about Trump's performance. McCain called it "one of the most disgraceful performances by an American president in memory. The damage inflicted by President Trump's naiveté, egotism, false equivalence, and sympathy for autocrats is difficult to calculate. But it is clear that the summit in Helsinki was a tragic mistake."[6]

Shortly before the 2020 election, Shultz criticized Trump's management of foreign policy. "After nearly four years of an administration that seems to have assumed that American relations with the rest of the world is a zero-sum game and that the game is based largely on the personal relations between national leaders, distrust abounds internationally," he wrote in an essay in the *Foreign Service Journal*. "The ability of the United States government to execute the president's foreign policies has become severely limited by the lack of a clear and coherent method of formulating policy. The president's use of social media to make frequent public reversals and revisions in policies has made the job of America's diplomats exceptionally complex."[7]

Sadly, Shultz did not publicly question Secretary of State Mike Pompeo's failure to defend the foreign service and Marie Yovanovitch, the US ambassador in Ukraine, after she came under baseless fire in 2019 from Rudy Giuliani, Trump's personal lawyer. At the time, Giuliani and Trump were trying to get Ukraine to investigate Joe Biden's son, Hunter, for his dealings with a Ukrainian energy company. Ambassador Yovanovitch was abruptly recalled and her career effectively terminated by the State Department.

As the years passed, I discovered that Shultz loved a good party and was quick to sing and dance in private and public settings, even look ridiculous when the occasion called for it, as occurred a few years ago when he donned a Superman costume in a skit in the grand lobby at San Francisco City Hall, rescuing a woman in distress, played by his wife, Charlotte, who descended in a harness from the ceiling while pleading for help.

Yet for all his success and competence, Shultz sometimes struggled to command a room, to get his way, to stand up for principles that he considered paramount. At times, he seemed guileless. These patterns were rooted in a tendency to defer to his bosses, a powerful sense of loyalty and a belief that manipulative efforts to outmaneuver opponents were destructive to orderly decision-making. The dynamics led to a puzzling degree of inaction at critical junctures in his career. This was evident in his reluctance to leave the Nixon administration as the Watergate scandal engulfed the president and Shultz himself was drawn into an improper, White House–instigated tax investigation of Lawrence O'Brien, a Democratic Party leader, by the Internal Revenue Service (IRS). That episode is for the first time fully revealed in this book.

As secretary of state, he was unable for several years to cut through the opposition and force Reagan to reckon with a dysfunctional national security policy-making team. Shultz opposed the sale of American arms to Iran in exchange for the release of American hostages held by Iranian proxies in the Middle East, but for months he stopped short of insisting that the operation be ended. Over time, unbeknownst to Shultz, profits from the arms sales were illegally diverted to fund antigovernment insurgents in Nicaragua.

In recent years, Shultz defended Theranos, a Silicon Valley biomedical company, after his grandson, who was employed there, informed him that the firm's widely touted claims about its blood-testing technology were exaggerated and deceptive. Shultz was enchanted with the company founder, Elizabeth Holmes, believed the new technology was a medical breakthrough and played a key role in drawing media attention and funding to the company. When Tyler Shultz came to his grandfather for help after Theranos threatened him with legal action for questioning its technology, George Shultz declined to disown Holmes. The episode sundered the Shultz family and shocked his friends. Shultz's conduct may have been partly motivated by financial considerations. His holdings in Theranos stock were worth nearly fifty million dollars at peak valuation.[8] On January 4, 2022, a federal jury convicted Holmes of wire fraud and conspiracy in her dealings with Theranos investors.[9]

Whatever Shultz's shortcomings and blind spots, the historical record shows that he was certainly one of the most influential, accomplished and sensible American leaders as the nation traversed the tumultuous decades of the late twentieth century. Thomas Simons, who worked closely with Shultz at the State Department and served as an American diplomat for thirty-five years, said, "George Shultz is the most distinguished servant of the American state of the twentieth century."[10] Henry Kissinger, who doubted Shultz's suitability to be secretary of state when nominated by Reagan in 1982, said some years ago, "If I could choose one American to whom I would entrust the nation's fate in a crisis, it would be George Shultz." About Shultz's collaboration with Reagan, Kissinger noted, "His contribution, first of all, was to bring the sort of diffuse thinking of the Reagan administration into a coherent pattern and to establish a method of work. George translated the instincts of a man he admired into operational policy, and in a very steady and very thoughtful way."[11] Colin Powell, Reagan's last national security adviser, put it this way: "George was magnificent in his ability to understand the president. I admired Shultz not only for his intellectual powers, but for the way he determinedly managed to put substance into Ronald Reagan's vision."[12]

Robert Gates, a senior CIA official at the time and later defense secretary, questioned the wisdom of Shultz's effort to warm up relations with the Kremlin, doubting the Soviet Union could fundamentally change. But he admired Shultz's ability to act on Ronald Reagan's inner impulse to tone down the cold war. Gates said, "Shultz, virtually alone in the administration's senior foreign policy team, perceived that Ronald Reagan saw America's resurgent military power and its challenge to Soviet assertiveness worldwide as a means to an end—to reduce nuclear weapons and, through a more constructive relationship, to take steps to promote a more peaceful world. When Reagan said these things publicly, most members of his own team, the press, and the public wrote it off as a political theater. Only Shultz seems to have grasped that Reagan was really serious and meant what he said."[13]

Eduard Shevardnadze's estimation of Shultz was more emotional. When I met him in Tbilisi in 2012, he was severely weakened by advanced Parkinson's disease. After struggling to walk from his desk to a sofa with the help of two aides, he instructed his longtime assistant to give him a small stack of papers at the far end of the large office where he had served as president of the newly independent Republic of Georgia after the disintegration of the Soviet Union in 1991. After briefly studying the materials, he handed them to me. They were Christmas cards from George Shultz and his wife, Charlotte. "I saved them," Shevardnadze said. "My friendship with George means so much to me."[14]

Much has been written over the years about the end of the cold war. Don Oberdorfer, the late *Washington Post* diplomatic correspondent, published a fine account before the ravages of dementia felled him. Though we worked for rival newspapers, Don warmly welcomed me to the diplomatic beat in 1983 and generously helped me navigate the fast-paced travels of a secretary of state. Other works include a compelling firsthand account by Jack Matlock, who served at the White House and in Moscow during the Reagan presidency; deeply researched histories by John Lewis Gaddis, a Yale historian, and Robert Service, an Oxford scholar; and George Shultz's own 1993 memoir, to name just a few.[15] I learned a great deal from all and have tried in this biography to help fill out the emerging history. In recounting Shultz's tenure as secretary of state, I have focused largely on his role in managing East-West relations, especially the Reagan administration's handling of the Soviet Union.

This book is the story of how an unexceptional boy born in New York City and raised in Englewood, New Jersey, who showed few signs of greatness in school or college, became a molder of history, played a singular role in unwinding the cold war and set a lofty standard for public service.

IN THE NATION'S SERVICE

PART I

Early Years

CHAPTER ONE

"Grow Up a Real Man"

GEORGE PRATT SHULTZ GREW up steeped in the history of his family and America and was proud of both. In 1640, twenty years after the *Mayflower* sailed, the Pratt family, his mother's kinfolk, arrived in Massachusetts from England. On his father's side, Mark Shultz, a Hessian mercenary who fought with the British during the Revolutionary War, eventually became a Virginia landowner. Over time, the Pratts and Shultzes moved west. "The Shultz family history is an American saga," George Shultz liked to say. "You can almost see a microcosm of United States history, at least that part with European roots. People came to the United States with motivation and they made their way in a new society."[1]

Birl Earl Shultz, George's father, was born in 1883 in Union City, located ninety-five miles northeast of Indianapolis in Randolph County, Indiana, on the state line with Ohio. Less than two decades earlier, five newly built rail lines converged in Union City, making it a major Midwest rail hub. His parents, William Edward and Cora Alexander Shultz, were natives of the county. Birl was raised as a Quaker on the nearby family farm. He became the first person in the family to attend college after winning a scholarship to DePauw University in Greencastle, forty miles southwest of Indianapolis. Birl Shultz played football and lettered for the DePauw Tigers for four years. From there he went on to earn a PhD in political science at Columbia University.

He clearly had further professorial ambitions. George Shultz remembers his father as an "instinctive scholar,"[2] and he might have "wanted to teach in a university but jobs were not so plentiful."[3] Instead, Birl became a different kind of educator in 1923, joining the New York Stock Exchange Institute as educational director. Located in the New York Stock Exchange building in Lower Manhattan, the institute was founded as the stock market began booming, with the Dow Jones Industrial Average increasing from 63 in August 1921 to 381 in September 1929. George Shultz's own academic aspirations, and early intent to make a career as a scholar, may well have been rooted in his father's academic ambitions and Shultz's desire to establish himself as a respected faculty member at academic heights that had eluded his father. Shultz's work as a professor at MIT, tenured faculty member and dean at the University of Chicago and part-time professor at Stanford business school seems at least partly inspired by an inner drive to overcome his father's thwarted Ivy League career aspirations.

In New York, Birl met Margaret Lennox Pratt, the daughter of Edward Pratt, a Presbyterian missionary, and Agnes White Welsh, an emigrant from Scotland.[4] Her father, a New York native, had journeyed west to extend the reach of the church, and Margaret was born in 1886 in Bellevue, Idaho Territory, and spent her early years in Shoshone, a tiny frontier town forty miles farther south.[5] Edward Pratt, who sported magnificently frizzy sideburns alongside a long, crooked nose, ministered to the many workers who toiled in the surrounding silver, gold and lead mines.[6]

After her parents died, Margaret was sent as a young girl to New York City to live with her uncle George Starkweather Pratt and his wife, Margaret Whitney Pratt.[7] George Pratt was an ordained Episcopalian priest who presided over the Church of the Archangel (All Souls' Church after 1906) at St. Nicholas Avenue and 114th Street in Harlem, a "very fancy parish" at the time, noted George Shultz.[8] Margaret Pratt grew up down the street at 88 St. Nicholas Avenue in the rector's "rather grand apartment," as her son remembered the place.[9] He recounted that she was "in effect raised as an only child" by her childless aunt and uncle,[10] reared with strong religious values and "very high standards for everything that she did or was involved in" during a childhood surrounded by missionaries, pastors and the church faithful.[11]

Margaret married Birl Earl Shultz on January 22, 1916, six months before Birl graduated from Columbia. The Reverend George Pratt, Margaret's uncle, officiated at the ceremony at All Souls' Church. The bride, wearing "a gown of white satin veiled with chiffon" and holding a bouquet of roses and lilies of the valley, was given away by her aunt, reported the *New York Times*.[12] Quite petite, she barely came up to her new husband's shoulder. Birl, the former football player, was a broad-shouldered man with large ears and round spectacles perched on a fleshy nose. Their son, George Pratt Shultz, was born at the New York Nursery and Child's Hospital at Amsterdam Avenue and Sixty-First Street at 2:24 a.m. on December 13, 1920. He was baptized three months later at All Souls' Episcopal Church, where his mother's uncle had long officiated. George Starkweather Pratt had died in July 1920, just months before George Shultz's birth.[13]

His earliest pictures show an alert infant, round-cheeked and sturdy. His mother diligently chronicled his developments in her slanted cursive hand, noting that his first tooth was "discovered right after breakfast" in July 1921. When George was two or three, the small family moved to Englewood, New Jersey, across the Hudson River from Manhattan.[14] Englewood was an affluent suburb, nicknamed "the bedroom of Wall Street" because its convenient location attracted powerful Manhattan bankers and financiers. These men built fabulous mansions on the desirable East Hill neighborhood and on the Englewood Cliffs overlooking the Hudson River.

The New York area, like much of the nation, enjoyed a burst of economic growth and prosperity in the decade after World War I. Between 1920 and 1929, the country's total wealth doubled, prompting Americans to rush to acquire new symbols of progress and comfort, especially cars. For the first time in the country's history, more Americans lived in urban areas than in rural regions. Englewood, too, was enjoying the boom. The town's population tripled between 1900 and 1930.[15] Its wealthy businessmen commuted to Manhattan on a ferry named *Englewood*, while artists and entertainers could easily get from Englewood to the studios in Fort Lee, home to America's first major film industry.[16] The construction trade was thriving, especially for East Hill estates, and the business district attracted shoppers from across northern New Jersey.

As Englewood grew and flourished, the Shultzes moved to Ward Three, one of the more humble sections of town. Shultz's lifelong friend Norman "Topper" Cook recalled that, as children in Englewood, they were well aware of the distance between the moneyed residents of Ward One's East

Hill and their own part of town: "We were not full of confidence. . . . It was sort of a struggle" to be so close to such affluence and yet stand apart from it all.[17] Birl Shultz had a good job—indeed, like many of the residents of East Hill, he also commuted to Wall Street—but their three-bedroom Dutch colonial house at 156 Rockwood Place was decidedly not a banker's mansion.

But even if they were "a little bit on the outs" in the stratified society of Englewood, as Cook reports, George Shultz loved his home. He played in its spacious attic. His mother grew grapes in the backyard, and he would eat them while lying on the grass in the summer.[18] Beyond its material comforts, the Shultz home was filled with warmth and security: Shultz affirmed that "my parents loved me, and I knew it. They made me a part of their life, so I was surrounded by whatever the conversation was when we were all at home."[19] He was an only child, and his parents consistently nurtured and encouraged him. His early life was steady and sheltered. "Basically, I lived all of my life growing up in that one house in Englewood with a constant set of friends around there."[20] The stability and warmth that permeated the Shultz household engendered a sense of self-confidence and equanimity in Shultz that grew stronger over the years. The love and trust that Birl and Margaret provided at home established a safe base from which Shultz could venture into the world and deal with successes and setbacks without losing his equilibrium, as well as relate to his environment and the people around him with a steady, open self-assurance.

As in many families of the early twentieth century, Birl worked while Margaret managed the house. Much of young George's interaction with his father took place beyond the confines of the house. On Saturdays, he would often accompany his father on the bus and subway to his office at the New York Stock Exchange. While Birl worked through the morning, his son would busy himself with small office tasks. Then the real fun began: the pair would go to a nearby deli called BMT for three-decker sandwiches, "the most wonderful sandwiches I've ever had in my life." Shultz recalled that he "would look forward to them all week long."[21]

Birl was "big on sports," his son said, and he encouraged athleticism and competition.[22] The pair played catch "endlessly" on the front lawn and regularly attended Columbia football games at Baker Field, at the northern tip of Manhattan.[23] One photo from 1928, when Shultz was seven years old, depicts a beaming, sandy-haired boy dressed in white standing next to his bespectacled father at San Francisco's new Kezar Stadium, a stop made possible by Birl's work travel.[24] Shultz's early introduction to sports instilled a strong sense of personal responsibility that he carried throughout his life: "I've come to feel that sports are a tremendous teacher of accountability and ethics, and it's built into you because there are rules and you follow the rules, and it's pretty relentless. If you drop a pass, you've dropped the pass. There it is: you dropped the pass. Accountability."[25]

At home, Margaret presided in an atmosphere of exacting standards, where, in her son's account, "whatever she did had to be first-class."[26] This made a lasting impression on her son, who set high standards for himself at work and at home as his life progressed. Raised in a strong religious setting, she exercised control over the family's churchgoing activities. They joined St. Paul's Episcopal Church in Englewood, the Quaker Birl with some reluctance. George Shultz was confirmed in the church and sang in its choir as a child, though his most vivid memory is of sneaking away from choir practice to see *Dracula* at the Englewood theater— which "scared the hell out of me," he remembered.[27] Margaret was "relatively quiet," her influence subtle but unmistakable:[28] George Shultz reflected that "she had standards and that . . . that affects you, you know. So you're supposed to do things right."[29]

While Birl took George into the city for sandwiches and sports, Margaret made the Englewood house a quiet refuge. She infused the home with the smell of delicious treats, such as spice cake and lemon chill, always made with an abundance of butter. She read aloud from treasured children's books. Decades later, Shultz could still quote verses from A. A. Milne's *When We Were Very Young*, the book that he remembered her reading "more than any other."[30] Over her son's protests, Margaret insisted that he attend Miss Florence's Dancing School. As Shultz remembered it, the boys had to ask the girl of their choice for a dance. Hanging back, uncomfortable in his white gloves, he "wound up with the girl left over."[31] That was a lesson, he laughed: "It's better to pick out the one you want and go after her."[32] And he did learn to dance, an activity he loved throughout his life, thanks to his mother's early perseverance. "She was wonderful," Shultz said. "I have a picture of her in my office where I sit and I look at it."[33]

Birl and Margaret emphasized the importance of education and ethics. George Shultz recalled, "As I look back, they put me in a position where I had to decide things, and then, whatever the consequences were, I had to recognize them."[34] They were supportive parents without being indulgent. Shultz's college friend Jim Baldwin contended that "George was an only child, and you'd never know it."[35] Birl and Margaret were not strict disciplinarians, and Shultz did not recall ever being spanked. Instead, they instructed him subtly, leading by example: "They didn't talk about ethical issues, but they lived an ethical life. I guess I'd put it that way. We were comfortable but not well off. But it was clear that they put a lot of value on education."[36]

In primary school, Shultz began attending the private Englewood School for Boys, newly opened in 1928 for fifty students in a rented house and barn in the most affluent part of town, East Hill. At school, as at home, excellence was expected. Shultz recalled an English teacher, Mr. Metzger, "whose motto was 'good enough is not good enough.' So he kept setting standards."[37] Sports were his primary pursuit in those days. Shultz acknowledged that "the academic program was good, and I liked it and did well, but I remember most vividly the athletics."[38] The school's athletic resources were limited. Its football field was less than full-scale and there was no basketball court, so Shultz and his friends used the next-door First Presbyterian Church's gym for practice. Although the school's sporting facilities were modest, Shultz says that "it provided the best kind of education" for a young athlete like himself.[39] His was an active childhood: basketball and football at school, tennis and baseball in the summers, skating in the winter, bicycling year-round. Shultz's childhood athletic experiences fostered a powerful, lifelong competitive spirit that remained strong throughout his life, often startling family and friends in its intensity on tennis courts, golf courses, executive suites and government offices. His son Alex mused, "I don't think any of us are as competitive as he is."[40]

When Shultz was about twelve, he was seized with an entrepreneurial spirit and started a neighborhood newspaper, an enterprise that "didn't last long," he laughed.[41] He peddled his *Weekly News* on Saturdays at the cost of five cents a copy, until one of his neighbors, waving a copy of the *Saturday Evening Post*, told him, "I got this for five cents. Do you think I should pay the same price for your paper?"[42] That episode marked the unceremonious end of the *Weekly News*, but his brief foray into the newspaper business provided him with his "first education on the creativity of the competitive market" and the dynamics of free-market economics.[43] His faith in the power of the marketplace grew over time and defined his economic outlook and an abiding faith in capitalism that shaped his work as an economist and a government official.

George Shultz's parents set exceedingly high expectations for their only child, expectations that left an enduring, if unrealistic, belief in him that others were guided by similar standards. In 1932, on the occasion of George's twelfth birthday, his father wrote him a typed letter conveying not only the joy George had brought to his parents but also their hope that "some day you would be a credit to your Mother and Father." It was a somber, portentous letter that must have registered profoundly with the boy and played an important, if unconscious, role in propelling him into a life of scholarship and public service. Living up to his parents' expectations put a great deal of pressure on Shultz as he entered adolescence. Birl Shultz's letter went on: "We hoped that you would be healthy, ambitious, successful and respected; a man worthy of our hopes. We planned for the time when you would attend College, that you may receive a real education which would inspire you to lofty ideals, noble deeds and great achievements and merit the respect of those who are interested in you, and also the community at large."[44]

Birl envisioned a clear path for George: Phillips Exeter Academy, Princeton, and then Harvard Business School or Columbia Law School, a sequence designed to "equip you with almost every possible weapon with which to tackle the field of business or law." These ambitions set a dauntingly high bar for a boy of twelve. The commanding tone of Birl's letter carried with it an expectation that George would defer to his parents' wishes and follow the path they had laid out. There seems little doubt that the letter, and the family atmosphere it reflected, engendered in Shultz a respect for authority that grew over time. Birl's exhortation to "merit the respect" of the community implied a reverence for social and professional status that he did not enjoy himself. His son inherited the itch.[45]

For Birl, who had journeyed from a rural Indiana farm to Wall Street, education was the vital resource to which his son should look to secure his future. In the event of Birl's death, a provision made through the Equitable Life Assurance Society would "supply the necessary money" for George's schooling through university. Birl reminded the twelve-year-old that "your

mother and I have made great sacrifices in order that you might have this
opportunity of receiving an education, in order to place you on equal foot-
ing with all educated men." In enjoining his son to "grow up a real man, a
pride to your family and a credit to yourself," Birl may have been reacting
to a recent distressing event: his own father, William Elwood Shultz, had
just died on August 27, 1932, at the age of seventy-five. This reminder of his
own mortality echoes through his birthday letter to George. Birl informs
his son that "life is uncertain" and evokes his own ephemerality and the
possibility of his "not [being] with you in person to help you acquire that
education" so greatly needed to meet one's "task in life." He goes on to note
that if "your mother does not survive me, you will be compelled to shift for
yourself."[46]

Beyond the death of his father, a national crisis may have been lurking
behind Birl's sobering words. George Shultz was eight years old when the
stock market collapsed in October 1929. By the time Birl wrote his birthday
letter in December 1932, over 20 percent of the American workforce was
unemployed. Birl's job and salary at the New York Stock Exchange Institute
were secure, but his son recalled being "very conscious of the drama on Wall
Street."[47] George Shultz was not among the three million American children who were forced by economic necessity to leave school,[48] but "it was
obvious that we had tough times" even at home in Englewood.[49] He was
deeply aware of the Great Depression, and it left a lasting impact on him.
He recalled, "You grow up in that period and what are people talking about
all through the 1930s is, 'What can we do about the economy?'"[50]

President Franklin Roosevelt's New Deal programs introduced Shultz
to the world of politics. Shultz's Republican identity is rooted in his view of
the New Deal, for his earliest consciousness of government was intertwined
with Roosevelt's policies, immersing him, he said, "almost without realizing it, in the debate of what's government's role in the economy: what works
and what doesn't work."[51] As far as he could see, the government programs
designed to put Americans back to work and revive the economy were not
generating a new era of prosperity as the months advanced. Tens of millions
of Americans remained unemployed two years after Roosevelt took office.
At the same time, the government was powerless in the face of the Dust
Bowl, as a combination of excessive plowing of prairie grasses, overgrazing
by cattle, drought and strong winds generated devastating dust storms in

the southwestern Great Plains that forced hundreds of thousands of Americans to flee their homes.

To Shultz, unlike many Americans who believed fervently in Roosevelt's decisive leadership, it added up to a stunning case of failed government action. "Here I am, it's in the 1930s," he recalled. "I'm in my teens. And of course you're aware there's a Depression. And here comes Roosevelt, and he has all these interventions in the economy and, as I remember, you sort of hoped they'd work but you could see they didn't. . . . So I was a Republican."[52] Birl was a lifelong Republican, though "not in any fierce way," his son clarified, so it was unsurprising that George would instinctively lean toward the GOP.[53] Margaret's political leanings were less clear. George Shultz remembered his father being afraid that she would "cancel his vote" after women's suffrage was legalized, suggesting that she may have voted Democrat.[54] Though political discussions don't seem to have been an overriding preoccupation at home, his father had an enormous influence on his own views. George Shultz was the son of a self-made man who had clambered up from the Indiana countryside to a Wall Street desk without government aid, where he trained stock exchange clerks in the art of the free market. His son regarded Roosevelt's big government actions warily, "seeing this big intrusion and hoping it would work and realizing it didn't work very well" to pull the country out of the Depression.[55]

Roosevelt forged on with these "intrusions" as his presidency moved into what is known as the Second New Deal. The Works Progress Administration, created in April 1935, employed more than three million people in its first year of operation.[56] The National Youth Administration, created in June 1935, aimed to reduce the school drop-out rate by providing part-time jobs to young people. Roosevelt signed the Social Security Act in August of the same year. By the 1936 presidential election, there were four million fewer unemployed Americans than the thirteen million jobless at the height of the Depression in 1933.[57] On November 3, 1936, Americans went to the polls. The Republican challenger, Kansas governor Alf Landon, was pulverized.[58] Roosevelt won every state except Maine and Vermont.

Most Americans were paying little attention to ominous developments in Europe. Three years before the 1936 American election, Adolf Hitler was appointed chancellor of Germany by President Paul von Hindenburg. Hitler, who had published his Nazi manifesto, *Mein Kampf*, in 1925, used a fire at the Reichstag and the resulting emergency decree in February 1933 as a pretext to consolidate Nazi power. In 1935, Hitler announced the Nuremberg Laws, which stripped German Jews of their civil rights as German citizens.

In the year of Roosevelt's reelection, the fifteen-year-old George Shultz left home for the first extended period. Both he and Topper Cook, his friend since early childhood, were dispatched to elite New England boarding schools—"finishing school[s]," in Cook's words—to "brush up in order to go to Princeton."[59] Cook went off to Phillips Exeter Academy in New Hampshire, while Shultz enrolled at the Loomis School in Windsor, Connecticut, for his last two years of high school. At Loomis, he was one of 331 students, all male, of whom 215 were boarders and 116 were day students. Shultz appreciated Loomis's demanding academic standards and enthusiastically enrolled in courses across an array of fields, including history, art, and French.

As in Englewood, he was drawn to the athletic fields at Loomis. He continued to play football and basketball, and after he didn't make the baseball team, he added tennis to his athletic program.[60] He was active in the badminton and table tennis clubs as well. His parents often came up to Loomis on weekends to visit. They watched him play sports for the school but didn't intrude on his school life. "It meant something to me that they were in the stands and rooting," Shultz recalled.[61] Shultz's competitive drive intensified after an encounter with Frank Boyden,[62] the long-serving headmaster of Deerfield Academy, another New England prep school. During a tennis match against a Deerfield student, Shultz recalled, "I was beating this guy and Boyden watched for a while. I thought I should butter him up. So I said, 'Well, it's a pretty good player over there,' and he said, 'Kid, with an attitude like that, you'll never win,' and he walked off. So of course then I really beat the hell out of him."[63]

From Loomis, Shultz enrolled at Princeton, which had long been a goal, with Topper Cook, whose father, an influential figure for both young men, was an enthusiastic alumnus.[64] The two Englewood boys roomed together their freshman year in Brown Hall, a neo-Renaissance/classic revival dormitory that dated from the 1890s.[65] Princeton was a clubby school with a distinctly Southern aura, a reflection of the many men from affluent Southern families who came north to study there. The names inscribed on the

Civil War tablet in Princeton's Memorial Hall were divided equally between North and South, despite the school's geographically north location.
The campus featured spacious lawns, Gothic arches and ornate carvings.
For some graduates, including F. Scott Fitzgerald, it conjured images of an
endless, carefree existence.[66]

Shultz arrived at Princeton in the fall of 1938, as the world was heading toward war. In March 1938, just months before Shultz resettled at
Princeton, Germany annexed Austria. During Shultz's freshman fall, Germany also began its occupation of the Sudetenland after the appeasement of
Britain, France and Italy. On November 9, 1938, Hitler unleashed Kristall-
nacht, the "Night of Broken Glass," as Nazi forces ransacked thousands of
Jewish homes, businesses and synagogues. As many as thirty thousand Jews
were arrested and sent to concentration camps. In the Soviet Union, Stalin
was strengthening his control over the Communist Party by purging party
members, government officials and Red Army generals. In Asia, Imperial
Japan was on the move.

At Princeton, safely ensconced amid the ivy-covered buildings, many of
Shultz's classmates harbored noninterventionist views. Their position mirrored that of much of America. With the sacrifices of the Great War still
vivid for many Americans, the nation was isolationist. Mired in economic
depression, Americans had little interest in engaging in another devastating international conflict when its domestic struggles were so acute. The
isolationist stance persisted even as Germany and the Soviet Union signed
the cynical Molotov-Ribbentrop nonaggression pact in August 1939 and
as Germany invaded Poland on September 1, 1939. Britain and France
declared war on Germany two days later. Although many American students wanted to provide some aid to beleaguered nations and to stem the
rising tide of fascism, they continued to agitate against American military
involvement.

Reportedly, six hundred Princeton students—the size of an entire undergraduate class—supported the American Independence League, an antiwar
organization, within days of its formation in the fall of 1939.[67] Princeton
men were not entirely removed from the possibility of war, of course. Enrollment in the Reserve Officers' Training Corps (ROTC) jumped to a new
high of 470 students that same fall.[68] This corresponded to the escalation
of the war in Europe. Between May and June 1940, German mechanized

forces swept across Belgium, Holland and France, demonstrating the brutal efficiency of blitzkrieg warfare.

Sheltered below the elms and red oaks of Princeton, Shultz focused on his studies in economics, his major, and took courses offered by the School of Public and International Affairs. Through his affiliation with that school, he received a "real orientation to public policy," especially in a role-playing course he took his senior year:

> What they did was take a project of some kind, and one semester it would be a domestic project and the next semester it would be an international one, and you had a role . . . you were assigned a role. You were the secretary of the Treasury or you were the foreign minister of Japan or you were something, so you had to study and try to figure out what . . . if you were in that role, what would your point of view be and why, and play that out. And I found it . . . I thought it was just terrific. I learned a lot from it.[69]

This interdisciplinary program provided Shultz with a taste of global affairs and government work and negotiation. At the time, though, he wasn't "totally oriented to government," he recalls. "Business applications of economics were also interesting."[70]

Between Shultz's sophomore and junior years at Princeton, he worked as a security analyst at a New York investment advisory house headed by Benjamin Graham. Shultz was impressed by the reach of Graham's knowledge. Here was a man who could have buried himself in numbers and details, but instead he was engaged in world events and thinking critically about their ramifications. For Shultz, immersed in his studies at Princeton, this was an impactful reminder that the outside world could not be shut out. Shultz recalled, "His book is full of the detailed way you do security analysis, but when he was looking at the investment picture, he was looking very broadly. That was a big lesson."[71]

Shultz appreciated the importance of finance and investment but knew early on that he did not want to throw himself into that world. Instead, he said, "I wanted to be in what I thought of as the real economy, and education was part of the real economy."[72] Birl was deeply versed in the language of Wall Street, but through an educational lens. His son wanted to integrate economics and education, applying economics to the real-life problems he observed in the midst of the Great Depression. It was a pivotal decision for the young Shultz, and it set him on an academic and career track that equipped him to operate successfully in the academic world, private sector and government service. The common element, as he realized early on, was to focus on developing practical answers to concrete problems rather than theoretical solutions to abstract challenges.

As Europe grew increasingly unsettled by Hitler's belligerence, life at Princeton remained tranquil. During his junior and senior years, Shultz lived at "lovely 13 Blair Hall,"[73] in Topper Cook's words, which was Princeton's first collegiate Gothic residence, adorned with brick chimneys and iron lantern brackets at each entry.[74] He shared a two-bedroom suite with Topper and another friend, John Brooks, in Blair entry number one.[75] Their Blair entry comprised mostly members of the Quadrangle eating club, whose atmosphere was less snobbish than that of some of the older Princeton clubs.[76] Shultz and Topper joined Quadrangle at the end of their sophomore year.[77]

Jim Baldwin considered their Quadrangle group to be fairly ordinary and down to earth: "They were a bunch of regular guys."[78] Quadrangle was a social group, not a political or academic one, and much of their time together was spent in fun. They ate lunch and dinner at Quadrangle and often played bridge or backgammon after eating. The group did well academically, but they "weren't a bunch of intellectual crazies," in Baldwin's words.[79] A trip to the city was a rare treat for this group.[80] Their interactions with women were fairly limited. Princeton did not admit women until 1969, so they had to find dates at women's colleges, such as Bryn Mawr and Vassar, or bring a woman from home to Princeton events. These barriers meant that "there weren't many women in our lives at that time," in Baldwin's estimation.

Neither of the two women Shultz recalled dating at Princeton proved to be a long-term prospect. One of them was Roxy Park, a girl from Shultz's hometown, whom he remembered bringing down to Princeton a few times. The other was Pinky Peterson. Pinky not only lived in Princeton, but she also had a car, which was quite a coup for Shultz: "At Princeton, you weren't allowed to have a car, so now I had a girl with a car."[81] On winter afternoons, the two would drive over to Lake Carnegie, a reservoir at the eastern end of the campus that had been donated to the university by Andrew Carnegie, the steel magnate and philanthropist. In a scene he later described with clear affection, Pinky would lace up her figure skates and swirl around the lake, dancing gaily to music playing on the car radio that Shultz set at high volume. Standing by the car in the afternoon cold, with the door swung wide open so the radio could be heard on the lake, Shultz would happily watch her skim across the ice. "She had a great capacity to enjoy herself and to help everyone around her do the same," he wrote to her daughter in 1996, after learning of Pinky's death. "She was a really lovely person and I only wish I had seen more of her."[82]

Shultz was not a standout in either Quadrangle or his Blair entry. He was well liked, but he was not a leader among the group. He was thoughtful and hardworking, and he earned good grades, but he did not make Phi Beta Kappa as Jim Baldwin or some of his other dormmates did. Decades later, when Shultz was serving as secretary of state, his former dormmate John Brooks noted, "Maybe he's brilliant now. He wasn't then. He had a steady, plodding intellect."[83] Shultz was considered "serious but not too serious," not an academic "grind" like some of his classmates, asserts Jim Baldwin. Simply put, he did not distinguish himself among his close friends as one destined for bigger things. He was, said Baldwin, simply "one of the guys."[84]

At the same time, though, his friends remember a certain consistent development on Shultz's part during their time at Princeton. Topper Cook, who had known him since early childhood, noted that though they were academically comparable in childhood and the "pretty average kind of kids,"[85] "the story of George Shultz is continual, continuous advancements. He got better at everything. Brighter."[86] Bob Young concurred, explaining that Shultz became "more and more focused."[87] When the group got together in the evenings, Brooks recalled that he and Topper would "say sort of half-baked, wisecrack things, and [Shultz] would think a long time and take them very seriously."[88] He showed no flashes of genius but rather a steady growth, marked by a sense of integrity that, to Bob Young, "stood out even when he was in college."[89]

Shultz's senior thesis—every Princeton student is required to produce one to graduate—provided an enduring lesson in the importance of learning through experience rather than just from books, theories and data. And it deeply impressed Shultz with the value of coming up with sensible solutions to challenging problems. These realizations led to a lifelong reliance on experiential learning and a proclivity to unpack complex problems dispassionately. Shultz's thesis examined "The Agricultural Program of the Tennessee Valley Authority." Congress and newly elected President Roosevelt had created the TVA in 1933 as a public corporation to manage the economic development of the Tennessee Valley. Shultz embarked on a summer of fieldwork to explore the TVA's impact.[90] Furnished with a scholarship for the summer before his senior year, he first journeyed to Washington, DC, to collect statistics before arriving in Knoxville, Tennessee, where the TVA was headquartered.[91] He then spent two weeks living in the Tennessee mountains with what he described as a "hillbilly family," Claud Young and his wife.[92]

By letting them talk and helping them fill out forms for the TVA, he uncovered the immense distance between TVA headquarters in Knoxville and the realities of life in rural Tennessee, to say nothing of the remoteness of Washington. The TVA practice was to provide farmers with fertilizer. The farmers were then expected to report back on conservation practices and agricultural progress. Far from the highbrow and cerebral haunts of Princeton, Shultz saw another side to the data that he had accumulated in Knoxville and in Washington. In helping the Youngs fill out their TVA forms, Shultz realized that "the farmers knew what the government wanted to hear. They wanted to keep the fertilizer coming, and they had a kind of ethic that you don't falsify things. On the other hand, everything is tilted, I began to see, so that they'd be sure that they got fertilizer, which they wanted. They got it free."[93]

He saw that "behind the numbers was a lot of plus or minus," unrecorded and unanalyzed by the theorists behind their desks:[94] "So I said, you know, a number is not what it looks like. And I've always felt that if you look at any number, your first question you have to ask is, where did it come from?"[95] He said he grew to respect the Youngs, who "taught me a lot."[96] Though the couple had received "no real education," he had observed their shrewd way of bending the TVA's aims to their own goals and way of making a living from the land.[97] In his thesis, dedicated to his parents and submitted in March 1942, Shultz noted that "the administering agency must recognize and respect the existing social patterns and values existing in the milieu where it plans to function" if the TVA hoped to function effectively.[98]

Returning to Princeton after his summer in the field, he began preparing for his senior season of football. At the beginning of his senior season, he was in the best shape of his life—the sandy-haired boy had grown into a nearly six-foot-tall dark-haired young man with broad shoulders. "[I] really felt that I was impressing the coaches and I had a crack at making the team" for the varsity roster.[99] In one of the first skirmishes of the year, he was blocked from behind at knee height, and his left knee was ripped apart. His running back hopes ended in an instant.[100] He was then asked to be the coach of the freshman backfield. It was his first management position, and he thrived in it. He delighted in fostering the skills of his players and was especially tickled when, in scrimmages against the varsity team, some of his freshmen outran and outmaneuvered the older athletes.[101]

He discovered the impact he could make by creating an inclusive and instructive environment, by encouraging his players to speak up and be engaged in the learning process. He also discovered that learning itself was an ongoing and essential process for all participants in an enterprise. As coach, he could not simply instruct his team—he also needed to actively learn just as much as his players did. "It showed me the importance of listening to people you work with, and the coaching spell laid the foundation for me of an inclusive, transparent, mutually respectful management philosophy that I have applied to all the jobs I have held," he said many decades later.[102] To the end of his life, Shultz called his coaching job "one of the great learning experiences of my life,"[103] and he acknowledged it had "something to do with my own orientation to the university and to a teaching career."[104]

On December 7, 1941, Japanese forces attacked the American naval base at Pearl Harbor. The following day, the United States declared war on Japan. Three days later, Congress approved a declaration of war against Germany and the and the Princeton class of 1942 found themselves preparing for battle. Topper Cook recalled that he and Shultz were "very eager to get into the war, to throw our bodies in front of the Nazi war machine."[105] About two weeks after Pearl Harbor, Cook said the two were "anxious to get in, to get into the war in the worst way," so they went up to New York City and tried to join the Royal Canadian Air Force.[106] They both failed the eye exam and headed to a city bar, where they drowned their sorrows first in beer and then in something more indelible. According to Topper, the barman was also a tattoo artist, so they followed him into the back room and "he administered tattoos, both of us in the same place, and the same animal, a tiger on our rumps . . . the tiger being the symbol of Princeton University and we carry those tattoos around forever."[107] For the rest of his life, Shultz was nearly always coy about the backside tattoo, neither confirming nor denying it was there.

His entry into the war delayed, Shultz returned to Princeton for his last semester. But he and his friends were "all oriented to the war," in Shultz's words, and biding their time until they could join.[108] He discussed his future with his adviser, Ed Lundy, who encouraged Shultz to study with Paul Samuelson at MIT, a rising star in economics. Shultz duly applied to the MIT PhD program in economics and was accepted. He intended to "continue his studies in economics, and to become a business or agriculture analyst," according to his graduation yearbook.[109]

Shultz looked back with "the fondest possible memories" of his time at Princeton, he said,[110] most of all about his senior spring. He remembered that "the tradition there was that the seniors every night—those who wanted to, and I did a lot of this—stood on the steps of Nassau Hall and sang all sorts of songs, Princeton songs and other songs."[111] He believed that the school motto, "Princeton in the nation's service," voiced nearly half a century before his own graduation by Woodrow Wilson, "undoubtedly had an impact on my own orientation toward readiness to serve in Washington."[112] First, however, he would serve in uniform. Shultz graduated from Princeton with departmental high honors on June 16, 1942, and then he went to war.

CHAPTER TWO

No Empty Threats

GALVANIZED BY THE ATTACK on Pearl Harbor and the US declaration of war, George Shultz, like millions of other Americans, was eager to defend his country. Newsreel footage and newspaper and radio accounts of the damage at Pearl Harbor made clear that the US Navy had absorbed devastating losses during the surprise air attack. Twenty navy vessels, including eight battleships, were destroyed or damaged, and more than twenty-four hundred Americans were killed.

After the Royal Canadian Air Force rejected Shultz, he turned to the US Marine Corps. On June 10, 1942, just days after graduating from Princeton, he impressed his right index fingerprint on a Marine Corps enlistment form at the recruiting post in New York City, signed the paper and became a private first class. Earlier that year, Birl and Margaret had sold the Shultz home in Englewood and moved to Pittsburgh, where Birl took a job at the War Production Board, which had opened a Pittsburgh office to manage steel production. After enlisting, George headed to the new family residence at 245 Melrose Street in a modest, working-class neighborhood to await call-up for basic training. Princeton mailed his diploma to him there. While in Pittsburgh, Shultz followed the war news from Europe and the Pacific as German forces extended their offensive in the Soviet Union nearly a year after invalidating the Molotov-Ribbentrop pact and invading Soviet territory in June 1941.

After six weeks at home, he reported to the Marine Corps training complex in Quantico, Virginia, on August 13 and enrolled in Officer Candidate School. With war mobilization gathering strength by the day, tens of thousands of young men were streaming into military boot camps around the nation, including many of Shultz's Princeton classmates. Norman Cook enlisted in the Coast Guard, Bob Young in the US Army and John Brooks in the US Army Air Forces. Shultz arrived at Quantico, located along the Potomac as it rolls south from Washington to the Chesapeake Bay, on a typically sultry summer day, where he spent ten grueling weeks in boot camp. The base was spartan, with corrugated-steel Quonset huts serving as barracks for marines in training.

Apart from the leg injury that had sidelined him during his senior year on the Princeton football team, he was in good physical condition. The late-summer heat and humidity at Quantico, coupled with the tough training regimen, left the new marine recruits drained by the end of each day, but Shultz weathered the challenging conditions. One drill sergeant left a lasting impression when he instructed the newly minted marines on how to handle their rifles. Years later, Shultz recalled the moment and its significance for him:

> "This is your best friend," the sergeant told me. "Take good care of it and remember: never point this rifle at anybody unless you're willing to pull the trigger." The lesson—no empty threats—was one that I have never forgotten. Its relevance to the conduct of diplomacy is obvious yet often ignored. If you say that something is unacceptable but you are unwilling to impose consequences when it happens, your words will lose their meaning and you will lose credibility. But the lesson is also broader, as in any deal making. If you are known as someone who delivers on promises, then you are trusted and can be dealt with. In the end, trust is the coin of the realm.[1]

Shultz completed basic training in mid-October, exiting as a second lieutenant, and soon was assigned to Student Base Defense Section, Artillery Course at Quantico. He was a leader now, whether or not he relished the role. "Suddenly, there you are, twenty-two years old and all of a sudden you're an officer and there are people who report to you. You're part of a unit. You have leadership responsibilities, but you're very integrated and interdependent. Marines are very much that way."[2]

Shultz finished the artillery course in January 1943. His next stop was more antiaircraft artillery training at the marine base at Camp Lejeune, North Carolina. Antiaircraft defenses were critical for the marines as they took a leading role in the American drive to dislodge Japanese forces from the Pacific islands they had occupied. As marines assaulted beaches and engaged in withering firefights with Japanese troops in strongpoint pillboxes and dug into jungle mountainsides, Japanese warplanes frequently counterattacked, bombing and strafing marines and other American troops on the ground. Early in the war, before the United States gained air superiority in the Pacific, antiaircraft fire was vital to blunting the Japanese air raids. In May, Shultz was assigned to an antiaircraft group in the 7th Defense Battalion, 3rd Marine Brigade, at Camp Elliott in San Diego to await instructions for deployment to the war zone in the South Pacific. On July 30, he was appointed a first lieutenant. In August, Lieutenant George Shultz headed for the Samoan Islands.

The Pacific War was slowly turning in America's favor by the spring of 1943. After the stunning Japanese attack at Pearl Harbor, Japanese forces had conquered Borneo, the Philippines and Dutch East Indies, extending Tokyo's control over a vast swath of the southwest Pacific. American troops on Wake Island, on Guam and in the Philippines and other outposts had been killed or captured, as had Dutch and Australian forces elsewhere in Japan's path. But after the US Navy prevailed in a pivotal showdown with the aircraft carriers of the Imperial Japanese Navy near Midway Atoll six months after Pearl Harbor, the Japanese advances were arrested and then agonizingly reversed, island by island, in a stepping-stone series of brutal battles expected to lead eventually to an American invasion of Japan.

The harrowing model for American and Allied success was the Guadalcanal campaign, a punishing six-month engagement with Japanese land, sea and air forces in the Solomon Islands to gain control of a strategically vital area and air base. The Allied forces finally prevailed in February 1943, not long before Shultz was dispatched to the Pacific Theater. By early 1943, the German invasion of the Soviet Union had stalled. The defeat of Nazi forces at Stalingrad in January 1943, after months of agonizing combat in and around the southern Russian city, left the depleted German army in retreat.

Shultz's first stop was Pago Pago, the capital of American Samoa. Like the two larger Samoan Islands to the east, American Samoa was located astride a critical shipping lane from Hawaii to Australia that was vital to America's prosecution of the Pacific War. Long a coaling station for the US Navy, the Pago Pago harbor was rapidly growing into an important American naval base by the time Shultz's ship steamed into port. Situated just outside the Pacific combat zones, Pago Pago, where lush green mountains rise from a turquoise sea, offered Shultz a tranquil introduction to the South Pacific.

He recalled his arrival: "We all heard about the marines who had been out in the Pacific for two years, and they'd all kind of become stir crazy and had what they called 'the thousand-mile stare' back to the States. I remember we came into American Samoa—Pago Pago. So we're coming up to the dock and the marines on the ship are standing and looking, and the marines on the dock looking at us, and all of a sudden it starts raining. The marines there—who had been there—don't pay any attention at all. It rains and nobody even moves. We thought, 'My God, it's true. They don't even know it's raining.'"[3]

Shultz soon learned more about marine culture and the sense of independence that the Marine Corps exercised. After a short stay in Pago Pago, he transferred to Western Samoa, known at the time as British Samoa. The two islands that make up Western Samoa, a short hop to the west from Pago Pago, were governed at the time by New Zealand. One of his first assignments at the marine compound was to help unload a supply ship. A marine captain named Red Miller instructed Shultz and his fellow marines to truck some of the supplies back to their base and hide them in the bushes. Shultz protested that they might be accused of stealing or hoarding. As Shultz recalled, Miller replied, "It doesn't matter. We barter. It gives us something to work with." Shultz said, "I remember hearing him talk to the quartermaster, once saying, 'Damn it, if you don't give it to me, I'll steal it from you!' So there was this notion that whatever it was belonged to us."[4]

During his time on Western Samoa, Shultz was troubled by social and economic inequalities and by an episode of cruelty toward a marine facing disciplinary action. His reactions to these events reflected a strong sense of fairness and sensitivity about civil rights that seemed instinctive to Shultz as he began to make his way in the wider world beyond home and college.

He was once instructed to drive a young Samoan woman to a dinner at the New Zealand governor's mansion, where she would be the companion of a marine general. Shultz met the woman and her parents at their simple home, a thatched roof above an open cement floor. The young woman was fashionably dressed for dinner, but she accompanied him to his jeep bare-footed, carrying a pair of shoes. She informed Shultz, who had learned a few words of Samoan, that the governor prohibited Samoan natives from stepping foot in his house unless they worked there as servants. Samoans customarily did not wear shoes, but she had acquired a pair so she could attend the dinner with the general. The governor was making an exception to let a Samoan come to his residence as a guest because the general had threatened not to attend if his Samoan date was not welcome.[5]

When a fellow marine was disciplined for falling asleep at his post one night, Shultz thought the case was unfair because the man was exhausted from doing day jobs, including grueling carpentry work. Shultz was appalled when he discovered the punishment—hauling a plow through farm fields as if he were an animal. While driving through the countryside one day, Shultz found the marine enduring this labor and told him to stop. Shultz then drove him back to base. "I just took him away and said, 'We're not going to do this to a human being.' It was one of these instinctive things where you see something you think is wrong so you try to do something about it."[6] The compassionate impulse reflected a humane quality in Shultz that the world later came to see as he tackled difficult domestic and international issues such as civil rights and human rights.

Shultz's peaceful sojourn in Samoa abruptly ended when he moved to Funafuti, a small atoll in the island cluster known today as the nation of Tuvalu. It was the launch point for his first combat engagement. The target was Nanumea Atoll in the Ellice Islands, Japanese-occupied territory southeast of Tarawa. Shultz and the platoon he commanded were part of an invasion force assembled for an attack planned in late November 1943. The assignment: land in the darkness, surprise the light Japanese forces and seize control of the island. The prospect of combat was bracing. Shultz had been following the Pacific War in newspaper coverage; now he was about to go into battle. He realized he was at the tip of one of many arrows he saw in newspaper maps showing the advance of American forces. "I thought to myself, I'm on the end of those arrows," he recalled. "I don't think the guys that drew the maps have any idea what it's like to be on the end of the arrow."[7]

The nighttime landing was slowed by an unmapped coral reef that forced Shultz and his unit to abandon their shallow boats and wade ashore. The delay eliminated the advantage of landing in darkness. By the time they got to the beach, the sun was up. The invaders were stunned to find a welcoming committee of islanders instead of armed Japanese defenders lining the beach. Employing a Samoan phrase he had learned, he greeted the man at the center of the group: "Taloka sol-li." "Good morning sir." The man replied in a clipped English accent, "Good morning Lieutenant. We've been expecting you. The Japanese left two days ago, and everything is arranged for your arrival."[8]

The peaceful tableau did not last long. A few days later, on September 7, ten Japanese Mitsubishi G4M bombers, dubbed "Bettys" by American forces, attacked the marine positions, thundering overhead at three to five thousand feet in three V-shaped formations. Shultz's unit had no warning of the raid. They responded with wildly scattered antiaircraft fire. Unprepared for the attack, the marines operated without any data about wind direction and velocity, and their antiaircraft guns, improperly anchored, shifted position during firing. Two of the guns jammed, and other technical breakdowns hampered the troops.[9] It was a debacle. Shultz recalled, "We had landed, and we were barely trying to get ourselves established, but we really weren't set. And they came and we had no defenses. There was no . . . nothing. They had a complete free rein."[10] One of Shultz's fellow marines urged the men to seek shelter in a nearby church. "There was only one building on the island," Shultz recalled. "It was a church with thick walls. And somebody yelled, 'Church!' I yelled, 'Disperse!,' which we did. And the Japanese put a bomb in the dead center of the church. So I remember afterwards telling the guys, 'OK. Two things we learned. Number one: never underestimate your adversary. They're pretty good marksmen. Number two: don't do what they expect you to do.'"[11]

By the time the raid ended, five marines were dead and seven wounded.[12] Shultz survived unscathed, but the attack left him shaken. "I remember it to this day." He said decades later, "I had a great sergeant named Patton, and I relied on him. He was a wonderful human being. And you become close to people in these kinds of things, very close. He's a fine person and smart, and he was one of these guys that could do things, could get people to do things. So I relied on him a lot. And things are going and I'm wondering, where's Patton, and rushed over to where I thought he went and said, 'Where the hell is Patton?' 'Patton's dead, sir.'"[13] "I'll never forget it."[14] "It hit me like a ton of bricks."[15] "The reality of war sinks in and you say to yourself, remember. Because it says to you when you're secretary of state or part of making decisions to send people into combat, that you'd better be careful and have a good mission that can be accomplished. Because people are going to get killed, and you owe it to them to look at it that way."[16]

Once the Americans secured the island and Japanese air attacks ended, Shultz's battalion headed to Kauai, Territory of Hawaii, in March 1944 to await reassignment. The quiet interlude lasted five months and turned into a life-changing moment for Shultz. The men wasted no time looking for female companionship. Shultz recalled, "Some of us said, 'This is a big island. If it's a big island, there must be a hospital. If there's a hospital, there must be nurses. So let's go find the hospital.'"[17] It wasn't long before Shultz was courting Helena Maria O'Brien, or "O'Bie" for short. She was a warm, modest and charming young woman, with brown hair, gray eyes, standing five feet, seven inches and weighing 135 pounds.[18] Five years older than Shultz, she grew up in a working-class family of Irish Catholics and was quite devout. Her grandparents had emigrated from Dublin and settled in New England. O'Brien's army record shows she began active duty on November 28, 1941, and shipped out as a general-duty nurse to the Central Pacific Base Command in Hawaii on June 7, 1942.

Their first date was unplanned—they attended a dance with other companions but were drawn to one another and left the dance hall together. When O'Bie was transferred to Schofield Barracks on Oahu, Shultz managed to relocate to Oahu himself and immediately started looking for a way to get from the marine base to Schofield Barracks, a sprawling army post adjacent to Wheeler Airfield, which had been one of the first Japanese targets during the first phase of the attack on Pearl Harbor. No jeeps were available, but he persuaded the marine logistics group to lend him a truck. For the next few months, he repeatedly took the wheel of a half-ton truck, not exactly a vehicle designed to impress a young lady, and rumbled across Oahu to see O'Bie.

By this time, the women he had dated at Princeton were committing to relationships with Shultz's classmates or other young men on the home front. "I got my Dear John letters. It was a little tough. You're overseas for two and a half years, and all these no-good guys that are back in the States are grabbing the girls."[19] Roxy Park and Pinky Peterson dropped off his short list. Peterson married first. "Pinky married someone else and she was the only active female interest I had when I left the states," he wrote to Norman Cook. Then Park. "I hear the last of 'my' girls bit the dust," he informed Cook. "Roxy Park got married. Tough war."[20] The disappointment was tempered by his discovery of O'Bie. He told a friend: "The big news is concerned with a Catholic, Irish, Army nurse with whom I've had quite a few dates in the last month or so. She's really superb company and I got to like her very much."[21]

Shultz missed life back home. While he was away at war, his parents had started spending breaks at a simple wooden farmhouse purchased on June 1, 1944, in the mountains of western Massachusetts. It was located in Cummington on a hillside above the Swift River where the stream winds through the Berkshires. Hearing about the property from his parents, Shultz advised Cook, his childhood and Princeton buddy, to come by when the war ended: "The crops are rolling in. So when you come up to New England on your second honeymoon, stop by the Shultz's and we'll get you healthy with plenty of fresh vegetables and swim in a newly discovered mountain pool. How about that!"[22]

The Hawaii fling with O'Bie was cut short when Shultz was assigned to temporary duty with the US Army 81st Infantry Division as a battalion liaison officer. The division was preparing for a major American assault in mid-1944 on Japanese-held territory in the Palau islands in the southwestern Pacific not far from the Philippines. Capture of the Palau islands would secure the waters and territory east of the Philippines for Allied operations under the command of General Douglas MacArthur to retake the Philippines. After some delay due to prolonged combat elsewhere in the Pacific, the Palau campaign was launched in September 1944, involving sixteen hundred warships and eight hundred airplanes, the largest amphibious assault in the Pacific up to that time.

The American assault proved to be one of the most grueling of the Pacific campaign. A formidable, heavily armed Japanese force was based on Peleliu, an island in the Palau archipelago and the site of a strategically important airfield. Japanese troops were dug in on the Umurbrogol heights, a commanding position. The American attack on Peleliu began on September 15, 1944, and initially stalled in the face of withering Japanese artillery and mortar fire. Shultz was spared the worst of it when his unit was dispatched to help seize Angaur, a speck of land with plentiful phosphate deposits located at the southern end of the Palau island cluster. Angaur was lightly but fiercely defended by Japanese forces. The 81st Division landing at Angaur, including Shultz's battalion, encountered limited resistance and the island was quickly secured. But the initial phase of the assault was no cakewalk, as Japanese troops, embedded in the cliffs above the beach, freely fired on the Americans as they hit the shoreline.

Shultz came ashore in the second wave of invading troops and immediately saw that the surge of military equipment and supplies was piling up on the beach, creating a bottleneck that would impede the American advance. It proved to be a formative moment for Shultz in his development as a leader. When Shultz talked about the battle scene years later, it was clear that the command role he exercised on the beach that day instilled a sense of confidence and competence that stayed with him the rest of his life. "People were taking refuge and the stuff was not moving off the beach," he recalled. "And these landings are really some piece of logistics because there are all these ships and the stuff is coming in and you can't stop it; it's coming. So somehow we had to get the beach cleared. And I sort of took charge, in a way, and I said, 'You aim for that place, and you aim for that place, and just keep firing at it, and that will keep the Japanese from coming out and shooting at our guys.' And people did it. I had no authority, no nothing, but it made sense and it did stop them and we did clear the beach and kept the logistics rolling."[23]

Shultz saw little, if any, combat action after Angaur. He remained in the Pacific Theater until August 1945, when he was ordered to return to San Diego to join marine units preparing for the invasion of Japan. Though separated from O'Bie, he remained smitten. He alluded obliquely to O'Bie in a letter to Norman Cook: "That brief oasis I ran into not long ago still has me reeling. I hope that it doesn't turn out to be another ship that passes after 'missing too many boats,' as they say."[24] He added wistfully, "I would have given anything to be at your wedding but still looking forward to seeing you if this damn war ever winds itself up."[25] A few months later, he reminded Cook about O'Bie. "Did I tell you about my

Army nurse? I met her some time ago and my great affection has lasted for 7 months now (7 mos. of not seeing her, damn it). She's been over almost three years with shipment to a new forward area but I hope and pray we'll be in the states together. She's quite large, Irish, older than I, and Catholic, but the important thing is—well you know all about that. She's wonderful!" Shultz's impatience to get home was growing. "At least one can see that it's possible for the damn thing to end, which is more than could be said a couple of years ago."[26]

In June 1945, less than two months after the German surrender and the end of the war in Europe, Shultz recorded his thoughts about the war. His belittling comments about Asians were typical of racist attitudes among many Americans at the time. "Nothing ever turns out too happily out here. . . . Don't forget these millions of detestable bastards holed up in caves from Hokkaido to Saluit to Bouqainville. They seem to be an eternal scourge to us. It seems to me very doubtful that the Japs will fold but I think we can really crush them anyway in not too many more years and I almost think the latter course is preferable. The Chinese boys seems [*sic*] to be the logical candidates for the extermination or what have you job once we get the Japs on their knees. Let the Orientals deal with the Orientals, then they'll have no bitch against the occidental races." He once again mentioned O'Bie to Cook. By then, she had been transferred to a hospital in the liberated Philippines. "I'm sold on her," he wrote. "Mother is all upset about the whole deal and considers my romance a 'calamity.' She's worried because O'Bie is a Catholic."[27]

As the war wound down, Shultz reflected on his experiences: "There is one outstanding impression which I've gotten out of this experience of leading men in the field and that is of their unfailing good sense and unlimited courage and ability when the chips are down."[28] He was well aware that his combat action had been relatively light compared to that of tens of thousands of marines and other American troops who had fought in the Pacific. "A place like Guadalcanal was a muddy, god-awful place . . . a hellhole. But I wasn't on Guadalcanal. I read about it and the heroic performance of the marines there."[29] Like so many men who engaged in combat operations and witnessed unspeakable violence and death during the war, he chose not to dwell on what he had experienced, rarely talking about his war service once the conflict ended. Many decades later during interviews for this book, he remained hesitant to revisit those years.

Clearly, the war changed Shultz, as it did so many men and women who survived the conflict. He emerged more mature, more cautious and more worldly. The war years planted in Shultz both an appreciation for American military power and a sense of restraint about how and when it could be used. Naturally, after his own combat experience, he was wary of war and the toll it inflicted on warriors and civilians. Yet he could see that military strength was critical to American security, and he was convinced that the judicious use of military power in support of American diplomacy would be essential in dealing with future adversaries. The courage and resilience of his fellow marines profoundly impressed him, giving him faith in the inherent goodness of his countrymen and making him a lifelong champion of the Marine Corps.

As he and his unit sailed toward San Diego in 1945 for what they knew would be reassignment to an invasion force to attack the Japanese homeland, news reached the ship about the atomic bombing of Hiroshima and Nagasaki:

> We're hardly out of port when we got word that something called an atomic bomb had been dropped. Nobody had a clue of what it was. But we thought, well, if it's been announced, it must be something of importance. And the ship lumbers on. And then we hear another one was dropped, and by the time we got to San Diego, the war was over. . . . We all knew we were going back to the states to be re-formed into the outfits that were going to go and assault the Japanese islands. And all of us had been involved in at least one landing, and so we can imagine what landing on the Japanese islands was going to be like, and the war's suddenly over. So you have to say, whatever the atomic bomb is, it probably has something to do with the fact that we're not assaulting those islands.[30]

The changes in Shultz were evident to family and friends as he returned to the family property in the Berkshires. "George Shultz has matured splendidly," Norman Cook's father, Norman Sr., observed after welcoming Shultz home from the war. "The aging, responsibilities and being on his own have done much for him." The senior Cook reported to his son that Margaret and Birl hoped George would settle for a while at the farmhouse in western Massachusetts. The younger Shultz had other ideas. "George has been among the trees and nothing else for two years. He said he found himself trying to recall what a woman looked like. I question his really wanting to put in many of his forty days resting among the trees of Swift River. After the last war the song was written, 'How are you going to keep him down on the farm after he's seen Paree.' Well, he hasn't seen Paree, but I'll bet he's been yearning for some of the things that are to be found in Paree—normal life, normal activities, old friends, girls, shows, and dozens of things that Pacific islands don't offer in any abundance."[31]

Shultz did not travel far. Instead of Paris, he returned briefly to the Berkshires, where his homecoming was momentarily marred when he sat down on an old chair at the farmhouse that instantly cracked and collapsed. He never forgot the dramatic moment. "I sat in that chair and I leaned back and broke it. And my mother must have died, but she didn't. She just said, 'Why don't you sit over there.' So we got it fixed up."[32] It was a telling incident. His mother, a precise woman who insisted on good manners, suppressed her anger and refrained from admonishing her son. Stoicism was a Shultz family trait. George Shultz admired it and made it a hallmark of his conduct as he ventured into the postwar world. He soon made his way to Boston, where he was reunited with O'Bie, and took the initial steps on an academic journey that vaulted him to national prominence.

CHAPTER THREE

The Real Economy

THE WAR WAS OVER, but Shultz was still in uniform when he arrived in Massachusetts in the fall of 1945. He had been assigned to the Boston Navy Yard with no clear release date. He arrived as the yard, which dominated the waterfront, was winding down after years of feverish shipbuilding and repair work during the war. Shultz recalled that, faced with the prospect of little activity at the Navy Yard, he approached his commanding officer with a solution to his restlessness: "You don't have anything for me to do, so to get off your hands, why don't I just go over and enroll at MIT?"[1] The commanding officer agreed, and Shultz headed down the Charles River to the Massachusetts Institute of Technology.

So began a period of his life that would profoundly deepen his conviction that his calling was developing commonsense solutions to national and international challenges, grounded in observing the real world rather than abstract theorizing. The years at MIT as student and teacher also reinforced a belief, instilled at Princeton and strengthened by his wartime experience, that serving the nation was an honorable and fulfilling vocation. At MIT, he found great satisfaction in a scholarly life. Shultz developed an aptitude for vigorous but civil debate; a restless curiosity about economic, political and social forces and organizations; an openness to new ideas and technologies; and a measured, patient approach to making decisions—intellectual habits that persisted throughout his life.

As Shultz began his coursework in the MIT economics department, he soon connected with Paul Samuelson, whom he had hoped to study with when he originally applied to the university. Completing his PhD work at Harvard in 1941, Samuelson had "shot to academic fame as a 22-year-old prodigy," the *New York Times* reported.[2] Given Shultz's doubts about Roosevelt's efforts to revive the American economy during the Depression and Shultz's faith in free-market capitalism, Samuelson was hardly a natural match for Shultz. Samuelson, just starting a career that would lead to a Nobel Prize, was not a free-market champion. Influenced by the economic theories of John Maynard Keynes, Samuelson believed that government intervention through fiscal policies such as federal stimulus spending and aggressive central bank monetary action such as interest rate reductions was sometimes needed to stabilize the economy and pull it out of recession. Shultz was one of just two students in the course, along with Charlie Holt, an electrical engineer who had worked with Samuelson in an MIT radiation laboratory during the war. While amazed to be in such an intimate seminar—"two guys with Paul Samuelson!"—Shultz was not won over by Samuelson's views.[3]

Shultz gravitated to the Industrial Relations Section of the economics department, where he discovered both his academic field and his closest colleagues. Shultz explained, "It's hard for people to realize that back at that time after World War II, labor unions were a huge factor in our economy, and the collective-bargaining process was a big deal. Strikes were common. People worried about them. And so this was a big component of society and the economy that you would want to address."[4] In the mid-1950s, union membership in the United States peaked at roughly a third of the workforce. Determined that "every member of our staff is actively engaged in some activity in industry," which "should keep our feet on the ground,"[5] the faculty and students of the Industrial Relations Section created links between the academy and the outside world. Shultz wanted his work to be grounded in reality, to look at the real-life applications of economics. "My idea was not so much economics in its abstract way, but I thought it was something I could use to analyze public policy issues or business issues. In other words, I wanted to go into economics because I thought it would be a useful discipline."[6]

At MIT, Shultz befriended an unusual figure in academia: Joseph Scanlon, the rough-hewn son of Irish immigrants who was a lecturer at the university. His work in union-management relations would have a lasting impact on the young labor economist and his practical approach to problem solving. Scanlon's commonsense analysis of labor-management relations seemed shrewd and down-to-earth to Shultz. Here was someone steeped in the workplace, familiar with the interaction of managers and workers, a man with a terrific instinct for how to motivate people and get them to work together productively. He became an important mentor for Shultz.

Born in 1899 in Cleveland, Joe Scanlon served in the navy from 1918 to 1921 and worked as a professional featherweight boxer instead of attending college. His rubbery face bore the scars of the boxing ring. With limited income prospects from boxing, Scanlon turned to the steel industry to make a living, starting as a cost accountant at Empire Steel in Mansfield, Ohio.[7] He left accounting to become an open-hearth tender at the same company. In 1937, he was elected president of Local Union 169 of the Steelworkers Organizing Committee. When Empire Steel teetered on the edge of bankruptcy, union leaders and company executives decided to create a Joint Research Committee to hear workers' suggestions for "cutting waste and improving productivity and profitability."[8] The company rallied, and one of its executives hailed Scanlon as the "sparkplug" of the recovery.[9]

His performance caught the attention of the Industrial Relations Section at MIT, which hired him as a lecturer. Scanlon was, in Shultz's words, "something of a genius in understanding people and how to motivate them."[10] Shultz explained that Scanlon would go to a financially troubled steel plant where the situation was "so dire that management might even listen to the people who are working there,"[11] and he would enlist worker input in improving plant conditions. In *Ideas and Action*, published in 2010, Shultz recalled that Scanlon "had a remarkable ability to change the atmosphere in the workplace by conveying to workers, *You matter. You have a stake.*"[12] Scanlon would "develop these participation plans where you organize things so that the workers involved could make suggestions about how to make work go more efficiently. And they wound up improving productivity by gigantic amounts—like thirty and forty percent. Saved quite a few companies."[13]

The presence of his parents at the family property in Cummington, a two-hour drive from Boston, was reassuring to Shultz and gave his father a chance to follow George's progress as a graduate student and aspiring scholar. Shultz said, "I always felt that my father wished that he had been able to follow an academic and scholarly career, so he was glad to see me doing so."[14]

On December 23, 1945, Shultz was relieved from active duty in the Marine Corps. O'Bie, released from her own military service, returned to the country that same month. On February 16, 1946, between semesters, they were married in O'Bie's hometown of Nashua, New Hampshire.[15] Since Shultz was not Catholic, the wedding took place next door to the church rather than within its halls. "It was a very small little thing," Shultz remembered. "You know, we had no money at all—zero." Their economical honeymoon took place in Boston and at the Shultz family farm in western Massachusetts.[16]

The newlyweds decided that O'Bie would continue working as a nurse, and "in that way we would have a little income to make a go of it."[17] But after being horrified at the unsanitary conditions on her first day on the job at a Boston hospital, she came home in tears and abruptly discontinued her career. Instead, she decided to return to school as her husband had and began studying at the Fannie Farmer Cooking School on the GI Bill. O'Bie never returned to nursing. Her daughter Margaret said "she was burnt out by the time she got back and really just wanted to settle down and have a family and put the war behind her."[18] By the time Shultz completed his PhD in industrial economics in February 1949, they had welcomed their first child, Margaret (in May 1947), and had a second on the way. Kathleen Shultz was born in June 1949, her arrival coinciding with MIT's graduation exercises.[19] Three additional children followed in subsequent years: Barbara, Peter and Alex.

As the Shultz family expanded and his graduate work progressed, George and O'Bie could see the Boston area—and the nation—slowly regaining economic equilibrium after the years of wartime stress and defense mobilization. Their lives were beneficially touched by the nation's postwar recovery. The arrival of the Shultz children was part of explosive, postwar population growth as the baby-boom generation made its debut. The migration of people from rural areas to urban centers; the development of suburban neighborhoods and shopping centers; growth in per capita income; and ownership of homes, automobiles and televisions all contributed to a rising sense of prosperity across many parts of the country.

The first postwar stirrings of the civil rights movement appeared as black men and women, repressed by racial barriers and the inequities of segregated life in the South and racial divisions in the North, demanded equality. In 1954, the Supreme Court declared that racial segregation in schools was unconstitutional. On December 1, 1955, Rosa Parks refused to yield her seat on a Montgomery, Alabama, bus to a white man and was arrested. Shultz was aware of the civil rights news and sympathized with the push for equal rights, but he did not get involved himself while at MIT. His sense of fair play, noticeable during his Marine Corps service, deepened during the years in the Boston area, providing a foundation for future civil rights action on his part.

Although international tensions did not directly affect George and O'Bie, they watched with concern as the cold war, which commenced soon after the end of World War II, intensified. North Korea's invasion of South Korea in June 1950 ignited a new hot war in Asia that quickly escalated into a grinding conflict involving hundreds of thousands of American troops operating under United Nations (UN) auspices. Meantime, tensions between the United States and the Soviet Union ominously heightened with the American and Soviet testing of hydrogen bombs far more powerful than the atomic weapons the United States had used against Japan. Airborne delivery systems for nuclear weapons, including intercontinental bombers and eventually ballistic missiles, soon created a frightening balance of terror that American and Soviet leaders struggled to manage.

While the United States was trying to revive Western European nations with assistance provided by the Marshall Plan, Europe quickly split into East and West camps. In June 1948, the Soviet Union and its East German allies blocked land access from West Germany to the divided city of Berlin, the first explosive crisis of the cold war. Less than a year later, the United States and it allies banded together to create the North Atlantic Treaty Organization (NATO) as a military counterweight to Soviet and Eastern European military forces. They, in turn, forged their own alliance, the Warsaw Pact, in 1955.

For his PhD dissertation, Shultz analyzed pressures in wage setting in the men's shoe industry, using Brockton, Massachusetts, as his case study because it was "a big men's shoe center in the postwar period."[20] As he compiled statistics on wages in Brockton, he was surprised to discover that pay rates had not declined during the Depression. They had, in fact, "showed very little movement" in those difficult years.[21] He met with "past and present principals in the union and manufacturer groups" to hear from them directly.[22] As in his Princeton thesis research, Shultz learned that the human dimension was vital—he could not glean the whole story from economic theory alone. In his Brockton research, he again saw "how clever people were if you really dug in. Again, that was a vindication of going and collecting material for yourself and trying to understand what was really going on and realizing people are smarter than you give them credit for."[23] After Shultz completed his PhD, several universities offered him a position, MIT among them: "It was considered a compliment if the university where you got your Ph.D. asked you to stay on and become a member of the faculty, which they did. I was flattered and I stayed."[24] In June 1949, at the age of twenty-eight, he became an assistant professor in the Department of Economics and Social Science.

By this time, Shultz no longer lived in temporary graduate housing. In the fall of 1948, George, O'Bie, and baby Margaret moved to Stow, Massachusetts, an hour's train ride away from MIT. At their little cottage on Red Acre Road, they became part of the community at Red Acre Village, the brainchild of Harriet Bird, daughter of a prominent local family, where the Shultzes luxuriated in the warm and communal atmosphere. Margaret Shultz remembers the sociability of the little community—"that generation," she recalls, "they were very social." Her parents, like many of their neighbors, had just returned victorious from war: the residents "were young, you know, twenties, won a war, lots of energy. No competition on the international horizon other than Russia." They came together in both communal service and neighborhood recreation. In winter, "the men would go out and clear this pond of snow and there would be skating parties, bonfires, and singing parties at Christmas," while "in the summer, in our backyard there was this gigantic garden and everybody would be out there" enjoying themselves together.[25]

Home life was simple. Shultz commuted to MIT for his day of teaching and research. When he came home, O'Bie had already made drinks. They would sip martinis straight up together in the evening, enjoying each other's company. Margaret says her parents' marriage was so successful because "my mother made her marriage her life's work. That was the key. She adored my father and he was always first. Her relationship with him was number one, and it was very clear, she adored us, she took care of us, made sure our homework was done, but when he came home, we were done, we were off in our rooms, we had been fed, unless it was a family dinner, and she had a cocktail ready, and they sat down and had adult time. Through their whole marriage."[26]

In May 1952, their third child, Peter, was born. George Shultz was a present, active figure in his children's lives. His lifelong friend and Red Acre Village neighbor Jim Baldwin emphasized that Shultz was always a strong family man, dedicated to his wife and children. Margaret concurred that her father "was around on weekends and in the evenings" and "was certainly part of the disciplinary process and certainly part of the family."[27]

Shultz devoted much of his energy to his academic career at MIT and was promoted to associate professor in 1955, one step short of a tenured post at the time. He also got involved in local affairs at home, and Stow became the seat of his first foray into politics. In 1953, he ran opposed for the Nashoba School District and won 253 votes. Though elected by an overwhelming margin, he was never installed because the voters turned down the establishment of the regional school board.[28] Though his school board career ended the same day it began, in the same election Shultz won a seat on the town's new planning board.[29] Two years later, he won a three-year term as a town selectman. His tenure as selectman was curtailed when Shultz, who was gaining a national reputation as an able labor economist, was appointed to the staff of President Eisenhower's White House Council of Economic Advisers (CEA). He resigned as a selectman in June 1955, just a few months after the election. These small-town public posts remained his only positions gained at the ballot box. He never again ran for elected office, though some Republican admirers later suggested he run for president.

When the thirty-five-year-old Shultz drove south to Washington in the summer of 1955, he was accompanied not only by O'Bie and their three children but by his parents as well, who followed along in their own car, creating what he recalls as "a little caravan of sorts." Birl and Margaret were thrilled at the idea of their son serving in the Eisenhower administration. George Shultz recalled that his father was particularly exultant. Birl loved Princeton's informal motto, "in the nation's service," and "was never more thrilled than when I was appointed to the CEA" to begin fulfilling that duty.[30] After arrival in the capital, the older Shultzes were amazed to find that George would be working in the Executive Office Building next to the White House. As they gazed out his office window, the Shultzes looked upon the White House's South Lawn. Birl couldn't stop beaming. He died just a few months later on November 9, 1955, at the age of seventy-two. Birl's quiet pride at his son's government service became a treasured memory for George Shultz.

George Shultz's time as a senior staff economist on the Council of Economic Advisers was a year of many firsts: his first foray into public service at the national level, his first sojourn in Washington and his first collaboration with Arthur Burns, chairman of the CEA, who would feature prominently in Shultz's later government work. By the early 1950s, the CEA, established in 1946, was withering. The *Washington Post* wrote in May 1950 that it was "created to meet an economic crisis which never came . . . like a fire department in a fireless town—willing but unsung."[31] Its analyses were "widely regarded as poor in quality and as slanted to fit the policy preconceptions of the chairman."[32]

When Dwight Eisenhower was sworn in on January 20, 1953, the CEA was fast running out of money. On March 6, Arthur Burns, a Columbia professor and director of the National Bureau of Economic Research, was named "a member of the Council of Economic Advisers,"[33] but he effectively stood alone as its only significant member. Burns and Eisenhower had met at Columbia during Eisenhower's sojourn as president of the university after the war. Just days after Burns's nomination, Congress "wiped out" the already-broke CEA, voting in March 1953 to appropriate fifty thousand dollars for a solo economic adviser and staff for the White House rather than the existing three-person council.[34] Burns, who was convinced that "a deliberative body would serve the President better than a single economic adviser,"[35] set out to create a reorganization plan for the CEA. While the plan endorsed a three-member panel, it also consolidated the authority of the chairman over the other two members, making the chairman "directly responsible" to the president.[36]

Arthur Burns had been born in Austria in 1904 and arrived in the United States when he was a small child. With his round glasses, neatly centered hair part and pipe, he retained a touch of the European throughout his life. He was determined to keep the council out of the political morass of Washington. Burns was a professional economist and a scholar, not a politician. He was a registered Democrat but apolitical in nature, and he noted that he had "no political connections whatsoever."[37] Burns refused to testify openly in front of Congress, convinced that speaking publicly would make him an administration spokesman.

Shultz came to know Arthur Burns well, and the older man became a mentor to the young MIT economist. Shultz was tasked with studying governmental statistical programs: "I learned what unemployment statistics represented—how the numbers were gathered and the statistics created—and I also learned about all the other issues that pertain to these figures."[38] Shultz considered Burns to be an excellent statistician, and he made a point of timing his memo submissions so he would have a chance to talk with the chairman. He explained, "I would try to turn it in around four o'clock in the afternoon, figuring Arthur would read it about four-thirty and call me in to discuss it. Then we'd sit toward the end of the day and I'd have a chance to spend time with him."[39]

One of Shultz's primary achievements was connecting Arthur Burns with organized labor leaders. Burns appreciated Shultz's efforts; Shultz, for his part, credited these Burns-labor meetings as "one of the things that led [Burns] to recommend me to Nixon as Secretary of Labor" over a decade later.[40] Shultz also embraced life lessons from Arthur Burns. He recalled his first government boss as not only "a very good economist, but he was a person of strong character." He was inspired by Burns's determinedly professional and apolitical stance as CEA chairman. Shultz explained, "When economists appoint themselves politicians, they're amateurs, and it's better off to leave that to the politicians and give your economic advice."[41] It was this approach to government service, more than anything else, that became Shultz's takeaway from his first episode in Washington.

He was also impressed by something Eisenhower told Shultz and his White House colleagues as they prepared to take part in an air-raid drill designed to get them to a safe spot if Washington came under Soviet nuclear attack. "You're taking part in a plan," the president told the staff members. "But if something happens, remember the plan is worthless. What's important is the planning process. And when things happen, they never happen exactly the way you thought, so your mentality has to be one of shifting. That's why planning and looking at alternatives is so important." Shultz recalled, "It was a very interesting statement coming from an experienced general."[42]

Shultz returned to Cambridge in July 1956. Not long after, the University of Chicago invited him to join its business school faculty as a full professor. John Burchard, dean of MIT's School of Humanities and Social Science, saw the Chicago offer as a good move for Shultz. He wrote to economics professor Ralph Freeman on January 29, 1957, "I am not sure that George is ever going to get tenure here, and I am certainly far from sure that he will ever get a professorship, and I think the number of years before he can expect a $12,000 professorship are so many that for him to count on this in any reasonable future would be bad, and that we would be really guilty of bad faith to him if we let him do so."[43]

Shultz was unaware of these calculations, and it is unclear if Burchard's doubts about Shultz's prospects at MIT were widely shared. "I didn't have the impression they were trying to get rid of me; quite the contrary," Shultz recalled.[44] But he was ready to move on. Shultz had been at MIT since the end of World War II, first as student and then as professor, and he was fresh off a successful year of government work in Washington. Now he was thirty-seven, a father of three (and expecting another child in December), and a newly named full professor at the University of Chicago Graduate School of Business. It was a step up in the academic world that turned into a step onto the national stage. Looking back at the move, Shultz said, "Chicago is what started me."[45]

CHAPTER FOUR

Pathway to Power

IN THE SUMMER OF 1957, the Shultz family packed up and left Massachusetts for Chicago. The move from a junior faculty post at MIT to a tenured professorship at the University of Chicago enhanced Shultz's reputation as a rising star in economics. His promotion to dean of the University of Chicago Graduate School of Business at age forty-one, five years after his arrival at the Hyde Park campus, raised his national visibility. The turmoil of the 1960s at home and abroad reverberated through the University of Chicago as the school, like the rest of the nation, struggled to cope with the assassinations of John Kennedy, Martin Luther King Jr. and Robert Kennedy; widespread urban rioting; the escalation of the Vietnam War; the threat of nuclear war; the Soviet invasion of Czechoslovakia; and other wrenching events. Shultz spent the decade concentrating on his work at the university and on his growing family.

The years immersed in the intense scholarly environment of the University of Chicago broadened Shultz's intellectual range and reinforced his natural inclination to ground policy views in the realities of the workplace and the world at large rather than in abstract theorizing. The powerhouse roster of conservative economists at the university, including Milton Friedman and George Stigler, both of whom would go on to win Nobel Prizes, deepened Shultz's faith in free markets and solidified his standing as a proponent of reduced government regulation and intervention in the economy.

This was consistent with the "Chicago school" of economic philosophy championed by Friedman and fellow Chicago faculty members. In their view, free markets are the most efficient way to distribute wealth. Shultz developed enduring friendships with Friedman and Stigler, even as he maintained a warm relationship with Paul Samuelson at MIT, whose belief in government intervention and Keynesian economics starkly conflicted with Friedman's views. For Shultz, differences of opinion and philosophy were grist for vigorous debate, not grounds for ideological warfare and the abandonment of friendships. He once said of Friedman's tennis game, "Milton didn't hit the tennis ball hard but it always came back, which was reflective of the way he argued, too."[1]

Finding a home in the Chicago area similar to the Shultz house in Red Acre Village outside Boston proved difficult. "There wasn't any place like it," Shultz said.[2,3] The dean of the business school, Allen Wallis, suggested that they find a place near campus. George and O'Bie bought a narrow three-story townhouse on Blackstone Avenue at Fifty-Eighth Street, just a ten-minute walk from Shultz's office. The city of Chicago was in transition as the Shultzes settled into their townhouse. Businesses were abandoning the city, lured to new suburban communities that offered tax breaks and new housing opportunities for executives and workers. The meatpacking industry, long an anchor of the Chicago economy, was moving out of town in favor of smaller plants closer to rural areas where livestock was raised, reducing their shipping costs. The McCormick Reaper Works, one of the city's largest industrial complexes, relocated to a new plant in suburban Hinsdale.

Racial tensions in Chicago and across the nation were rising as Shultz started work at the University of Chicago. Civil rights leaders such as Martin Luther King Jr. initially focused their campaigns on systemic segregation across the South but watched widening racial discrimination in northern cities with growing alarm. In 1966, King and the Southern Christian Leadership Conference unveiled plans for a major campaign to address racial and socioeconomic inequities in Chicago. King moved to the North Lawndale neighborhood of Chicago, about thirteen miles northwest of Hyde Park, to lead the Chicago Freedom Movement, a series of nonviolent marches and other demonstrations in the city.

Shultz and fellow faculty members were well aware of racial inequities in the city. The university was a privileged enclave in Hyde Park, surrounded by blocks of dilapidated housing and economically struggling residents, many black. Though Shultz did not join the civil rights marches in Chicago, he witnessed racism firsthand through his association with meatpacking companies and unions. He launched programs to increase the number of black students admitted to the business school and worked with corporations and unions to expand job opportunities for African Americans. In 1968, violent rioting broke out on the west side of Chicago after the King assassination.

After arriving in Chicago, Shultz quickly found fellowship among his new colleagues at the university, many of whom also lived on or near campus. The Shultz children remember that their parents often hosted dinners and cocktail parties for colleagues and visiting academics. "Dad would throw out ideas," remembers Margaret, clearly relishing his role as host and "stir[ring] up conversation and controversy."[4] Attendees included Milton Friedman, George Stigler and other "economic luminaries," as Alex Shultz puts it, "all doing their own research" and "feeding off of each other."[5]

George Shultz found the school "the most extraordinarily intellectual experience you'll ever have because it's very intense all the time." As a full professor of industrial relations in the Graduate School of Business, he was able to connect with thinkers across different disciplines. "There are no real boundaries" at the school, he explained. "There's economics, business, law, sociology. We had an anthropologist on our business school faculty."[6] This was a familiar setting for him, coming from the equally interdisciplinary MIT, with its economists, psychologists and former union leader Joseph Scanlon.

Chicago was an exciting place to be as a young economist, especially as Shultz rode in on the wave that reinvigorated the business school. Shultz showed up just as the notion of a Chicago school of economics, dominated by Friedman, began to attract attention and adherents. Friedman, eight years older than Shultz, had earned his master's at Chicago before returning to the East Coast for a PhD at Columbia. He came back to Chicago in 1946 and stayed for the next thirty years, standing as "an ardent crusader for capitalism and economic freedom," as the *New York Times* wrote in 1976 when he won his Nobel. "Adam Smith is generally hailed as the father of modern economics and Milton Friedman as his most distinguished son."[7] Upon his death in 2006, the *Economist* called him "the most influential economist of the second half of the 20th century."[8]

Shultz later explained that the Chicago school "stands for the fundamental value of freedom," for "free markets, freedom of enterprise, freedom from undue regulation."[9] During his time there, he taught classes such as Business 340: Personnel Management and Industrial Relations and Business 344: Government and Industrial Relations. In Business 344, which focused on "issues of public policy in the areas of labor-management relations and the labor market," Shultz's detailed syllabus tackled such topics as the organization of unions; "the use of economic coercion: strikes, picketing, and boycotts"; mediation of labor disputes; and "direct action by the government in the labor market."[10] Several of the reading selections came from Shultz's recent book, *Labor Problems: Cases and Readings*, published with his former MIT colleague Jack Coleman in 1959.

The following year, Shultz coauthored another book, *Management Organization and the Computer*, with Chicago business policy professor Thomas Whisler. Shultz and Whisler held a conference on a similar theme in anticipation of the rise of the computer. Shultz explained that "the thesis of the book was, You guys in management are using this device to do payrolls and personnel records. Wake up. It's going to change the way you manage your company." The book did not attract many readers, he recalled with a laugh. "The book was a total dud. . . . My mother bought a copy, but she didn't read it. That was the extent of it."[11] But Shultz's interest in computers was prescient, emblematic of his willingness to explore new vistas of technology and scientific development and his openness to changes in perspective.

Even as he immersed himself in the business and economics community in Chicago, Shultz continued to build on his professional work in Washington, acting as a consultant to Eisenhower's labor secretary in 1959 and 1960. After John F. Kennedy became president in 1961, Shultz chaired a task force of the US Employment Service, and he also attended meetings of Kennedy's Advisory Committee on Labor Management Policy.

When Lyndon Johnson assumed the presidency in 1963, following Kennedy's assassination, Shultz was again asked to direct a government task force: "He asked me to chair one on unemployment in the ghetto and what to do about it. And it was a subject that I had worried about—an important subject." Shultz and his team decided that rather than create training programs without a guaranteed job at the end, "you had to get employers to bring these people on board and train them on the job."[12] After they pitched the idea to Johnson, the president convinced Henry Ford II to chair this new jobs program.

Shultz's association with Johnson came with an important insight that he kept very much in mind as his association with political leaders expanded. During a conversation with the president at the beginning of the project, Johnson informed Shultz, "George, if you have a good idea, and it's your idea, it's not going to go very far. But if it becomes my idea, it just might go somewhere. Do I make myself clear?"[13] Once the jobs program became Johnson's idea, Shultz said, "he ran with it brilliantly, and it made a difference."[14] "I learned a good lesson from that," Shultz said.[15] He saw the benefit of subsuming his own ego in service to a higher goal and higher-ranking officials, a self-effacing attitude that would reappear repeatedly as he attained higher office.

After five years at the business school, Shultz became its dean in 1962. His six years as dean were his first leadership role since his service in the Marine Corps two decades earlier, and he had many more constituents to satisfy now. He was responsible for seventy faculty members and thirteen hundred students, and administrative abilities were paramount.[16] Shultz explained, "The ethic at a place like Chicago is that administration is a lousy thing to do, and you shouldn't want to do it but sometimes you have to. . . . But I enjoyed it, and I didn't want to let on that I enjoyed it."[17]

Shultz was jolted by racism while helping the meatpacking industry resolve racial challenges as it dispersed to smaller plants in rural areas. The shift during the 1960s threatened to leave many employees in Chicago and other cities unemployed, including thousands of African Americans. One of the biggest firms and lynchpin of the city's meatpacking industry, Armour and Company, founded in 1867, collaborated with two unions, the United Packinghouse Workers and the Amalgamated Meat Cutters, to create an outside committee, the Armour Automation Fund Committee, to examine the economic and social ramifications of decentralization. Company and union leaders appointed Shultz and Clark Kerr, president of the University of California, as cochairs. The committee mission was to tackle the problem of plant closures and worker layoffs in a changing industry. Shultz recalled, "The traditional pattern was the cattle were driven to big centers in Fort Worth and Kansas City and the famous Chicago stockyards, and they woke up to the fact that when they do that, the cattle all lose weight. And they didn't have to have big stockyards, so they were changing the whole pattern and locating smaller stockyards out more where the cattle were."[18]

In March 1962, Armour announced that it would close its primary plant, located in Fort Worth, Texas, dismissing about a thousand workers in the process.[19] Shultz, along with a University of Chicago colleague, Arnold Weber, and a union official, traveled to Fort Worth. At their hotel, Shultz and Weber quickly registered for their rooms. When the union representative, an African American man, stepped forward, the hotel clerk announced there were no additional rooms available, Weber recalled. Shultz told the clerk that he and Weber would share a room, freeing up space for the union representative. When the clerk rejected the proposal, Shultz said, "We'll move a cot into our room." After disappearing into a back office, the clerk reappeared. "Well, we've just had a cancellation."[20] Shultz later said, "It turned out that's the first time any black guy was registered in that hotel."[21]

The direct encounter with the ugliness of racism left a deep impact on Shultz: "Intellectualizing about the issue is one thing," he said. "Having it happen to you is something else again. You get it in your stomach in a way that is different from getting it in your head."[22] When asked about his 1964 establishment of the Careers for Negroes in Management program, Shultz's response recalled his experience in Fort Worth. He said, "I think I somehow was brought up with the idea that people should be treated on their merits, and obviously they're not being treated on their merits. If you don't treat people on their merits, you're going to lose out on a lot of talent. But then, it's wrong. At the hotel, when the guy wouldn't register, that was just plain wrong."[23]

In 1964, following his experience in Fort Worth and his work with Johnson on jobs creation, Shultz developed one of the first minority scholarship programs at an American business school. It was his proudest achievement as dean. When he became dean, there were two business school programs available at Chicago, a regular on-campus MBA program and a "downtown program" (literally located downtown) for full-time workers who wanted to earn a business degree through night-school classes. Shultz observed that "we had a number of blacks in our downtown program but we had zero on campus, and I thought there was something wrong with that."[24] He knew they were not rejecting these applications—they were not receiving any.

For Shultz, "that was a problem that was solvable."[25] He approached the leaders of a dozen prominent companies, including the First National Bank of Chicago, Inland Steel, Proctor and Gamble, Standard Oil and United Airlines.[26] He convinced them to offer scholarships for African American students, as well as summer internships between the first and second years of the MBA. "The recipient didn't have to take it, but the job was there." With that encouragement, "we managed to recruit some outstanding people to come" earn their business degrees on campus, Shultz remembered.[27]

At home on Blackstone Avenue, Shultz faced division over the Vietnam War. He supported it, but daughter Margaret did not. Margaret left home for college in 1964, then a Democrat "enthralled with Jack Kennedy."[28] She participated in antiwar demonstrations at the University of Massachusetts. At the University of Chicago, Shultz grappled with a student protest against Dow Chemical Company, among the firms that came to campus to recruit and interview students. The Dow protest was one of many antiwar eruptions at the university in the late 1960s, including sit-ins, student strikes and other actions. Disruptions at the university were milder than upheavals at other schools around the country.

Students were protesting against Dow because it was producing Napalm, an incendiary chemical brew that American forces were using in Vietnam. Its use in military operations resulted in horrifying civilian casualties and news photos of severely burned Vietnamese noncombatants fleeing Napalm attacks. The business school faculty, hoping to avoid a paralyzing student protest, asked Shultz to bar Dow Chemical from campus recruiting. Shultz refused, recalling his position in a 1983 interview: "I said, 'Absolutely nothing doing. Communists come here. Nazis come here. Anybody the students want to invite comes, and they say their piece, whatever it is. That's what a campus is about—openness, argument. And, in effect, this company has been invited by these students, and this is where they are going to be interviewed.'"[29] A university trustee suggested that they rent a suite and ferry students there for interviews with Dow rather than hold them on campus, but Shultz again refused. Two prominent professors stood by him, Milton Friedman and George Stigler. The three economists held out, and Dow Chemical came to campus to recruit.

As protests over the war in Vietnam intensified, Shultz met a young man from another conflict-riven region who willingly put himself in harm's way to defend his country, Israel. The contrast with American students who opposed the Vietnam War and resisted the draft was striking to Shultz. His association with Joseph (Yosef) Levy, a thirty-year-old PhD student at the Chicago business school, profoundly affected Shultz. Levy's all-too-short life, and his sudden death during the Arab-Israeli Six-Day War in 1967, had an enduring impact on Shultz's attitude toward Israel and American interests in the Middle East. Levy's story, lodged in Shultz's memory in a partially distorted form, took on a mythological aura for him and ultimately influenced American policy in the Middle East during the Reagan administration.

Shultz had a tradition of inviting students on the dean's list to his home at the end of each quarter, where they would enjoy O'Bie's cooking, including baked beans, or "Dean's beans" as they came to call them. Levy always attended with his wife, Tzvia, and he stood out to Shultz: "Lots of kids are smart, and you had to be smart or you wouldn't have made the dean's list," Shultz explained. "But this young man was different. He was not only smart; he was really one of these savvy young people that you meet and you just know: This kid is destined for big things."[30]

Many of Levy's intimates at home in Jerusalem would have agreed with Shultz's assessment. Yossi, as they called him, was an only child, the son of a successful lawyer, "a self-made man whose own father was a barber," recalls Levy's cousin Shmuel Shay.[31] Levy graduated at seventeen and joined the Academic Reserves, a small number of citizens who studied for several years before fulfilling their draft requirements. Levy studied law and economics at the Hebrew University of Jerusalem before fulfilling his military service. In 1956, when Israel invaded the Sinai to regain access to the Suez Canal, twenty-two-year-old Levy took part in the military campaign.

Levy began his PhD in operations research at the University of Chicago business school in 1963. He completed his degree in a record two and a half years and promptly returned to Israel. Levy and his wife lived in Tel Aviv, where Levy began teaching at Hebrew University. In May 1967, Egyptian troops began massing on the border with Israel, soon followed by mobilization of other Arab militaries. Israel called up its reserves as the tension grew. Levy wanted to play a role. He talked his way into a combat unit in the Jerusalem Brigade just days before the war began. Itzik Nir, a twenty-three-year-old commander in the same battalion, remembers telling Levy that they did not need any officers. But Levy, ranked as a second lieutenant at the time, insisted on staying even as a common soldier. "I think everyone loved him from the very beginning," Nir says.[32]

On June 5, 1967, with more than 230,000 Arab troops lining Israel's borders, the Israeli Air Force launched an air strike that decimated the Egyptian, Syrian and Jordanian air forces. The Jordanians began shelling Israeli Jerusalem. Nir moved his unit toward UN Headquarters. Levy was selected to remain behind but soon rejoined the unit. He was among the men who settled on an exposed stone terrace near their command post. In the morning, when the shelling resumed, incoming munitions shattered the terrace, killing Levy and wounding several soldiers. Four months later, his son, Nadav, was born. That is not exactly how Shultz remembered it. In Shultz's recollection, Levy was still living in Chicago during the tense weeks leading up to the war and had rushed home at the last moment to serve. "I hardly had learned that the Six-Day War had started when I heard he was killed," Shultz said. "He had gotten word of it, went back to Israel, was a tank commander and was killed."[33] Shultz was "stunned" to learn of Levy's death: "He had such talent to be wiped out at such a young age—a loss to mankind, let alone Israel."[34]

A half century later, Shultz still held on to this distorted memory of a young man who rushed headlong from a safe academic position in Chicago to an early death in Jerusalem. "I learned that Israelis have an almost instinctive depth of loyalty to their country, at least Joseph did," Shultz said. "I learned that he lived in an area where conflict was all too prevalent, and it has tragic consequences."[35] For Shultz, Yossi Levy incarnated Israel and the Middle East conflict: "You say to yourself, 'What kind of a country is this that can command the loyalty of such talent?' There's got to be something special there. And then, 'What kind of a world is this—region is this—where such talent can be snuffed out by the animosities there?' It gives you a respect for Israel, and it gives you a concern about the conflict in the region."[36] In February 2016, Shultz traveled to Jerusalem to meet with Levy's widow, Tzvia, and Nadav Levy. He joined the family at events commemorating the service and death of Levy, including the unveiling of a monument at the site where Levy and his comrades died during the Six-Day War. "He was a great man," Shultz told Nadav as the two men descended along a path below the monument. "I am so glad to see him commemorated."[37]

When Shultz was selected as a fellow at Stanford's Center for Advanced Study in Behavioral Sciences for the academic year 1968–1969, he embraced the opportunity, so the family moved west again in the fall of 1968. When shown to his small office on a hill overlooking campus and San Francisco Bay, he was surprised to find that there was no telephone in the sparsely furnished room. The director smilingly explained that they didn't "believe" in phones at the center. Shultz was bewildered at first but soon he found this liberating. He realized that "what I did was what I decided to do, not what somebody rang me up on the telephone and asked me to do." He resolved to hold on to this lesson, where he could "block out periods of time when nothing was scheduled, think ahead about key problems, ways of getting at them, what I wanted to work on, and what I wanted to cause others to work on. This was my own personal version of policy planning."[38]

His old boss at the Council for Economic Advisers, Arthur Burns, had a busier life in mind for Shultz. At Burns's suggestion, Shultz was asked to chair a task force on labor issues for presidential candidate Richard Nixon as the 1968 election approached. His modest role was enough to impress Nixon. By the end of 1968, Shultz cut short his sojourn at Stanford and headed to Washington and a cabinet post as Nixon's secretary of labor.

PART II

Nixon Administration, Bechtel

CHAPTER FIVE

Equal Opportunity

THEY WERE AN UNLIKELY pair, Richard Nixon and George Shultz. Nixon hailed from Yorba Linda, California, at the time of his birth a sleepy, nondescript town in the shadow of Los Angeles; Shultz, from urbane Manhattan and its prosperous northern New Jersey suburbs. Nixon earned an undergraduate degree from Whittier College. Shultz graduated from Princeton. Nixon was consumed by politics; Shultz showed little interest in politics. Nixon was suspicious of academics and intellectuals. Shultz was an academic and an intellectual. Nixon was scheming and insecure; Shultz, trusting and sure of himself.

Despite the differences, the two men improbably developed a productive working relationship during the Nixon presidency. Though Nixon and his tight circle of White House aides never entirely trusted Shultz, and privately ridiculed him for being insufficiently expedient, they dealt Shultz ever more authority as he ascended from labor secretary to inaugural director of the Office of Management and Budget to Treasury secretary. As Shultz transited from one cabinet post to another over six years, the leadership traits that became the hallmark of his government service began to emerge. He was a problem solver, not a zealous ideologue; he combined policy expertise with an instinctively inclusive and effective feel for managing large organizations; he was unflappable; and he worked with a quiet competence and steadiness.

For the most part, he maintained a healthy degree of independence and used his influence to temper some of the Nixon administration's hard-edged domestic policies. But a sense of duty and responsibility, and a subtle, perhaps unconscious, affinity for occupying powerful Washington jobs, kept Shultz coupled with Nixon as the Watergate scandal engulfed the president. He lingered even as his doubts about Nixon's character grew, and his determination to preserve his own integrity was challenged by the rising paranoia and lawbreaking of the president and his henchmen.

Looking back at Nixon years later, recalling a Longfellow verse, Shultz said of Nixon, "He's like the little girl that had a little curl in the middle of her forehead, and when she was good, she was very, very good, and when she was bad, she was horrid."[1] Overall, Shultz said, his relationship with Nixon was positive. "All everybody thinks about with Nixon is Watergate, but Nixon did a lot of really extraordinary things, and a lot of them were in my area."[2] "He developed confidence in me, I think it's fair to say."[3]

As his presidency unfolded, Nixon told H. R. Haldeman, his chief of staff, that Shultz was among the most brilliant minds in his government.[4] In 1970, when Nixon promoted Shultz and moved him into the White House by naming him the director of the newly formed Office of Management and Budget, Nixon said, "I want you here because I track well with you."[5] The *New York Times* reported, "Every White House eventually produces an individual who is relied upon so heavily that he becomes, in effect, Assistant President."[6]

Though Shultz may have met Nixon during the Eisenhower administration when Nixon was vice president and Shultz served for a year on the staff of the Council of Economic Advisers, the Nixon-Shultz relationship began in earnest during the turbulent 1968 presidential campaign, a time of convulsive upheaval in America. Lyndon Johnson, faced with a tidal wave of protests against the Vietnam War, declined to run for reelection after Senator Eugene McCarthy nearly won an upset victory in the New Hampshire Democratic presidential primary. On April 4, James Earl Ray, a small-time criminal and racist, assassinated Martin Luther King Jr. in Memphis. Rioting soon erupted in dozens of cities, including Washington, Chicago, Baltimore and Kansas City. Order was restored only with the intervention of National Guard forces and, in some cases, thousands of active-duty infantry and marines.

On June 6, Sirhan Sirhan, a mentally troubled Palestinian, killed Bobby Kennedy at the Ambassador Hotel in Los Angeles moments after Kennedy celebrated his victory in the California Democratic presidential primary. Two months later, the Democrats nominated Vice President Hubert Humphrey as their presidential candidate during a quarrelsome convention in Chicago that was marked by bloody clashes between demonstrators and the police outside the convention hall.

The national violence and disorder—rioting in Los Angeles, Detroit and Newark had previously shaken the nation in the mid-1960s—coupled with rising crime rates, provided an ideal environment for a law-and-order candidate. Richard Nixon was well prepared to seize it, and did. He had served as vice president for eight years under Dwight Eisenhower, making a mark as a dogged, resilient conservative and anti-Communist. After barely losing the 1960 election to John Kennedy and enduring a humiliating defeat as candidate for California governor in 1962, Nixon assiduously rebuilt his political career by tirelessly courting Republicans to prepare the groundwork for another presidential run in 1968. With pioneering use of modern public relations techniques, including carefully staged television appearances, Nixon refashioned his image, supplanting his reputation as a loser with a vision of a "new," more likable Nixon. Lyndon Johnson's landslide victory over Barry Goldwater in 1964 left the Republican Party shattered, opening the way for a Nixon resurgence. Ronald Reagan, just stepping onto the national political stage after his election as California governor in 1966, was not yet a serious presidential contender.

Nixon made restoration of law and order a primary campaign theme as he appealed to citizens, especially disaffected white voters, unsettled by antiwar protests, civil rights demonstrations, rising crime rates and inner-city rioting. Decades later, Donald Trump would copy the Nixon 1968 campaign playbook with a virulent populist appeal to citizens estranged from the political establishment. Nixon called these Americans "the silent majority" and appealed to them with promises of middle-class empowerment. Though Alabama governor George Wallace was running for president with a blend of color prejudice and economic grievance,[7] Nixon nevertheless campaigned hard to wrest Southerners from their long-standing allegiance to the Democratic Party. His "Southern Strategy" relied on veiled but unmistakably racist appeals to white voters. In the end, Wallace carried five Southern states—Arkansas, Louisiana, Mississippi, Alabama and Georgia—but Nixon won North and South Carolina, two traditionally Democratic states. Nixon edged Humphrey in the popular vote, 43.4 percent to 42.7 percent, but handily prevailed in the electoral college with 301 votes to Humphrey's 191. Wallace collected 46 electoral college votes.

Shultz's labor expertise won him a role in the 1968 Nixon campaign. Arthur Burns, a top economic adviser to Nixon during the campaign, connected the two men. In 1968, Burns invited Shultz to help develop labor policies for a potential Nixon administration, putting him in charge of a planning group on labor affairs, including strikes, wage and price issues and related matters. Shultz assembled a small team of labor specialists who submitted a set of policy recommendations to Burns shortly after Nixon won the election. The role brought Shultz to Nixon's attention and put him in play for a job in the new administration. "I was a Republican and I'd helped during the campaign, but I was not part of the political process," Shultz said.[8]

As a Republican, Nixon owed little politically to labor unions and George Meany, the hard-boiled leader of the AFL-CIO, the nation's largest and most influential labor organization. Union membership, which peaked at over 34 percent of the American workforce in 1954, was rapidly declining by the time Nixon was elected president. Nixon's model for labor secretary was James Mitchell, who served in the post throughout Eisenhower's two terms. While labor leaders considered Mitchell to be a friend, the former New Jersey and New York businessman also commanded respect in the corporate community and gained a reputation as an honest broker on labor-management issues. Shultz had developed a similar reputation from his perch in the academy and his mediation work. H. R. Haldeman recalled, "If we can get George Shultz in the administration, that would be a real coup."[9]

Not long after Shultz and his family relocated to the Bay Area in the fall of 1968 for his fellowship, Burns got in touch after Nixon's election to ask if Shultz would accept an invitation from the president-elect to be labor secretary. Shultz discussed the proposition with O'Bie and their children and decided he would take the job, if formally offered. Nixon soon called Shultz to ask him to serve. Shultz agreed but asked to meet with Nixon to be sure that Nixon was comfortable with the policies that Shultz expected to advance as labor secretary. A few days later, Shultz flew to Los Angeles and the two men talked at the Century Plaza Hotel. Shultz recalled, "I wanted to be sure the president-elect knew my views on labor matters and saw what kind of labor secretary I would be. I would get along with the unions, try to make collective bargaining work, play down high-level and White House intervention in strikes, work on retraining programs for displaced or disadvantaged workers, advocate equal employment opportunity."[10]

If Nixon was not satisfied, Shultz recalled, he could ask someone else to take the job. Shultz's appointment had not been announced. Nixon planned to unveil his entire cabinet simultaneously for dramatic effect. The conversation at the Century Plaza went well, but Shultz noted to himself that Nixon seemed oddly defensive and insecure, selling himself to Shultz rather than vice versa. "I remember reflecting, the guy has just been elected president of the United States and he's got something of an inferiority complex. Turned out to be a penetrating observation about him. He was a brilliant man in many ways, but odd."[11]

On December 11, 1968, Nixon introduced his cabinet to the nation in a nationally televised appearance. When he got to Shultz, Nixon said he had looked for a man "in the tradition of" James Mitchell. Nixon went on, "He is a man who is a great educator, but more than that, he is a man who will speak for labor as did Jim Mitchell, but who also has demonstrated in his mediation capacities that he can gain the confidence of both labor and business. . . . Here is a man who may be able to mediate some of those devastating labor-management crises before they come to the strikes that paralyze our economy."[12]

Actually, mediating potentially crippling nationwide strikes was one thing that Shultz did not plan to do. While at the University of Chicago, he had often opined that Presidents Kennedy and Johnson had intervened too quickly in labor-management conflicts, eliminating the incentive for the dueling parties to negotiate their own settlements. Postwar presidents had frequently wrestled with debilitating strikes. To break a national railroad strike in 1946, Harry Truman threatened to order strikers to be drafted into the armed forces. In 1952, he took control of the nation's steel mills to end a strike that the White House said was impeding prosecution of the

Korean War. John Kennedy grappled with steel industry labor-management disputes, and Lyndon Johnson intervened to avert a railroad strike in 1964.

At Nixon's invitation, O'Bie and the children, along with the families of other cabinet designees, attended the announcement of the cabinet at the Shoreham Hotel in Washington. Shultz thought the invitation was a nice personal touch by the president-elect. With the sabbatical plan abruptly upended, the Shultz's Chicago furnishings packed up for the move and the new Shultz home in Arlington, Virginia, not yet ready for occupation, George and O'Bie decided to take the family to the farm in western Massachusetts for Christmas. Just as they arrived, a powerful snowstorm hit the Berkshires, draping the mountains in a thick layer of snow. The family's Christmas decorations were in Chicago, and the hazardous roads made it tough to go Christmas shopping, so the family settled into the modest farmhouse for a cozy holiday. Peter Shultz remembers it as a magical visit, the best Christmas they ever had. They flew down the slippery hillsides on snow saucers and sat by the fireplace. Peter said, "We threaded popcorn, we got construction paper and made different things to decorate the tree. I don't think we had any lights or anything. We just made it work."[13]

Though Shultz had successfully run a business school, the Labor Department was far larger, with over ten thousand employees and a $3.69 billion budget.[14] Managing a cabinet department also put Shultz at the mercy of the Senate and House Labor and Finance Committees and the political machinations of Washington. He thought his experience as a dean would be useful. "A dean has a lot of responsibility and you don't have much authority," he said. "Your authority over the faculty is very limited; you've got to persuade them. And you can't tell students to learn. You've got to create an environment where they learn, and they have to be the ones who learn. And you have a central administration you have to cope with somehow or other. And you can't order the alumni to give you money; you've got to persuade them that it was a good investment. So everything is persuasion. And when you're in the cabinet, you find the same thing."[15] Not quite. Frederick Livingston, a New York lawyer and longtime Shultz friend, warned Shultz that his lack of political savvy could be a problem. "You have no experience," Livingston told Shultz.[16] He was right, as Shultz soon discovered to his dismay.

Shultz's first task as incoming labor secretary was to hire a team of officials to help run the department. He started by recruiting Arnold Weber, a fellow economist at the University of Chicago and former Shultz graduate student at MIT. Initially, the two men looked at people they knew, then realized that was not a wise approach. "We started thinking about friends of ours who might be good at something, and all of a sudden it hit us: that's not the way to go about it. This is a diverse constituency we're dealing with, and we needed to find people with different experiences from us who would have contacts with others."[17] Shultz and Weber, who agreed to serve as assistant secretary for manpower, wanted high-caliber labor economists and experts, regardless of party affiliation. They soon assembled an impressive group. They selected James Hodgson, a senior executive at Lockheed Aircraft Corporation, as undersecretary, the number-two post. Geoffrey Moore, a top official at the National Bureau of Economic Research, a highly regarded nonpartisan organization, would serve as commissioner of labor statistics. To direct the women's bureau, Shultz appointed Elizabeth Koontz, an African American who was president of the National Education Association. He tapped William Usery to be assistant secretary for labor-management relations.

Shultz and his appointees were invited to the Pierre Hotel in Manhattan, where Nixon and his transition team were based. After meeting with Nixon, Shultz and his team headed to a ballroom downstairs to announce the appointments to the press. The unveiling did not go well. After Hodgson was introduced, a reporter asked about his party affiliation. He was a Democrat. Ditto with the next appointee, and the next. And so it went, with each of Shultz's selections disclosing that he or she was a Democrat or an independent. Not a single one was a Republican. "Naïve me," Shultz recalled. "It had never occurred to me to ask."[18] When he got back to his hotel room, he recalled, "My phone is ringing off the hook—all the Republicans on the Senate Labor Committee saying, 'Don't you know there was an election, and we won?' And I said, 'Well, I checked them with the White House and I checked them with the ranking member on the committee.'" Senator Jacob Javits, a moderate New York Republican, was the ranking Republican. One of the unhappy senators who phoned Shultz told him, "Oh, Javits. He's no Republican!"[19]

Figuring that he needed some savvy public relations advice, Shultz hired Joseph A. Loftus, a veteran labor reporter at the *New York Times*, as special assistant for communications. Before accepting the job, Loftus told Shultz he would need unfettered access to Labor Department policy-making discussions and a free hand in dealing with reporters. He presented Shultz with a list of enlightened, if uncommon, PR practices he would follow if appointed. Dubbed "Loftus's Laws," they included "Don't lie. Don't mislead. Credibility is very precious; it can never be misused. Once destroyed, it cannot be recaptured. The press is an important way you communicate with the public. Don't act as if they are your enemy, however tempting at times."[20]

Shultz got another early lesson in Washington politics when Senator Russell Long, a powerful Louisiana Democrat and chairman of the Senate Finance Committee, confronted Shultz over a Nixon initiative to downsize the Job Corps, a program to train young men for decent-paying jobs. One of the training camps designated for elimination was in Louisiana. At the time, Shultz was also proposing a change in the unemployment compensation law. Senator Long summoned Shultz and Arnold Weber to his office. They sat on the sofa and Long pulled up a chair across from them. "Let me tell you something," Long said, as Shultz recalled. "According to your announcement, you're fixing to close the Job Corps camp in such and such a place. I want you to know I have a personal stake in that camp. If that camp closes, your unemployment compensation bill is going nowhere. Am I making myself clear?"[21] Just in case Shultz and Weber didn't understand, Long went on, "You haven't been in this town very long, have you Mr. Secretary? Well, I ought to tell you, there's two types of people in Washington. The fuckers and the fuckees, and I don't presume to be the latter."[22] Weber recalled that Shultz was startled by the coarse language. In twenty-five years of working with Shultz, Weber had never heard him say anything harsher than "that son of bitch."[23] As they headed back to the Labor Department, Weber dryly noted, "I didn't read about this in the civics books."[24]

Shultz was on firmer ground dealing with substantive issues. He and Nixon faced an early leadership test on the labor-management front as they took office. East and Gulf Coast longshoremen had started a strike the previous summer, but President Johnson, fearing the walkout would endanger the economy, had intervened. Acting under provisions of the 1947

Taft-Hartley Act, he enjoined the strike and won a quick Supreme Court ruling in his favor. The injunction expired a few days before Christmas. Docks from Maine to Texas had been shut down by striking longshoremen for a month as Shultz took office. Firmly believing that presidents should not get involved in labor-management disputes unless a genuine national economic crisis seemed imminent, Shultz urged Nixon to let the long-shoremen and shipping companies resolve their differences without White House help. "If the president hangs out his shingle, he'll get all the business," Shultz said.[25]

He told Nixon, "Mr. President, your predecessor was wrong and the Supreme Court was wrong. This strike will cause a lot of kerfuffle, particularly around New York City, but the economy's very resilient and the problems that it causes will be the pressures that we can use to get the parties to settle this for themselves. And if we do that, we'll teach a big lesson that we want people to face their own problems and make their own agreements." The argument was canny. Shultz recognized that Nixon thought of himself as a strategist rather than a solver of specific problems. "I think what he liked about it was that I explained what I wanted to do in strategic terms. It wasn't just about this dispute. It was about changing our way of going about these things." Nixon did not intervene. Instead, federal mediators worked with the union and management representatives. By the end of March, the strike was over. "Nixon went along with me and he took a lot of heat, particularly from the New York area, but he stood up to it and it worked out just as I said: it wasn't a national emergency. The marketplace is amazing, what it does. That was my first experience with him, and it worked and he liked it."[26]

Not long after the longshoremen returned to work, the Brotherhood of Railroad Signalmen threatened to strike. This time, somewhat contradicting his own advice to Nixon, Shultz invited railroad union and management representatives to the Labor Department for marathon negotiations directed by William Usery. Working with the help of federal mediators, the negotiators reached agreement, avoiding a strike.[27]

Shultz soon found himself working seven days a week, clocking ten to twelve hours a day. "I'm busier than I have ever been in my life," he told the *Wall Street Journal*. He had no time for exercise, reading newspapers or tennis or golf. And he spent less time with the family. "He wasn't around as much," his daughter Barbara recalled. "I remember him being home for some dinners and then having to go back in."[28] Peter Shultz, sixteen years old when his father became labor secretary, said years later, "When it came to being a dad, he didn't have much time. In Chicago, one of the things we used to do is we would go to the museums on the weekend, or during the winters I would ice-skate on the Midway and he'd walk with me there and then go into his office, and then an hour or so later walk by and pick me up and we'd walk home, so we were together a lot of the weekends and things. Dad always had time for me. He taught me to drive in the parking lot of Soldier Field. That didn't happen in Washington. He didn't have as much time."[29]

As Nixon took control of the government, he was determined to scale back many of the social welfare and civil rights programs that the Kennedy and Johnson administrations had created or enhanced. With Democrats in control of the House and Senate, Johnson had successfully launched a series of Great Society initiatives designed to alleviate poverty, expand the social safety net and advance school integration. In his inaugural address on January 20, 1969, Nixon noted the importance of civil rights: "No man can be fully free while his neighbor is not. To go forward at all is to go forward together. This means black and white together, as one nation, not two. The laws have caught up with our conscience. What remains is to give life to what is in the law: to ensure at last that all are born equal in dignity before God, all are born equal in dignity before man."[30]

The words were inspiring, but Nixon's interest in civil rights was limited at best. The lawyer in him understood that civil rights laws had to be honored and enforced; the political Nixon realized his chances to win a second term, with George Wallace expected to run again, would depend partly on replaying the Southern Strategy that had attracted traditional Southern Democrats to vote Republican in 1968. Nixon and his aides also thought many of the Great Society programs were bloated and ineffective and gave the federal government too much power over state and local matters. His domestic agenda meshed with his conventional Republican view that the economy would fare better if government regulation were reduced and market forces unleashed. Shultz shared this Republican perspective about the role of free markets.

For all the political and policy considerations, the truth was that Nixon was not all that interested in domestic policy. The president's passion was foreign affairs. He soon made clear to aides that the less he had to deal with domestic policy, the better. He told H. R. Haldeman, "You handle domestic without me."[31] In July 1969, he gutted the Urban Affairs Council, the high-level group he had created as a domestic counterpart to the National Security Council. Arthur Burns and Daniel Patrick Moynihan, a voluble Harvard scholar and Democrat who had joined the White House staff, served as cochairs of the council. Nixon quickly grew weary of Burns's rambling disquisitions about the economy and long-winded policy arguments between Burns and Moynihan. Over a mid-July weekend at Camp David, Nixon, Haldeman and John Ehrlichman decided to create a Domestic Council, headed by Ehrlichman. Burns, Moynihan, Shultz, Secretary of Health, Education, and Welfare Robert Finch and other domestic cabinet members would henceforth report to Ehrlichman.[32]

The change, in effect, demoted Shultz. But his value to the White House as a social and economic policy thinker and effective emissary to a large block of blue-collar voters made him a valued colleague who could take the lead on a number of fronts. These included restructuring the Job Corps, efforts to increase federal contracting with minority-owned construction firms, court-ordered integration of large urban school systems in the South and welfare reform. Shultz tackled these assignments as a largely apolitical official, often to the consternation of his highly political White House bosses. Nixon often viewed the world through a political prism. Policy choices were often dictated by how much political mileage they would generate for Nixon and his hopes of winning a second term in 1972. The president and his praetorian White House court considered Shultz inexplicably insensitive to political dynamics. "How could Shultz be non-political?" Ehrlichman wondered aloud to Nixon at one point. Nixon replied, "It's almost impossible."[33]

While Shultz championed civil rights, he did so quietly for the most part, absent passionate rhetoric about the issue. He never presented himself as a zealot about civil rights. The progressive minority employment and school integration agendas he supported during the Nixon administration seemed driven more by his sense of fair play and adherence to the law than a burning desire to protect and enhance the rights of minority groups. This followed the pattern established when he was at the University of Chicago, where he remained aloof from the tumultuous civil rights campaign that

Martin Luther King Jr. led in the city but quietly and effectively worked to bring more African American students to the university's business school.

As politically motivated domestic policy edicts were handed down by Ehrlichman, Shultz and his leadership team at the Labor Department quietly remade them into more balanced policies and programs, sometimes defying the White House intent. Their work on the Job Corps was typical. Instead of gutting or abolishing the program, as Nixon wanted, they examined the program carefully, identified strengths and weaknesses and reformed it. Democrats were unhappy with the changes, but Shultz made a defensible case that the Job Corps needed adjustment and he executed sensible changes.

Lyndon Johnson had created the Job Corps as part of his sweeping Great Society campaign to enact progressive domestic programs, including the development of Medicare, a government health insurance program for senior citizens. To help economically challenged Americans, Johnson promised a "War on Poverty." One of the first steps was passage of the Economic Opportunity Act of 1964, establishing the Office of Economic Opportunity (OEO), an agency charged with administering several new programs. One was the Job Corps, designed to provide vocational training to unemployed young men and women fourteen to twenty-two years old who had dropped out of school or were struggling in other ways to get working careers started. Other new federal programs initiated by the OEO in the same period included Head Start, designed to assist kindergarten students from economically distressed homes, and Volunteers in Service to America, a domestic counterpart to the Peace Corps. By 1968, the Job Corps was operating 124 residential training centers, or camps, around the nation, most "conservation" centers for men, located on US Forest Service lands. They had a total enrollment of nearly thirty-five thousand men and women.

Nixon, impatient with the OEO programs, transferred the Job Corps to the Labor Department's Manpower Administration and ordered Shultz to review it. "He wanted to kill it," Shultz recalled.[34] Shultz, familiar with the Job Corps after examining federal job training programs for the Nixon presidential campaign, decided to see if it could be salvaged and improved. He assigned the work to Arnold Weber. The record was spotty. Job Corps centers were troubled by disciplinary problems, high per capita training costs and rising dropout rates, among other problems. A March 1968 audit report by the General Accounting Office (GAO), the investigative arm of Congress, found that the volume of men and women attending camps was falling short of expectations, and record keeping and quality control were largely absent. The GAO proposed remedial steps, but its overall finding was downbeat. "We have doubt, however, that, in light of our findings and the cost of this type of training, the resources now being applied to the Job Corps can be fully justified. Our doubt in this regard is especially applicable to the conservation center component of the program."[35]

Weber's review confirmed the flaws. "They'd have 100 trainees, and eight would get jobs six months later," he recalled. "And a year later only four had jobs. That's what made it inefficient, that they weren't training people for realistic positions and didn't have the connections to the labor market. The cost of training at that time was $4,000, $5,000 a kid, and you were doing an injustice to the kids who were going in there."[36] The GAO offered three primary recommendations: better coordination between the Job Corps and other federal, state and local training programs; a steep reduction in the number of Job Corps centers; and the establishment of thirty new, model centers at inner-city sites.[37] Democratic senators greeted the proposed changes coldly. Fifteen senators appealed to Nixon not to close fifty-nine Job Corps centers. When Shultz appeared before the Senate Subcommittee on Employment, Manpower and Poverty in April 1969, he was assailed. Democrats were outraged by plans to cut the program's annual budget by one hundred million dollars, or more than a third. Senator Gaylord Nelson, Democrat from Wisconsin and the subcommittee chairman, denounced the plan, noting that the Clam Lake center in Wisconsin had been thrown into turmoil as corpsmen, concerned about its imminent closure, were "piling on buses to get the hell out of there."[38]

Shultz, maintaining the sangfroid that was becoming the hallmark of his congressional appearances, defended the Labor Department plan. He conceded that the announced closings would produce a "period of chaos" at the affected center but argued that the administration had the authority to shutter some camps and restructure the Job Corps. As Weber recalled, Shultz's quiet, stoic style was quite effective in handling grandstanding lawmakers. "I used to be able to read the muscles in his neck when he was mad. You'd see a tenseness, but you'd never see it on his face. He'd say, 'Well

Mr. Chairman, you certainly have made a good point.' He wouldn't say, 'You're completely wrong.'"[39] In the end, the Shultz plan prevailed in the Senate when a Democratic resolution to postpone the closing of fifty-nine Job Corps centers was defeated by a coalition of Republicans and Southern Democrats. Senator Long, still simmering over the planned closing of a Louisiana Job Corps camp, voted for the postponement resolution.[40] After the final vote, he declared that Shultz "couldn't find his ankle with his hands. That man doesn't know zero from nothing."[41]

Despite the victory, Shultz recognized that he had much to learn about political maneuvering. He took the verbal lashing from Senator Long, coupled with the decision to move ahead with closing the Louisiana camp, as evidence that he, at least, was willing to move ahead with politically unpopular decisions. "It established a reputation for me as not being very smart politically, but at least having some integrity," he later said with a smile.[42]

When the *Wall Street Journal* checked in on the new labor secretary six months after Shultz assumed the job, the front-page headline declared, "Shultz, an Ex-Professor, Wins General Acclaim as Secretary of Labor." The story opened by reporting:

> George Pratt Shultz is a comer.
> The new Secretary of Labor, little known outside academic circles when he was selected, is establishing a reputation as one of President Nixon's ablest Cabinet choices.
> This soft-spoken ex-professor, occupying one of the hotter spots in Washington, is operating in a quiet but generally effective way that is drawing more bouquets than brickbats from business, labor and his colleagues in Government. One management man predicts he'll be "the best Secretary of Labor in many a moon." A union chief says "he's a lot better than we expected" from the Nixon administration.[43]

George Meany, the gruff, powerful head of the AFL-CIO, was one of the union bosses who respected and liked Shultz. That was no accident. Shultz courted Meany, understanding that his effectiveness as labor secretary depended on maintaining good relations with the unions, especially Meany. Shultz's friendship-building work with Meany was also a reflection of Shultz's belief that men and women of good faith can bridge political, social and economic differences if they trust one another, even when in policy conflict.

Golf brought the two men together. During the AFL-CIO Executive Council's annual meeting in Miami on February 21, 1969, Shultz and

Meany took time out for a round of golf. Shultz shot an 80, ten strokes better than Meany.[44] More important, Shultz helped Meany get a seat at Dwight Eisenhower's state funeral at the Washington National Cathedral on March 31, 1969. Shultz knew that Meany, who was not a Nixon favorite, would cherish an invitation. The two men had talked about Eisenhower one day while they were waiting for a meeting to begin in the White House Cabinet Room, where Eisenhower's portrait hung. Meany told Shultz how much he admired Eisenhower, how they had met during World War II and stayed in touch after the war. "It was harder than I thought," Shultz said, "but I worked on it pretty hard because I knew he didn't want to go there to be seen. He wanted to go because he genuinely admired Eisenhower." He recalled, "Little things like that, when the guy knows you really went out of your way and got something done that was worthwhile, that registers."[45]

While Shultz was restructuring the Job Corps, he waded into another racially charged arena by leading an administration effort to alleviate discrimination in the building trades. The move was an early step toward the development of affirmative-action plans to aid African Americans and other minorities in a variety of fields, including higher education and the labor market. Like other Nixon administration initiatives involving civil rights, the construction jobs program grew out of a mélange of motivations, including a genuine desire to assist minorities and a politically calculated attempt to drive a wedge between two major Democratic constituencies, labor and minorities. Construction sites around the nation had long been overwhelmingly a white man's world. Construction unions were notoriously allergic to recruiting black and other minority workers, and most commercial developers across the nation were uninterested in pressing unions to enroll minority laborers. The Johnson administration tried through the Office of Federal Contract Compliance to require federally supported construction projects to hire minority workers, but the US comptroller general ruled the plan invalid because it violated competitive bidding principles.

As Shultz took office, less than 10 percent of construction trade union members were African American. He recalled: "I found that discriminatory policies against blacks were rampant in the skilled building trades. In Philadelphia, for example, despite the existence of perfectly capable black workers, there were none to be found in the hiring halls of the skilled construction unions."[46] He was determined to change that. "I am deeply interested in civil rights matters and feel the Department of Labor can—and should—play a significant role in assuring equal opportunities to all Americans," he said at the time.[47] In one of his first acts as labor secretary, Shultz announced he would withhold federal contracts from Southern textile mills that failed to adopt affirmative-action programs.[48]

Shultz and Arthur A. Fletcher, an assistant labor secretary and one of the most senior African Americans in the administration, selected Philadelphia as the battleground for their affirmative-action effort. They modified the "Philadelphia Plan," the name for a program the Johnson administration had launched and later abandoned in the city after the comptroller general's ruling. Shultz and Fletcher made it the centerpiece for the Nixon administration drive. To get around the adverse ruling, they cleverly announced that a new Philadelphia Plan would only set race-based hiring goals and timetables rather than hard quotas for integrating the building trades. John Mitchell, the attorney general, bought the distinction, issuing a legal opinion holding that the proposed scheme fell well within Title VII of the Civil Rights Act, the law that the comptroller general had said the Johnson administration plan violated. The plan would apply to contractors with federal or federally supported contracts exceeding five hundred thousand dollars. It covered iron workers, plumbers and pipefitters, elevator construction workers, electricians, steamfitters and sheet metal workers. The goals for minority hiring started in the 4 to 6 percent range and grew to 20 percent after four years. The plan offered an escape hatch, excusing contractors from compliance if they showed a good-faith effort to meet the hiring goals.

Shultz artfully addressed the quota issue at a news conference in which he appeared with Mitchell and Fletcher. "Our approach is to say, 'Here are objectives.' It isn't an exact number. It represents a target to shoot at during a given period of time, and we set these ranges, targets, by a means that make us feel they are reasonable, they are attainable. Then we sit down and work with people to try to help them attain those goals. We are certainly willing to look at a fair effort that somebody makes to get there." He then explained, like a college dean, that any endeavor is best pursued by setting goals, targets and timetables. "It is a very common thing across the board in government and business. Even universities set objectives for themselves."[49] Nixon supported the plan, up to a point. While serving as vice president during the Eisenhower administration, he chaired a committee on government contracts that Eisenhower set up to counteract discrimination in the execution of federal contracts. The committee's charge was anemic—use persuasion rather than coercion—but the group's work gave Nixon an education in discriminatory practices that were common at the time. Using federal persuasion to help African Americans get jobs appealed to Nixon more than coercive steps toward integration.[50]

Civil rights advocates in the Nixon administration, including Stanley Pottinger, the civil rights chief at the Department of Health, Education, and Welfare (HEW) and later at the Justice Department, favored the revised Philadelphia Plan as a matter of principle. Nixon's political advisers liked it because they knew it would irritate George Meany and other labor leaders and put them at odds with civil rights leaders like Roy Wilkins, executive secretary of the National Association for the Advancement of Colored People (NAACP). Meany spoke disparagingly of black workers, referring to them in racist terms when recalling that earlier in his career "it would never have occurred" to him to invite African Americans to join the plumbers' union.[51] Shultz defended the plan in an appearance before the Senate Labor Committee that he vividly recalled decades later. Philip Kurland, the committee counsel and a law professor at the University of Chicago, accused Shultz of favoring a quota system. "I said, 'I'm not trying to *start* one; I'm trying to *replace* one.' And he stormed at me, 'What do you mean?' I said, 'There's been a quota system in place for a long time, and it's been very effective. Zero: that's the quota.'"[52]

When opponents tried to kill the Philadelphia Plan, Shultz spoke at a White House news conference about the importance of federal affirmative-action programs. Recalling his efforts to enroll more minority students at the University of Chicago business school and the work he did to assist African American meatpackers find new jobs when their industry was automated, he said, "Both those things hit me very hard."[53] Two days before Christmas in 1969, Shultz watched the debate and vote from the Senate gallery. Liberal Democrats and moderate Republicans teamed up to defeat the killer rider attached to a supplemental appropriations bill. Republican senator Hugh Scott from Pennsylvania, the minority leader, handed Shultz the tally sheet after the vote. Shultz proudly displayed it on the wall of his conference room to the day he died. Shultz savored the victory. "I'd had a lot of prior exposure to racial discrimination, so it was an issue I cared about and I thought I was on the right side. So I was competitive, but I was really saying, 'Well, here's something that is right, and I'm fighting for it . . . hard.'"[54] He did not care that Nixon might have supported the Philadelphia Plan for political rather than moral reasons. "I got total support from the White House," he recalled in recent years. "This was in spite of the so-called Southern Strategy and everything that was written about so much. But I never asked him, 'Why did you support me?' I just knew that he did."[55]

The same could be said of Nixon's role in desegregating Southern school systems, one of Nixon's—and Shultz's—most significant domestic achievements. When Nixon became president in January 1969, 5.2 percent of African American children in eleven Southern states were enrolled in integrated schools. Two years later, 90 percent attended integrated schools. The dramatic shift did not bring an end to racial and educational inequities in Southern school systems, but the progress was remarkable. "There's no doubt about it—the Nixon administration accomplished more in 1970 to desegregate Southern school systems than had been done in the sixteen previous years, or probably since," Tom Wicker, the former *New York Times* columnist and Washington bureau chief and no fan of Nixon, wrote in a 1991 book about Nixon.[56]

Shultz deserves much of the credit. Under his direction, a cabinet task force on school desegregation cleverly employed presidential and federal power to bring opposing sides together in biracial committees in seven Southern states and helped white and black leaders see that a cooperative approach to desegregation would be far better for their communities than involuntary integration. Raymond Price, Nixon's chief speechwriter, put it this way: "We did what people said couldn't be done; we integrated the schools peacefully. Nixon did that by deliberately reversing the conventional way of doing it, which had been to demonize the white South and beat these people over the head and demand that they rise to a higher moral plane; he made a point of treating them with respect—making them part of the process—and it worked."[57]

As they were in other civil rights matters, Nixon's motivations were mixed. And he probably would not have acted absent the force of a 1968 Supreme Court ruling that left no escape route. Yet Shultz never pressed him to explain the paradoxes inherent in his commitment to integrate Southern schools while courting segregationist white voters. Shultz simply accepted Nixon's strategy and set about executing it. He succeeded far beyond what he or Nixon might have expected when Nixon took office. In May 1968, as Nixon was closing in on the Republican nomination for president, the Supreme Court, impatient with the pace of school desegregation, had ruled, "The burden on a school board today is to come forward with a plan that promises realistically to work, and promises realistically to work *now*." The court emphasized "now."[58] The ruling was a rejection of "freedom-of-choice" plans that Southern school districts, and Nixon, supported. The freedom offered was, in reality, simply a way to postpone integration. White families had no interest in sending their children to integrated schools, and black families were unenthusiastic about putting their children in white schools, fearing a hostile reception.

Nixon showed little interest in advancing school desegregation in the first months of his presidency. If anything, he tried to assuage Southern concerns about federal integration efforts by ordering his administration to delay or roll back a denial of federal school funding that the Johnson administration had employed to coerce school districts to desegregate. Just days after Nixon took office in January 1969, Robert Finch, the newly installed secretary of health, education, and welfare, granted a sixty-day extension of funding to five segregated school districts in Mississippi that had failed to produce desegregation plans. In May, Nixon told Finch that desegregation plans ought to be "inoffensive" to the people of South Carolina and other Southern states.[59]

The message was clear: we are not going to force the South to desegregate schools with the same vigor as the Kennedy and Johnson administrations had. "I support the law of the land," Nixon said in a press conference soon after taking office, while suggesting he was in no hurry to do so. "Before we use the ultimate weapon of denying funds and closing a school, let's exhaust every other possibility to see that local school districts do comply with the law."[60] He put it more bluntly in handwritten comments on a memo from a White House staff member who described complaints about zealous enforcement of civil rights laws that Herb Klein, the White House communications chief, had heard during visits to Dallas and Richmond. "My express policy," Nixon wrote, is to "do what the law requires and not one bit more."[61] Nixon instructed administration spokesmen to adhere to this formulation: "We are opposed to segregation in any form, legal and moral, and we will take action where we find it, and where it amounts to a violation of an individual's rights—but our opposition to segregation does not mean we favor compulsory or forced integration; and we remain opposed to the use of federal funds to bring about some arbitrary racial balance in the public school system."[62]

The federal courts were not so considerate. On July 3, 1969, the Fifth Circuit Court of Appeals, based in New Orleans, ordered the desegregation of thirty-three Mississippi school districts when the new school year opened in September. It set an August 11 deadline for submission of desegregation plans to the court. The decision infuriated Senator John Stennis, a Mississippi Democrat. As chairman of the Senate Armed Services Committee, Stennis had considerable leverage with Nixon, as he supported development of an anti-ballistic missile (ABM) program that Nixon championed. The next step in funding the ABM system required Senate approval of a defense authorization bill. In response to the Fifth Circuit ruling, Stennis warned Nixon that he would temporarily vacate the committee chairmanship to go home to fight the desegregation order, leaving Senator Stuart Symington, an opponent of the ABM system, in charge of the committee. If that happened, Symington was likely to try to scuttle funding.

On August 6, the Senate approved ABM funding by a vote of 51 to 50, with Vice President Spiro Agnew casting the decisive vote in his role as the presiding officer of the Senate. (Under the Constitution, the vice president can vote in the Senate only to break a tie.) Stennis voted for funding. Two weeks later, the administration petitioned the Fifth Circuit to extend the deadline for the Mississippi school districts to December 1. The NAACP quickly appealed to the Supreme Court. Acting swiftly, the Supreme Court unanimously ruled on October 29, 1969: "The obligation of every school district is to terminate dual school systems at once and to operate new and hereafter only unitary schools." Warren Burger, recently appointed chief justice by Nixon, joined the ruling, making it a powerful rebuke to the administration. With further delaying options blocked, Nixon declared he would carry out the law, even though he disagreed with the Supreme Court ruling.[63]

The court ruling served Nixon's political interests. He had sided with white Southerners by opposing the Fifth Circuit decree. Now, he had no choice but to comply with the Supreme Court decision. The role of reluctant enforcer of desegregation orders was a perfect fit—it allowed Nixon to demonstrate his sympathy for Southern concerns about school integration while simultaneously honoring his oath to "preserve, protect and defend the Constitution of the United States." The mechanism Nixon selected in February 1970 to enforce the law was a cabinet task force, headed by Vice President Agnew, former governor of Maryland, who was less than enthusiastic about school desegregation himself. Nixon appointed Shultz as vice chairman. Other members included John Mitchell and Robert Finch. Robert Mardian, the HEW general counsel, was named executive director.[64] Civil rights groups regarded Mardian, a Barry Goldwater organizer in 1964 and Republican Party official in California, as a desegregation opponent. Indeed, he had roundly criticized the Johnson administration for withholding federal funds to try to coerce Southern school districts to desegregate.

In announcing creation of the task force, Nixon issued an extended statement about his administration's views on desegregation. He embraced a community-based approach, calling on business, labor, education and religious leaders to work together and in cooperation with the federal government to ensure that local school systems remained a vital source of educated men and women in their communities. Rather than threaten to withhold federal funds if districts failed to desegregate or impose busing plans that would require students to attend schools outside their neighborhood or local community, he promised to make $1.5 billion available to help pay for integration efforts. At the same time, he made clear that the federal government would take uncooperative school districts to court to require them to desegregate. The strategy essentially was to desegregate voluntarily with federal financial aid or face court-ordered federal enforcement actions.

Agnew was leery of the entire enterprise and quickly distanced himself from the task force, without formally relinquishing his role as chairman. It quickly became clear to Shultz that Agnew was withdrawing. Shultz recalled, "Agnew said, 'I don't want to have anything to do with this. It's going to be bloody, and I won't participate.' So I became the de facto chairman."[65] As Shultz took over the task force, he worked closely with two top White House aides, Daniel Patrick Moynihan and Leonard Garment. Moynihan, a loquacious Harvard professor, initially played a leading role in Nixon domestic policy making until John Ehrlichman supplanted him. Shultz, a fellow academic, liked Moynihan. "He was very lucid and a brilliant writer, an interesting man, interesting mind," Shultz said.[66] The two men had together devised a welfare reform proposal for Nixon that never gained traction. Shultz also liked Garment, a skillful lawyer who was a proponent of integration.

Recognizing that the support of community leaders was essential to successful desegregation, Shultz and the task force placed their bets on the establishment of a biracial committee in each of the seven states targeted for integration. They selected Mississippi as the first case, realizing that it would be among the most difficult. If the strategy worked there, it would work elsewhere. Shultz and his colleagues insisted that the Mississippi committee include desegregation proponents and opponents. When reporters learned that a Ku Klux Klan member had been appointed to the Mississippi committee, they jumped on Robert Mardian during a visit to Los Angeles. Asked if it was true that a KKK member served on the committee, Mardian replied, "I don't know. I have heard there are five. I certainly hope so." He added, "You can report that if you also report that the vice chairman of the committee is the president of the Biloxi NAACP chapter."[67]

Shultz recalled, "We decided the key is to involve respected people—black and white—and try to work with them. Our effort was to create a committee in each state, half black, half white. And by agreement with the president, we weren't even going to ask anybody whether they were Republicans or Democrats; we didn't care. What we wanted were people who were respected in their respective communities and who, if they said something, they would be taken seriously."[68]

Mardian and several other administration officials made several trips to Mississippi to consult with white and black leaders and to narrow a list of possible committee members. On June 24, 1970, the Mississippi committee—nine white, six black—assembled in the Roosevelt Room of the White House, across the hall from the Oval Office. Shultz, Robert Finch, John Mitchell and a gaggle of White House aides joined them. Shultz welcomed the wary Mississippians. The atmosphere was tense and grew more strained after Albert Fielder, a black man from Meridian, asked the attorney general how he planned to remedy the fact that there was not a single black member on any Mississippi school board. One of the white Mississippians pulled a White House aide aside to complain that the composition of school boards was not a matter he was prepared to discuss and would walk out of the meeting if Fielder brought it up again. Mitchell bluntly informed the group that if Mississippi failed to integrate its schools, he would enforce the law and leave them no choice.

The atmosphere improved a few minutes later when the group was escorted into the Oval Office for a meeting with Nixon, who recalled meeting Fielder during a visit to Meridian. Then another black committee member told Nixon, "Day before yesterday, I was in jail for going to the wrong beach. Today, Mr. President, I am meeting you. If that's possible, anything is possible."[69] The next stop was lunch in the ornate Jefferson Room at the State Department. Shultz had invited the two senators from Mississippi, John Stennis and James Eastland, and the state's five congressmen to attend the lunch. They all declined. One of them told Mardian, "You've been around long enough to know I'm against desegregation." He refused to attend a lunch with African Americans, referring to them with a racial slur.[70]

Shultz and Mardian sat together at a table that included the two men they hoped would agree to serve as chair and vice chair of the committee, Warren Hood, president of the Mississippi Manufacturers Association, and Dr. Gilbert Mason, a black physician from Biloxi. As the lunch conversation progressed, Shultz unexpectedly stood up and headed for the door, motioning Mardian to follow him. "Why are we leaving?," a stunned Mardian asked. "They're ready to come to agreement." Shultz replied, "I learned long ago in labor negotiations that when parties get that close to a decision, there is only one way they can complete it—by themselves."[71] Shultz also thought that an agreement reached by men on their own would become their agreement rather than an agreement imposed on them by Shultz or the White House.[72] As Shultz and Mardian exited the Jefferson Room, Mason told Hood, "If you and I can't do this, nobody else in Mississippi can. We're probably the only black and white men in the state who can get together on something like this." Mason and Hood shook hands. The Mississippi committee was a go.

Over the next few weeks, the other six Southern states followed suit, each led to desegregation by a biracial committee like the one in Mississippi. Louisiana was the last state to fall in line, and only after Nixon traveled to New Orleans on August 14 to encourage the desegregation committee to move ahead. Agnew advised Nixon not to go. Shultz recalled the moment, a meeting in the Oval Office. "Agnew says, 'Mr. President, don't go. There's going to be blood through the streets of the South, and the blood will be on your hands. Stay away. The blood should be on the hands of all these liberals from the North that have been pushing this.' So Nixon looks at me. I'm the nonpolitician in the room. I say, 'Well, I don't know. Maybe the vice president's right. But, Mr. President, whatever happens, it's on your watch, and you've met with these people who've come up here. You can see for yourself they are good people and we have been working with them. So I think you should go.'"[73] Nixon agreed with Shultz.

Shultz credits Nixon with coaxing the Louisiana committee into action despite strong misgivings among its members. As Air Force One landed in New Orleans, Shultz, already meeting with the committee at a hotel, realized that the committee chemistry was not favorable. John Mitchell had not made the trip, leaving Shultz without the attorney general to lean on the committee with his threat to enforce the law. The hotel site lacked the White House aura that lent meetings a sense of historical significance. "All these things are dawning on me," he recalled. "We're getting along, but it's not quite as good. And all of a sudden I hear, 'The president has just landed.' Then, 'The president's ten minutes out.'"[74] Shultz feared the Louisiana meeting would fail.

Nixon made a strong closing argument with the committee, telling them that Louisiana schools would be integrated on opening day, August 31, whether the state approved the move or not. But he promised the committee that the federal government was ready to support a peaceful, voluntary transition. "You can have good schools, inferior schools or no schools," he told them. When Nixon was finished, the committee agreed to support desegregation. Nixon later emphasized that his approach to desegregation "treated this part of the country with the respect it deserves."[75]

The outcome across the South was the ideal resolution for Nixon. Schools were desegregated, as the Supreme Court had ordered, allowing Nixon to claim accurately that he had upheld the law. Yet he could also legitimately say he had respected the dignity of Southern states and worked cooperatively with them. A vital national goal—desegregation—had been powerfully advanced without undermining Nixon's future political appeal to Southern white voters. While Nixon set the course and dedicated his administration to realizing the goal, Shultz provided the smart strategy that made it work. "It's a principle I got from my labor relations," he said. "As long as people are arguing about principle, you can't get anywhere. If you can translate it into problems, people are pretty good at solving problems."[76]

On the flight back to Washington Nixon joined his team in the staff section of Air Force One. Shultz, Moynihan, Garment and Bryce Harlow, a Southerner who served as a presidential counselor, were talking. Nixon asked Harlow how he thought the desegregation effort was going. Shultz still remembered the exchange decades later:

Harlow: "Well, Mr. President, I think it will go pretty well in the South. Your problem's going to be in the North."

Nixon: "What do you mean by that?"

Harlow: "In the South, we hate the Negro as a race but we love the Negro as a human being. When they get sick, we help them. When we get sick, they help us. They help take care of our children. We worry about their children. We have strong, direct human relationships, so we get along. In the North, it's the other way around. They exalt the Negro as a race but they have no human experience."

Thinking about the moment later, Shultz said, "It turned out to be a pretty prophetic remark."[77]

CHAPTER SIX

Treasury Travails

SHULTZ'S MANAGEMENT OF THE Labor Department turned out to be an audition for higher office, first as the inaugural director of a powerful new government agency, the Office of Management and Budget (OMB), and then as Treasury secretary and simultaneously Richard Nixon's chief economic policy adviser. The jobs put him at the vortex of critical and controversial economic actions that rocked the nation and the world. The Treasury post also gave Shultz a fiery baptism in Richard Nixon's abuses of power. He passed one test, refusing to unleash the IRS against a list of Nixon opponents. He fell short on another, succumbing to White House pressure to turn the IRS on Lawrence O'Brien, chair of the Democratic National Committee.

As the Watergate scandal closed in on Nixon, Shultz was clear-eyed about Nixon's misconduct but remained loyal to him. He stayed on as Treasury secretary until May 1974, three months before Nixon resigned. Loyalty trumped principle, or so it seemed. Shultz disputed that interpretation, but even his friends wondered why he chose not to part company with Nixon sooner. When he did leave, the last of Nixon's original cabinet members to go, he mused, seemingly without irony, about top government officials who have a "tendency to stay too long."[1]

Impressed by Shultz's performance as labor secretary, Nixon put him in charge of the OMB in 1970. The organization reflected Nixon's desire to refashion the Bureau of the Budget, creating a successor agency with greater sway across the executive branch. Its director would assume a leading role in management of the government. To underscore the point, Shultz moved into a West Wing office on July 1, 1970. "I want you to have your meetings there," Nixon told him, advising Shultz that a White House office would underline the authority of the OMB director. If the office was not large enough for some meetings, Nixon invited Shultz to use the Roosevelt Room.[2] *BusinessWeek* described Shultz as "one of the president's three or four top confidants. He is a pivotal man in the drive to restructure the government."[3]

At OMB, Shultz found himself cast with Caspar Weinberger, a rising California attorney–cum–political figure who had supported Nixon's 1968 presidential campaign, served as chair of the California Republican Party and worked as Governor Ronald Reagan's state finance director. Nixon brought him to Washington in 1969 to lead the Federal Trade Commission, then moved him to OMB to be deputy director as the new agency opened. The Shultz-Weinberger pairing was the first of several occasions when they worked warily alongside each other as their careers advanced. The higher they rose, the more they clashed.

Two policy issues dominated Shultz's tenure at OMB and Treasury— combating inflation and disconnecting the value of the dollar from the price of gold. In intense administration debates about these matters, Shultz became the primary advocate of free-market solutions, reflecting his faith in the Chicago school of economic philosophy and his trust in Milton Friedman. As Shultz took command of OMB, the White House was growing increasingly concerned that inflation was proving more persistent than it had been in recent economic cycles. Alarmed that businesses were laying off workers and limiting capital expenditures and that the consumer price index was rising, Nixon feared inflation would stall the economy and imperil his 1972 reelection hopes.[4]

John Connally, the Treasury secretary, favored government intervention. Connally, a Democrat, had joined the Nixon administration after serving as Texas governor. He had hosted John F. Kennedy's visit to Dallas on November 22, 1963, and was wounded during the assassination as the two men rode together through Dealey Plaza in the president's open limousine. More a politician than a policy maker, Connally gained Nixon's trust and became a dominant figure in economic policy deliberations. Shultz admired his brashness but thought he lacked depth. "He was less interested in content than he was in presentation," Shultz recalled. Ron Ziegler, Nixon's press secretary, told Shultz that Connally had assured him, "Ron, I can sell it flat or I can sell it round, just tell me."[5]

Arthur Burns was Connally's improbable ally in the inflation debate. Appointed Federal Reserve chair by Nixon in early 1970, Burns surprised fellow economists by favoring government action to hold down inflation. As chief economic adviser during Nixon's first year as president, Burns endorsed free-market approaches to tackling inflation. He reversed course as he became convinced that inflation had become an intractable problem immune to natural forces in the economy that would normally temper it. He called for the adoption of wage and price controls. "We face a problem unknown to earlier generations—namely a high rate of inflation at a time of substantial unemployment," he told the Senate Banking Committee in March 1971.[6]

Shultz disagreed. Although concurring with Burns on many economic issues and respectful of him as a mentor and the person who had recommended him to Nixon, Shultz strongly opposed the controls. He did not believe the federal budget was fueling inflation and counseled patience to let market forces bring down inflation. He summarized his outlook a month after Burns's Senate testimony. In a speech titled "Steady as You Go," Shultz told the Economic Club of Chicago, "A portion of the battle against inflation is now over; time and the guts to take the time, not additional medicine, are required for the sickness to disappear. We should now follow a noninflationary path back to full employment."[7]

Time magazine put the dueling duo of Burns and Shultz on its cover in early August 1971: a cartoon depicted the two men, bloodied by combat, wrestling under the headline: "Battle of the Economy: Stand Pat or Do Something?" Burns and Connally won the debate. Along with Shultz and other economic advisers, they hashed out the issue with Nixon at Camp David, the presidential retreat, on August 13. Two days later Nixon ordered a sixty-day price freeze followed by wage and price controls. Newspaper headlines called the decision the "Nixon Shock." Milton Friedman, siding with Shultz, said Nixon "has a tiger by the tail. Reluctant as he was to grasp it, he will find it hard to let go."[8] Shultz soon was holding the tail himself as Treasury secretary.

Looking back on the activation of controls, Shultz said, "In the short term, the consumer price index, which measures inflation, declined and real GDP rose. All this led to the landslide reelection of President Nixon. But trouble lay ahead. The economy sputtered, and prices were a problem. The Cost of Living Council, the bureaucracy responsible for administering the controls, was intrusive. No wage or price change could take place without approval of the Pay Board or the Price Commission, so the gears of the economy ceased working in the normal and natural way that produces an efficient system."[9]

The Cost of Living Council reported to Shultz as Treasury secretary. He wanted to ease the controls, as did the two young men who ran the council: Dick Cheney and Donald Rumsfeld. Both men would go on to serve as secretaries of defense, twice in Rumsfeld's case, under Presidents Gerald Ford and George W. Bush. Cheney, who was defense secretary under President George H. W. Bush, was elected vice president in 2000 and 2004 as George W. Bush's running mate. Nixon lifted the measures but then reinstated them in June 1973. Shultz remained unconvinced and told Nixon he needed to find a new Treasury secretary who supported the president's policy. Shultz backed off the threat when Nixon asked him to stay on to help host a visit to the United States by Leonid Brezhnev, the Soviet leader. He ended up staying in office until May 1974.

To Shultz's obvious delight, Friedman inveighed repeatedly against the controls. In March 1974, Friedman told a group of bankers, "There is hardly a person today who will not recognize that price and wage controls meant more inflation—not less—that they mean disruption, distortion, a reduction in output, and an increase in the power of the government over the individual."[10] The convulsions over inflation left Shultz more convinced than ever of the vital importance of free markets: "The free market system is, at its core, a system of accountability. If you let it work, the accountability is relentless in punishing bad performances and rewarding good ones. If you intervene in this accountability system, though, you inevitably change it and can easily wind up moving responsibility to the intervener, usually the government."[11]

While dealing with wage and price controls, Shultz played a central role in altering the way currencies were valued. Under the 1944 Bretton Woods Agreement, reached by delegates from forty-four nations who gathered in Bretton Woods, New Hampshire, the external value of national currencies was set in relation to the value of the dollar. The value of the dollar, in turn, was fixed by the value of American gold reserves, thirty-five dollars per ounce. This fixed exchange rate system started to crumble in the 1960s as the number of dollars in worldwide circulation outgrew the US gold stock-pile to back up the dollar, leaving the dollar overvalued. By the early 1970s, the stress on the Bretton Woods system neared a breaking point. West Germany withdrew from the agreement, and foreign central banks struggled to convert their dollar holdings to gold at the fixed rate. The number of dollars controlled by foreign governments reached an unsustainable point that was more than three times the dollar value of the gold reserves housed at Fort Knox.[12]

The developing crisis had enormous global and domestic implications. The stability of both the postwar world economy and the American economy rested in critical ways on the Bretton Woods foundation and the fixed value of the dollar. Delinking the value of the dollar from American gold reserves would not only alter the international monetary system but also somewhat reduce the role of the United States in that system. Administration policy making dramatically culminated in mid-August 1971 at Camp David when Nixon and his top aides, including Shultz, decided to end America's commitment to link the dollar to the fixed-rate value of gold. Instead, as Shultz proposed, there would be a system of floating exchange rates that, in effect, relied on market dynamics—the demand for dollars relative to its supply—rather than the fixed price of gold. The August 15, 1971, decision sent shock waves around the world.

Milton Friedman later described the shift. "Nixon closed the gold window and ended the commitment which the United States had to buy or sell gold to foreign governments, at a fixed price. The ending of this commitment paved the way for ending controls on the price of the dollar in terms of the mark, franc, yen and the pound. So, this measure opened the way to a free market, where there was none before."[13] The Shultz-designed architecture remains in place today, some forty years later. Jeffrey E. Garten, the former dean of Yale's School of Management, described the shift as signaling the world that "the near-omnipotent role that the United States had played since the war was over."[14]

When Shultz moved into the Treasury secretary's spacious office overlooking the White House South Lawn and the Ellipse, he knew he would face a variety of economic challenges. He had no idea his authority over the Internal Revenue Service would draw him into one of the most acute ethical crises of his government career. Managing the IRS is one of the most sensitive jobs in Washington. Few government agencies hold such sway over so many Americans, with the power to bend taxpayers to its will through administrative measures ranging from audits to the garnering of wages, seizure of property and other draconian steps, not to mention criminal prosecution of taxpayers for felony violations. The agency's extensive access to the most intimate financial details about individuals, couples and businesses is an invitation to abuse.

It was a temptation that Richard Nixon and his aides could not resist. In 1971, Nixon bluntly told his two most trusted White House aides, Robert Haldeman, the White House chief of staff, and John Ehrlichman, assistant to the president for domestic affairs, precisely what kind of IRS commissioner he wanted: "I want to be sure he is a ruthless son of a bitch, that he will do what's he told, that every income tax return I want to see I see, that he will go after our enemies and not go after our friends. Now, it's as simple as that."[15] Nixon, Haldeman and Erlichman soon started pressing Shultz and the IRS commissioner, Johnnie M. Walters, a South Carolina tax lawyer appointed to the post by Nixon, to use the IRS as a flamethrower against their opponents. The demands were brazen, the pressure unremitting and the growing impatience with Shultz and Walters increasingly intense as 1972 unfolded, all secretly recorded in a series of conversations among the president, Haldeman and Ehrlichman.

Shultz and Walters admirably rejected one attempt, a stunning 1972 demand by John W. Dean III, the White House counsel, to urge the IRS to pursue a list of several hundred George McGovern staff members and campaign contributors. At the time, Senator McGovern was the Democratic presidential nominee. When Dean presented what became known as the "Nixon enemies list" to Walters on September 11, 1972, the IRS commissioner was appalled. Walters told Dean, "If I did what you asked, it'd make Watergate look like a Sunday school picnic."[16] He immediately took the list to Shultz for consultation. Shultz instructed him to ignore it and to tell Dean to call him if Dean leaned on Walters to take action. "That was totally out of line, and we said no," Shultz recalled.[17] When Dean pushed Walters a few weeks later, Shultz reiterated that nothing should be done. Walters put the list in an IRS safe and took no further action, infuriating Dean and the White House.[18]

Shultz also backed Walters when the IRS, in randomly selecting complicated tax filings to audit, picked Nixon's returns. "Guess whose name came up?" Walters announced to Shultz one day. Shultz told him to go ahead. He informed Alexander Haig, who in May 1973 had replaced Haldeman as the White House chief of staff. Haig told Nixon. The president was furious. "He's really steamed," Haig informed Shultz. "He thinks the IRS is trying to harass him and wants to know by eight o'clock tomorrow morning whether any sitting president has ever been audited." Walters provided the answer at seven o'clock the next morning: Franklin Roosevelt and John Kennedy had been audited while in office. They, too, had complicated returns that fit the random selection metrics. "Whew!" Shultz thought to himself.[19]

Shultz acted less nobly when the White House pressured the IRS in 1972 to investigate the tax returns of Lawrence O'Brien, a leading Democrat. In contrast to his defiant stance about the "enemies list," Shultz expressed discomfort about the pursuit of O'Brien but did not stand in the way of an extensive IRS investigation. The White House assault sent the IRS into a frantic scramble during the summer of 1972 to come up with damaging financial information about O'Brien and his business associates before the November presidential election. As the confidential data flowed into IRS headquarters in Washington, Shultz passed some of it along to the White House and relayed impatient demands from Ehrlichman to Walters.[20] In the end, O'Brien was cleared, but the episode was an abuse of power by the White House and a misstep by Shultz that left Walters furious and disappointed with Shultz.

Shultz's entanglement with the IRS and White House was one of many pieces of the Watergate affair that eventually forced Nixon to resign the presidency on August 8, 1974. Over time, the term "Watergate" came to cover a variety of misdeeds and crimes committed by Nixon, several of his cabinet members, his top aides and an array of other Nixon supporters. Most of the unethical activity grew out of Nixon's paranoia about his opponents and his reliance on underhanded maneuvers to sabotage his critics and gain reelection in 1972. The core of the Watergate scandal started when burglars broke into the Democratic National Committee headquarters at the Watergate office complex in Washington on June 17, 1972, in hopes of replacing wiretapping devices previously installed in the offices of its chairman, Lawrence O'Brien. The break-in was detected midstream, and the five burglars were arrested. Prosecutors soon linked them to the Nixon reelection campaign committee. From there, the investigation, and tireless reporting by Bob Woodward and Carl Bernstein of the *Washington Post*, unveiled a series of illegal acts, including the diversion of campaign funds to finance the break-in and payment of hush money intended to keep the burglars from disclosing the role of the reelection committee.

Nixon and his top aides tried feverishly to cover up White House involvement in the affair. Nationally televised Senate hearings dramatically depicted the lawlessness, including testimony by John Dean, who turned against Nixon in a crisis of conscience and for fear he would become the scapegoat for Watergate. On October 20, 1973, Nixon ordered Attorney General Elliot Richardson to fire Archibald Cox, who had been appointed as a special prosecutor to investigate the case. Richardson refused and resigned, as did his deputy, William Ruckelshaus. Robert Bork, the solicitor general, dismissed Cox. The bloodletting quickly became known as the Saturday Night Massacre. The House Judiciary Committee drafted articles of impeachment, and former Nixon attorney general John Mitchell, who headed his reelection committee, and Maurice Stans, a former commerce secretary who became reelection finance director, were indicted. The endgame came after Alexander Butterfield, a White House aide, disclosed that conversations about the plot were recorded on a secret taping system in the Oval Office and other White House locations. Nixon resigned not long after the Supreme Court unanimously ruled that the recordings had to be turned over to investigators.

Shultz had no involvement in the Watergate break-in or the cover-up, but Nixon turned his malign attention to Shultz less than two months after the botched Watergate burglary when the president fixated on O'Brien and tried to commandeer the investigative and enforcement divisions of the IRS to pursue O'Brien for tax evasion and fraud. Nixon told Haldeman he wanted to "dirty up O'Brien."[21] Nixon viewed him as the Democrat's most effective political operative and a threat to his reelection prospects. O'Brien, born and raised in Springfield, Massachusetts, the son of Irish immigrants, was, indeed, a skilled political operative, one of the best of his era. After earning a law degree from Northeastern University in 1942, he quickly made his way into politics, becoming a key campaign aide to John F. Kennedy during Kennedy's successful runs for a Senate seat in 1952 and 1958. O'Brien served as the director of organization during Kennedy's 1960 presidential campaign.

O'Brien was running the Democratic National Committee in 1972 as Nixon was preparing his reelection campaign and unleashing a variety of underhanded maneuvers designed to disrupt the Democrats and their leading presidential contenders, Senator Edmund Muskie from Maine and Senator George McGovern from South Dakota. One way to subvert the Democrats was to disable O'Brien. John Ehrlichman, Nixon's chief accomplice in this effort, put it this way in an Oval Office conversation with Nixon: "We just want O'Brien to quit sleeping nights."[22] Nixon and his aides figured the best way to intimidate O'Brien was to enlist the IRS in a campaign of harassment, investigation and, if possible, prosecution for tax malfeasance. In their warped view, using the IRS as a weapon against Nixon's political opponents was perfectly reasonable and legitimate, just another way of exercising presidential power. The White House attitude was captured in a memo that John Caulfield, an aide to John Dean, prepared for Haldeman before Haldeman met with Shultz to talk about the IRS.

Contending that Democratic administrations had used the IRS effectively against political opponents, Caulfield reported that the Nixon team had failed to do so. "We have been unable." It went on:

"The Problem"

Lack of guts and effort. The Republican appointees appear afraid and unwilling to do anything with IRS that could be politically helpful. For example:
  We have been unable to crack down on the multitude of tax exempt foundations that feed left wing political causes.

We have been unable to obtain information in the possession of the IRS regarding our political enemies.

We have been unable to stimulate audits of persons who should be audited.

We have been unsuccessful in placing RN supporters in the IRS bureaucracy.[23]

Caulfield advised Haldeman to tell Shultz that Johnnie Walters "must be more responsive" by hiring staff recommended by the White House. Moreover, the memo stated: "Walters should be told that discreet political action and investigations are a firm requirement and responsibility on his part. John Dean should have direct access to Walters, without Treasury clearance, for purposes of the White House. Walters should understand that when a request comes to him, it is his responsibility to accomplish it—without the White House having to tell him so."[24] George Shultz did not agree and initially tried to shield the IRS from White House interference but eventually succumbed in handling O'Brien.

Walters seemed an unlikely defender of IRS independence when the White House selected him as commissioner in 1971. John Mitchell, the attorney general, soon to become chairman of the Committee for the Re-election of the President, recommended Walters for the job, impressed by his performance as assistant attorney general for tax policy. "Mitchell said he was the guy who would cooperate," Haldeman recalled in 1972.[25] The White House agreed, thinking he would be more malleable than Randolph Thrower, who was fired as commissioner for resisting White House pressure.[26] The White House's assessment proved mistaken. A modest, bookish, bespectacled man, Walters was a sharecropper's son, a farm boy from rural South Carolina whose primary ambition as a young man was to get a law degree and make a decent living in his home state. He was a Boy Scout and scoutmaster, a member of the Rotary Club and lay preacher at his local Baptist church. After graduating from Furman University in 1942, he joined the US Army Air Forces and served as navigator on more than fifty perilous combat missions in Europe, winning a Purple Heart. When the war ended, he enrolled at the University of Michigan Law School. Strom Thurmond, the long-serving South Carolina senator, liked Walters and encouraged the Nixon administration to give him a job.

As Walters took over as IRS commissioner, his top goals were to simplify the paperwork for tax returns and to crack down on tax evaders. Contrary to White House expectations, he understood that manipulating the IRS for political purposes was wrong and quite possibly illegal. As it became clear to the White House that Walters would not be its obedient, ruthless servant, Nixon and his advisers grew increasingly impatient with him and eventually decided to fire him.

The possibility of a tax case against O'Brien grew out of his dealings with Howard Hughes, the wealthy, eccentric businessman and aviator who spent the latter decades of his life in near-hermetic isolation in a penthouse complex atop the Desert Inn, one of his Las Vegas properties. The isolation was self-imposed by the paranoid Hughes, who feared germs and dust that might be transmitted by contact with other people. Hughes, who inherited his Texas family's oil tool business, Hughes Tool Company, was one of the richest men in America. During a lifetime of dizzyingly varied pursuits, he founded the Hughes Aircraft Company; acquired and expanded TWA Airlines; designed, built and piloted the *Spruce Goose*, the largest airplane ever constructed or flown; and produced several Hollywood movies. As a rakish young man, he frequently made the gossip columns, dating Hollywood stars Katherine Hepburn, Ava Gardner and Ginger Rogers. Along the way, he also established the Howard Hughes Medical Institute, which became a respected biomedical research center and remains so today.

With business enterprises spread across the nation, including Texas, California and Nevada, Hughes was anxious to wield political influence at the national and state levels to protect his corporate interests. O'Brien's political connections made him a natural magnet for Hughes. In 1968, the top executive at Hughes Enterprises, Robert Maheu, got in touch with O'Brien because Howard Hughes wanted to hire him. Maheu invited O'Brien to spend a weekend in Las Vegas so they could discuss the proposition.[27] The employment offer came directly from Hughes, Maheu told O'Brien, once O'Brien and his wife and son had checked into the Desert Inn. He explained to an amazed O'Brien that he never met with Hughes in person but nevertheless handled his business affairs. O'Brien said he did not want to work full-time for anyone but planned to open a consulting firm in New York. That led to a conversation about contracting with the O'Brien firm for advice, among other things, about how to draw attention to Hughes's support of medical research through the Howard Hughes Medical Foundation.[28]

After several false starts with Maheu, O'Brien eventually sealed a fifteen-thousand-dollar-per-month consulting deal and started work for Hughes Tool Company in January 1969, along with two colleagues, Joseph Napolitan and Claude Desautels. The three men ended up working on a variety of matters that intersected with Hughes's business interests, including Nevada water projects; underground nuclear weapons testing in Nevada; prevention of dumping nerve gas in the ocean; Las Vegas airport development plans; Nevada educational television; communication satellites; Air West, a commercial airline company; and the Howard Hughes Medical Institute.[29] In 1970, Hughes Tool Company paid $190,000 to Lawrence F. O'Brien and Associates and $163,000 to Joseph Napolitan Associates.[30] The IRS conducted routine audits of O'Brien's 1969 and 1970 tax returns, found nothing that warranted further investigation and closed the audits.[31]

In late 1971 or early 1972, the IRS opened an intensive investigation of the Howard Hughes organization and operations. Unbeknownst to the IRS at the time, the White House was already taking an active interest in O'Brien's financial affairs after learning in early 1971 that he was representing Howard Hughes. Nixon was especially interested in Hughes's business affairs because Hughes had financial dealings with Donald Nixon, the president's younger brother, and Bebe Rebozo, one of the president's closest friends. When the White House learned that the IRS had opened a criminal investigation into possible kickback schemes involving Hughes, Nixon demanded that he be kept up-to-date on developments. The prospect of an IRS investigation of Howard Hughes that might involve Donald Nixon, Bebe Rebozo and Lawrence O'Brien seized Nixon's attention. The president and his top aides talked several times about the confluence of individuals and the potential for embarrassing revelations about Donald Nixon and Bebe Rebozo. Indeed, Nixon ordered Haldeman to tip off Rebozo about the investigation.

The two separate investigative streams—the White House inquiries about Hughes and O'Brien and the IRS investigation of Hughes—intersected during the summer of 1972 when the White House learned that the IRS probe of Hughes involved payments to O'Brien from Hughes. Roger Barth, an IRS aide, tipped off the White House after reading an IRS Sensitive Case Report about the Hughes investigation that noted the O'Brien link. Barth had been sent to work at the IRS by the White House to keep the president and his aides informed about politically sensitive cases. After hearing about the Sensitive Case Report, Ehrlichman told Shultz that the Hughes payments to O'Brien might be campaign contributions improp-, erly reported by O'Brien and should be investigated by the IRS. Shultz, in turn, instructed Walters to do exactly that. Walters then told the IRS assistant commissioner for compliance, John F. Hanlon, to see if O'Brien's tax returns reported the Hughes income. Hanlon informed Walters that O'Brien's tax returns for 1970 and 1971 had been routinely reviewed and that they included significant revenue from Hughes, O'Brien had paid a small deficiency and the examination was closed. Walters soon recounted all this to Shultz.[32]

Shultz reported back to Ehrlichman what he had learned. Ehrlichman was dissatisfied and made his irritation plain to Shultz.[33] Shultz looped back to Walters, telling him that the White House insisted more be done and that O'Brien should be summoned for an interview with IRS agents. O'Brien was not immediately available but offered to send his son, who was familiar with his business and tax returns. When Ehrlichman heard about this plan, he objected to Shultz, who told Walters that O'Brien, not his son, should be interviewed.

While the IRS was struggling to corral O'Brien for an interview, Nixon was fuming about the agency in general, its handling of O'Brien and Shultz's reluctance to order the IRS to pursue Nixon's critics. "We have all this power and we aren't using it," Nixon complained to Haldeman and Ehrlichman during an Oval Office conversation on August 3, 1972: "Now, what the Christ is the matter? . . . What is being done? Who is doing this full-time? That's what I'd like to know. Who is running the IRS? . . . What, if anything, is being done on the Democratic candidate? I mean, for example, on his income [tax], on O'Brien? . . . That's why I say on O'Brien, just to use him as an example, if you could dirty up O'Brien now I think that might be a lot better than waiting until later."

When Ehrlichman informed Nixon that some of his cabinet secretaries, including Shultz, were reluctant to cooperate with the White House, Nixon vented, "It's so Goddamn frustrating." He asked Haldeman if the cabinet secretaries "are afraid?" Haldeman answered: "I would think we could get some people with some guts in the second term, when we don't care about the repercussions." When the conversation returned to Shultz and his reluctance to manipulate the IRS, Nixon seemed baffled by his Treasury secretary's innocence. A few hours later, Nixon and Ehrlichman revisited the subject of Shultz's queasiness about delving into O'Brien's tax returns. "George has got a fantasy," Nixon scoffed. "What's he trying to do, say that you can't play politics with the IRS?"

Nixon's impatience grew as Ehrlichman informed him that Shultz was hesitant to promote Roger Barth, assistant to the commissioner for public affairs, to serve as deputy general counsel of the IRS. IRS managers, wary of Barth and his loyalty to the White House, complained that Barth was not qualified to be deputy general counsel, giving Shultz pause.

Ehrlichman told Nixon: "George called up and said, 'Geez, I'm really having trouble with this. My bureaucracy is really wild about this; this guy is known to be a loyalist and hard-ass and so on, so I've had a lot of flack.' I said, 'George, that's the only guy we've got in the whole IRS.'"

Nixon was furious. "Out with them, every one of those bastards, out now. I think the whole bunch goes out just because of this. Don't you agree?"

Ehrlichman: "Sure, it would be a great move. It would be a marvelous move."

Nixon: "We'll kick their ass out of there."

Ehrlichman: "We've got four more years."

Nixon: "That's right. And they can learn it. It isn't all that difficult. But out their asses go, and then investigate the bastards. They're probably on the take."

On August 7, Ehrlichman informed Nixon that O'Brien was being audited and had failed to show up for a meeting with the IRS. "Shultz wanted some guidance as to how to play this. I said, 'Okay, invite him in one more time, this week before Wednesday, while the National Committee is meeting. If he doesn't show up, then subpoena him.'"

Nixon: "Yes, sir, absolutely."

Ehrlichman: "So Wednesday we'll know."

Nixon relished the thought that O'Brien would be hit with a tax violation, but he fretted that the case, because it involved Howard Hughes, might reopen the investigation of Donald Nixon. He asked Ehrlichman if there was any indication that Donald had received additional money from Hughes. "Not that I know of," Ehrlichman reported, "and none that shows up in this thing." On August 11, while Nixon was at Camp David, the president, Haldeman and Ehrlichman returned to the O'Brien case. The three men talked about Shultz's handling of the matter.[34]

O'Brien and his son met with two IRS special agents on August 17 at the Sheraton Park Hotel in Washington. The lead agent described O'Brien senior as "cordial and quite friendly throughout the interview." During the seventy-minute meeting, O'Brien recounted the history of his association with Hughes and Maheu and the issues he had handled while acting as a consultant for Hughes. When asked if he had passed any of the money he received from the Hughes company to anyone else for political contributions, O'Brien said he had not. That was the question that the White House found so tantalizing.[35] Claude Desautels, who had worked with O'Brien on the Hughes consulting deal, met with the same two special agents in Washington the same day.[36] The IRS had interviewed Joseph Napolitan in Boston on July 29.

On August 19, while Nixon was at Camp David, Haldeman gave Nixon an update over the phone about O'Brien: "I got the report on the O'Brien audit. John [Ehrlichman] said he had forgotten to tell me about it and I'd forgotten to ask him this morning. But O'Brien showed up yesterday as instructed, with his son and all their records, and asked that his case be postponed until after the election and they declined. They said, no, they had to pursue it right away. . . . And he's quite shook up about the whole thing. A cursory examination . . . would indicate that, if everything that he says is true, he is clear. But he left all the records there and they're starting through them. And our guy, Roger Barth, will be going through them also. So we've got his files and now we can do some exploring."

Nixon: "But it looks as if you say . . ."

Haldeman: "On the basis of what he says, if what he says is true. But this is true of almost anybody when they come in. He's not going to come in and say, I've not paid my taxes. He's going to say I have it all covered."

Nixon: "At least we've got a guy working on it like Barth that's not going to give it a cursory examination."

Haldeman: "That's right. It will be very thoroughly examined on the merits, and also for the political interest of anything that might be in there. See, that was the other thing. We wanted to rummage through the records . . ."

Nixon: "That's a lot of nerve, to say to put it off until after the election."

The White House's impatience with the IRS's handling of O'Brien escalated on August 29 when Ehrlichman angrily berated Shultz and Walters during a phone call with the two men. Shultz and Walters, and Roger Barth, the White House informant at the IRS, gathered in Shultz's office.[37] Ehrlichman was at the White House. The conversation was recorded at Ehrlichman's end at the White House.

Ehrlichman, increasingly impatient as the conversation progressed, rebuked Shultz and especially Walters for not moving faster and harder on O'Brien's tax returns. Walters, incensed by the criticism, sharply responded. Shultz, while supporting Walters, flipped through O'Brien's tax filings, giving Ehrlichman a detailed account of what the IRS had found. Though both Walters and Shultz told Ehrlichman they saw no evidence of tax fraud, the discussion makes clear that Shultz bowed to White House pressure to rummage through O'Brien's tax returns and to enlist the IRS in hot pursuit of O'Brien.

During the call, Shultz updated Ehrlichman on the IRS investigation of O'Brien and described various financial transactions involving Howard Hughes, O'Brien and two O'Brien associates. He read from a confidential memorandum prepared by IRS agents for internal use about their interview with O'Brien on August 18. "Now, I'm turning to a paper I have here that's a memorandum of the interview with O'Brien Sr.," Shultz told Ehrlichman. After going through the O'Brien documents, Shultz informed Ehrlichman that Walters and the IRS would examine them closely and should have a more complete reading on them in about a week.

Ehrlichman erupted: "Well, that should take 20 minutes, why will it take a week?"

Dismissing Walters's insistence that a week was needed, Ehrlichman suggested giving the tax returns to Barth and that he "would be able to have all that done by tomorrow night."

Walters warned that giving the job to Barth rather than to a team of IRS agents would be politically fraught and might get "pie in our face."

Ehrlichman: "Well, I'm willing to take a little pie in my face, John, and I think you should, too. This is very big stuff."

Shultz intervened at this point, noting again that there seemed to be nothing questionable about O'Brien's tax returns or his financial dealings.

Unconvinced, Ehrlichman renewed his criticism of Walters. "I'm very impatient with the way the IRS has handled it thus far. I think there's been foot-dragging. I think you've been way too lenient with this guy in granting him extensions of those interviews; it's sort of business as usual around the IRS and that's not good enough."

"And that's directed at Johnnie, not at anybody else. And Johnnie, I must say, I would like to see that the IRS was really with us on this."

Shultz: "So far there's nothing wrong."

Ehrlichman: "I know, I'm not quarreling with that George; it was just attitudinal."

Outraged by Ehrlichman's accusations, Walters testily explained that he is trying to keep the IRS out of politics. "John, I'm sorry you feel that way, because let me tell you, I'm busting my gut . . . to do everything to protect the president."

Ehrlichman: "No, no, no, wait a minute . . ."

Walters: "With this one, we're playing with fire."

Ehrlichman: "We've been protecting the president for years and years at the IRS and that's an excuse not to do something."

The Ehrlichman-Walters argument ended when Shultz assured Ehrlichman, "The interviews are going forward and we will look at these returns and we'll do it promptly."

Before turning to another topic, George Meany, the AFL-CIO chief, Ehrlichman asked Shultz if the Treasury Department could check if the money that Hughes paid O'Brien might have been turned over to members of Congress, a potential violation of the Corrupt Practices Act regulating campaign finance in federal elections. Shultz said the lobbying issue would be explored.

Ehrlichman: "Let's be extraordinarily diligent and thorough on this and please do let me hear from you as soon as you have any indication one way or the other."

Shultz brought the discussion to an end by asking Walters and Barth if they had anything to add. Neither did. "If you do, don't hesitate," Shultz said, "because the whole purpose of this is that we're all informed and got the same information and any ideas that anyone has are all expressed."

In the days immediately following the phone call with Ehrlichman, IRS officials scrambled to track down financial information about O'Brien and copies of his tax returns. Three IRS couriers carrying O'Brien IRS paperwork rushed the materials to Washington from IRS offices around the nation. In one case, the regional commissioner of the North Atlantic Region, who supervised ten thousand IRS employees, was ordered to carry O'Brien's tax returns to Washington himself. From August 29 to September 5, Walters and several top aides drafted a report on O'Brien and his ties to Hughes. The report's bottom line echoed what Shultz and Walters had told Ehrlichman: the O'Brien tax returns were clean, and there was no reason to pursue the matter further.[38] Treasury Department records, including Shultz's calendar, indicate that Barth delivered the report to Shultz on the afternoon of September 5 and that the two men discussed it with Ehrlichman over the phone.[39]

On September 7, Ehrlichman was still seething over the IRS's and Shultz's handling of O'Brien. The issue came up during a conversation with Nixon and Haldeman about providing Secret Service protection for Senator Edward M. Kennedy. Nixon, eager to catch Kennedy in some compromising behavior, insisted that his aides make sure the Secret Service reported to the White House about all of Kennedy's activities and that the security detail monitor the senator twenty-four hours a day. Ehrlichman made clear he did not intend to work through Shultz, who oversaw the Secret Service as Treasury secretary. "I'm not going to have Shultz do it. He screwed up the O'Brien thing."[40]

The next day, Ehrlichman informed Nixon that he had new information about O'Brien. "I got the Larry O'Brien numbers, and they are quite interesting. The guy has a hell of an income. In '69, he got $43,500 roughly from Hughes, but he had adjusted gross income of $173,800."[41] It is not clear whether the information came from Shultz or Barth or some other source. Ehrlichman ran through some additional details for Nixon about O'Brien's income and tax returns. He then described O'Brien's 1970 tax returns, noting that O'Brien received about $100,000 from Hughes.

On September 15 in an Oval Office discussion, Nixon, Haldeman and Dean talked about purging the Justice Department, Treasury Department and the IRS after the election so they could appoint officials who would be responsive to White House political imperatives. Nixon complained that Attorney General John Mitchell, Shultz and Walters had become captives of entrenched bureaucracies at their agencies, most staffed by Democrats.

"I'll look forward to the time when we have the entrance to the Department of Justice and the IRS under our control," Nixon said.[42]

Nixon vented about Shultz. "He should be thrown right out of the office. . . . He didn't get to be Secretary of the Treasury because he's got nice blue eyes and not for any other reason." Frustrated by the White House's inability to get tax returns of its opponents, Nixon suggested, "God damn it, sneak in in the middle of the night. If Walters will not cooperate, get rid of him," Nixon said. "He's finished, he's finished November the eighth believe me. Out." As for Shultz, Nixon warned, "We're not going to have a secretary to the Treasury who doesn't do what we say." Two years later, in testimony about the O'Brien matter, Ehrlichman succinctly summed up the affair. Referring to O'Brien, he said, "I wanted them to turn up something and send him to jail before the election and unfortunately it didn't materialize."[43]

In writing and talking publicly about White House pressure on the IRS, Shultz said little about the O'Brien affair over the years until questioned about it during preparation of this biography. Looking back on the O'Brien case in 2017, Shultz seemed stricken as the details of the affair were laid out for him. It was clearly not a topic he relished discussing. Shultz recalled that he was unhappy with the White House pressure. "They wanted us to harass Larry O'Brien, and I thought that was a lousy idea and resisted," he said. "An audit was made, and there was no problem. And Johnnie's view was, we've had the audit, there's no problem, case closed. So I was very supportive of that, and finally the White House accepted that. So that was the end of that, although I didn't like it."[44]

Walters thought the matter should have ended immediately after the first White House inquiry about O'Brien because the IRS had already audited O'Brien. "I informed the Secretary that the returns had been filed, IRS had audited the returns, and IRS made a small refund to Mr. O'Brien. Instead of ending the situation, the secretary came back and said that Mr. Ehrlichman was not satisfied and wanted more detail."[45]

Shultz acknowledged in 2017 that his resistance stopped well short of telling the White House that targeting O'Brien was improper. "I suppose I could have said, 'Hang up the phone. It's none of your damn business,' or something. But, you know, the White House is the White House; you're going to talk to them. Ehrlichman I knew very well. He was head of something called the Domestic Council, and that was created when the OMB was created. So I worked with him, and I had a very good opinion of Ehrlichman. They worked with me on civil rights issues and other things like that that were controversial, and they supported me."[46] He offered to serve as a character witness for Ehrlichman when Ehrlichman went on trial in federal court in 1974 for his role in Watergate. Ehrlichman was convicted of conspiracy, obstruction of justice and perjury on January 1, 1975.

Shultz did not threaten to resign or publicly expose the wrongdoing. He soldiered on, increasingly disillusioned with Nixon and his team as Watergate enveloped the White House. He believed he could help keep the government from unraveling as Nixon's abuses of power were exposed, the prospects of impeachment grew and Nixon's drinking and psychological instability became ever more evident. He also thought that a new Treasury secretary might permit far more extensive White House meddling at the IRS. "I remember thinking about that and saying to myself, 'I'm standing between the White House and the IRS. As long as I'm standing here, the problem is not going to arise. Who knows what my successor might do?' And we had put the issue to rest; that is, they got an answer and they didn't like it, but they didn't do anything about it."[47] Shultz's commitment to prevent an executive branch meltdown may have seemed of paramount importance to him as the Nixon presidency disintegrated. But his unwillingness to quit a corrupt president and White House staff, even as the misconduct bore down directly on the Treasury Department, also seemed to reflect a misplaced sense of loyalty to Nixon and an affinity for high office and the status and privileges that come with it.

Margaret Shultz, his eldest child and an insightful observer of her father, recalled an instance when Nixon subtly tried to gain Shultz's support on a policy issue unrelated to the IRS matters by offering Shultz a weekend at Camp David. "At one point where Nixon was trying to court my father, convince him, sway him, and I didn't know the issues or any of that, but I just remember Camp David being available, and it was obvious he was trying to persuade him. You know, there's my dad on a government salary with five kids, jumping at it. And my mother just loved it there." Margaret thought her father was deeply offended by Watergate and Nixon's unethical conduct. In particular, she recalls that Shultz was indignant when Nixon encouraged his elder daughter, Julie, to defend him in public appearances and television interviews. "What kind of man has his daughter speak for him when he knows he's wrong? I remember him saying that to me. Puts his daughter out in front of the camera to speak for him when he knows he's wrong."[48]

Yet, the most outrage Shultz could muster when questioned about the O'Brien episode by the Watergate Special Prosecutor's office in 1974 was to call it "an unpleasant and distasteful experience."[49] Shultz's account to prosecutors of his involvement in the O'Brien matter suggested that the matter was closed at the end of August 1972. In fact, recordings of White House discussions and phone calls, and IRS records, show that the IRS actively continued to examine O'Brien's tax returns into September and beyond, with Shultz's knowledge and approval.

Shultz's role in the pursuit of O'Brien was mitigated by his firm, repeated declarations to Ehrlichman that he saw no evidence of tax evasion, tax fraud or, for that matter, any irregularities in O'Brien's tax returns and financial records. In the end, the O'Brien case was closed without penalty or adverse finding. In recounting his conduct, Shultz correctly recalled his resistance to the "enemies list" presented by John Dean and his support of Walters to audit Nixon. In his narrative of his behavior as Watergate engulfed Nixon, Shultz sees himself as a stalwart of integrity standing against improper White House pressure.

Walters, the IRS commissioner, did not agree. Though he thought his work with Shultz, in general, was "pleasant and productive," he found Shultz's handling of O'Brien disappointing. Looking back on the O'Brien episode and other Watergate issues that buffeted the IRS during Shultz's tenure as Treasury secretary, Walters said of Shultz, "He always seemed to have a halo around his head. Following his government service, the media and almost everyone praised him highly. He clearly was a very able man and he served the country well in various high level spots. I had a slightly different view of him. He did not protect the IRS the way he should have." Walters added that Shultz seemed surprised when he learned that Walters told a grand jury that he had shown Shultz a copy of the enemies list. "When I informed Secretary Shultz of this, his immediate remark was, 'Did I see that list?' My immediate response to him was, 'Damn right you did, Mr. Secretary.' In my view, Secretary Shultz liked to please the boss."[50]

In early 1973, as pressure was building on Nixon to fire H. R. Haldeman and John Ehrlichman because of their involvement in the Watergate case, Shultz thought he was a candidate to succeed Haldeman as White House chief of staff. That prospect, and the ambition behind it, undoubtedly contributed to his reluctance to break with Nixon. Shultz intimated as much to Arthur Burns, chairman of the Federal Reserve and a Shultz confidant, at lunch on April 16, 1973. "He whispered to me that the Watergate case is going to blow wide open, that his own involvement in White House affairs would become vastly larger," Burns noted in his private diary on April 22, 1973. "He implied but did not say that he may have to give up Treasury post. Swore me to secrecy. I interpreted all this to mean that Haldeman is about to leave, but I kept my own counsel."[51] The post went instead to Alexander Haig in May 1973 after Haldeman was forced to resign.

As Watergate closed in on Nixon in 1974 and he began behaving more erratically, Shultz started meeting regularly with Burns and Secretary of State Henry Kissinger to make sure White House decision-making did not veer off in dangerous directions. Shultz recalled their thinking at the time, "It's a tough time and the president isn't paying as close attention as he might, so let's get together fairly frequently and talk about what's going on. Not that we're trying to usurp power, but we're trying to get ourselves into a position to give him good advice in case anything comes up."[52] Kissinger said, "We wanted to prevent some erratic move being made. . . . You want to make sure that nobody comes into the office [the Oval Office] with some hot plan and gets it approved."[53]

Shultz's loyalty to Nixon, and his dutiful effort to keep the government from unraveling, reflected Shultz's public-spirited commitment to his job and his own sense of honor, then and throughout his career, even when it became evident that his advice was being ignored or rejected and his colleagues were acting dishonorably. These are admirable traits. But they can come with a downside. In the case of Nixon and Watergate, Shultz's steadfast loyalty left him at the side of a wounded president long after it became abundantly clear that Nixon was engaged in criminal misconduct and acting in violation of constitutional constraints on the executive branch.

Shultz stepped down as Treasury secretary on May 8, 1974, ostensibly over the reimposition of wage and price controls that he opposed. His handwritten farewell letter to Nixon said, "You have accomplished a tremendous amount for the country and the world and I know that further achievements lie ahead. I have been proud to be a part of what has been done and will be supporting your efforts in the times ahead."[54] Such effusive thanks are common among Washington officials when corresponding with presidents they have served. Yet in the context of the Watergate affair, which was rapidly accelerating toward Nixon's demise by May 1974, more subdued prose might have been appropriate from a cabinet member parting company with Nixon. Shultz said not a public word about Nixon's misconduct. Nixon resigned three months later.

Margaret Shultz watched her father struggle with his conflicting principles at the time. Did Shultz stay too long in the administration before resigning? "It's hard to judge," Margaret said. "I mean you're not in his shoes; you don't know the stakes. He's a very loyal person, a committed person. When he did leave, it was very hard for him and on him."[55]

Bob Young, a Princeton classmate, caught up with Shultz during this period, and the two talked on the White House grounds after playing tennis on the White House court. "My impression was he was pretty depressed by what was going on, and he said that," Young recalled. "One of the things I remember him saying is that this is a job where you work like hell. You get in at eight in the morning and you often don't go home until eight or nine o'clock at night. It's exciting because you're dealing with significant national issues and you're having a good time and giving it your all. But it's a little depressing when you realize the everybody thinks you're a jerk because you're part of this administration, which has suddenly lost all of its public acclaim and because you were connected with this crooked guy."[56]

Arthur Burns watched Shultz struggle, too, and saw how it wore him down. "Shultz is a very sad man," Burns noted in his journal on June 9, 1973. "He is thoroughly disillusioned with the President—believes he is up to his neck in Watergate affair, and he is devious, unprincipled. I don't understand why he puts up with it all."[57] Six months later, Burns wrote: "Shultz keeps talking about reportedly leaving. I'm hardly convinced—especially now, since after a long lapse—the President is seeing him again. Shultz is tired, but I think he likes being Secretary too much to give it up. I may be wrong. If he goes, I will miss him. Shultz has no use for the President, morally. He does not miss many opportunities to tell me this."[58]

For all his confidence and independence, Shultz was susceptible to the accoutrements of power and enjoyed the stature and status accorded cabinet members. It can be a heady experience to serve as a cabinet member, traveling the country and world in a security bubble with attendants and staff, surrounded by world leaders, treated as the guest of honor by kings and potentates. "I think he was attracted to the glamour of it and the prominence of it, of course," one colleague said. "Who wouldn't be?"[59]

The seductive mores of power never intoxicated Shultz, but for a man who grew up during the Great Depression and participated as a marine in South Pacific battles of World War II, the dazzling life of a Washington celebrity was clearly appealing. More than Shultz may have realized or acknowledged to himself, the status he gained in high office drew him to Washington and may have kept him there during trying times when his better instincts told him to go home.

When he finally exited the Nixon administration, Shultz did not know what he would do next. Believing it was unethical to entertain private-sector job offers while still in a government post, Shultz declined to consider a variety of corporate and academic employment options until he left office on May 8, 1974. Several big banks offered him senior executive posts, including Citicorp and J.P. Morgan. He eventually narrowed the choice to a corporate post with Bechtel, the global engineering and construction company based in San Francisco. "I got offered chairs at various universities, and I said I've been working hard, I don't want a chair, I want a couch, and nobody had a couch available. Then I thought, you know, I've had an academic career, I've taught classes, I've written books, I've been a dean, and I've had a government career, why not try business?"[60]

Stephen D. Bechtel Jr., the CEO of the family-owned company, invited Shultz to come aboard as a top executive. The opportunity to do some teaching on the side at Stanford and live in the Bay Area made the offer especially appealing. O'Bie and the children applauded the plan to return to the San Francisco area. Steve Bechtel's bet on Shultz was a gamble. He was a prestigious hire with global connections and an accomplished record as a scholar, dean and cabinet member. But as Shultz was the first to admit, he knew little about construction and engineering or the inner workings of a family-owned business that was anything but publicly transparent about its finances and operations. "I said to Steve, 'You know, I don't know anything about this business,'" Shultz recalled. "He said, 'Well, you'll learn, but you know a lot about human relations and personnel, and you know a lot about labor relations and you know a lot about finance, and those are big elements of our business.'"[61]

Steve Bechtel was the grandson of Warren Bechtel, an enterprising Kansas native who ventured west in 1898 in search of construction work. He found it in Nevada, Oregon and California on railroad, road and pipeline projects, eventually establishing W. A. Bechtel Co. Formal incorporation came in 1926. A few years later, Bechtel joined a consortium of companies to build Hoover Dam. The firm grew over the decades into one of the nation's largest construction and engineering corporations. It also attracted a good deal of critical media coverage for its work for autocratic regimes abroad, such as signing up for large projects in Saudi Arabia. In 1976, the Justice Department accused Bechtel of violating antitrust laws by participating in an Arab League boycott of companies doing business in Israel. Bechtel agreed to a settlement of the case a year later, neither admitting nor denying that it had violated US antitrust laws.

In accepting the Bechtel job, Shultz made clear he would not try to leverage his connections in Washington on behalf of Bechtel, a condition that Steve Bechtel readily endorsed. After an orientation period, Shultz dived into the intricacies of Bechtel's mining and metals division, tutored by veteran Bechtel executives unaccustomed to welcoming an outsider to their realm. He emerged from the crash course, which included reading assignments and travel to mining projects, with sufficient mastery of the business that his colleagues presented him with an informal diploma that he treasured for the rest of his life. "Best diploma I ever got," he said.[62]

Before long, Steve Bechtel named Shultz president of Bechtel, making him the second ranking executive to Steve. Shultz and the Bechtel family found they could learn a lot from each other. For Shultz, the comparison to working in the academy and government was sharp. "In government, demands made are likely to take years to be met; in universities, demands are taboo; and in business, you'd better take care in making demands because of the high probability they'll get done."[63] Looking back years later, he said, "As an executive at Bechtel, I had seen what a well-run organization looks like and what leadership looks like and what you do, how you make it work.[64]

Riley Bechtel, who succeeded his father, Steve, as CEO in 1990, spotted the problem-solving aptitude that was an enduring Shultz strength throughout his career. "George was absolutely a wonderful problem solver," Riley said. "And he was as good a problem anticipator as problem solver, and there are not a lot of people that can do that. There are even fewer that can do both." Riley called Shultz "a wonderful, over-the-horizon thinker" who helped Bechtel develop long-term growth strategies by thinking about environmental, social, technological and geopolitical trends and how to anticipate them.[65] Riley recalled that Shultz guided Bechtel to better understand the importance to its business of local cultures, local businesses, diversity and sustainability.

Shultz pressed Bechtel to be less secretive about its operations. "When I came, Bechtel was not just a private company; it was very secret," he said. "You couldn't find out anything about Bechtel. And one of the results of it was scandal-type stories about the company. I kept arguing with them that we shouldn't be secretive: We're proud of what we're doing."[66] The company gradually made more data available, including an annual report, but stopped well short of the disclosure standards of publicly traded corporations. Shultz also recommended that Bechtel create an investment vehicle for surplus cash the company had cautiously been putting in low-yield Treasury bills. Over time, the more aggressive strategy advocated by Shultz led to establishment of an in-house investment group, Bechtel Investments, that later turned into Fremont Investors, Inc., a very successful Bechtel family private-equity fund. Alan Dachs, Steve Bechtel's son-in-law, joined the construction company in 1982 and managed Fremont for years.

Through all of Shultz's time at Bechtel, he well understood that the family owned the corporation and that Steve Bechtel was the paramount boss. "He knew where the ultimate responsibility was and he respected it," Dachs said.[67] Accepting a subordinate role, even one as elevated as president of Bechtel, helped Shultz earn the trust of the family. The same understated quality had been a hallmark of his work during the Nixon administration. When asked about his self-effacing instinct, Shultz would recount the story of Lyndon Johnson once telling him the best way to advance his ideas was not to claim credit himself but to let Johnson take ownership of them. In 1982, eight years after going to work at Bechtel, Shultz got an unexpected chance to see if his management style would work well with another president of the United States.

PART III

Reagan Administration

CHAPTER SEVEN

Odd Man Out

SHULTZ'S LIFE CHANGED ABRUPTLY on June 25, 1982. In London on Bechtel business, he was handed a note that "George Clark" in the United States was calling. He brushed it aside, unfamiliar with the name. Soon, another call came from Clark, this time "William Clark." Shultz instantly knew that name—William Clark was President Reagan's national security adviser. He took the call. Clark asked if Shultz could go to the American embassy on Grosvenor Square as soon as possible to talk on a secure phone line with the president. Before heading to the embassy, Shultz talked to O'Bie. "I don't know what it's all about, but it's the president calling," he told her. "What it is he wants, I should be willing to do, whatever it is."[1]

Reagan quickly got to the point: Alexander Haig had resigned as secretary of state, and Reagan wanted Shultz to take the job. Startled by the invitation, Shultz asked if Haig had already quit or was threatening to. "I did not want to get into the position of saying yes to the president's request and then having Al Haig told he was out," Shultz recalled. "He has resigned," Reagan reported. "It hasn't been announced, but it has happened. I have accepted his resignation, and I want you to replace him."

In fact, as Haig later reported, he had not resigned but had been fired by Reagan. Knowing his relationship with the White House and Reagan had reached a breakpoint, Haig had drafted a resignation letter but not submitted it and had told Reagan on June 24 that he was prepared to resign. After a National Security Council luncheon meeting at the White House on June 25, Haig was told to step into the Oval Office. In Haig's account, he found the president standing at his desk. "'On the matter we discussed yesterday, Al,' he said. 'I have reached a conclusion.' He then handed me an unsealed envelope. I opened it and read the single typed page it contained. 'Dear Al,' it began. 'It is with the most profound regret that I accept your letter of resignation.' The President was accepting a letter of resignation that I had not submitted." Reagan asked Haig to remain as secretary until the Senate confirmed his successor and told Haig he would soon offer the post to George Shultz. Haig thought staying on as a lame duck was a bad idea but reluctantly agreed.[2]

Not long after Reagan dismissed Haig, White House operators connected the president to Shultz on a secure line at the London embassy. As the conversation progressed, Shultz realized Reagan was waiting for him to accept on the spot. He asked if that were so. "Well, yes I am, George," Reagan said. "It would help a lot because it's not a good idea to leave a post like this vacant." Shultz momentarily hesitated, thinking about his Bechtel responsibilities, his part-time teaching role and his busy but satisfying life in California. But just as he did when Richard Nixon summoned him to service in Washington in 1968, Shultz thought a job offer from the president of the United States was a command performance. "Mr. President, I'm on board," he told Reagan.[3] Shultz tried unsuccessfully to reach Steve Bechtel to tell him of his imminent resignation from the company, then headed to a dinner at the home of Andrew Knight, editor of the *Economist* and a good friend. When Knight greeted Shultz and asked him what was new, Shultz slyly told him, "I'll tell you at 6:30," the time when the White House planned to announce Haig's resignation and Shultz's appointment as the new secretary of state.[4]

After months of simmering White House tension with the combative Haig, Reagan was relieved to get a new secretary of state. He noted in his diary:

> Today was the day—I told Al H. I had decided to accept his resignation. He didn't seem surprised but he said his differences were on policy and then said we didn't agree on China or Russia, etc. I made a simple announcement to the press and said I was nominating George Shultz for the job. I'd called him & like the patriot he is he said, "yes." This has been a heavy load. Up to Camp David where we were in time to see Al read his letter of resignation on T.V. I'm told it was his 4th re-write.

Apparently his first was pretty strong—then he thought better of it. I must say it was O.K. He gave only one reason & did say there was a disagreement on foreign policy. Actually, the only disagreement was over whether I made policy or the Sec. of State did.[5]

Haig's decapitation startled the capital. Though his differences with Reagan and quarrelsome style had been extensively noted in news accounts over preceding months, few people outside the White House inner circle realized that the president had lost patience with Haig and wanted a new secretary of state. The *New York Times* bannered the news across the top of the front page: "Haig Resigns over Foreign Policy Course, but Cites No Issues; Reagan Names Shultz." The *Times* reported: "Mr. Reagan's announcement was stunning, coming as it did during what may be the culmination of the Israeli campaign against the Palestine Liberation Organization in Lebanon. Mr. Haig, who appeared before reporters in the State Department's main auditorium an hour and a half after the President's statement, did little to clear up the mystery over the circumstances of his resignation."[6]

The *Times* recalled running tensions between Haig and the White House. "Mr. Haig, 57 years old, had been involved in a continuing series of disputes with other senior Administration officials almost from the start of the Administration. In the past, he reportedly threatened to resign over what he perceived as encroachment by other officials on his responsibilities."[7] Shultz's appointment drew generally favorable coverage. The *Times* described Shultz as

> a labor economist whose service in government during the Nixon Administration led him into the international business world, including significant involvement in the Middle East.
>
> While there are some questions about how this experience will help shape policies on the Middle East, East-West relations and other matters, there seems no doubt that Mr. Shultz will operate well in the Administration. And there is also no doubt about his experience in government.[8]

Walter Heller, former chairman of the White House Council of Economic Advisers and a Democrat, told the *Times*, "I am very high on George Shultz. He is not one of those guys who wiggles and waggles in the wind. He has good balanced judgment. He is the kind of conservative I really go for."[9]

Donald Rumsfeld, Gerald Ford's defense secretary, said, "He's an un-flamboyant person. He doesn't have any sharp edges. He works in a manner that does not call attention to himself."[10] The *Washington Post* reported:

> The biggest potential differences that Shultz might seek to make are likely to involve Mideast policy. His position as chairman of the Bechtel Group Inc., which has major construction interests in Saudi Arabia, gives him a reputation as favoring the Arab side in the Middle East conflict.
>
> Several pro-Israeli senators, noting that Weinberger also came from Bechtel, said last night that they intend to question Shultz closely during his confirmation hearings about whether his move into the secretary's post will lead to a cooler and tough line in U.S. relations with Israel.[11]

The next morning, after a wakeful night in London with O'Bie at the Stafford Hotel near Green Park, where reporters descended in search of Shultz, the couple caught the morning supersonic Concorde flight to Washington. It whisked them across the Atlantic in four hours. Eight years and two months after he resigned as Treasury secretary, Shultz was headed back to the fulcrum of power and all the privileges and machinations that come with it.

The Washington of Ronald Reagan appeared to be anything but a hospitable environment for a moderate, nonideological problem solver like Shultz. "Government is not the solution to our problem; government is the problem," Reagan had declared in his inaugural address on January 20, 1981. In his first year as president, even though sidelined for several months after a March 1981 assassination attempt that nearly killed him, Reagan jolted the capital with his hard-right agenda. He pressed for domestic budget cuts, deregulation and other conservative policies incubated over the years in conservative think tanks that Reagan wholeheartedly embraced during his rise as a political leader. Just weeks after taking office, he fired thousands of government air traffic controllers after they went on strike, signaling that he was unafraid to shake up the capital.

His foreign policy was no less jarring. Always-volatile relations between the United States and the Soviet Union had worsened after the 1979 Soviet invasion of Afghanistan. President Carter had suspended arms control talks with the Kremlin, brought other diplomatic discussions with Moscow nearly to a standstill and barred American athletes from participating in the 1980 Summer Olympics in the Soviet capital. Reagan went much further.

He committed the United States to a fundamentally new vision for dealing with the Soviet Union. Reagan abandoned the strategy of containment that American leaders had employed since Harry Truman. It called for the vigorous use of political power and military strength to prevent the expansion of Soviet influence around the globe. Reagan moved to a policy aimed at rolling back Soviet gains abroad and actively maneuvering to undermine the Soviet Union itself. The new strategy was codified in National Security Decision Directive (NSDD) 32, approved by Reagan on May 20, 1982. One of the stated goals: "To contain and reverse expansion of Soviet control and military presence throughout the world, and to increase the costs of Soviet support and use of proxy, terrorist, and subversive forces."[12]

The strategy was contemptuous of détente, an effort favored by multiple presidents to reduce cold war tensions and seek arms control and other agreements with the Soviet Union. Just two weeks before Shultz's appointment as secretary of state, Reagan boldly told the British parliament that Communism would wind up on "the ash heap of history." Richard Perle, a top Pentagon official in the new administration, called the Reagan approach "a breathtaking shift in policy." The United States, he said, was moving from "a policy whose central proposition was that the Soviet Union is a permanent establishment, and the task of American policy is to figure out how to get along with it, to the view that it was ephemeral and the task of American policy is to figure out how to hasten its demise."[13] To that end, Reagan quickly expanded a Carter administration covert effort to support restive workers in Poland who were challenging the Communist regime in Warsaw. Collaborating secretly with the Vatican and Pope John Paul II, a Pole, the CIA funneled money and other assistance to the Solidarity shipyard workers in the Polish port city of Gdansk. Led by Lech Walesa, a charismatic, gutsy dissident, the workers' resistance grew into a nationwide movement that deeply alarmed the Kremlin and led Polish leaders to impose martial law in 1981.

Hard-liners on the Reagan team like Perle—Defense Secretary Caspar Weinberger, CIA Director William Casey, National Security Adviser William Clark, among others—were ascendant. More moderate figures like James A. Baker III, the White House chief of staff; Michael Deaver, guardian of Reagan's public image; and First Lady Nancy Reagan exercised little influence over foreign policy. Shultz was a relative newcomer to national security

policy. The uncompromising policies of the Reagan administration had hardened over Reagan's first year in office. Alliances among conservatives within
the administration had formed, many contemptuous of diplomacy. Access
to the president was tightly controlled by a national security adviser who rejected Shultz's worldview. Although Shultz was an experienced government
official, he was not temperamentally suited to waging and winning internal
power struggles. As O'Bie once said of her husband, he dreaded confrontation and far preferred to talk through problems. He was surprisingly innocent
about the Reagan White House and the world. A number of colleagues found
Shultz unexpectedly credulous, noting that this trait reflected, as one put it,
"an American quality that is naïve in the rough and tumble and meanness of
the world."[14] Shultz believed in the fundamental goodness of people.

He was joining a team driven by ideological fervor and a commitment
to upend decades of American foreign and domestic policy. While Shultz
had followed the headlines about Reagan's unyielding policies toward the
Soviet Union, he did not realize that he was joining a government in which
his natural impulse to seek common ground, to rely on patient negotiation
to resolve seemingly intractable conflicts, was fundamentally at odds with
the Reagan administration's approach to managing the cold war. Unlike
the national security team in the Nixon administration, in which Shultz's
pragmatic approach to governing was roughly in sync with much of the
executive branch, the Reagan dogmatic national security team was determined not just to constrain the Soviet Union but to defeat it.

Shultz's primary goal, even if still gestating in his mind at the time,
was nothing short of curtailing the cold war. He hoped to stabilize and
then improve relations with the Soviet Union and diminish the threat of
nuclear war. Prevailing in the administration cauldron would depend on
whether Shultz could command the support of the president and overcome
the formidable opposition of much of the Reagan national security team.
The outlook looked inauspicious, to say the least. Stepping off the Concorde
into the sticky heat of the Washington summer, he did not know if Reagan
shared that hope. It was an improbable mission. As Jim Gordon, the character played by John Wayne in the 1942 film *Flying Tigers* said of a heavily
damaged American warplane returning from combat, "She's coming in on
one wing and a prayer."

Several members of the White House top command assembled at Dulles Airport to greet the Shultzes: Baker, Clark, Deaver and Edwin Meese, counselor to the president. Shultz recalled the scene on the Dulles tarmac, where one of the presidential aides told him, "The president wants to see you up at Camp David. He has a chopper to take you and there's a car that will take your wife into town. She can find a hotel room." "I said, 'Well, this is a package deal. We'll both go to Camp David or we'll both go find a hotel room. Take your pick.' So we both went to Camp David and Nancy was expecting O'Bie, I could see. So I said that was my first indication you've got to fight with the White House staff a little."[15]

As the helicopter sped over northern Virginia's undulating hills toward Maryland's Catoctin Mountain and Camp David, Shultz was naïvely confident that he could work effectively with Reagan and his entourage. As a fellow California Republican, he had served off and on over the years as a Reagan adviser on economic affairs. The two men first met in 1974 while Reagan was California governor and Shultz a recently retired member of the Nixon cabinet. At lunch at the governor's mansion in Sacramento, Reagan, already a presidential aspirant, quizzed Shultz about the federal budget and government. "I got the most severe grilling for about three hours on how the federal government worked. How does the budget get put together? What does the budget director do? What does the president do? What do the cabinet officers do? How does this thing work? And I came away saying, 'I know the guy wants to be president, but he wants to do the job. He doesn't want to be president because he wants to be president; he has an agenda and he wants to execute it.'"[16]

A few years later, while actively campaigning for the 1980 Republican presidential nomination, Reagan came to dinner at Shultz's home on the Stanford campus. Shultz invited a number of fellow economists who served as senior fellows at the Hoover Institution, including Milton Friedman, the economist. Reagan at the time was an honorary fellow at Hoover. After dinner, the guests settled into sofas and armchairs in the living room for a spirited discussion about economics. Shultz found the conversation bracing and Reagan's performance impressive. "Reagan was the target and everybody was after him about this and that—not afraid to argue with him. And he just stood up to everything. And what came through to me was this man has views, but he understands why he has the view. He doesn't have the view because he thinks this is a good political thing to do. He had an underlying rationale. And it always seemed to me that was why he was basically so consistent."[17]

As the presidential campaign accelerated, Reagan invited Shultz to chair an economic advisory committee. Shultz also helped Reagan prepare for his first televised debate with Jimmy Carter. "I could talk to Ronald Reagan candidly, and he would listen," Shultz said. "He had strong views and I respected them. I felt we could work together."[18] After handily defeating Jimmy Carter in the election, President-Elect Reagan considered appointing Shultz as secretary of state. Richard Nixon, disgraced by Watergate but working hard to rehabilitate himself, lobbied Reagan to appoint Haig, a former four-star general and NATO commander who had served as a Nixon aide and White House chief of staff. Nixon told Reagan, "George Shultz has done a superb job in every government position to which I appointed him. However, I do not believe he has the depth of understanding of world issues generally and the Soviet Union in particular that is required for this period."[19]

Not long after questioning Shultz's qualifications, Nixon assured Shultz he had done nothing of the kind. "In talking to a mutual friend the other day," Nixon wrote to Shultz, "I was quite disturbed to learn that you had been told that I had opposed your appointment as Secretary of State or other positions in the administration. To be sure my memory had not been doing tricks on me I checked my files and found a letter I wrote to Bill Smith [appointed attorney general by Reagan] after the election. As I had remembered I had observed that you were superbly qualified to serve in any post which you might receive. I also gave high marks to Al Haig—because of his experience in foreign policy, but in no way was that derogatory to you. As an old friend and one who often told people that you were superb in every post you held in the White House years, I thought it well to set the record straight."[20] Shultz, probably aware of Nixon's hypocrisy, nevertheless thanked Nixon for the letter. "I am really pleased to have this word directly from you," he replied.[21]

Henry Kissinger was another Shultz doubter. Over dinner at the River Club in Manhattan, he confided to Arthur Schlesinger, a former Harvard colleague and close associate of John Kennedy, "George has no knowledge of foreign policy, none at all; worse than that, he has no feel for it. In the dozen years I have known him we have never had a conversation about foreign policy. He just doesn't think in terms of foreign policy. Making him Secretary of State would be like making me Secretary of the Treasury. Hard as I might work to master the subject, I would never be sure in my bones that what I was doing was right. This means that George will be at the mercy of the State Department bureaucracy."[22]

Despite Nixon's reservations and the doubts of several Reagan aides who also thought Shultz lacked the policy chops and backbone to deal with the Kremlin, Reagan seemed inclined to offer the job to Shultz. He stopped short in a phone call, apparently misinformed that Shultz had no interest in returning to Washington. "He called me after the election," Shultz recalled, "and said, 'Well, I'd love to have you in my administration, but I know your life is good and you've been here before.' And I said, 'Yeah, I've had cabinet jobs before, so somebody else should have a chance, and I'll help you any way I can.' Mike Deaver later told me he was supposed to ask me to be secretary of state on that call but didn't."[23] James Baker described the misunderstanding as a "busted signal." Baker said that during the presidential transition period when Reagan selected his cabinet, some Reagan aides got the impression that Shultz was not eager to serve a second time as Treasury secretary, if offered the job. The version that got to Reagan was that Shultz, broadly speaking, did not want a Washington encore, so Reagan was reluctant to press him, leading to the abortive phone call.[24]

As Reagan settled into the Oval Office in 1981, Shultz attended several White House meetings in his role as chair of the president's Economic Policy Advisory Board. After a White House social event in November, Shultz wrote to Reagan, "What a pleasure it was for me and my wife, O'Bie to be your guests at the White House. Your touch is everywhere. We felt an unusual combination of warmth and relaxed elegance. You both are giving to the United States and to the world extraordinary leadership and example."[25]

Once it became clear to Reagan that Haig could not last as secretary of state, the White House inner circle conferred about possible successors. The short list included Henry Kissinger; Weinberger; Robert McFarlane, the deputy national security adviser; and Shultz. Weinberger was settled at the Pentagon. The Reagan team did not entirely trust Kissinger, who had already served as secretary under Presidents Nixon and Ford. McFarlane, who had spent much of his career as a congressional aide, was integral to White House operations and lacked the national stature common to most candidates selected as secretary of state.

Although it was unclear to some Reagan aides whether Shultz shared the administration's philosophy about aggressively waging the cold war, he was a safe bet and considered sure to be a loyal Reagan aide. He was a battle-hardened veteran of the Nixon administration, fluent in international economic issues and familiar with a number of leading players on the world stage, including Helmut Schmidt, the German chancellor; Lee Kuan Yew, the prime minister of Singapore; Valery Giscard d'Estaing, the former French president; and several Arab leaders with whom he had done business at Bechtel. He was widely traveled and had interacted with high-level Soviet officials while serving in the Nixon administration.

But in other ways, Shultz seemed ill suited for the post. As Nixon and Kissinger had suggested, he lacked experience in defense, intelligence and other national security issues, including the most critical challenge he would face—helping manage the volatile nuclear weapons standoff with the Soviet Union. He had given little thought to nuclear arms control strategy and weapons negotiations with Moscow and was not a student of cold war diplomacy or the intricacies of Middle East tensions, relations with China and a host of other international security matters. "He's just a goddamned economist. What does he know?" Haig said about Shultz.[26]

Members of the State Department press corps, many of whom had covered Henry Kissinger's high-wire diplomatic initiatives and Haig's erratic but colorful performance, wondered if Shultz could successfully navigate the right-wing ideological rapids and interagency feuding of the Reagan team.[27] Haig was a casualty of the disorder and internecine battles. His departure after just eighteen months in office reflected his own impatience with the turbulent decision-making process and the mounting frustration of Reagan's inner circle with Haig's brazen efforts to seize control of foreign policy. Haig later said that the "vacuum of authority, combined with a babble of leaks to the press and palace intrigues, soon produced a dangerous incoherence in our foreign policy, finally, I decided I could not stay unless the situation was regularized."[28]

To some extent, the wounds were self-inflicted, as Haig, possibly psychologically affected by heart bypass surgery, often seemed to lunge for power, at one point describing himself as the "vicar" of foreign policy. He clashed frequently with White House aides and Defense Secretary Weinberger and William Casey, the director of the Central Intelligence Agency (CIA). Haig made plain his contempt for his colleagues in a conversation with Leslie Gelb, the *New York Times* chief national security correspondent, during the first months of the Reagan presidency. Gelb recalled: "We start talking about how decisions are made in the Reagan administration, and he says, 'I'll tell you how they're made, by the triple-headed cyclops that doesn't know shit about anything. Meese, Baker, and Deaver, and those guys they were trying to get into my pants all the time, and they don't know nothing, they're just a total pain in the ass, and Reagan, he doesn't know anything either, so he pays attention to them.'"[29]

Haig irreparably damaged his standing on March 30, 1981, when John Hinckley Jr., a mentally disturbed college dropout, shot and wounded Reagan as the president stepped toward his limousine after an appearance at the Washington Hilton Hotel. With Reagan in emergency surgery at George Washington Hospital and Vice President Bush in the air over Texas without voice communication connections, Haig rushed to the podium at the White House pressroom, declaring to reporters, "Constitutionally, gentlemen, you have the president, vice president and the secretary of state, in that order, and should the president decide he wants to transfer the helm to the vice president, he will do so. As of now, I am in control here, in the White House." Fellow cabinet members were shocked. "What's this all about?" demanded Donald Regan, the Treasury secretary. "Is he mad?" Defense Secretary Weinberger scoffed, "He's wrong. He doesn't have the authority."[30] Haig later explained he was merely trying to make clear that the government was still operating, but his comment sounded to many like an unconstitutional seizure of executive powers.

The chaotic policy-making process was foreshadowed by Richard Allen's short tenure as national security adviser. Allen, a scholar at the Hoover Institution and veteran of the Nixon administration, was an early Reagan disciple who helped shape Reagan's foreign policy positions during the 1980 presidential campaign. He was rewarded for his loyalty with the security post, but the job was downgraded to report to Meese rather than directly to the president. Outranked, he struggled to manage heavyweight cabinet members like Haig, Weinberger and Casey. He then came under fire for accepting gifts from a Japanese magazine that wanted to interview Nancy Reagan. He resigned in January 1982 after less than a year on the job.

Allen's successor, William Clark, was an amiable foreign policy neo-phyte but a trusted colleague of the president. As *Time* magazine reported, "He lacked training for such a role: he dropped out of two colleges and law school and had no academic or professional foreign policy experience."[31] A fifth-generation Californian, Clark was born in 1931 in Oxnard, a farm-ing and cattle-ranching community northwest of Los Angeles where his grandfather had served as sheriff and his father as police chief. A sturdy, square-faced man with bushy eyebrows and a cowboy mien, he started un-dergraduate studies at Stanford, then transferred to Santa Clara University but did not graduate. He was accepted at Loyola Law School in Los Ange-les, left school when he was drafted into the army in 1953, and though he resumed legal studies at Loyola after a two-year stint in the army, he did not finish his studies and failed to get a law degree. He nevertheless passed the California bar exam on his second try in 1958 and opened a successful private practice.

Like Reagan, Clark hailed from a Democratic family and swerved rightward as he aged. They met at a fund-raising event for Reagan in the mid-1960s, and Clark signed on to run his 1966 gubernatorial campaign operations in Ventura County, just up the coast from Los Angeles. When Reagan was elected, he named Clark his chief of staff in Sacramento, over-seeing a group of aides including Edwin Meese and Michael Deaver. Clark forged an almost brotherly relationship with Reagan. "To lighten the paper flow into the Governor's office," *Time* reported at the time of his appoint-ment as national security adviser, "Clark developed the famous 'mini-memo' system of single-page briefings, which is still in use at the White House. When aides groused that many ideas were too complex to be boiled down to a one-page memo, Clark replied, 'If you can't get it on one page, you are unable to understand your problem.'"[32]

Governor Reagan eventually put Clark on the California Supreme Court. The two men shared a passion for horseback riding, cowboy boots and Stetson hats. When Reagan became president, he brought Clark to Washington, improbably making him deputy secretary of state. The Senate confirmed him despite a rocky confirmation hearing that exposed Clark's limited knowledge of international affairs. The rationale for the appointment was clear: the Reagan inner circle wanted one of its own at the State Department to keep an eye on Haig. With Allen's departure, Reagan moved Clark to the White House as national security adviser, simultaneously announcing that Clark, unlike Allen, would report directly to the president, as did two powerful predecessors, Henry Kissinger under Nixon and Zbigniew Brzezinski under Jimmy Carter. Kissinger and Brzezinski had spent their lifetimes engaged with foreign policy issues. Clark had but one year of international affairs education as deputy secretary of state.

Although Clark's foreign policy outlook was still developing, his instinctively uncompromising views about the cold war made him a natural ally of Weinberger, Casey and other ardent cold warriors around the president. His long-standing friendship with Weinberger, rooted in the years they spent together in Sacramento working for Reagan, created a personal bond that inhibited collaboration with officials who did not share their policy views. The Clark-Weinberger bond was evident in Weinberger's strenuous but ultimately futile effort to persuade San Francisco's exclusive Bohemian Club to admit Clark as a member.[33]

Unbeknownst to Shultz, Clark thought Weinberger ought to be secretary of state and had advocated the appointment in late 1980 as Reagan put together his team before inauguration. Weinberger thought so, too, and had made his ambition clear to Clark and other Reagan advisers. Weinberger wound up as defense secretary, hardly a consolation prize, but as Haig flamed out as secretary of state, Clark favored moving Weinberger over from the Pentagon. "My first choice was Cap, with whom I've felt since 1980 really a very close friend, and I thought he'd make the perfect secretary of state," Clark recalled years later. "Shultz had held Cabinet roles, but very little foreign policy, so there was a void there, but a good diplomat. So by consensus it finally came down to Shultz."[34]

Weinberger, a compact man with dark hair and an engaging smile, was gracious and courteous with family and friends, stubborn and demanding with colleagues and subordinates. His father, Herman Weinberger, was a prosperous San Francisco lawyer. Caspar Weinberger was born in 1917 and attended Harvard, where he served as president of the *Harvard Crimson*, the student newspaper. He earned a law degree at Harvard Law School in 1941, then enlisted in the army. Assigned to the 41st Infantry Division, he participated in several intense battles in the Pacific Theater. After the war, he launched a legal career in San Francisco and ran successfully for a seat in the California Assembly; during the 1950s he hosted a weekly panel-discussion television program on KQED-TV, the local public station, and did book reviews for the *San Francisco Chronicle*. After Weinberger lost a 1958 bid to become California attorney general, Richard Nixon engineered his selection as chair of the state Republican Party.

Like Clark, Weinberger was impressed when he first encountered Reagan in 1966 while the movie actor was campaigning to be governor. "He stood out immediately in the crowd and had an enormous amount of charm and excited a great deal of almost immediate support just by being there," Weinberger recalled.[35] Reagan won the election and named Weinberger state director of finance. From there, it didn't take Weinberger long to make the leap to Washington. Nixon, who admired Weinberger, named him chair of the Federal Trade Commission (FTC).

So began a long, and sometimes uneasy, relationship between Weinberger and Shultz as they ascended to ever-higher posts in the Nixon administration. At each step of their oddly twinned Washington careers, Shultz held the more senior post. When Shultz served as Nixon's labor secretary, Weinberger was chair of the FTC. When Nixon made Shultz the inaugural director of the Office of Management and Budget, Weinberger was appointed his deputy. As Treasury secretary under Nixon, Shultz outranked Secretary of Health, Education, and Welfare Weinberger. After Nixon was reelected in 1972, Weinberger told the president he would like to be defense secretary. His wish was not granted.[36] The Shultz-Weinberger dynamic continued after the Nixon presidency, when both men landed jobs at Bechtel, the international construction company. Shultz was Bechtel president; Weinberger, the general counsel. Even their respective camps at the secretive Bohemian Grove in Northern California were stratified, with Shultz at the elite Mandalay Camp and Weinberger at the lesser Isle of Aves Camp. Shultz, it seemed, always ended up in the more powerful or prestigious position. That seemed to rankle Weinberger, generating a simmering resentment toward Shultz.

The rivalry did not augur well for cooperation between the secretaries of state and defense, a relationship easily frayed because of divergent institutional imperatives and inherent policy friction. The secretary of defense is responsible for maintaining American military strength and sending armed

Figure 1. Shultz with his father, Birl, at San Francisco's Kezar Stadium, 1928.
Source: George P. Shultz Personal Photo Album.

Figure 2. Birl and Margaret
Shultz, date unknown.
Source: George P. Shultz
Personal Photo Album.

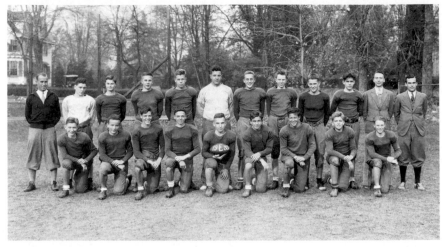

Figure 3. Shultz (first row, third from right) on the Englewood School for Boys football team, 1935. Source: George Pratt Shultz papers, Hoover Institution Library & Archives.

Figure 4. Shultz as a Princeton football player, 1941. After a senior year injury sidelined him, Shultz became the freshman team's backfield coach. Source: George Pratt Shultz papers, Hoover Institution Library & Archives.

Figure 5. In the summer of 1941, Shultz traveled to Tennessee to conduct on-site research for his Princeton senior thesis, "The Agricultural Program of the Tennessee Valley Authority." Source: George Pratt Shultz papers, Hoover Institution Library & Archives.

Figure 6. US Marine Corps Captain George P. Shultz, 1945. Source: George Pratt Shultz papers, Hoover Institution Library & Archives.

Figure 7. Helena "O'Bie" Shultz and George Shultz at the time of their wedding, 1946. Source: George P. Shultz Personal Photo Album.

Figure 8. Shultz as a faculty member at the University of Chicago, 1962. Source: George Pratt Shultz papers, Hoover Institution Library & Archives.

Figure 9. Shultz is sworn-in as Secretary of Labor by Chief Justice Earl Warren, as President Richard Nixon and Helena "O'Bie" Shultz look on in Washington, DC, January 22, 1969. Source: DPA Picture Alliance/Alamy Stock Photo.

Figure 10. Flanked by AFL-CIO leader George Meany and Shultz, President Nixon signs Executive Order 11491, which expanded federal employees' rights to collective bargaining through labor unions. October 29, 1969. Source: George Pratt Shultz papers, Hoover Institution Library & Archives.

Figure 11. Shultz plays a round of golf with Georgy Meany, leader of the AFL-CIO, date unknown. Source: George Pratt Shultz papers, Hoover Institution Library & Archives.

Figure 12. As Director of the Office of Management and Budget, Shultz meets with President Nixon and Milton Friedman in the Oval Office, June 1971. Source: Milton Friedman papers, Hoover Institution Library & Archives.

Figure 13. As the new secretary of the treasury, Shultz "shakes hands" with the first treasury secretary, Alexander Hamilton, 1972. Source: George Pratt Shultz papers, Hoover Institution Library & Archives.

Figure 14. Shultz (right) with Bechtel Corporation colleagues, 1975. Source: George Pratt Shultz papers, Hoover Institution Library & Archives.

Figure 15. Luncheon meeting at Camp David with (left to right) White House Chief of Staff James Baker; Shultz; President Reagan; National Security Advisor William Clark; and Presidential Counselor Edwin Meese, June 26, 1982. Source: Ronald Reagan Presidential Library.

Figure 16. After taking the oath as Secretary of State, Shultz is congratulated by President Reagan in the Rose Garden, July 16, 1982. Source: George Pratt Shultz papers, Hoover Institution Library & Archives. Ronald Reagan Presidential Library.

Figure 17. Shultz with President Reagan and Vice President Bush at the White House, date unknown. Source: Ronald Reagan Presidential Library.

Figure 18. Shultz briefs President Reagan on Middle East developments in White House Deputy Chief of Staff Michael K. Deaver's office, September 18, 1982. Source: MediaPunch Inc/Alamy Stock Photo.

Figure 19. President Reagan teases a sleeping Shultz aboard Air Force One, December 4, 1982. Source: Ronald Reagan Presidential Library.

Figure 20. Shultz and Vice President Bush on the White House South Lawn, 1983. Source: David Hume Kennerly via Getty Images.

Figure 21. Seeking a "renewal" of US-China relations, Shultz meets with Chinese leader Deng Xiaoping in Beijing, February 1983. Source: George P. Shultz Personal Photo Album.

Figure 22. Shultz visits the demilitarized zone dividing the two Koreas on February 8, 1983, reaffirming the US commitment to the defense of South Korea. Source: George P. Shultz Personal Photo Album.

Figure 23. Shultz and President Reagan raise a toast to Queen Elizabeth II at the de Young Museum in San Francisco, March 3, 1983. Source: Ronald Reagan Presidential Library.

Figure 24. Opening a diplomatic mission to secure the withdrawal of foreign armies from Lebanon, Shultz meets with Egyptian President Hosni Mubarak in Cairo, Egypt on April 26, 1983. Source: Chip Hires, Gamma-Rapho via Getty Images.

Figure 25. Shultz inspecting bomb damage at the American embassy in Beirut, April 28, 1983. Source: George Pratt Shultz papers, Hoover Institution Library & Archives.

forces into combat. The secretary of state's job is to assert American interests abroad through diplomacy and to seek, where possible, the resolution of conflict by peaceful means. But a role reversal is not uncommon at an operational level. Defense secretaries, responsible for the welfare of American forces, can be understandably reluctant to send them into combat, especially in circumstances where they are vulnerable to attack. And secretaries of state can favor "coercive diplomacy," the use of military force to bring adversaries to the negotiating table. Weinberger recalled, "Oddly enough, I was generally on the side of more caution and more concern about the safety of the troops."[37]

Reagan had assigned Weinberger the high-priority job of bolstering American forces with new weapons and added manpower. He did so with skill and relentless determination. No one in the administration was more determined to resist the Soviet Union. The best way to do so, in his view, was by intimidating Moscow with America's military might. With Reagan's enthusiastic endorsement, he proposed whopping budget increases for the Pentagon and sponsored publication of a voluminous annual report, *Soviet Military Power*, that warned darkly about rising Soviet military might and the Kremlin's aggressive global intentions. Weinberger did not want to launch a war against the Soviet Union, but he was highly skeptical of arms control efforts and diplomatic overtures with the Kremlin. As Haig foundered at the State Department, Weinberger quickly established himself as the most powerful member of the Reagan cabinet. That did not augur well for Shultz.

At first glance, William Casey, the CIA director, looked to be a potential Shultz ally. A tall, jowly, ungainly figure whose suits and ties perpetually bore stains from recently consumed meals and drinks, Casey had an intellectual bent and was an avid reader. Stacks of books, some precariously balanced, cluttered his desk at CIA headquarters in Langley, Virginia. Some were about the business of spying; others, about economics and politics. He authored several books about tax law and securities and two volumes about the American Revolution, a reflection of his keen interest in American history. A man of high energy and restless curiosity, he often astonished his CIA employees by citing data from obscure books. He spoke rapidly and sometimes indistinctly, leaving listeners puzzling over his comments. His short temper and gruff management style did not endear him to colleagues.

Shultz would later say of Casey, "I was almost afraid to have him come for lunch because he would say things and I wouldn't understand what he was saying and maybe he'd think I agreed with him. People said he was the one guy in Washington who didn't need a secure phone."[38]

Casey was born in Queens, New York, in 1913. His grandfather had moved to the United States from Ireland in 1849 during the Potato Famine. Casey attended parochial school and Fordham University and earned a law degree from St. John's University. His parents were Democrats and devout Catholics. Though a lawyer, Casey gravitated to finance and economics after serving effectively in the Office of Strategic Services (OSS), America's World War II spy service. Disillusioned with the Democratic Party, he became a Republican and played an active role in Republican politics on Long Island. He unsuccessfully challenged a Republican incumbent for a congressional seat in 1966. Over the decades, he became wealthy by smartly aggregating legal and financial data of use to corporations and through his own shrewd venture capital investments.

During the Nixon administration, when Shultz was Treasury secretary and Casey chair of the Securities and Exchange Commission and later undersecretary of state for economic affairs, they got along well. The friendship was sealed during a 1973 trip to Moscow when the two men brought along their wives. They stopped for rest and recreation at the Black Sea resort of Sochi. On the way home, during a refueling layover at Shannon, Ireland, Casey guided the two couples to the seat of the O'Brien clan in Drogheda, O'Bie's ancestral homeland. They consumed some Irish whiskey at a local pub and were quite jolly by the time they returned to their air force plane for the flight to Washington. "They all seemed tipsy," said Thomas Dawson, a Casey aide who made the trip with them. "Secretary Shultz was dancing in the aisle."[39]

The bonhomie did not guarantee that Casey and Shultz would work together smoothly nine years later as Shultz joined the Reagan administration. Warning signs were visible that the two men might not agree on national security issues. Casey's path to the CIA—serving as chair of Reagan's 1980 presidential campaign—stirred concern at the agency that he would politicize intelligence. By elevating the job to cabinet level, Reagan gave Casey a policy-making perch, adding to alarm that the CIA's analytical work would be bent to support administration policy objectives and that dissenting views would be suppressed. Shultz believed that the role of intelligence agencies was to present unbiased information to the president and stay out of policy-making debates.

As Casey took command of the agency in 1981, he made clear that his goal was to put the agency at the vanguard of Reagan's aggressive challenge to the Soviet Empire throughout the world. From the outset, Casey, a devout Catholic, worked to deepen the CIA's secret alliance with the Vatican to support Lech Walesa and the striking workers in Poland. He also took the lead in warning that the Communist threat was metastasizing in Central America and would soon, as he told colleagues, arrive at America's doorstep in Mexico.

The Clark-Weinberger-Casey worldview was shared by other influential officials surrounding Reagan. Jeane Kirkpatrick, the administration's UN ambassador, the first woman to hold the job, was a Democratic political science professor turned hawkish Republican. She had flipped parties after growing disillusioned with liberal critics of the United States. A 1979 Kirkpatrick essay in *Commentary*, a neoconservative journal, brought her to Reagan's attention. The essay argued that the United States should not have abandoned right-wing dictators like the shah of Iran and the Somozas in Nicaragua, leaders who were supportive of American interests in their region. Her professorial outfits and coifed gray hair gave her a grandmotherly demeanor. It was deceiving. She was a person of strong convictions and tart pronouncements who was not shy about asserting American interests. She quickly feuded with Haig and leveraged her cabinet rank to maneuver around and even defy the secretary of state. Her blunt defense of American policies at the UN impressed Reagan and made her an Oval Office favorite.

Richard Perle fueled the aggressive approach to the Soviet Union with his doubts about the nuclear arms control measures endorsed by previous administrations. Perle had mastered the intricacies of arms control issues while serving as an adviser to Senator Henry "Scoop" Jackson, a conservative Democrat from Washington State who saw little gain in trying to make balanced arms deals with the Soviet Union and used his seat on the Senate Armed Services Committee to push for large Pentagon budget increases. Over time, Shultz came to respect Perle even though he often disagreed with him.

Richard Pipes, the White House director of East European and Soviet affairs, was another hard-liner. A Russian historian at Harvard and émigré from Poland, Pipes gave scholarly weight and stylish prose to the bellicose policy toward the Kremlin. In 1976, he had led a group of foreign policy and defense specialists appointed by CIA director George H. W. Bush to take a fresh look at the Soviet threat. The group, dubbed "Team B," found the danger much greater than estimated by the CIA. In Pipes's view, seeking common ground with Moscow was futile and likely to undermine American and Western interests. He doubted Shultz could handle the Kremlin. Pipes's disdain, later recorded in his memoirs, brightly highlighted the administration's preference for ideological battle and its contempt for pragmatic problem solving.

Pipes said dismissively of Shultz, "Being primarily an economist and businessman, he lacked a deeper understanding for the whole ideological and political dimension of our relationship with the Soviet Union. Like most corporate executives, he tended to treat our conflict with it as a CEO might treat disagreements with his firm's labor union: that is, assume that the two parties shared a common interest in the enterprise and only haggled over the division of profits. But in dealing with the USSR there really was no room for compromise, except on minor issues of no consequence, because the Soviet Union acted on the principle that foreign relations were a zero-sum game." Pipes added that Shultz wanted "'to try to turn the relationship [with the Soviet Union] around: away from confrontation and toward real problem solving.' He thought in those commonsensical terms, unaware that the real problem was the Soviet regime with its ideology and its *nomenklatura* and that one could not negotiate with it its own destruction. This had to happen despite itself."[40]

Pipes and most of his fellow national security officials were members of the Committee on the Present Danger, a bipartisan conservative group initially formed in the early 1950s and reconstituted in 1976 to warn Americans that Washington was insufficiently vigilant about the Soviet threat. Shultz himself was a member and had been elected to the committee's board of directors in 1979, but he had not been propelled by the ideological ardor of other members like Pipes, Casey and Kirkpatrick.

The phalanx of hard-edged Reagan aides represented a potential source of serious trouble for Shultz, but the threat was not on his mind as he dived into preparations for his Senate confirmation hearings. Like a college student cramming for exams, Shultz needed to master a dizzying array of foreign policy issues on short notice. While O'Bie looked for a new Shultz home in the Washington area, the Shultzes accepted an invitation from Donald Regan, the Treasury secretary and a Shultz friend, to live in a guesthouse at the Regan home near Mount Vernon in northern Virginia. Shultz reported daily to the State Department, temporarily making use of a vacant, spacious office usually occupied by the undersecretary for economic affairs, located just steps from the seventh-floor suite of the secretary of state. Between cram sessions, he fretted about personal issues such as delivery and registration of the family Oldsmobile and preparations for closing on the purchase of a house in Bethesda, Maryland, later in the summer.[41]

He needed an executive secretary. After interviewing several candidates, he quickly selected Raymond Seitz, a veteran diplomat. Seitz found Shultz "somewhat inscrutable" and humorless during their conversation and was surprised to be selected. "He was taking a chance," Seitz recalled. "He didn't know anything about me, and I didn't know him at all."[42] The selection of an experienced foreign service officer was no accident. Shultz was signaling the State Department that, unlike some of his predecessors, he would rely to a considerable extent on the judgment of experienced diplomats rather than political operatives well connected at the White House and in Congress.

Seitz, an urbane man born in Hawaii and educated at Yale, had served at embassies in Canada, Kenya, Zaire and Britain and worked in senior staff posts at State Department headquarters under four secretaries of state. He was a shrewd student of foreign policy making and had a fine feel for the flow of power in Washington. Though twenty years younger than Shultz, he immediately became a discreet sounding board for Shultz as he began to engage with his fellow cabinet members, White House aides and State Department colleagues. Once installed in a small office immediately adjacent to Shultz's, Seitz started keeping detailed notes of daily developments and meetings, beginning a confidential chronicle of Shultz's work. Within a few weeks, it turned into a full-scale journal filled with unvarnished accounts of successes and setbacks.[43]

On July 5, while still preparing for his confirmation hearings, Shultz and Reagan agreed while meeting in California that the time had come for Haig to step down as secretary and become a consultant to the State Department. Reagan would temporarily make Deputy Secretary Walter Stoessel acting secretary. When Shultz called Haig to discuss the plan, Haig rejected the consulting proposal, saying he would prefer to serve as secretary until Reagan instructed him to leave. Shultz called back an hour later to say the president had reached that decision. Later that day, Reagan called Haig himself to tell him Shultz had acted on his behalf and to thank Haig for his service.[44]

Haig's exit made Shultz even more acutely aware that he was inheriting a daunting job. As the days passed, he was inundated with troubling news. Robert Ames, the CIA's highly respected senior Middle East expert, told him the region was in disarray. The State Department's European specialists advised him that the Reagan administration's opposition to construction of a natural gas pipeline from the Soviet Union's abundant gas fields to energy-dependent Western Europe was threatening to fracture relations between Washington and its allies. The fight could undermine American hopes of basing nuclear-tipped intermediate-range missiles in Germany to counter Soviet bases with similar missiles within range of Western European capitals.

Public opposition to nuclear weapons in Europe and the United States was increasing as citizens joined the nuclear freeze movement, a rapidly growing campaign to pressure Washington and Moscow to suspend the production of new weapons and begin drastic reductions. Just days before Reagan invited Shultz to become secretary of state, more than a million people had marched against nuclear weapons in New York. Meantime, American relations with the Kremlin were at a standstill, with little communication between the two superpowers.[45]

Apart from heightened tensions in American-Soviet relations, other parts of the world were in turbulence. Middle East instability was rising dangerously after Israeli forces had moved into Lebanon to combat the Palestine Liberation Organization (PLO). The overthrow of the shah of Iran and his American-backed government by fundamentalist Islamic forces in 1979 had deprived Washington of a vital, if undemocratic, ally in the Middle East. As Reagan took the oath of office on January 21, 1981, Iran freed fifty-four American diplomats whom it had held hostage for more than a year, but the ruling clerics in Teheran remained hostile to the United States.

Nixon's overtures to China had led to the establishment of formal diplomatic relations during the Carter administration, including the opening of a highly secret US intelligence listening post in western China, designed to monitor long-range Soviet missile tests. But relations between Washington and Beijing had cooled during Reagan's first year as tensions increased over American arms sales to Taiwan. Lee Kuan Yew told Shultz that the US-China diplomatic dialogue was static and emphasized form over substance. Though China's economy was still weak and its political system traumatized by Mao's long rule, Deng Xiaoping, Beijing's paramount leader since 1978, was introducing liberal economic reforms and harnessing the energy of a nation of one billion people. Clearly, China was emerging from decades of internal turmoil and on its way to becoming a global economic force, adding to its considerable influence as a military power with nuclear weapons and counterweight to the Soviet Union.

Political unrest was spreading in Central America, where leftist insurgent forces were trying to destabilize the government in El Salvador and the left-leaning Sandinista leadership in Nicaragua was welcoming economic and military assistance from Cuba and the Soviet Union. The Reagan national security team, fearing Communist advances near America's doorstep, initiated a series of covert military and intelligence programs in the region designed to support the Salvadoran regime and undermine the Nicaraguan government.

The lethargic state of the American economy added to the disheartening picture. Shultz was well aware that the economy was becalmed, suffering from an unholy combination of high inflation and business stagnation. Intentional cutbacks in petroleum production by Saudi Arabia and other Middle Eastern oil-producing nations, which resulted in long lines at American gas stations, had undermined the Carter administration. Reflecting on the wobbly state of the nation, Jimmy Carter had bemoaned a "malaise" in America in a nationally televised address permeated with pessimism. It helped kill his reelection hopes. While Reagan had taken the White House partly on the strength of a more optimistic vision of America, a year into his presidency the economy remained mired in recession, unemployment was running at 8.8 percent and interest rates were hovering above an eye-popping 15 percent.

Faced with all these global challenges, plus an administration pursuing national security policies more hard-line than his own views on some issues, Shultz needed to establish his authority quickly. The power of secretaries of state depends greatly on their relationship with the president. Absent a tight partnership between a secretary and president, secretaries of state can be outmaneuvered and overshadowed by other top officials such as the defense secretary and national security adviser. Shultz did not have to look far to see failed secretaries of state who had never won the full trust of their presidents. William P. Rogers never gained traction as Richard Nixon's first secretary of state, thwarted by Nixon's faith in his own judgment and the advice of Henry Kissinger, his national security adviser. Cyrus Vance was outweighed as Jimmy Carter's secretary of state by National Security Adviser Zbigniew Brzezinski and abruptly resigned after a failed attempt in April 1980 to rescue the American diplomats in Iran. Haig had been undone by his own missteps, a coterie of top White House aides who did not trust him and a shaky relationship with Reagan.

Shultz also knew that successful secretaries of state understood that their job was to execute the foreign policy of the president, not to act as the architect of American policy themselves, especially in public. The quickest way to fail was to suggest in word or action that the secretary was setting policies. Haig was Exhibit A. But how much could Shultz count on Reagan's support if he advocated a more conciliatory approach to the Kremlin or questioned the emphasis on covert military and intelligence operations to prevent the spread of Soviet influence in Central America? Shultz's encounters with Reagan over the years provided few clues. Most of their discussions had focused on economic and budget matters. They had not talked extensively about national security issues. Indeed, Shultz did not really know where Reagan stood on many fundamental national security challenges, beyond Reagan's pronouncements as a presidential candidate and as president. On the central matter of American-Soviet relations, Shultz was uncertain if Reagan's bellicose rhetoric about the Kremlin was his core view or whether behind the harsh words and policies, Reagan wanted to ease East-West tensions and slow, even end, the superpower nuclear arms race.

Unsure where his president stood, uncertain if he could count on presidential support, unallied with other powerful officials, unsuited to handle bruising internal policy conflicts—it was hard to imagine how Shultz could have a chance to alter the course of the cold war.

CHAPTER EIGHT

A Common Foundation

HAD SHULTZ HAD TIME to examine the development of Reagan's views about the Soviet Union over the years, he would have found much in common with his own. In fact, although they did not know it when Shultz was appointed secretary of state, the two men had remarkably similar instincts about the Soviet Union and how to manage the cold war. Reagan's belligerent rhetoric about the Soviet Union overshadowed an underlying impulse to ease tensions that could be found from time to time in Reagan's public pronouncements. That impulse coincided with Shultz's own intuition that the cold war could be moderated. The convergence was a fortuitous alignment with the potential to reshape East-West relations—if Reagan and Shultz could spend enough time together to see how much their views overlapped and if Shultz could overcome the united front of hard-liners around the president who actively discouraged diplomatic overtures to Moscow. In effect, the Reagan national security team was doing its best to prevent Reagan from acting on his temperate instincts.

Shultz was only vaguely aware of the evolution of Reagan's thinking about the Soviet Union across the decades of his career as a movie actor and politician. Reagan was not a student of American foreign policy—his understanding of American history came partly from movie roles he played and remembered. At times, he even seemed to think his movie roles and the history his films loosely told were actual events he had witnessed or participated in. But he had a gut instinct for how to deal with the Kremlin: Be stout in combating Communism. Avoid nuclear war. Brook negotiations and Soviet-American agreements if they advanced American interests. Apply pressure to the Soviet Union's greatest vulnerability, its weak economy. See the Soviet Union as a fatally flawed state destined to fail.

These were, on one level, boilerplate cold war views embraced by Republicans and Democrats. They reflected mainstream sentiments among the American people, reinforced over the early decades of the cold war by East-West tensions that erupted periodically into volatile crises and even armed conflict. This history included the 1948–1949 land blockade of West Berlin by Soviet-backed East German forces, the 1950 North Korean invasion of South Korea, Soviet armed suppression of democratic reformers in Hungary in 1956, construction of the Berlin wall in 1961, the 1962 Cuban Missile Crisis, Soviet military intervention in Czechoslovakia in 1968 to crush a democratic movement and Soviet pressure on Poland to impose martial law in 1981 to silence democratic forces. When Reagan took office as president in 1981, the Soviet Union, belying the utopian visions advertised by its founders during the 1917 Bolshevik Revolution, was a hardened totalitarian state brutally shaped by Stalin and sustained with only minimal modifications by his successors. It maintained the largest land army in the world and a nuclear weapons arsenal that matched, and in some weapon categories exceeded, the American nuclear triad of intercontinental ballistic missiles, bombers and submarine-launched missiles.

Reagan's anti-Soviet outlook made no allowance for America's role in initiating and sustaining the cold war, including the tragically misguided Vietnam War. Nor did he harbor doubts about Washington's extravagant investment over the years in military hardware, much of it assembled to deter and, if necessary, combat Soviet forces. In fact, he was determined to increase military spending. His oft-repeated version of postwar history was a chronicle of unbroken American altruism and generosity, undergirded by defense forces required to counter the Soviet threat. Yet Reagan coupled his anti-Communist views with a hopeful, if simplistic, belief that the American and Soviet people yearned for peace and a better life and wanted their leaders to do the same. He was prone to reducing big ideas and policy debates to human scale through stories and anecdotes. The allusions sometimes left the impression he did not understand policy nuances. Indeed, according to many Reagan aides, he did not fully grasp the subtleties of some of his administration's policies. But the impulse to simplify issues, and talk about them in terms that the average person could understand, gave his leadership a power and appeal that more detail-minded presidents like Jimmy Carter lacked.

Reagan's outlook developed haphazardly over the years, and it would be imposing a strategic order on his thinking to suggest with the benefit of hindsight that each piece was carefully constructed and woven into a coherent strategy by the time he became president. But they are visible as he moved from college to making movies to governing California and eventually being elected president. Reagan's strident anti-Communist rhetoric as president echoed his campaign declarations and long history of outspoken opposition to Communism. As a young man in rural Illinois growing up in a Democratic household that revered Franklin Roosevelt, and as an activist actor in Hollywood in the 1940s and 1950s, Reagan was a progressive on domestic policy and largely silent about foreign policy. He awakened to the Communist threat after World War II while working in Hollywood and serving as president of the Screen Actors Guild:

> These were eye-opening years for me. When I'd come back to Warner Brothers after the war, I'd shared the orthodox liberal view that Communists—if there really were any—were liberals who were temporarily off track, and whatever they were, they didn't pose much of a threat to me or anyone. I heard whispers that Moscow wanted to infiltrate the world's most powerful medium of entertainment, but I'd passed them off as irrational and emotional red baiting. Now I knew from firsthand experience how Communists used lies, deceit, violence, or any other tactic that suited them to advance the cause of Soviet expansionism. I knew from the experience of hand-to-hand combat that America faced no more insidious or evil threat than that of Communism.[1]

Though still a Democrat, he supported Republican Dwight Eisenhower's 1952 bid to become president and campaigned for him, an early Reagan dip into electoral politics. Traveling the country in the 1950s as a pitchman for General Electric's *General Electric Theater* television show, Reagan drifted to the right. Nancy Reagan recalled, "He became increasingly concerned about government interference in the free enterprise system—and also in the lives of individuals. One day he came home from a speaking trip and told me he was starting to realize that the Democrats he had campaigned for in election years were responsible for the very things he was speaking out against between elections."[2]

By the early 1960s, Reagan was sounding off about the Communist threat, attracting attention as a possible candidate for public office. He claimed to have firsthand knowledge of a Communist effort to capture control of the American entertainment industry, Hollywood in particular, from his days serving on the board and leading the Screen Actors Guild. A number of Hollywood screenwriters and other movie industry workers were blacklisted at the time, part of the national anti-Communist fever stirred up by Senator Joseph McCarthy and his allies. In a 1961 speech in Phoenix, Reagan said, "One of the foremost authorities on Communism in the world today has said we have ten years. Not ten years to make up our mind, but ten years to win or lose—by 1970 the world will be all slave or all free."[3]

During the 1964 presidential campaign, he barnstormed around the country extolling the virtues of Barry Goldwater, the Republican candidate. In a speech titled "A Time for Choosing," which vaulted Reagan into national prominence as a politician and set the stage for his 1966 candidacy for California governor, he said the United States confronted a fateful choice in responding to the Soviet empire:

> We are faced with the most evil enemy mankind has known in his long climb from the swamp to the stars. We cannot buy our security, our freedom from the threat of the bomb by committing an immorality so great as saying to a billion human beings now enslaved behind the Iron Curtain, "Give up your dreams of freedom because to save our own skins, we're willing to make a deal with your slave masters." Alexander Hamilton said, "A nation which can prefer disgrace to danger is prepared for a master, and deserves one." Now let's set the record straight. There's no argument over the choice between peace and war, but there's only one guaranteed way you can have peace—and you can have it in the next second—surrender. . . .
>
> You and I know and do not believe that life is so dear and peace so sweet as to be purchased at the price of chains and slavery. If nothing in life is worth dying for, when did this begin—just in the face of this enemy? Or should Moses have told the children of Israel to live in slavery under the pharaohs? Should Christ have refused the cross? Should the patriots at Concord Bridge have thrown down their guns and refused to fire the shot heard 'round the world?[4]

Yet even as he fueled his political career with anti-Communist broadsides, Reagan grew alarmed at the prospect of nuclear war. Exactly when, and how, this concern developed is difficult to trace in Reagan's life. The origin may well have been the August 1945 American nuclear bombing of Hiroshima and Nagasaki. Four months after the attacks, he signed up to speak at an antinuclear rally in Hollywood. He withdrew from the event when Warner Bros. informed him the appearance would violate his contract with the studio. Reagan's concern was evident three decades later when he addressed the 1976 Republican Convention. His insurgent campaign to snatch the nomination from Gerald Ford, the incumbent president, had failed, but many convention delegates saw Reagan as the future leader of their party. Outlining the challenges that the nation faced, Reagan said, "We live in a world in which the great powers have aimed and poised at each other horrible missiles of destruction, nuclear weapons that can in a matter of minutes arrive at each other's country and destroy virtually the civilized world we live in."[5]

In a 1978 radio broadcast, he told listeners, "If the Soviets push the button, there is no defense against them, no way to prevent the nuclear destruction of their targets in the United States."[6] On July 31, 1979, Reagan made a visit to the headquarters of the North American Aerospace Defense Command, housed deep inside Cheyenne Mountain in Colorado. His tour of the site, outfitted with huge radar tracking screens and other equipment designed to display Soviet missiles streaking toward American targets, including Washington, DC, seemed to deepen his fear of nuclear war. Reagan aides later claimed the visit as the wellspring for his dream of building a defense system to shield the United States from incoming missiles.

In addition to his florid anti-Communist pronouncements and his concern about nuclear war, Reagan dabbled with another notion about the Soviet Union—that its economy was weak and an American military buildup might put added strain on the Kremlin as it tried to match Washington's defense spending. In a 1963 address at the Orange County Press Club, Reagan alluded to this somewhat inchoate idea:

> If we relieve the strain on the shaken Russian economy by aiding their
> enslaved satellites, thus reducing the danger of uprising and revolution,
> and if we continue granting concessions which reduce our military
> strength giving Russia time to improve hers as well as shore up her
> limping industrial complex—aren't we perhaps adding to the commu-
> nist belief that their system will through evolution catch up and pass

ours? If we truly believe that our way of life is best aren't the Russians more likely to recognize that fact and modify their stand if we let their economy come unhinged so the contrast is apparent? Inhuman though it may sound, shouldn't we throw the whole burden of feeding the satellites on their slave masters who are having trouble feeding themselves?[7]

Reagan returned to the theme intermittently. In 1977, he said, "The Soviet Union is building the most massive military machine the world has ever seen and is denying its people all kinds of consumer products to do it. We could have an unexpected ally if citizen Ivan is becoming discontented enough to start talking back."[8] During the 1980 presidential campaign, Reagan told the *Washington Post*: "I think there's every indication and every reason to believe that the Soviet Union cannot increase its production of arms. Right now we're hearing of strikes and labor disputes because people aren't getting enough to eat. They've diverted so much to military [spending] that they can't provide for the consumer needs. [It] would be of great benefit to the United States if we started a buildup."[9]

After taking the oath of office at noon on January 20, 1981, Reagan, in his first address as president, focused primarily on domestic issues but said of the Soviet Union, without naming it:

> As for the enemies of freedom, those who are potential adversaries, they will be reminded that peace is the highest aspiration of the American people. We will negotiate for it, sacrifice for it; we will not surrender for it—now or ever.
> Our forbearance should never be misunderstood. Our reluctance for conflict should not be misjudged as a failure of will. When action is required to preserve our national security, we will act. We will maintain sufficient strength to prevail if need be, knowing that if we do so we have the best chance of never having to use that strength.[10]

As Reagan settled into the White House, his national security team quickly began to construct an unyielding approach to the Kremlin that stressed Reagan's hard-edged, anti-Communist impulses. Yet for all the tough rhetoric and the military buildup, Reagan seemed drawn at times to a less strident, almost innocent approach. Just months after taking office, he shocked Haig, Pipes and other aides by presenting them with a handwritten response to a boilerplate letter he had received from Leonid Brezhnev, the Soviet leader. Drafted by the president in April 1981 as he was recovering from the assassination attempt, the letter hinted at a private Reagan anxious to avoid a nuclear conflict, open to constructive diplomacy and seeking a way to wind down the cold war. It was sappy and simplistic and seemed utterly unrealistic, yet it offered a glimpse of a more peaceful world that stirred Reagan. The letter reminded Brezhnev that he and Reagan had met a decade earlier in California, as President Nixon and Brezhnev were wrapping up a round of talks at Nixon's residence in San Clemente, a coastal community between San Diego and Los Angeles. The Reagan letter offers a look at his personal outlook, unfiltered by White House aides and Soviet experts in the administration:

> Mr. President: When we met, I asked if you were aware that the hopes and aspirations of millions of people throughout the world were dependent on the decisions that would be reached in those meetings. You took my hand in both of yours and assured me that you were aware of that and that you were dedicated with all your heart and soul and mind to fulfilling those hopes and dreams. . . .
>
> Is it possible that we have permitted ideology, political and economic philosophies, and governmental policies to keep us from considering the very real, everyday problems of our peoples? Will the average Soviet family be better off or even aware that the Soviet Union has imposed a government of its own choice on the people of Afghanistan? Is life better for the people of Cuba because the Cuban military dictate who shall govern the people of Angola?
>
> It is often implied that such things have been made necessary because of territorial ambitions of the United States; that we have imperialistic designs, and thus constitute a threat to your own security and that of the newly emerging nations. Not only is there no evidence to support such a charge, there is solid evidence that the United States, when it could have dominated the world with no risk to itself, made no effort whatsoever to do so. . . .
>
> Mr. President, should we not be concerned with eliminating the obstacles which prevent our people, those you and I represent, from achieving their most cherished goals?[11]

Reagan's advisers were stunned. "I found myself astonished by [Reagan's] attitude when I measured it against the backdrop of what he was saying publicly, and what was attributed to him as a classic Cold Warrior," Haig later recalled.[12] Pipes was equally astounded. He found the letter "mawkish" and said later, "I could not believe my eyes. . . . It was written in a Christian turn-the-other-cheek spirit sympathetic to the point of apology, full of icky sentimentality."[13] Despite the objections and State Department preparation of a conventional response to Brezhnev, Reagan did not yield. He instructed aides to send both the State Department letter and his version to Brezhnev.

A few months later, Reagan publicly disclosed the letter, proudly reading aloud portions of it during an appearance at the National Press Club on November 18, 1981. His speech that day outlined a four-part agenda for reducing American and Soviet nuclear and conventional forces and for equalizing troop levels in Europe. A *New York Times* story about the appearance observed, "The emphasis in the speech, as it was in Mr. Reagan's most recent news conference, was on his desire for peace around the world. He sought to ease concerns abroad and at home about the possibility of war."[14]

His inclination to seek a better relationship with the Kremlin surfaced here and there throughout his first fifteen months as president, often overshadowed by his bellicose attacks on the Soviet Union. In a commencement speech at Eureka College, his alma mater, on May 9, 1982, Reagan told the graduates, "I'm optimistic that we can build a more constructive relationship with the Soviet Union." He described a five-point strategy for managing East-West relations: "Military balance, economic security, regional stability, arms reductions and dialogue."

On June 8, 1982, eighteen months into his presidency and two weeks before he invited Shultz to serve as secretary of state, Reagan and his speechwriters crystallized his long-gestating views about the Soviet Union into a memorable speech delivered to the British Parliament in London. As the text was drafted and revised, nuclear freeze organizers were preparing for a mass march in New York on June 12 that was expected to draw as many as a million supporters into the streets. While the movement seemed unlikely to compel Washington to trim the American nuclear arsenal, it clearly had the potential to fuel public opposition in West Germany to Washington's plan to base medium-range nuclear missiles there.

The Westminster speech, as it became known, featured slashing rhetoric coupled with a desire to avoid a nuclear confrontation, as well as a sense that the Soviet Union was structurally unsound and might be effectively undermined by forcing the Kremlin to make unsustainable investments in defense. Reagan reprised his tough anti-Communist line: "We see totalitarian forces in the world who seek subversion and conflict around the globe to further their barbarous assault on the human spirit. What, then, is our course? Must civilization perish in a hail of fiery atoms? Must freedom wither in a quiet, deadening accommodation with totalitarian evil?"

In words that might blunt or assuage nuclear freeze supporters, Reagan underscored his alarm over the threat of nuclear war and offered a reassuring endorsement of arms control negotiations:

> There is first the threat of global war. No President, no Congress, no Prime Minister, no Parliament can spend a day entirely free of this threat. And I don't have to tell you that in today's world the existence of nuclear weapons could mean, if not the extinction of mankind, then surely the end of civilization as we know it. That's why negotiations on intermediate-range nuclear forces now underway in Europe and the START talks—Strategic Arms Reduction Talks—which will begin later this month, are not just critical to American or Western policy; they are critical to mankind. Our commitment to early success in these negotiations is firm and unshakable, and our purpose is clear: reducing the risk of war by reducing the means of waging war on both sides.

Then he spoke of the internal weaknesses of the Soviet Union:

> In an ironic sense Karl Marx was right. We are witnessing today a great revolutionary crisis, a crisis where the demands of the economic order are conflicting directly with those of the political order. But the crisis is happening not in the free, non-Marxist West, but in the home of Marxist-Leninism, the Soviet Union. It is the Soviet Union that runs against the tide of history by denying human freedom and human dignity to its citizens. It also is in deep economic difficulty. The rate of growth in the national product has been steadily declining since the fifties and is less than half of what it was then.

Near the end of the speech, Reagan dramatically predicted that "the march of freedom and democracy" would "leave Marxism-Leninism on the ashheap of history."[15]

Not surprisingly, press coverage of the speech emphasized Reagan's pugnacious language and his call to resist Communism and the Kremlin. "President Urges Global Crusade for Democracy," the *New York Times* headline declared.[16] Reagan's bold prediction about the eventual fate of Marxism-Leninism immediately became the shorthand reference for the speech. Less noted at the time were Reagan's references to danger of nuclear war and the importance of seeking agreements to limit the nuclear arms race. No one doubted that Reagan was determined to confront the Soviet Union and buttress the American military with new weapons. But with Secretary of State Haig rapidly fading as a force in the administration, the question was who could deliver on Reagan's commitment to negotiate nuclear arms accords and make the cold war less combustible. Arms control negotiations were at a virtual standstill.

Shultz, though unaware that the White House might soon be looking for a new secretary of state, heard about the Westminster speech. He read the text and agreed with it.[17] To a surprising degree, it echoed his own thoughts about the need to blend military strength and firmness with a faith in dialogue with adversaries and a willingness to seek common ground and ease cold war tensions. He thought a different kind of relationship with the Soviet Union might be possible. Not friendship, partnership or even collaboration. But perhaps a more civil discourse about disagreements and some cooperation to check, even reverse, the frightening growth in nuclear arsenals on both sides and the reliance in Washington and Moscow on doctrines on fighting a nuclear war that called for the obliteration of American and Soviet societies.

His own dealings with the Soviet Union during the Nixon administration, while limited and focused on economic issues, gave him a strong sense that improved relations with the Kremlin might be possible. He also saw evidence that the Soviet economy was shaky and that arms expenditures were creating consumer goods shortages and civilian discontent. Shultz first stepped on Soviet soil in 1973 as Treasury secretary. Despite being whisked around Moscow in a security bubble and housed in government guesthouses or hotels, he could see long lines of shoppers waiting outside shops with mostly bare shelves. He noted street lanes reserved for black ZiL limousines ferrying officials to and from the Kremlin. He was struck by the absence of civilian cars. While Shultz attended meetings, O'Bie, a former nurse, was taken by Soviet guides to Moscow hospitals and other medical facilities that the government thought would impress her. "She came back from these visits horrified at the lack of basic hygiene and sterilization procedures considered routine in any US hospital," Shultz recalled. "So, I saw, the health care system was not working."[18]

His reaction was not unlike that of American diplomats, business executives and journalists based in Moscow. A common refrain among these Americans was that one had to live in the Soviet Union for only a few months to see how inert the economy was, how few consumer goods there were, how most Russians, even those living in the capital, subsisted on potatoes, cabbage and other root vegetables, rarely getting access to decent meats, fresh fish, fruits and vegetables. Medical and dental services were rudimentary. Soviet-manufactured television sets were inferior to Western models and had a tendency to explode. The running joke among Americans was the Soviet Union was a backward nation with nuclear weapons.

The gap between Soviet boasts about the advantages of Communism and the reality of Soviet life was underscored for Shultz during a brief break in Sochi, the Black Sea resort. "I was going from the World Bank–IMF meetings in Nairobi to meetings the following week in Moscow. The Soviets proposed to give me a weekend in Sochi. They took me to the grounds of what was clearly an old estate and to a rather substantial building that had obviously replaced whatever had been there before. I remarked on the building and my Soviet friend said, 'We wanted to bring you here so you could see that not everything good in the Soviet Union was built by the czars.' What a revealing comment."[19]

Another impactful moment for Shultz—one that made him think he could work with the Kremlin—came during a 1973 visit to Leningrad. Nikolai Patolichev, the Soviet foreign trade minister, accompanied Shultz, surprisingly agreeing to make the flight from Moscow on Shultz's US Air Force plane. When Shultz announced he wished to see the art collection at the Hermitage and take a tour of the Summer Palace, one of the czars' monumental homes, Patolichev insisted they first go to Piskaryovskoye Memorial Cemetery, the resting place of 420,00 civilians and 50,000 soldiers killed in the Leningrad area during World War II.

As Shultz and Patolichev walked past rows of mass graves and funeral music played from loudspeakers, he realized their interpreter was no longer walking alongside them. He looked back. Overcome by the scene, she had stopped and was sobbing. Patolichev, a hardened Kremlin veteran whose father was a friend of Stalin, had stopped too, tears streaming down his face. Shultz placed a wreath at the memorial statue at the end of the long row of graves. The two men then walked back and climbed the stairs to a platform overlooking the cemetery.

"I have a great sense of community with the people here. I also fought in World War II as a marine in the Pacific," Shultz said to Patolichev. "And I also had comrades get killed alongside me so I feel for these people. These are the people who stopped Hitler." Shultz then walked to the front edge of the platform. Standing as erect as he could, he gave his best Marine

Corps salute as he stared out at the mass graves. Patolichev watched closely. As Shultz returned to his side, Patolichev said, "Thank you. That shows respect." Shultz recalled, "Later I heard others make comments suggesting that they had heard about this visit. I learned an important lesson in dealing with the Soviets: don't be afraid to show respect when respect is deserved. That adds credibility to your views, including critical ones."[20]

As Treasury secretary, Shultz also came to realize that Soviet leaders were capable of conducting negotiations in good faith and honoring commitments they made. He learned this from talks with Andrei Kosygin, the Soviet premier, about grain purchases the Kremlin was making from American farmers. Grain shortages were a chronic Soviet problem produced by limited lands suitable for farming, the failed collectivization of agriculture, periodic droughts and other unfavorable conditions. In an effort to buy as much grain as possible, the Kremlin had started buying it throughout the United States, in effect, cornering the grain market before American officials realized what had happened. Once the pattern became evident, grain prices skyrocketed, increasing the cost of bread and other grain-based foods for Americans. "We can't tolerate this," Shultz told Kosygin. The Soviet premier said he understood. Their conversation, Shultz said, led to "the long-term grain agreement, which provided for a negotiation at the start of each season to produce an agreement for the amount of grain the Soviets would buy. This was announced publicly so the monopsony power was taken away."[21]

Nixon asked Shultz to host a group of Soviet economic officials at Camp David in June 1973 while Nixon accompanied Leonid Brezhnev to California. With little on the agenda at Camp David, the Russians devoted most of their time to recreational activities, scattering golf balls through the woods as they wielded golf clubs for the first time in their lives. Shultz's State Department interpreters reported to him that the Russians, talking freely among themselves, griped about the anemic state of the Soviet economy. Based on these encounters, Shultz thought, "I had seen enough of conditions to realize that their system was not very good, on life support, really."[22] "People thought it was an evil place, and it was. But then I had enough experience to know that the system wasn't working, and everybody knew it, including people in the Soviet Union. And so, somehow or other, it would change."[23] Beyond that, he said, "I also learned that the Soviets were tough negotiators but you could negotiate successfully with them. In my experience, they did their homework and had skill and patience and staying power. I respected them not only as able negotiators but as people who could make a deal and stick to it."[24]

As Shultz learned more about Reagan's views, he found that "Reagan's judgment was that the Soviet Union was not a stable system and would change, and that's what I thought. Most people in Washington didn't think that."[25] Indeed, Reagan and Shultz were in a distinct minority. The prevailing view, publicly embraced by the Reagan administration, was that the Soviet Union was irrevocably committed to dictatorial rule at home and expansionist policies abroad. That a milder Soviet Union would embark on internal reforms, subdued by its own economic and social strains, seemed highly unlikely, if not inconceivable. Soviet analysts at the CIA generated a steady stream of classified reports in the early 1980s describing a dysfunctional Soviet economy, shortages of consumer goods, unsustainable defense spending and disappointing harvests. But the reports offered little hope that the Soviet Union could reform Communist customs or become less truculent in international affairs, even as the Communist Party's aging leaders entered a period of transition.

An August 1981 CIA report was typical. Noting the likelihood of increased Soviet defense spending in the mid- to late 1980s, the report stated: "In the near term, investment in some civilian sectors would suffer. Cutbacks would occur mostly in such areas as consumer durables, services, housing, and machinery and equipment for the food and soft goods industries. Such cuts would worsen already poor prospects for improving labor productivity over the next five years and could increase worker discontent. Despite these consequences, we believe the Soviet leadership would be inclined to continue the current mix of cosmetic concessions, short-term fixes, and patriotic appeals and, if necessary, adopt repressive measures to ensure both continued growth of the defense effort and domestic control."[26]

While Reagan's and Shultz's views about the cold war aligned, more so than they realized as Shultz assumed his new job, there were equally important intangible factors that made them natural partners. If these qualities were given a chance to come into play, Reagan and Shultz seemed likely to develop good chemistry and might discover that what they could accomplish together exceeded what either man could achieve on his own. This was so despite their very different backgrounds. Just as Nixon and Shultz seemed to have little in common, so it looked with Reagan and Shultz. Reagan came from humble, rural Midwest origins; Shultz, from a modestly prosperous urban and suburban family. Reagan attended Eureka College; Shultz, Princeton. Reagan was a movie star, gifted pitchman and dazzlingly natural politician; Shultz, an academic, business executive and dry government official. Yet there were qualities that made them natural allies.

In Shultz, Reagan had brought aboard a man of quiet yet sure-handed competence, unswerving loyalty, great decency and a rare blend of sound judgment and unassuming leadership. Unlike Haig, he would never try to challenge the supremacy of the president or grab the spotlight. "I don't have a foreign policy," Shultz liked to say. "President Reagan has one. My job is to help him formulate it and to help him carry it out."[27] In Reagan, Shultz was working with a man whose core instinct was to reduce the threat of superpower nuclear war and improve relations with the Kremlin, despite the president's hot rhetoric. Reagan, while inattentive to detail and seemingly oblivious to the disarray within his administration, shared Shultz's impulse to seek solutions to international problems. If Shultz could grow confident that Reagan and he shared a worldview, he might have a chance to overcome the opposition of administration hard-liners.

Reagan already knew from past dealings that Shultz was totally dependable and trustworthy. Almost everyone who dealt with Shultz trusted him and knew he would do what he promised. As Helmut Schmidt said, "George Shultz is a dependable human being. I could always rely on him."[28] Shultz also brought to the relationship with Reagan a natural penchant for listening intently and patiently and a gift for quiet diplomacy and skillful management. He understood the benefits both of careful reflection and decisive action in domestic and international affairs. He tried to set aside thirty minutes every workday to retire to an intimate private den adjacent to his spacious State Department office to read and think about the big picture of American foreign policy, telling his secretary to hold all calls except those from his wife and the president. When he wanted to learn more about an issue, he organized Saturday-morning seminars at the State Department with government and academic experts.

Like Reagan, Shultz framed public policy issues on a human scale, and he knew that resolving differences required working with people, even antagonists. "He understood that it's all about relationships at the end, and you're not going to change somebody's mind by not having a relationship with them," Margaret Shultz, his eldest daughter, said. "You have to treat them with respect, and you have to confront the issues in order to move forward. If it had become personal, which it did apparently for others, he would have not accomplished as much as he did in the end. And I think he learned from the Nixon administration that in government you have to keep your eye on the bigger picture and not get sucked into the morass. Otherwise you're doomed."

She traced his ability to work with people, even opponents, to his service as a member of the Board of Selectmen in the small suburban community outside Boston where Shultz lived and started a family while teaching at MIT in the early 1950s. "'All politics is local,' as Tip O'Neil always said," Margaret noted, referring to the Democratic Massachusetts congressman who served as House Speaker during the Reagan presidency. "My father was able to set the stage so you could have relationships with people in all camps. You are working with people. You have to present ideas to convince them, and that means you have to be in a dialogue."[29] Alan Dachs, who married into the Bechtel family and watched Shultz help lead the Bechtel Corporation, detected the same instinct. "Shultz tackled global issues and humanized them," Dachs said. "He understands that ultimately somebody has to do something."[30]

Reagan and Shultz shared another related trait: they learned predominantly through experience rather than abstract theory or policy debate. They saw the world through stories and used them to persuade listeners, professional and casual, about the truths that they found self-evident. With little prompting, often without any, both men would recount stories from their lives, the lives of others and, in Reagan's case, from experiences that sometimes seemed to be drawn from the characters he and fellow actors played in films. The stories were often illuminating and instructive, sometimes rambling and confounding to colleagues. Reagan stunned more than a few foreign leaders with anecdotes that seemed bizarrely tone-deaf and off point. But he loved telling them, as did Shultz.

Shultz recalled:

Sometimes President Reagan simply did not seem to care that much about facts and details. That bothered the press and it bothered me. On

occasion I would try to correct the inaccurate chronology of a favorite
story about something he had done earlier in his presidency.

Over time I began to see another side to his love of storytelling: he
used a story to impart a larger message—and sometimes this message
was simply more important to him than the facts. He was a gifted sto-
ryteller, who could use a story effectively to make his point take on a
deeper and more vivid meaning or to defuse a tense situation. People,
he felt, believe in and act on the stories they hear and tell about the past.
Stories create meaning. Facts are the unassembled parts of the apparatus that do not operate until put together in an individual's own unique
way. Stories bring fact to life. To Ronald Reagan, today's events always
seemed rooted in some piece of wisdom, some story he had incorporated
long ago.[31]

Late in life, Shultz collected dozens of his stories in a book. It offered a
telling insight into the importance of stories and how they forged a bond
with Reagan. Describing a foreign policy speech he drafted and showed to
Reagan, Shultz reported the president's reaction: "He picked up the speech,
flipped it open, and edited a page. He inserted a caret and wrote: 'Story.' He
had skillfully personalized the page. Why the story? He said, 'That is the
most important point on this page. If you want to get across an important
point to people, you want to get it into their heads but also into their gut,
and the way to do that is to tell them an appropriate story. Then they'll realize what you're talking about.'" So, Shultz noted in his manuscript, "these
stories illustrate the theme, learning from experience, that can help you
work your way through a myriad of often tense and important policy issues
and events."[32]

Perhaps most important to developing a productive partnership with
Reagan, Shultz firmly believed that even the most difficult disputes could
be abated, if not resolved, through dialogue and negotiations. He had seen
this approach work repeatedly during his days as an economist, university
dean, labor secretary and Bechtel executive. He would often tell friends and
colleagues that the magic formula for easing the most stubborn conflicts
was to stop arguing about principles and start talking about how to solve a
problem. Almost everyone who worked with or alongside Shultz over the
years watched him put this philosophy into action. Raymond Seitz recalled
that when Shultz faced a difficult challenge, he would say, "You got a problem? Solve it!" Seitz watched "with wonder" as Shultz went to work solving
problems: "George had this wonderful way of taking a problem that would

seem utterly intractable and entangled, and he would say, 'All right now, let's just break it all down, get all the pieces down, and let's just see if we can put it back together.'"[33]

Shultz also understood that adversaries such as the Soviet Union were likely to act in their self-interest rather than in response to hectoring demands from the United States. "I think fundamentally if you want to get people to do really big important things, it's not likely to happen because you're hammering on them. It's much more likely to happen if, from the inside out, they think it's a good idea for them. Big things have to happen because you decide that it's in your interest to do that."[34]

As Shultz moved into the State Department in the summer of 1982, the makings of a strong partnership with Reagan were present, if only faintly understood by each man. Making it a reality would require a reordering of White House dynamics to give Shultz private access to the president and a chance to overcome the powerful forces driving Reagan toward confrontation with the Kremlin.

CHAPTER NINE

Stumbling Start

SHULTZ SAILED THROUGH HIS Senate confirmation hearing less than a month after his appointment, but the auspicious start did not last long. Within a few weeks of moving into the secretary's spacious seventh-floor office suite at the State Department, Shultz collided with powerful fellow cabinet members over American policy in the Middle East. The rancorous conflict made clear that his opponents were tenacious and determined to outmaneuver him. The disputes also served as an early warning sign that Reagan administration foreign policy making was broken and the president was either unwilling or unable to fix it. It quickly became apparent to Shultz that White House aides were limiting his direct access to Reagan, but he saw no immediate way around the roadblock.

The Senate Foreign Relations Committee convened on July 13 to consider the Shultz nomination. Room 1202 in the Dirksen Senate Office Building was packed. As Shultz, wearing a natty light-colored pinstripe suit, took his seat, a scrum of news photographers huddled between the nominee and the Senate members, led by chairman Charles Percy, an Illinois Republican. Reporters filled the seats at press tables behind Shultz, and television cameras recorded the event for evening network news broadcasts. In his opening statement, and in response to senators' questions, Shultz straddled the administration's militant approach to the Kremlin and his own instinct to seek a more stable, productive relationship with Moscow. In a low-key performance that contrasted with Haig's sometimes combative appearances before the committee, Shultz largely hewed to the administration line on most foreign policy matters, but some subtle distinctions were evident.

He began by emphasizing the Soviet threat and the importance of restoring American military strength that Reagan and his supporters maintained had been neglected by President Carter:

> Today most Americans are uncomfortable with the fact that we spend so much of our substance on defense, and rightly so, and yet most Americans also recognize that we must deal with reality as we find it, and that reality in its simplest terms is an uncertain world in which peace and security can be assured only if we have the strength and will to preserve them.
>
> We have passed through a decade during which the Soviet Union expanded its military capability at a steady and rapid rate while we stood still. President Reagan has given us the leadership to turn that situation around, and just in time. The past decade taught us once again an important lesson about United States-Soviet relations. In brief, it is that diminished American strength and resolve are an open invitation for Soviet expansion into areas of critical interest to the West and provide no incentive for moderation in the Soviet military buildup.[1]

Shultz then made clear that military strength, in his view, should support a broader policy of engagement:

> Thus it is critical to the overall success of our foreign policy that we persevere in the restoration of our strength; but it is also true that the willingness to negotiate from that strength is a fundamental element of strength itself.
>
> The President has put forward arms control proposals in the strategic theater and conventional arms areas that are genuinely bold and that will, if accepted, reduce the burdens and the dangers of armaments. Let no one doubt the seriousness of our purpose, but let no one believe that we will seek agreement for its own sake without a balanced and constructive outcome.
>
> We recognize that an approach to the Soviet Union limited to the military dimension will not satisfy the American people. Our efforts in the area of arms reduction are inevitably linked to restraint in many dimensions of Soviet behavior, and as we enter a potentially critical period of transition in Soviet leadership, we must also make it clear that we are prepared to establish mutually beneficial and safer relationships on the basis of reciprocity.[2]

The Shultz statement echoed the themes of Reagan's Westminster speech a month earlier, absent the belligerent rhetoric. It would have been an overstatement of his comments during the two days of confirmation hearings to suggest he would steer the administration toward a more constructive relationship with the Soviet Union, and journalists and commentators made no such assertions about his appearance. But Shultz's milder tone was suggestive. News coverage of the hearings paid more attention to Shultz's criticism of Israel and his ties to Bechtel, which did a great deal of construction business in the region, including Saudi Arabia. A number of Democratic and Republican senators, concerned that Shultz's work at Bechtel had left him hostile to Israel, pressed him about his views on Israel. Bernard Gwertzman reported in the *New York Times*:

> In his two days of hearings, Mr. Shultz avoided statements that directly contradicted existing Administration policy. But he seemed to suggest that he would seek to modify some key aspects of that foreign policy.
>
> The most evident shift that Mr. Shultz appears to have in mind is in American policy toward the Middle East. After Israel invaded Lebanon, Mr. Haig was able to prevail within the Administration to block any public condemnation of the Israelis, arguing that verbal attacks on Israel would only stiffen Prime Minister Menachem Begin's resistance to change.
>
> But Mr. Shultz, in his remarks to the Senate Foreign Relations Committee on Tuesday, not only criticized the Israelis for their invasion of Lebanon but also expressed concern about Israeli settlements in the West Bank and the ouster of Palestinian mayors in the West Bank and the Gaza Strip.[3]

While unafraid to criticize Israel, Shultz also challenged the widely accepted view that he would favor Arab interests in the Middle East after his service at Bechtel. He made clear that he greatly admired Israel's commitment to democracy, the patriotism of its people and their desire for peace. In a moment that went largely unnoted by media coverage of the hearing, Shultz recalled Joseph Levy, the Israeli student at the University of Chicago who had been killed in Jerusalem during the Arab-Israeli War in 1967. He recounted the Levy story as it had fixed in his memory, a somewhat inaccurate but nevertheless powerful morality tale for Shultz. For anyone seeking to understand how Shultz experienced the world and approached policy decisions, his account about Levy provided clear clues that people and their stories mattered more to him than bloodless theories and cold data.

The other experience that made an enduring impression on Shultz was a 1977 visit to Israel with O'Bie and Irving Shapiro, the CEO of Dupont, and his wife. The two couples arrived just a week after the historic visit to Israel by Anwar Sadat, the Egyptian leader. As they attended meals and meetings with Israelis, Shultz found many people, particularly women, encouraged by the peacemaking process between Israel and Egypt initiated by Sadat's visit, the first by an Arab leader since Israel's founding in 1948. Shultz told the Senate committee, "I believe that there is in that troubled part of the world a yearning for peace that is very deep, and a recognition of how much better we will all be and they will be if we can attain a peace."[4]

On July 15 the Senate voted unanimously to confirm his nomination, 97–0, with three senators absent. Senator Percy said, "He has the potential to be one of the greatest Secretaries of State of all times." The *New York Times* noted:

> More striking, perhaps, than Mr. Shultz's possible policy shifts was his style. He made it clear that unlike Mr. Haig, he was uninterested in becoming "the vicar" of foreign policy. His approach, stated in his matter-of-fact way, was pragmatic.
> "The essential point," he said, "is that the same President, the same man, is calling the shots." He said the job of a secretary of state was to help advise the President because "he's the boss." Mr. Shultz, who is 61 years old, said he would work with William P. Clark, the national security adviser; Caspar W. Weinberger, the Defense Secretary, and other aides.[5]

After Shultz was sworn in as secretary of state on July 16, Haig asked him sarcastically, "Do you think you can handle it?"[6] Richard Nixon, continuing his schizophrenic pattern of flattering Shultz directly while undermining him indirectly, told Shultz in a letter: "This is just a note to tell you that I thought your handling of your confirmation hearing was nothing less than brilliant in every respect. Looking back over 35 years in and out of public life, I cannot think of a Cabinet officer getting off to a better start."[7]

On July 22, Shultz surprised his new administration colleagues by heading to California and the annual summertime gathering of members of the Bohemian Club at the Bohemian Grove, a secluded set of camps nestled in the redwood groves north of San Francisco. The club, founded in 1872 by journalists, artists and other cultural figures, had morphed over the decades into an elite group of corporate executives, government leaders and other prominent men. The club admitted no women, a policy it maintains to this day. The trip, so soon after assuming his post, seemed oddly frivolous for a man known at the time for an absence of frivolity, but Shultz insisted that he keep a commitment to host Helmut Schmidt at the Grove. It would also give him a chance to see old friends and get a last taste of privacy and fellowship before plunging into his new duties. Gerald Ford, Henry Kissinger and Haig would all be present.

The Grove was known for its rustic accommodations and alcohol-fueled festivities. Seitz, relegated to a nearby motel where his room was outfitted with encrypted communications gear, could not help noticing that the establishment seemed to be swarming with hookers who had come to service club members.[8] He was allowed onto the Grove grounds only for short meetings with Shultz. "I am having a hard time getting traffic from Washington and equally difficult time getting into the Grove so I can consult with the secretary," Seitz noted in his journal.[9] "The campsites are set in a dark forest of huge redwood trees. It is steamy. The various camps are set behind little fortress barricades and look like something out of Swiss Family Robinson. I found the secretary at the Mandalay Camp and we spoke outside on a small terrace."[10] Once when Seitz was reviewing classified material with Shultz, Haig happened to walk by, making for an awkward moment.[11] While at the Grove, Shultz instructed Seitz to see if Diane Sawyer would like to serve as the State Department spokesperson.[12] Sawyer, at the time a CBS News correspondent and morning anchor, had worked in the press office at the Nixon White House. She declined.

Shultz's discussions with Schmidt at the Grove and during a conversation a few days later at his Stanford home with Schmidt, Henry Kissinger and Lee Kuan Yew, the prime minister of Singapore, made Shultz realize how precarious Soviet-American relations were. "No one is talking; that is dangerous," Schmidt told Shultz.[13] Schmidt also warned Shultz that West Germany and other NATO members were troubled by the Reagan administration's opposition to construction of a pipeline that would supply much-needed Soviet natural gas to Western Europe. The dispute threatened to undermine NATO support for American plans to place nuclear-tipped medium-range missiles in Western Europe to counter comparable weapons Moscow had based in the Western territory of the Soviet Union. Shultz disagreed with the administration's opposition to the pipeline, fearing it would divide NATO at a critical moment.

Lee Kuan Yew advised Shultz that the Reagan administration was mishandling relations with China by emphasizing superficial issues. Shultz asked Seitz to invite Winston Lord, a China expert and experienced American diplomat, to organize a seminar for him on China and to invite Hal Sonnenfeldt, one of Washington's top Soviet experts, to do the same on Soviet affairs. After an encounter with Isaac Stern, the violinist, at the Grove, Shultz mused, "Sometimes you need soothing and friendly musicians." He told Seitz to arrange for a Dixieland band to perform from time to time at State Department events. He also showed Seitz a sweater that he wanted placed aboard his air force plane for all his foreign trips.[14]

Shultz got his first exposure to dysfunctional policy making just a few weeks after becoming secretary. Israeli-Palestinian tensions erupted early on the morning of August 4 when Israeli forces, which had moved into Lebanon in early June, rolled into South Beirut from their positions around the Beirut airport. As Israeli artillery pounded sites in South Beirut and Israeli troops advanced, aides awakened Shultz at home to inform him about the escalation. A few hours later, at 4:00 a.m., the Saudi ambassador in Washington, Prince Bandar, phoned Shultz at home, appealing to him to lean on Israel to stop the bloodshed. Shultz quickly dressed and headed to the State Department operations center.

Over the next forty-eight hours, Reagan aides debated how strongly the United States should respond to Israel's move. Though Shultz was fundamentally sympathetic to Israel's beleaguered status as a Jewish state surrounded by hostile Arab neighbors, he was troubled by the Israeli invasion of Lebanon and favored a strongly worded condemnation of the latest Israeli military move. Jeane Kirkpatrick argued that the PLO, which had essentially taken control of Beirut, was a Soviet surrogate and deserved no American sympathy. The wording of a UN Security Council resolution about the Israeli action became the focal point of discussion at a series of White House meetings. Reagan seemed ill informed about developments and wavered about how to respond. Shultz was puzzled that colleagues across the administration failed to see that Israel was acting in defiance of Reagan's previous calls for restraint.

After a White House meeting, Shultz reported that Clark had failed to brief Reagan adequately about the developments in Lebanon; General John Vessey, chairman of the Joint Chiefs of Staff, had downplayed the significance of the Israeli military advance; and Kirkpatrick had complained about the PLO. Though Reagan had seemed to agree with Shultz on a tough

American response, Shultz watched with dismay as the Reagan-Shultz approach was watered down.

Once the harshest language in the UN resolution was eliminated—it would have equated Israel with the illegal white colonial regime in Rhodesia—Shultz pushed to approve the resolution. Kirkpatrick resisted. Shultz insisted and called Clark at the White House to tell him that the United States would vote for the resolution. He then called Kirkpatrick to inform her. He was kept on hold for four or five minutes, hardly the response a secretary of state expected when calling an ambassador. When Kirkpatrick finally came on the line, she informed Shultz she was going to abstain rather than vote for the resolution and had cleared her decision with Clark. After the call ended, Seitz noted in his journal later that day: "Shultz stared wearily out the window for a long time as it dawned on him that Kirkpatrick had gone around the back of the barn to get Clark to overrule him."[15]

After the sleepless night and long day, Shultz and Seitz reflected on the fast-moving developments. They agreed Shultz needed direct access to the president rather than work through Clark. They also thought Shultz had spent too much time personally trying to manage the crisis, in effect, acting as if he were a Mideast policy desk officer rather than secretary of state. And Shultz confessed that he had grown progressively more tired as the day unfolded and was not at his best operating on just a few hours of sleep. "He finally left for home a little after 8:00 p.m., slightly bedraggled and slightly bewildered," Seitz noted.[16]

The next day, Shultz made plain his irritation to Kirkpatrick about her end run. She shot back that Reagan had instructed her to report to him, not the secretary of state. Shultz grumbled, "There can't be two chains of command. In a crisis situation, there can only be one chain." When the tense conversation ended, he told Seitz, "We haven't heard the last of that."[17] Kirkpatrick saw no need to appease the secretary of state. One of her aides said, "We told Jeane to cultivate him. She wouldn't do it. She saw Shultz as a rival and her attitude was that she wasn't going to waste her time with people who bored her."[18] A few days later, Seitz presented Shultz with some ammunition for the next showdown with Kirkpatrick: a copy of a secret National Security Agency intercept in which Argentina's ambassador in Washington informed his foreign ministry about a conversation with Kirkpatrick. The ambassador reported that she had described secret internal

State Department deliberations about possibly lifting the arms sale embargo Washington had imposed on Argentina when it invaded the Britain's Falkland Islands off the Argentine coast. Shultz told Seitz to hold on to the intercept for the next encounter with Kirkpatrick.[19]

If the dawning recognition that Shultz would have to fight to get control of American diplomacy were not worrying enough, a few days later at a Pentagon briefing Shultz got his first, sobering look at America's plans for fighting a nuclear war. The session began with a brief history of the plan, known as the Single Integrated Operations Plan (SIOP). It had been revised several times over the years as presidents pressed for ways to wage a limited nuclear conflict rather than a full-scale global conflagration. The military briefer told Shultz that the president and his national security team would have twelve minutes to decide whether to launch American missiles after the firing of Soviet ground-based missiles was detected, eight minutes if the attack came from sea-based missiles carried by Soviet submarines. The menu of American options included unimaginable variations such as "withhold Poland" and "execute" the Soviet Union. The assembled military brass then played an audio recording of a nuclear-attack simulation conducted daily at the Pentagon. When the president asked during the simulation how many minutes remained before Washington was destroyed, the answer was "four minutes." The last words of the simulation came from an office giving the order, "turn the key," the command to launch America's missiles.[20]

Shultz was just weeks into the job, and the challenges confronting him seemed enormous, more than he had bargained for. He turned to an anecdote to lighten the mood. At an internal State Department meeting on Latin American affairs, he recounted a story about Bryce Harlow, a well-known Washington figure who had served as an adviser and speechwriter for Dwight Eisenhower and Richard Nixon and worked as a corporate lobbyist. Shultz admired Harlow's inside knowledge about Washington. He related that Harlow, a diminutive man, once asked Rogers Morton, a very tall man who served as secretary of the interior, to stand up at a meeting of newly appointed government officials that Harlow was addressing. "Twenty years ago when I first came to Washington," Harlow quipped, "I was as tall as Rogers Morton."[21] It was a bittersweet tale for Shultz. At the end of the day, he opened a small brown box that one of his children had given him. It was labeled "Foreign Policy Kit." The box contained a pacifier, a compass, a whistle, a thermometer, an American flag and some aspirin.[22] Seitz noted in his journal, "For the first time since he arrived in the [State] Department, the Secretary was so tired that he left all his papers and his yawning brief-case behind and took the rest of the evening off."[23]

For a man who had witnessed at close hand the scheming of Nixon aides and the disintegration of a presidency, Shultz seemed surprisingly flummoxed by the chaotic foreign policy operations of the Reagan admin-istration. He looked outmatched by his opponents and unable to count on decisive support from the president in policy debates. His talent for dispas-sionate analysis, careful deliberation and consensus building seemed irrele-vant in the ideologically propelled councils of the administration. Perhaps most troubling, Reagan seemed to float above the policy battles and often failed to intervene when aides undermined or ignored his decisions. Though it was still very early in Shultz's tenure at State, a refrain was already becom-ing familiar in the secretary's seventh-floor suite—Shultz was stymied; he needed to spend more time with the president. The problem was that he and his top advisers were not sure how to make that happen.

The frustrations soon escalated as he tangled with Defense Secretary Weinberger, who was a far more powerful opponent than Jeane Kirkpat-rick and had a much longer personal history with Shultz. Weinberger's ap-pointment as defense secretary lifted him out of Shultz's shadow at Bechtel and in the Nixon administration, where he had always been subordinate to Shultz. Neither man ever said much about their differences over the years, but Weinberger offered some clues in recounting his relationship with Shultz at Bechtel: "George Shultz joined Bechtel about a year before I did. As seemed to be the case every time we worked together (before and since Bechtel), we often had differing viewpoints. This was most evident when lawsuits were brought against the company, particularly large class-action suits. . . . Generally I would recommend that we fight rather than yield, but invariably George would want to settle."[24]

Colin Powell, who knew both men well and was aware of their career histories, said of the Bechtel relationship, "Cap was the general counsel and George was the big boy. I think Cap always kind of resented that a little bit, was always jealous of that."[25] Shultz recognized the tension. "Cap and I had a long history. When Nixon started the OMB, I was the director and he was my deputy, so we worked together for two years very effectively. He was working for me, however. Then we both wound up at Bechtel, and I was president and he was our general counsel, so once again he's working for me. And I always wondered, when we got into office and he has one cabinet post and I have another, if there isn't a kind of a 'I'm not working for you anymore, pal.'"[26]

Now that the two men occupied the most critical cabinet posts in the making and execution of US foreign policy, disagreements between them could have far-reaching implications. With the possible exception of the national security adviser, no senior official had a greater ability to thwart Shultz than the defense secretary. Ostensibly, the Shultz-Weinberger relationship seemed amiable enough following Reagan's election. When Reagan nominated Weinberger as defense secretary in December 1980, Shultz dispatched a gracious note to his Bechtel colleague: "Congratulations to you and to us all on your nomination as secretary of defense at this most critical time. You have the gift of intellect, the capacity for prodigious work, the habit of honesty, and the toughness of steel in your backbone. You also have my very best wishes, my respect and admiration as you move into the Washington scene."[27]

Just a few weeks after Shultz became secretary of state, he enjoyed an elaborate Pentagon dinner hosted by Weinberger that featured the Air Force Strolling Strings and the Army Chorus. "Last night's dinner was very elegant and you were a most gracious host," Shultz wrote to Weinberger the next day. "Most of all the warmth of your own welcome to Washington increases my pleasure at the prospect of working with you once again."[28] The bonhomie did not last long. On the morning of August 19, little more than a week after the "elegant" dinner, Shultz arrived at the Pentagon for one of the first of his weekly breakfasts with the defense secretary and several top Defense and State Department aides. Weinberger launched into an extended pitch for selling M-1 tanks to Saudi Arabia. Shultz feared the sale would upend the delicate diplomacy he and State Department colleagues were conducting to decrease tensions in the Middle East. Brusquely dismissing Weinberger's arguments, Shultz declared, "Cap, I find everything you said incomprehensible." It was a stunning rebuke. Once back at the State Department, he vented to aides, "We spent the whole time arguing about the timing of tank sales to Saudi Arabia."[29]

John Howe, the State Department's director of politico-military affairs, who attended the breakfast, told colleagues that Shultz had been in a bad mood and, at one point, seemed about to end the breakfast abruptly and take the issue to Reagan to decide. As Howe recalled, Shultz angrily told Weinberger, "Go ahead and send your letter [to Saudi Arabia]. I don't know why we have these breakfasts." Walter Stoessel, the deputy secretary of state, also present at the breakfast, was shocked by the heated confrontation. It did not take long for word of the combative breakfast to reach the White House. William Clark called Stoessel. "What's happening?" he asked the deputy secretary of state. "I thought relations between State and Defense were going to get better."

Later that day, musing on his encounter with Weinberger, Shultz told Seitz that Weinberger thinks small things and is unable to consider them in a broader context. He went on: "I know Cap well. He spends half an hour talking to refute arguments that haven't been made." Reflecting on his long association with Weinberger during the Nixon administration and at Bechtel, Shultz observed, "The hardest thing is that I used to be his boss, and at the conclusion of any discussion, I would say, 'Cap, this is the way it is going to be done.'" Shultz sighed, "I guess I can't do that anymore."[30]

The Shultz-Weinberger relationship under President Reagan was already combustible—and the men had not even been talking about the Soviet Union, on which their views diverged most sharply. When Weinberger makes up his mind, Shultz later said, "that's it, very hard to argue with him."[31] When Seitz counseled Shultz that the secretaries of state and defense had to find a way to work together or American national security strategy would splinter, Shultz replied that, at least, the White House national security staff could make decisions when the State Department and Pentagon disagreed. Seitz dryly noted that the Reagan White House seemed incapable of making and sticking with decisions.[32]

Weinberger's headstrong style soon generated new concerns for Shultz. The defense secretary proposed that he visit the Middle East. Shultz and his fellow diplomats were aghast. Giving Weinberger license to tour the volatile region at a moment of delicate diplomacy there and festering Mideast policy disagreements in Washington seemed ill-advised. Shultz made clear his opposition. Weinberger pressed ahead with planning. In late August, word reached the State Department that Clark had approved the trip after Weinberger told him that Shultz, at a breakfast with Weinberger earlier in the day, had endorsed the visit. Shultz had done nothing of the kind. Shultz was irked and unsure if Weinberger had misinformed Clark or if Clark had made up the story to justify his approval of the trip. "Why don't we just close up till Weinberger gets back from his trip?" Shultz groused.

Shultz told Seitz he was making a list of Weinberger transgressions and planned to discuss them with Reagan. "If this is the way it is, he can get a new boy," Shultz declared. Then, reflecting on the threat for a moment, he pulled back. "No, I can't threaten to resign." A few moments later, Weinberger called on a secure line to update Shultz on a just-completed meeting with Ariel Sharon, the Israeli defense minister. As Seitz was exiting Shultz's office to give the secretary some privacy, he heard Shultz say, "Before we get into that Cap, I just want to let you know how unhappy I am with the way you handled this trip." When the call ended, Shultz told Seitz that Weinberger had insisted that he had not reported to Clark that Shultz had approved the trip, and, in fact, as far as he could recall, the subject of the trip had never come up at the breakfast with Shultz. Either Clark or Weinberger was lying. It was hardly a reassuring moment for the newly installed secretary of state. Seitz noted in his journal, "The Secretary cannot get over the fact that he objected to the trip on serious and legitimate foreign policy grounds, yet the trip was approved."[33]

Shultz's irritation about the Weinberger trip reflected a territorial view of the role other national security officials could play on the secretary of state's turf, an attitude that did not endear him to other officials. "Shultz was not a team player unless he could be coach, captain, and quarterback," observed Robert Gates, the deputy CIA director at the time. "Unlike Haig, he always remembered who owned the team. He acknowledged the primacy of the President. . . . With all others, however, he wanted to call the shots. For Shultz, foreign policy and national security policy were virtually synonymous, and anytime Defense or CIA or anyone else stepped beyond the narrow roles Shultz regarded as appropriate for them, there was hell to pay."[34] Actually, as Gates may not have known at the time, Shultz frequently found himself outmaneuvered and outgunned by the Pentagon and CIA and seemed unable to do anything about it.

Weinberger, too, chafed at Shultz's broad definition of the secretary of state's domain, particularly on matters involving the use of American military force. Soon after taking office, Shultz argued for sending a contingent of marines to Lebanon as part of a multinational peacekeeping force designed to discourage further conflict between Israeli troops and the PLO as Palestinian fighters prepared to withdraw from Lebanon. Weinberger opposed the idea, fearing the marines would be vulnerable to attack from various militia forces operating in Lebanon. "I felt that we could not either guarantee their safety, nor give them the means to provide for their own security, under the arrangements and conditions then prevailing in Lebanon."[35]

Weinberger was not alone in questioning Shultz's impulse to apply military force in the service of diplomacy. The Shultz attitude was antithetical to the natural caution of military commanders reluctant to put their troops at risk. Colin Powell, the senior military assistant to Weinberger during this period, recalled, "The secretary of state was often ready to commit America's military might, even in a no-man's land like Lebanon. What was the point of maintaining a military force if you did not occasionally demonstrate your power? On the other side was the man responsible for the forces that would have to do the bleeding and the dying, arguing against anything but crucial commitments."[36] The bitter quarrels over Middle East policy augured even nastier infighting over Soviet policy, as Shultz soon discovered to his dismay.

CHAPTER TEN

Soviet Policy Standoff

WHILE MIDEAST AFFAIRS WERE consuming much of Shultz's attention—
far too much, he thought—his initial efforts to influence relations with
Moscow proved halting and frustrating. Issues requiring urgent attention
included arms control talks, which were becalmed, and the Reagan administration's opposition to the proposed natural gas pipeline from Siberia
to Western Europe. Scheduling one-on-one meetings with Reagan proved
nearly impossible, preventing Shultz from raising critical Soviet policy
issues with the president absent instant objections from hard-line aides.
As the weeks passed, Shultz grew increasingly irritated by the roadblocks,
and although unsure of Reagan's support, he failed to devise a strategy to
outflank his opponents. His natural inclination to play by the rules, work
within organizational constraints and assume that calm deliberation and
common sense would prevail in policy debates left him looking indecisive
and vulnerable to the guerrilla tactics employed by his opponents.

Shultz's instincts about the Soviet Union were sound, but his knowledge
about Soviet-American relations was shallow, shaped by his limited dealings
with the Kremlin on economic issues during the Nixon administration a
decade earlier. While that experience left Shultz convinced that constructive
diplomacy with Moscow was possible, he lacked background about the
panoply of national security issues at the core of Soviet-American relations,

including nuclear weapons policy and arms control. To remedy these deficiencies, he devoted Saturday mornings to seminars featuring Soviet experts that were actually tutorials for Shultz, and he tried to master the arcane web of arms control topics. To overcome the views of hard-line aides such as Richard Pipes, who had spent a lifetime studying Soviet history and behavior, he would need to enhance his own knowledge quickly.

Braced by his July discussions with Helmut Schmidt at the Bohemian Grove and Shultz's Stanford home, he was anxious to reopen lines of communication with the Kremlin, fearing the absence of high-level dialogue could lead to a potentially volatile miscalculation or misunderstanding. Not long after the California discussions, Schmidt doubled down on his advice by telling Shultz's son, Peter, during a meeting in Bonn, that his father had unique leverage with Reagan, whom Schmidt considered to be a "dilettante" on national security matters.[1] As Peter recalled, Schmidt told him, "I want you to bring a message to your dad—just for your dad from me through you. Tell him that right now he is the most powerful person in the world because Ronald Reagan cannot afford to get another secretary of state, so he has to listen to your dad."[2]

Sensing that his father wanted to put his imprint on Soviet policy, Peter thought, "I think he was sending a message to Dad that this was his chance to do something about the Soviet Union, and he could really do it."[3] Shultz thought so, too, but he faced a minefield of opposition in Reagan's inner circle as summer turned to fall in 1982. Clark limited Shultz's access to Reagan. When Shultz thought he had an opening to make policy recommendations directly to Reagan, he invariably found critical White House meetings stacked against him. He would make his way to the White House expecting to see Reagan privately, or in the company of Clark, only to find the Oval Office, Cabinet Room or Situation Room filled with aides such as Richard Pipes who opposed any effort to ease relations with Moscow.

Nixon, weighing in from post-Watergate exile in northern New Jersey, added to Clark's wary view of Shultz. Shortly after Shultz's appointment as secretary of state, Nixon called Clark to warn him about a perceived Shultz character flaw that had concerned Nixon during his presidency: "'Bill, I want you to tell President Reagan one problem with your new secretary of state. My experience was, and I'm sure you are going to experience the same thing, a wonderful ability to, when things look iffy or are going wrong, he'll contend he never heard about the issue and was never briefed and was not a part.' I said, 'I'll tell the president,' and I wish I had," Clark recalled.[4]

Beyond Nixon's warning, Clark grew concerned that Shultz was being manipulated by his State Department colleagues, a view that he said was reinforced by Henry Kissinger and Zbigniew Brzezinski, Jimmy Carter's national security adviser. "I kept pushing that he was the premier foreign policy person, and yet as Kissinger said, 'No one has ever been more overtaken by the department and the bureaucracy than George Shultz.' I thought he gave the impression of being tough, but he was, in my opinion, and certainly Kissinger and Brzezinski as well, pretty much the tail wagging the dog at State. I think the President, while not commenting frequently, realized that as well."[5]

Clark's criticism echoed a recurrent theme among national security advisers during the postwar period that secretaries of state who welcomed counsel from assistant secretaries of state, ambassadors and other diplomats had been "captured" by institutional timidity and were insufficiently responsive to White House direction. Kissinger and Brzezinski were often contemptuous of the State Department during their tours as national security adviser, undermining the authority of Secretaries of State William Rogers and Cyrus Vance. White House disdain for the State Department was fueled by a broader White House assertion of authority over cabinet departments that accelerated during the Nixon administration and continued beyond as the Office of the President grew larger and larger. Since Shultz openly welcomed advice from State Department colleagues and was unwilling to take orders from the national security adviser, it was not surprising that Clark and the White House national security staff viewed him with suspicion.

Clark's doubts about Shultz only intensified friction within the administration over Soviet policy. Richard Perle, among the senior officials wary of softening American policy, recalled, "There was a group within the administration that was not eager to take steps that would diminish the confrontational aspect of the relationship with the Soviets because that was part of the strategy at that point, and it would have included Pipes. Clark would make sure that there were other voices in the room. So there were battles, no question about it."[6] Rozanne Ridgway, who served as ambassador to East Germany and later as assistant secretary of state for European affairs, was alarmed by the forces arrayed against Shultz. "The national security circles were heavily dominated by people who truly believed that it was wrong to engage the Soviet Union and the Warsaw Pact countries. They laid out a set of conditions for Eastern Europe, namely that they had to eschew their membership in the Warsaw Pact before we would talk to them. That wouldn't take you anywhere, which suited them just fine."[7] Leslie Gelb, who closely tracked Reagan administration policy making for the *New York Times*, thought Shultz was outgunned by the hard-liners. "When he went to the NSC meetings with that crowd, they knew much more about the Soviet Union than George did. Not that he couldn't hold his own intellectually, but they knew more."[8]

Shultz fretted about the obstacles, telling Seitz that the White House national security staff—Clark, Pipes and others—enjoyed frequent access to Reagan and used it energetically to reinforce the president's most belligerent attitudes about the Kremlin. Shultz mused that if he pressed to join regular morning Oval Office meetings with the president, Weinberger and Casey would insist on attending, too. When Seitz reiterated his view that Shultz's relationship with the president was "fundamental to the success of your office," Shultz replied, "That's right, and that's the problem."[9] Faced with determined, inflexible opponents and a lack of access to Reagan, Shultz seemed powerless on a number of critical Soviet policy issues. "George really had a hard time," Seitz recalled. "Everybody was so suspicious and small-minded and just bloody difficult or very right-wing. George is a conservative man, but these were conservatives of a different ilk. George has this instinct of saying, 'Gee, if there's a problem, let's see if we can work it out,' whereas the attitude of a lot of these people was, 'If there's a problem, what's the point of working it out?' George was a problem for a lot of these people, whether it was Perle, Weinberger, Kirkpatrick, Casey. His biggest challenge was just trying to get something done and have people stick to it and not undermine it."[10]

One of the most contentious issues was nuclear arms control. Shultz tangled for months with the White House and Pentagon over control of the arms control agenda with the Kremlin. By the time Reagan assumed office in 1981, decades of rising alarm about the danger of nuclear war had motivated the United States and Soviet Union to agree on a number of arms control treaties. The 1963 Limited Test Ban Treaty, initiated after the frightening 1962 Cuban Missile Crisis, banned nuclear tests in the atmosphere, outer space and underwater. It was signed by the United States, Soviet Union and United Kingdom. The 1968 Nuclear Nonproliferation Treaty, advanced by the United Nations and ultimately approved by dozens of nations, aimed to prevent the spread of nuclear weapons beyond the five existing nuclear weapons states: the United States, Soviet Union, China, United Kingdom and France.

In an effort to limit, though not reduce, Soviet and American nuclear arsenals, Washington and Moscow negotiated two strategic arms limitation treaties, known as SALT I and SALT II, the first under Nixon in 1972, the second during the Carter administration in 1979. Also in 1972, the two nations agreed to limit the development of an anti-missile system in the Anti-Ballistic Missile Treaty (ABM Treaty).

The arms control architecture, produced after prolonged and contentious debate in the United States, left Washington and Moscow with absurdly large nuclear arsenals as Reagan became president. The US inventory totaled twenty-three thousand nuclear weapons; the Soviet Union, thirty-three thousand. Each country maintained multiple ways to deliver the weapons, including intercontinental ballistic missiles (ICBMs), submarines loaded with nuclear-tipped missiles that could be launched from underwater (SLBMs) and intercontinental bombers. The combined firepower was enough to destroy civilization and plunge the planet into a protracted "nuclear winter" in which skies darkened by smoke and debris would prevent photosynthesis, extinguishing most vegetation and animal life on earth.

Beginning with Harry Truman, presidents had struggled to find a way to manage nuclear weapons, rely on them without firing them to deter American enemies and contain public anxiety about them. For the most part, American leaders had failed to stop the nuclear arms race from escalating wildly. They had acquiesced to defense strategy based on the theory of mutual assured destruction, an Armageddon formula designed to deter nuclear war by making clear to the Soviet Union that it would be eviscerated if it attacked the United States. The Soviet Union adopted a matching strategy. Adding to this nuclear balance of terror, the president of the United States was authorized to launch nuclear weapons absent consultation with Congress or anyone else, for that matter. If Soviet missiles were detected in flight toward the United States, the president would have thirty minutes at most to decide how to respond. It was a chilling scenario.

The immediate question for Reagan, and now Shultz, was whether the number of strategic, or long-range, weapons could, and should, be trimmed. They also faced the corollary issue of how to handle the planned placement of American intermediate-range nuclear-tipped missiles in Western Europe to counter similar Soviet weapons that could reach European targets and whether a treaty to reduce the number of intermediate-range missiles, or eliminate them entirely, was advisable. Before Shultz's arrival, Reagan had approved a so-called Zero-Zero Option negotiating proposal on intermediate-range missiles in Europe. This formula called for Washington and its Western European allies to cancel the planned installation of new American missiles in Western Europe if Moscow would eliminate its arsenal of six hundred similar weapons based in the western regions of the Soviet Union.

Just as Shultz was taking office, Paul Nitze, Washington's lead negotiator on intermediate-range missiles, formally known as Intermediate-Range Nuclear Forces (INF), infuriated administration officials by going off script with his Soviet counterpart, Yuli Kvitsinsky. During talks in Geneva, including a stroll in the woods, Nitze and Kvitsinsky explored an informal compromise that departed from the "Zero-Zero Option" proposal. Nitze, a widely respected cold warrior and skilled Washington infighter, survived the imbroglio. Eugene Rostow, nominally his boss as director of the Arms Control and Disarmament Agency, came under increasing fire. "Rostow doesn't know how to handle the president," Shultz privately told his colleagues after meeting with Rostow and Reagan in the wake of Nitze's unauthorized talks with Kvitsinsky. "Instead of arguing the merits of the position, Rostow conveyed the impression that the Germans would be unhappy if we did not continue these exploratory talks. There is nothing more calculated to turn off the president's attention. The president said we should stick with the zero/zero because he had not been shown anything better."[11]

The larger issue for Shultz was a lack of clarity about arms control goals and who was running arms control policy and negotiations—the State Department, the Pentagon or the White House. Parallel to the INF negotiations in Geneva, Washington was in discussions with the Kremlin about terms of a treaty to reduce strategic weapons. These questions mattered a great deal because the administration was divided over how to pursue negótiations with Moscow, or even if there should be arms talks at all. Understandably, Shultz thought the secretary of state should take the lead on arms talks. Instinctively, he believed that Washington and Moscow would have to settle for accords short of their maximal goals. Weinberger and his colleagues, led by Richard Perle, were not so sure. Compromise accords that balanced American and Soviet interests were anathema to the Pentagon team. "Cap's primary focus was on getting the budgets necessary to implement the rebuilding program," Perle recalled. "Arms control was a contentious issue. Weinberger was not against agreements with the Soviet Union. He wanted agreements that were in the American interest, and he wasn't shy about wanting agreements that were lopsidedly in our interest."[12]

James Goodby, another senior arms control negotiator, recalled, "It was clear that the Defense Department, despite the President's wishes, was fighting tooth and nail against any serious negotiation on any terms, practically, except their own."[13] Clark, while partly sympathetic to the Pentagon view, referred in a memo to Reagan about a "very deeply-felt ideological bias with your administration against arms control." He wrote, "This small group of professionals—centered in the Defense Department—believe that arms control generally is bad." Clark warned Reagan, "These individuals will resist any serious negotiation and if given the opportunity, will undermine it with leaks."[14] In Perle's view, the efforts of previous administrations to reach accords with the Kremlin to slow the growth of nuclear arsenals were based on the false premise that a failure to limit weapons would allow the Soviet Union to tip the nuclear balance in its favor. Perle and Weinberger believed the Kremlin was already straining financially to maintain its military forces, so Washington could, in Perle's words, "just wait until they came around."[15]

In an effort to break the policy impasse within the administration, Shultz in mid-September seized on a Clark memo about Rostow in which Clark unexpectedly argued that the secretary of state should direct the Geneva talks about intermediate-range missiles. Shultz was thrilled. He told Seitz, "I will assure the president that all the views will get through to him, but I have to be confident that Bill Clark will stand in the way of any end runs."[16] Reagan seemed to buy the argument and told Shultz he wanted him to be in charge. But the initiative quickly dissolved absent clear instructions from Reagan to other officials, which never materialized. The standoff continued.

Meantime, Shultz's initial efforts to untangle the gas pipeline dispute quickly ran into opposition from Weinberger and others despite Shultz's warning that American sanctions designed to prevent construction of the pipeline could severely damage Washington's relations with its closest European allies just as the United States needed allied support to station intermediate-range nuclear missiles in Western Europe. The Reagan administration's handling of the pipeline reflected the strength and weakness of the tough, anti-Soviet stance Reagan embraced after taking office. The idea of a pipeline carrying natural gas from Siberia to West Germany, France, Italy, Austria and other countries had obvious appeal to the Kremlin, eager to expand trade with Western Europe, generate hard currency revenue and gain leverage in the West. Western European leaders saw clear benefit in importing much-needed natural gas and giving Moscow an incentive to cooperate with Western Europe rather than threaten it. European leaders decided in September 1981 to move ahead with the pipeline project.

The trade-offs looked very different in Washington, where Western European dependence on Soviet natural gas seemed unwise, a concern that was validated decades later when Russia invaded Ukraine in 2022 and America's European allies struggled to curtail their reliance on Russian gas. Anxiety about the pipeline plan spiked in December 1981 when the Polish government declared martial law to suppress rapidly rising anti-Communist opposition propelled by the striking shipyard union workers in Gdansk. The discontent in Poland was the first Soviet-bloc uprising since democratic forces shook Czechoslovakia in 1968 and drew a crackdown by Soviet military forces. Acting on December 29, 1981, following the imposition of martial law in Poland, the Reagan administration tightened restrictions on American corporate business dealings with the Soviet bloc. In June 1982, it ratcheted up the sanctions after François Mitterrand, the French president, publicly rejected reports that the United States and its allies had agreed at an economic summit at Versailles just days before to further restrict trade with the Soviet Union.

The *New York Times* reported: "This so irritated the President that, at the urging of his National Security Adviser, William P. Clark, and Mr. Weinberger, he ordered that the sanctions be expanded. He ordered that foreign affiliates of American companies and independent companies under license to American companies also be barred from participating in the pipeline construction, even if they were doing so under contracts signed prior to the Polish crisis. This was a political move to show that the United States was not backing down on Poland."[17]

European leaders were furious, as Shultz had quickly discovered directly from Chancellor Schmidt at the Bohemian Grove. Shultz recalled:

> I returned to Washington knowing full well that resolving the pipe-line problem was a top priority for me. There was no reason to expect the Europeans to back down. At best, our sanctions might slow down the project while American parts and other American supplies were engineered out, itself an action setting a terrible precedent for our export capabilities. An unreliable supplier becomes a pariah in what is, increasingly, a truly global economy. At a Senior Interagency Group meeting on August 5, Cap Weinberger was militant. In response to comments about some of the legal issues involved, he said,"I don't want to hear about legalities." Cap was against the very idea of a negotiation to resolve this bitter dispute with our allies.[18]

The Europeans refused to back down. In quick succession, British, French and Italian companies moved ahead with contracts for pipeline parts and assistance, all with the public blessing of their governments. It was a rare act of defiance by America's closest allies. Shultz worked the issue with his European counterparts and inside the administration, trying to come up with a plan that he could sell to Weinberger and other officials and that would be acceptable to the Europeans. By mid-October, he thought he had gained approval for a compromise formula from Reagan and Weinberger, but Weinberger astonished Shultz by questioning the plan at a National Security Council meeting on East-West trade issues. "Old Cap loves those sanctions," Shultz complained after the meeting.[19]

Shultz was unnerved when Edwin Meese, one of Reagan's closest aides, told a television interviewer that he knew of no trade package that might be negotiated with the Europeans in exchange for Washington dropping the sanctions. Was Meese signaling that Shultz's proposed resolution of the pipeline dispute might not gain White House approval? "I hope Meese's comments don't reflect the president's views," Shultz confided to Seitz. "I can't reach an understanding with our allies and then not be able to deliver. That would destroy me."[20] In an encouraging, if limited, victory for Shultz, Reagan ultimately approved the Shultz plan, which called for substituting an American-European agreement on limiting trade with the Soviet Union for the pipeline sanctions. On November 13, Reagan announced that he was lifting the sanctions. While that eliminated the issue as a potential obstacle to the placement of American intermediate-range missiles in Europe, French leaders irritated Shultz by continuing to resist the accord. "The damn French are trying to block us every inch of the way," Shultz muttered to Seitz one afternoon.[21]

The death of Leonid Brezhnev, the longtime Soviet leader, on November 10 gave Shultz his first opportunity to visit Moscow as secretary of state and to press Reagan to use the occasion to signal a more conciliatory approach to Soviet relations. To that end, he recommended that Reagan lead the American delegation to Brezhnev's funeral. "It would be a ten strike if the president went to Moscow," Shultz told Clark. "It would accomplish a lot with the Europeans and the new Russian leadership. . . . The president's action would speak volumes."[22] Despite a personal appeal from Shultz, Reagan declined and instead dispatched Bush and Shultz.

That did not stop Shultz from making several conciliatory gestures himself to Anatoly Dobrynin, the Soviet ambassador in Washington. He stopped by the Soviet embassy in Washington to sign the condolence book and asked Dobrynin if the Kremlin would let the United States send a four-member delegation, one more than the limit Soviet officials had set. Shultz explained that he wanted to bring along a leading Democrat as a show of bipartisan support. Dobrynin said he thought that would be possible. Within a few hours Shultz was forced to withdraw the request after Clark informed him that the White House would be sending only three representatives to the funeral, Bush, Shultz and Arthur Hartman, the American ambassador in Moscow. To make his intentions plain, Shultz then told Dobrynin that he favored a broader delegation that would have conveyed bipartisanship to the new Soviet leader, Yuri Andropov, longtime head of the KGB.[23]

On November 13, just hours before his air force plane was due to depart for Moscow, Shultz gagged on a chunk of his lunch. After twenty minutes of coughing he was driven to the emergency room at George Washington University Hospital. When doctors examined Shultz, they informed O'Bie, who had rushed to the hospital, and Seitz that Shultz most likely would need to spend the night and could not travel to Moscow. Moments later, the prognosis suddenly improved. In the course of swallowing a barium liquid that would enhance X-ray images of his abdomen, Shultz dislodged whatever was stuck in his esophagus. He happily told aides he was going to Moscow and phoned Clark at the White House to say the trip was on. He let Clark know that O'Bie, a former nurse, had advised him to take plenty of milk of magnesia during the flight to overcome the constipation the barium would cause. "I'd rather get loose on the plane than in Red Square," he told Clark. While his fellow passengers dined on steak and potatoes, Shultz settled for mashed potatoes and ice cream.[24]

The November weather in Moscow was cold and dreary, but Shultz's brief visit seemed to invigorate him and strengthen his desire to put relations with the Soviet Union on a more positive track. He was struck by Andropov's energy and unmistakable sense of command at Brezhnev's funeral. At the Kremlin reception that followed, a Soviet protocol official pulled Bush, Shultz and Hartman from the back of a long receiving line and escorted them to the front, directly in front of Pierre Trudeau, the Canadian prime minister. Trudeau quipped that he was accustomed to "following the Americans." When the three Americans greeted Andropov, Shultz thought the new Soviet leader seemed genuinely touched by the high-level delegation.[25]

After a brief meeting with Andropov, Shultz told his colleagues that Andropov looked strong, decisive, self-confident and human. "This man is a power-house," Shultz said. Andropov told the Americans that he would welcome a constructive relationship with the United States, then launched into a litany of familiar complaints about American conduct. He joked with Bush, saying that Shultz and Andrei Gromyko, the veteran Soviet foreign minister, were "warriors" who engaged in mutual combat, while he and Bush were "peacemakers." Bush, Shultz and Hartman were unaware that Andropov's kidneys were failing and his long-term outlook was not promising. The American interpreter who attended the meeting noted to Shultz that Andropov looked surprisingly old, apparently sensing that he was not in good health, an insight that Shultz did not detect as he talked with the Soviet leader.[26]

Shultz was impressed with Andropov, but wary. He told his State Department associates that he thought Andropov wanted to improve relations. "Whether it's a mousetrap, I don't know." When Shultz emphasized the good tone of the discussion with Andropov, aides reminded him that the conversation had been very general and ought not be interpreted as the beginning of a new era in Soviet-American relations. The cautionary note registered. A few days later, back in Washington, Shultz said that Bush's written account of the Andropov meeting was too euphoric. When Reagan asked Shultz to describe the most significant outcome of the meeting, he replied it was to stick with increased defense spending.[27]

Shultz was not the only one trying to divine if Andropov wanted to recalibrate East-West relations, whether he enjoyed sufficient support within the Communist Party's ruling Politburo to do so or if his initial comments were merely a propaganda feint designed to make the Kremlin appear less threatening. The CIA's classified assessment:

> Andropov is reputed to be an intelligent, competent and relatively urbane party functionary, with sophisticated artistic and literary tastes; it is most unlikely, however, that he is "liberal" in our sense of the term. He is not known to have visited the West, yet is reputed to take a pragmatic, non-ideological approach to foreign policy issues—perhaps as a result of his access to relatively undistorted information about world events while KGB chairman. In the same capacity, however, he presided over the (still continuing) crackdown on dissent and non-conformity, and in a previous job—as Ambassador to Hungary in the 1950's—over the repression of the Hungarian revolution. In short, he evidently is tough-minded and capable of ruthlessness. While committed to Marxism-Leninism, he may prove to be more flexible and subtle in applying doctrine to strategy and tactics than was the late ideologue [Mikhail] Suslov.[28]

George Kennan, the respected former ambassador to Moscow, said in a *New York Times* op-ed article: "From the standpoint of Soviet-American relations, the new Andropov leadership may well be preferable to any conceivable alternatives, especially since it promises no early or drastic departure from the Brezhnev line. This is important, because in the first days following the change of regime, both parties have possibilities for conciliatory moves that would involve no significant sacrifice of their own interests but might well represent a turning point in an otherwise tragically strained relationship."[29] The notion that Andropov was a devotee of jazz and English literature seemed alluring but doubtful and was never confirmed. It was lampooned in the *New Republic*: "What emerges from these attempts to piece together a version of Andropov's life is a portrait worthy of 'Saturday Night Live': the head of the K.G.B. as one wild and crazy guy. After a hard day at the office repressing dissent, Brezhnev's heir spends the evening at home, telling anti-regime jokes in fluent English and playing jazz for dissidents."[30]

While Washington was consumed with speculation about Andropov, Shultz focused on a November 22 lunch with Dobrynin that had been scheduled before Brezhnev's death. He thought it might provide the opening he needed to get Reagan's blessing to reactivate diplomatic discussions with the Kremlin. When State Department aides offered Shultz a detailed road map for the lunch meeting, he rejected it, arguing that a more general conversation about Soviet-American relations would be better. Shultz consulted Reagan, who agreed that Shultz should dwell on a single overarching point: Reagan was committed to keeping America strong but equally serious about trying to develop a more constructive relationship with Moscow. Reagan and Shultz agreed that Shultz should also take note that Andropov seemed ready to improve relations.[31]

Dobrynin was a Washington fixture, having served as Soviet ambassador to the United States since 1962. Tall, balding, witty and a fluent English speaker, he represented Soviet interests with a blend of toughness and charm. Since his arrival in Washington just months before the Cuban Missile Crisis, he had developed effective working relationships with five presidents and six secretaries of state. But after the Soviet invasion and occupation of Afghanistan in late 1979, his access to senior American officials was restricted. Twenty-two months into the Reagan presidency, his only meeting with Reagan had been a fleeting encounter when the president stopped by the Soviet embassy to express condolences about the death of Brezhnev.

The lunch went well. Shultz reported, "Dobrynin agreed but said the question is how to go about it. We reviewed the agenda and proposed meeting occasionally. It's important for Dobrynin to have a 'feel' for the U.S. government. I said it was equally important for Art Hartman to have the same feel in Moscow. We talked about a possible meeting with Gromyko in the spring. Dobrynin raised a summit."[32] Shultz thought the door was open to explore a variety of ways to ease cold war tensions. He was eager to try. "I felt we had to turn the relationship around: away from confrontation and toward real problem solving."[33]

The critical question for Shultz was whether Reagan would support a shift in direction. "I needed a much clearer sense of where Ronald Reagan stood if I was to be able to move us from rhetoric to real engagements with the Soviets. I knew the White House staff would oppose such engagement."[34] During a presidential trip to Brazil in early December, Shultz thought he secured Reagan's approval to revitalize arms talks with the Kremlin but remained uncertain if Reagan would affirm that decision with his other national security aides. As 1983 began, Shultz clearly understood that his most urgent challenge was determining if Reagan truly shared his desire to refashion relations with Moscow. He told Seitz, "The problem is I don't know exactly what Reagan thinks. I haven't talked to him in a structured way." Seitz noted in his journal that "the secretary's tone showed an urgency to begin to engage the president and a reluctance to postpone this until mid-February."[35]

As Shultz struggled to get control of arms talks with Moscow, White House impatience with Rostow crested. Clark informed Shultz in early January that Rostow had to go. He said Helene von Damm, a long-time Reagan associate who served as director for presidential personnel, would ask Rostow for his resignation. Shultz was appalled that Rostow, a former undersecretary of state and dean of Yale Law School, would be dismissed by von Damm rather than the president. He offered to do the deed himself. "He is a person of tremendous distinction. He deserves every dignity he can get in the process." Shultz looked drained after delivering the news to Rostow. "It was tough," he told Seitz. "I don't think he's ever been asked for his resignation before and he's 69. He asked me if there was a bill of particulars. I said no, just that the president wishes it. He took it with grace and dignity. This is a cruel town. When you're out, you're out. The town loses interest in you right away. I guess we're really just too busy for the regular civilities, but these are human beings and the civilities are important." Later that day, still depressed by his encounter with Rostow, Shultz confessed that arms control issues did not catch his imagination.[36]

While Shultz privately was sharing his doubts with Seitz and arms control leadership remained fiercely contested within the administration, Reagan, in a statement announcing Rostow's departure, blithely said the new leadership at the Arms Control and Disarmament Agency "will report to and through the Secretary of State."[37] That was technically accurate, but far from the reality facing Shultz. The next day, John Hughes, the State

Department spokesman, told Shultz that news of Rostow's departure had upset the Europeans and "created an image of the administration in disarray." Shultz instructed Hughes to insist to reporters that Reagan was in charge.[38] Confidentially, Shultz compared Reagan's slack leadership with Richard Nixon's more decisive style. "President Nixon was very effective in cutting through such difficult problems. He would study the issue, listen to his advisers, and then say, 'Here's the problem and this is what we will do about it; one, two three.' At some point, President Reagan has to say what he thinks."[39]

Seitz noted in his journal a few days later: "The secretary, sounding discouraged, then said it was lamentable that the Secretary of State cannot see the President for one hour on US-USSR relations."[40] Shultz's irritation was compounded by lingering disagreement within the administration over how to unlock the intermediate-range missile talks in Geneva. The "Zero-Zero Option" advocated by the administration seemed dead. Shultz wanted presidential approval to explore other formulas. Vice President Bush favored consideration of new options, as did Paul Nitze, the chief INF negotiator. The Pentagon military high command seemed neutral. Weinberger was opposed, as was Edward Rowny, the lead negotiator at talks about limiting strategic nuclear forces, including long-range missiles.

As 1983 began, Shultz seemed unable to bring the issue to a conclusive decision point with Reagan. He encouraged Nitze to discuss the INF talks with Helmut Kohl, the new German chancellor, hoping that clarification about Kohl's position on the talks might help move the issue in Washington.[41] When Bud McFarlane, the deputy national security adviser, questioned whether Nitze should see Kohl, Shultz vented, alluding sardonically to Reagan's recent statement that the secretary of state directed arms control policy. "Now that I'm in charge of arms control, I wish I knew how to get into the act."[42]

His hopes for a more conciliatory policy hit a new obstacle on January 17, when Reagan signed National Security Decision Directive 75, a summary of American policy on the Soviet Union in the post-Brezhnev era. The secret document, drafted by Pipes, echoed the hard-line principles outlined the previous May in NSDD 32, which had set overall American national security strategy. NSDD 75 spelled out three primary tasks for dealing with the Kremlin:

1. To contain and over time reverse Soviet expansionism by competing effectively on a sustained basis with the Soviet Union in all international arenas—particularly in the overall military balance and in geographical regions of priority concern to the United States. This will remain the primary focus of U.S. policy toward the USSR.

2. To promote, within the narrow limits available to us, the process of change in the Soviet Union toward a more pluralistic political and economic system in which the power of the privileged ruling elite is gradually reduced. The U.S. recognizes that Soviet aggressiveness has deep roots in the internal system, and that relations with the USSR should therefore take into account whether or not they help to strengthen this system and its capacity to engage in aggression.

3. To engage the Soviet Union in negotiations to attempt to reach agreements which protect and enhance U.S. interests and which are consistent with the principles of strict reciprocity and mutual interest. This is important when the Soviet Union is in the midst of a process of political succession.[43]

As a manifesto of American policy, the NSDD did not look like a policy blueprint conducive to the kind of positive diplomacy Shultz had in mind. Although it allowed for the possibility that Brezhnev's death might lead to moderation by the Kremlin and an easing of cold war friction, the policy statement read more like a battle cry generated by Weinberger, Casey, Clark and the other ideological warriors around Reagan.

In an effort to work around White House inflexibility, Shultz sent Reagan a memo on January 19 proposing a new diplomatic initiative designed to test Andropov's willingness to reduce tensions. The memo opened by noting "increased Soviet activism" under Andropov. "This memo sets forth a strategy for countering this new Soviet activism by using an intensified dialogue with Moscow to test whether an improvement in the US-Soviet relationship is possible. Even if no improvement ultimately takes place, the dialogue would strengthen our ability to manage the relationship and keep the diplomatic initiative in our hands."[44]

Shultz recalled, "I set out to him for the first time what was to become our four part agenda: human rights, arms control, regional issues, and bilateral relations, including the problem of managing domestic (largely agricultural) pressures for increased trade. I set out four possible levels of contacts: specialists at 'departments and desks'; ambassadors with Gromyko and me; foreign ministers directly; and eventual summit if substance warranted.' Shortly after my paper reached the White House, Bud McFarlane let me know that the NSC staff over there was 'fly specking' it. 'There are so many ideologues around here that they are picking it to pieces,' he said."[45]

Several days after sending the memo, Shultz discussed it with Clark and McFarlane. They were leery of opening too many communication channels with Soviet officials and wary of considering a Reagan-Andropov summit, but they told Shultz to move ahead with his own meetings with Dobrynin.[46] Clark told Reagan, "I have grave reservations not only about the overall thrust of the proposed strategy for 'improving U.S.-Soviet relations,' but I also disagree with some of the policy initiative set forth."[47] Clark delivered the same verdict directly to Shultz, pointedly informing Shultz that Reagan had asked him to respond. It was another disappointing setback for Shultz.

In the State of the Union address on January 25, Reagan tried to strike a balance between belligerence and moderation in relations with Moscow. His words, negotiated among the contending camps in his administration, masked the torrid debates boiling behind the scenes:

> We're prepared for a positive change in Soviet-American relations. But the Soviet Union must show by deeds as well as words a sincere commitment to respect the rights and sovereignty of the family of nations. Responsible members of the world community do not threaten or invade their neighbors. And they restrain their allies from aggression.
>
> For our part, we're vigorously pursuing arms reduction negotiations with the Soviet Union. Supported by our allies, we've put forward draft agreements proposing significant weapon reductions to equal and verifiable lower levels. We insist on an equal balance of forces. And given the overwhelming evidence of Soviet violations of international treaties concerning chemical and biological weapons, we also insist that any agreement we sign can and will be verifiable.[48]

Three days after the State of the Union, Shultz, frustrated by the NSC staff meddling with his January 19 memo to Reagan and Clark's dismissal of it, ordered aides to withdraw it. He instructed Seitz to destroy all but one copy.[49]

As January came to an end, Shultz prepared to head to Japan and China. After hearing from a range of China experts, Shultz wanted to move relations with Beijing to a problem-solving phase where the two nations could try to resolve specific trade, technology transfer and other issues rather than repeat stale arguments about Taiwan. Shultz the economist could see that China was destined to become a global economic power that would eventu-

ally rival the United States. He told aides, "In a generation, China's going
to be the significant economic force—the most dynamic economic force
in the world, and Asia and everyone will have to adjust to the fact of this
burgeoning economy."[50]

As Shultz gathered up his briefing books before departing for Tokyo and
Beijing, his impatience with the White House and even Reagan over Soviet
policy was evident. He wanted to start talking to the Kremlin in a pragmatic way, free of the ideological passions of his administration colleagues.
He startled aides just before leaving the State Department to head to Andrews Air Force Base just outside Washington for the flight to Asia. "Here's
a screwball idea," he told Seitz and Larry Eagleburger, the undersecretary
of state for political affairs. "I've been thinking about Poland. We're in a rut
on that, too. Let's suppose the talks with Dobrynin shape up. Suppose we
say we'll do something in an area near you and you do something in an area
near us. The respective areas should be a long way from each of us. I could
suggest, 'Here's what we'll do on Poland; you get off our backs in Central
America.' We might also suggest that we get together to resolve the problems in southern Africa."[51] Seitz, astonished, called the idea "highly dangerous." He said, "We should not propose to the Soviet Union that there is
any kind of trade-off we are interested in and that equivalency is the wrong
way to approach the problems. Moreover, the idea of slicing up the world
or suggesting a kind of co-dominion is anathema to our allies and others."[52]

As Shultz's plane turned toward the northwest and its path across North
America and the North Pacific to Tokyo, Shultz could not reflect with
much satisfaction on his first six months as secretary of state. Although he
was America's chief diplomat, he exercised little command over American
foreign policy and was besieged by opponents across the Reagan administration. His relationship with Reagan was distant. The president seemed
inattentive and indifferent to the policy combat fracturing his government
and hampering America's global leadership. The Reagan-Shultz partnership that seemed inherent in their core views about tempering the cold war,
and their complementary character traits, was nowhere in sight. Improbably, a mid-February blizzard that buried Washington under several feet of
snow provided a breakthrough that empowered Shultz to take the first steps
toward tilting the administration internal power balance in his favor.

CHAPTER ELEVEN

Nancy Reagan to the Rescue

THE SNOW BEGAN FALLING on Friday, February 11, and piled up quickly. State Department security officers advised Shultz in the late afternoon that he should head home before roads became impassable. Washington typically struggles to cope with even a dusting of snow. With the snow falling at a rate of several inches an hour, the city's lean fleet of snowplow trucks could not keep pace. By Saturday, Washington was essentially paralyzed. Cross-country skiers took to normally busy thoroughfares, such as Wisconsin and Connecticut Avenues, that were blanketed by three feet of snow. With helicopter and car travel to Camp David blocked by the storm, the Reagans unexpectedly faced an unstructured weekend at the White House. They improvised. Nancy Reagan phoned the Shultz residence in Bethesda on Saturday morning. "I picked up the phone, and it was Nancy Reagan," Shultz said. "She said, 'Can O'Bie and you come over to dinner?'" It would be just the two couples, dining in the family quarters on the second floor of the White House.

State Department security agents managed to make it through the snow-clogged streets to pick up the Shultzes at their Bethesda home. Even though the dinner would be informal, Shultz donned a suit and tie in deference to the stature of their hosts. "I would not go to the White House in a sweater," he said. As dinner was served, the president and first lady peppered Shultz with questions about his recent visit to China, where he had

met with Foreign Minister Wu Xueqian and Deng Xiaoping, China's paramount leader. Shultz vividly recalled the White House scene decades later:

> They started asking me about the Chinese leaders and what were they
> like and then started asking me about the Soviet leaders. And suddenly
> I'm sitting there saying to myself, "This guy has never had a real con-
> versation with a big-time Communist leader, and he's dying to have
> one." And that totally was not his image. . . . So I said, "Well, Dobrynin
> is coming over next Tuesday at five o'clock. Why don't I bring him over
> here and you can talk to him?" And the President says, "That's a good
> idea. It won't take long because all I want to tell him is if Andropov is
> interested in a constructive dialogue, I'm ready." That's totally different
> from what Casey, Weinberger, everybody thought.[1]

After all the frustration, all the obstacles placed in his way by Clark, Weinberger and others, Shultz for the first time could see that Reagan actually
wanted to tamp down the cold war. "That was a turning point in how we
worked together because after that, I knew I had a bond with him, whatever anybody else said," Shultz recalled. Most important, it gave Shultz the
sense that the president shared his impulse to drain some of the tension
from Washington-Moscow relations and to look for steps, however modest,
to put the relationship on a more constructive course. "One of the things
that evening did for me was I felt that maybe Weinberger and everybody
thought we shouldn't talk to the Soviets, but I knew my guy did."[2]

While the White House conversation was encouraging, it offered no
guarantee that Shultz could prevail in administration debates about handling the Soviet Union, much less that Reagan would take decisive action
to support Shultz and end the internal feuding. Shultz was encouraged but
recognized that the path ahead was far from clear or easy. He would need
frequent access to Reagan to gain his full confidence, trust and support—
and Shultz was still unsure how to get it. His tendency to be patient, to play
the long game, remained his natural impulse. But it seemed insufficient to
the challenge he faced. Reflecting on the dinner two days later, Shultz told
Seitz he thought that Reagan felt trapped by his own rhetorical blasts about
the Soviet Union, the Defense Department and a White House national
security staff opposed to any overtures to the Kremlin.[3] Or as Shultz himself thought, "All this crap that the NSC staff has does not reflect Reagan's
true feelings."[4]

The melding of minds was precisely the outcome that Nancy Reagan wanted. The blizzard was unexpected, but the idea of putting the Reagans and Shultzes together in a cozy setting squared perfectly with Nancy Reagan and Mike Deaver's growing sense that the bristling relations between Washington and Moscow, including deadlocked arms control talks, threatened to undermine the president's record and his legacy. They saw themselves as protectors of Reagan amid a coterie of ideologues trying to box the president into rigid national security policies that precluded any warming of relations with the Kremlin. They believed Shultz would encourage Reagan to pursue a more pragmatic path with the Soviet Union. As did James A. Baker III: "I think Nancy appreciated George, and I know she supported the idea of talking to the Soviets, and I did, and certainly Deaver did," Baker recalled. As chief of staff, Baker could see that Shultz was contending with "an appallingly adversarial environment."[5]

Deaver's association with the Reagans dated back to Reagan's first term as California governor. He was a gifted public relations practitioner who became the minder of Reagan's public image and followed him to Washington, where as White House deputy chief of staff he worked closely with Nancy Reagan. Ideological issues were secondary to Deaver. His job was to burnish Reagan's persona and promote the proposition that the president was a statesman. He and Nancy Reagan talked frequently, gossiping and scheming to protect the president from internal and external threats. He joked, "I always imagined that when I died there would be a phone in my coffin, and at the other end of it would be Nancy Reagan."[6]

Baker, a politically savvy Texan who was a longtime counselor and close friend of George H. W. Bush, was a quintessential pragmatist and consummate deal maker. He was a loyal Republican, but not driven by an ideological fervor as were many Reagan aides. He served as manager of Bush's failed campaign for the 1980 Republican presidential nomination. Once Reagan selected Bush as his vice presidential candidate, Baker became part of the Reagan-Bush campaign operation and emerged as a strong contender for a top White House post. Nancy Reagan, regarded by Reagan advisers as the unofficial personnel director of the Reagan campaign, operated quietly behind the scenes to get Baker installed as White House chief of staff despite his ties to Bush. Baker's appointment blocked Edwin Meese, a staunch conservative and longtime Reagan associate in Sacramento, from getting the pivotal post.

Once Ronald Reagan became president, Nancy Reagan carefully monitored administration machinations, collecting information and gossip from a vast network of social friends in Washington, New York and California and presidential aides she trusted. Her circle included several longtime Reagan friends from Southern California who served as members of an informal kitchen cabinet for Reagan while he was governor and a presidential candidate. Largely at Nancy's instigation, the Reagans developed good relations with the Georgetown social set, an eclectic group of journalists, lobbyists and former government pooh-bahs. Many of these people were Democrats, but they welcomed the convivial access to the president and first lady after the standoffish Carter presidency. Jimmy and Rosalynn Carter were largely uninterested in the elegant Georgetown dinner party culture that John and Jackie Kennedy had enthusiastically embraced and come to symbolize.

Even though the *Washington Post* had endorsed Jimmy Carter for reelection in 1980, Katherine Graham, the *Post* publisher, was invited to a dinner of Washington insiders with the Reagans at the exclusive F Street Club less than two weeks after Reagan's election in November 1980. Graham could not attend due to travel. She was surprised when Nancy Reagan's press aide encouraged her to invite the Reagans to dinner at her Georgetown mansion. She did, and they came. So began an enduring friendship between the first lady and Graham.

As it happened, Shultz also enjoyed a cordial friendship with Graham. Her mother, Agnes Meyer, had met Shultz during the Kennedy administration when she served on an advisory panel he chaired. When Shultz reappeared in the capital as Nixon's labor secretary, he developed a warm relationship with Graham, despite the frosty relations between the Nixon White House and the *Post* as the Watergate scandal unfolded. In cheeky defiance of Nixon, Shultz frequently invited Graham to the White House tennis court, an act of brazen insubordination that both Shultz and Graham clearly relished. "One of the great bonds I have with George is that he invited me to play tennis on the White House court while Nixon was president, an act of extreme courage and even defiance," she later said.[7] Shultz was a frequent guest at her dinner parties during both the Nixon and

Reagan administrations. Recalling a Shultz visit to her Martha's Vineyard summer home, Graham could not resist telling Shultz that one of his fellow Vineyard dinner guests had subsequently referred to him as the "sexy sec."[8] Whether Graham and Nancy Reagan compared notes about Shultz is not known, but their mutual admiration of him was a timely coincidence that may have reinforced the first lady's attitude toward Shultz.

Nancy Reagan did not attend policy meetings or immerse herself in policy issues. But she was fiercely protective of her husband. After the 1981 assassination attempt, she started consulting an astrologer in hopes of divining when and where it would be safe for the president to travel. She was intently interested in how history would judge her husband, and she had a finely honed instinct for sensing whether officials were selflessly serving her husband or pursuing their own interests. She grew concerned that the administration's aggressive stance with the Soviet Union would prevent Reagan from accomplishing anything positive as a cold war president. She wanted, as she later said, to encourage "Ronnie to consider a more conciliatory relationship with the Soviet Union." She added, "For years it had troubled me that my husband was always being portrayed by his opponents as a warmonger, simply because he believed, quite properly, in strengthening our defenses."[9]

"Nancy Reagan was just keeping track of everything that was going on with respect to Ronnie—who was undermining him, who was supporting him," said Richard Helms, a social friend of the Reagans who had served as director of the CIA.[10] She distrusted Haig from the start, thought he was more interested in amassing power and controlling foreign policy than in supporting the president. "I never liked Haig," she told *Vanity Fair* years later.[11] She also did not like Clark. "Bill Clark, who came in in 1981 as deputy secretary of state, was another bad choice, in my opinion. I didn't think he was qualified for the job—or for his subsequent position as national security adviser. I wasn't the only one who felt that way; he embarrassed himself in front of the Senate Foreign Relations Committee when he couldn't name the prime minister of Zimbabwe. Clark had been in Ronnie's administration in Sacramento, but even then I had never really gotten along with him. He struck me as a user—especially when he traveled around the country claiming he represented Ronnie, which usually wasn't true. I spoke to Ronnie about him, but Ronnie liked him, so he stayed around longer than I would have liked."[12]

She once bluntly described how she perceived her role to Brian Mulroney, the Canadian prime minister: "I protect Ronnie from himself. You know, he has a big Irish heart. He trusts everybody and he doesn't see when he's being blindsided, or when people are acting out of motives that are less than noble. And he never acts upon it once he does. I do."[13] Though Shultz did not know Nancy Reagan well when he became secretary of state, he did understand that she exercised outsize influence at the White House. "If you have any intelligence, you don't make an enemy of the first lady, particularly Nancy Reagan, because she was so strong."[14] "If someone were to say, 'Who's the biggest influence on Ronald Reagan?,' it would be Nancy, without a doubt," Shultz said. "I think substantively she wanted constructive outcomes. She saw Reagan as a person who could accomplish things."[15]

Over time, he artfully cultivated his relationship with her. "George was good at creating these kind of indispensable connections," said Colin Powell.[16] Shultz and Nancy Reagan developed a bantering camaraderie about his seat assignments at state dinners. She recalled, "He was always trying to do the seating chart at our State Dinners so he could sit next to the prettiest girl in the room! At every State Dinner, George would take me aside and remind me that I promised to sit him next to the 'glamour girl' of the evening. At one such dinner, he was in 'seventh heaven' to have the opportunity to dance with Ginger Rogers."[17] Years later, he still treasured a signed and inscribed photo of Rogers dancing with him: "What a joy this was for me! You know, for the first two minutes I could swear I was dancing with Fred! Here's to another round sometime. My warmest regards, Ginger." Rogers and Fred Astaire famously costarred and danced together in a series of musical movies filmed in the 1930s. Shultz's eyes sparkled decades later when he recalled the dinners. "Nancy Reagan put on the most elegant White House dinners. I doubt anyone has done it as well. She always fixed me up with a Hollywood starlet as my dinner partner." At one dinner with a high-ranking Chinese official that the president could not attend due to illness, Shultz got to dance with Nancy. She sent him a photo of the moment with the inscription, "Dear George, my turn."[18]

Shultz's eldest child, Margaret, sensed the rapport. "I knew how much he liked her. And how much she liked him. There was kind of a flirty, in a nice way, relationship."[19] Nancy Reagan came to rely on and trust Shultz. She recalled:

I respected and admired George Shultz. It's a good thing George was there, because he was very practical in dealing with so many of our international problems in the 1980s, especially the Soviet Union. . . .

I trusted George completely and knew that he wouldn't take Ronnie down the wrong path out of some desire for personal recognition or fame. My "job" as a wife was to look out for Ronnie, especially when Ronnie wasn't looking out for himself. . . .

George played a very important role in our very successful relationship with the Soviet Union during this period. Ronnie came into office knowing this was one of his top priorities, and it wasn't until George came along that he felt he had a good ally at the State Department to accomplish this.[20]

Seitz watched raptly as Nancy Reagan and Shultz operated. "She would call on occasion," he said. "She would say, 'You know, I think Cap or Clark was way out of line and I'm going to tell Ronnie about it.' It was never, 'Well, what do you think our position ought to be on deploying the Pershing II missiles?'"[21] Deaver said, "She would call George Shultz up on the phone and say, 'You've got to get in and talk to Ronnie.' Because he would come home at night over dinner and say, 'I've talked to someone. They brought these people in from the National Security Council.' And she'd call Shultz or me or George Bush and say, 'You've got to get in there and talk to Ronnie. You can't let these people dominate the conversation, because that's not what Ronnie wants to do.'"[22]

But at the time of the blizzard dinner with the Reagans, Shultz did not know that Nancy Reagan and Deaver were plotting to enhance his access to the president and his authority within the administration. At the dinner, he did sense that the first lady approved of his proposal to bring Dobrynin by the Oval Office. More important, he knew that Reagan had endorsed the suggestion and seemed to share Shultz's desire to improve relations with the Kremlin. That knowledge steeled him as hard-liners immediately tried to abort the Dobrynin-Reagan meeting and diplomatic steps that followed it.

Clark was not happy when Shultz informed him that Reagan had agreed to meet with Dobrynin in the Oval Office on February 15. "Clark is very negative about the RR-Dobrynin meeting," Seitz noted. "Clark's nose is out of joint. The meeting was set up in his absence and he is peeved that Mike Deaver seems to have encouraged RR to schedule the meeting. Clark told GPS that he will recommend to RR that the meeting be postponed."[23] A few hours later, Clark called to say that Reagan wished to go ahead with the meeting despite Clark's opposition.[24]

When Dobrynin got to the secretary of state's office suite on the seventh floor of the State Department, Shultz delivered the surprising news that they were going to the White House. To avoid detection by reporters stationed in the pressroom near the West Wing, an unmarked White House car dropped off the two men at the entrance to the East Wing and they made their way across the White House to Reagan's private quarters on the second floor rather than to the Oval Office.

Shultz's reading of Reagan's interest in talking to Communist officials proved correct. "Rather than the brief meeting I expected, the president talked with us for almost two hours," Shultz recalled.[25] The conversation ranged across an array of issues, including the stalled arms control talks, Soviet conduct in Poland and Afghanistan, human rights issues such as the Kremlin's harsh treatment of dissidents and the possibility of better relations now that Andropov was Soviet leader. Reagan told Shultz and Dobrynin he wanted to open a personal and confidential communication channel with Andropov, working through Shultz and the Soviet ambassador. As coffee was served, Reagan and Dobrynin argued vigorously over the postwar roles and intentions of Washington and Moscow, with Reagan stressing what he said were the benign and generous efforts of the United States to heal rather than dominate the world. Dobrynin countered with the Soviet view that it had honored its commitments to its wartime allies and had not attempted to bully Western Europe. Dobrynin rejected Reagan's assertions about Marxist-Leninist doctrine and its inherent drive to spread Communism around the world.

In Dobrynin's retelling, Reagan told him: "Please tell Andropov that I am also in favor of good relations with the Soviet Union. Needless to say, we fully realize that our lifetime would not be long enough to solve all the problems accumulated over many years. But there are some problems that can and should be tackled now. Probably, people in the Soviet Union regard me as a crazy warmonger. But I don't want a war between us, because I know it would bring countless disasters. We should make a fresh start."[26] In Shultz's account, Reagan "spoke with genuine feeling and eloquence on the subject of human rights, divided families, Soviet Jewry, and refuseniks," the term used for Soviet citizens who applied unsuccessfully for permission to emigrate. Reagan brought up the Pentecostals, a small group of Christians who had sought refuge in the American embassy in Moscow five years earlier and were still housed there. 'If you can do something about the Pentecostals or another human rights issue,' Reagan told Dobrynin, 'we will simply be delighted and will not embarrass you by undue publicity, by claims of credit for ourselves, or by 'crowing.'"[27]

On June 27, 1978, seven Pentecostals from Siberia who had unsuccessfully appealed to the Kremlin for permission to emigrate had surged into the consular wing of the American embassy in Moscow after Soviet guards stationed outside refused to let them in. An eighth Pentecostal, age seventeen, was blocked outside by the guards, thrown to the sidewalk and detained. The seven inside the consulate refused to leave the reception area. They remained there for eight weeks, living off supplies provided by the embassy, and then moved to a cramped basement space where they remained indefinitely, in effect, wards of the United States. "It's like the isolation cell in a prison," one of them told the *New York Times*. "We can't complain about the way we have been fed and clothed, but we will never go out here and submit to Soviet law again."[28] As a presidential candidate and as president, Reagan repeatedly called for the Soviet Union to promise safe passage for the seven Pentecostals to emigrate, citing their case as a human rights violation.

Shultz and Dobrynin continued the conversation for another hour when they returned to the State Department, agreeing to work together initially on the Pentecostal impasse. Shultz was pleased. He thought that Reagan "had the time of his life" talking with Dobrynin. "The president was personally engaged," Shultz recalled. "I felt this could be a turning point with the Soviets."[29] Reagan was enthusiastic, too. "Shultz sneaked Dobrynin into the W.H," he noted in his diary. "We talked for two hours. Sometimes we got pretty nose to nose. I told him I wanted George to be a channel for direct contact with Andropov—no bureaucracy involved. Geo tells me that after they left, the ambas said, 'this could be an historic moment.'"[30] Reagan's hopes were justified but soon undermined by his own aides.

CHAPTER TWELVE

Shultz's Opponents Strike Back

REAGAN'S PERSONAL ENGAGEMENT WITH Dobrynin represented a grand opportunity for Shultz to press his pragmatic agenda. But it also generated high anxiety for Clark and others for precisely that reason. They feared that Washington's stony stance on Soviet-American relations would crumble if Shultz prevailed. Instead of quieting dissension within the administration, the Reagan-Dobrynin meeting set off a new round of internal warfare over Soviet policy, deepening Shultz's doubts about Reagan's willingness to end the bickering. Yet, as earlier, Shultz was paralyzed by his high-minded deference to organizational structures, particularly the role of the National Security Council staff led by Clark. For a man serving in his fourth cabinet post, Shultz seemed surprisingly naïve. He even hesitated when Michael Deaver renewed his invitation to put Shultz together privately with Reagan on a weekly basis.

Clark's dismay over the Reagan-Dobrynin-Shultz meeting was evident when Larry Eagleburger filled in Clark and Bud McFarlane on the president's encounter with the Soviet ambassador. Clark, apparently miffed that he was not consulted in advance about the meeting, had declined to attend despite Shultz's suggestion that he participate. Nancy Reagan and Mike Deaver's role in arranging the Dobrynin session also seemed to unnerve Clark. Clark told Eagleburger that he wanted to talk directly to

Shultz about the meeting and that Clark and McFarlane were "worried about 'detenteniks,'" a reference to the period of détente when Washington and Moscow sought to reduce tensions and negotiate mutually acceptable agreements on a variety of issues. Shultz assured Eagleburger he would talk with Clark, Casey and Weinberger. "The President is not a loner," Shultz observed. "He certainly does not want to be the subject of an end run. In this instance, however, he end ran himself."[1]

With tensions escalating between Clark and Shultz, Seitz counseled Shultz to reduce the temperature by meeting with Clark. "I urged GPS to get together with Bill Clark as soon as possible. I said there were bad feelings around and they would benefit from a good discussion. I said that even if the decision to see Dobrynin was RR's, Clark nonetheless will think the President was encouraged in this direction on Saturday night. His animosity may be directed at Deaver, but the Secretary doubtless is blamed as well. I also said to GPS that Clark's and McFarlane's discomfort with the decision to move ahead on US-Soviet relations has some justice. We can't start giving things away unless we get something for it. We have to be clear about that. The Secretary nodded."[2]

The discord unsettled Shultz. He returned to it that evening, musing at length about the role of the White House staff and the harmful implications for Reagan. Yet, instead of choosing to assert himself with the president and demand time to discuss critical policy issues with Reagan, Shultz worried about trampling on White House staff operations. Faced with an unexpected opening to expand his influence, Shultz seemed seized by good governance practices and a surprising degree of timidity. Seitz recorded the moment:

> At 6:15 pm GPS, looking troubled, came to my door and gestured me into his office. With his hands folded on the crown of his head he said he wanted to ruminate out loud. He spoke quietly and reflectively. "A President needs his staff. A staff is not simply another bureaucracy that gets in the way. The President's staff is essential to bring order to the time and attention of the President. Sometimes, however, a staff prevents a President from getting engaged in an issue when he wants to. You (meaning me) have urged me ever since the beginning to work directly with the President, but when I do this I seem to get in trouble with the staff. It's a fact of life that if the President's staff does not support a policy, the policy won't succeed. The President by himself can't make sure that a policy works or is being implemented. So the staff has

to be brought along. Bill Clark is feeling pressed now. He is devoted to the President and has always been, even when he did not work directly for him. Naturally, Bill concentrates on the substance of an issue. He has to. He cannot let the President make mistakes. Deaver, however, concentrates on image. That's his job. Sometimes these two concerns cannot be reconciled. It leads to conflicts. Then there is the problem of the other agencies. DOD is just plain dumb."[3]

Shultz worried out loud about whether Reagan would forcefully make his intentions clear to Clark and the National Security Council staff or just let the disorder continue and avoid tangling with Clark, Weinberger, Casey and others who opposed any overtures to the Kremlin.

The problem with all this is really more difficult now because the President wants to be engaged. He doesn't have immediate access to the problems, however, so he doesn't quite know how to get engaged. The staff, in a way, has cut him off. Even if he were engaged, the President doesn't like to take decisions in isolation. He likes the staff around him as he is making decisions and he likes general agreement. This is what got Al Haig in such trouble. He tried to get the President to make decisions on his own. The President likes to talk things through with others and doesn't like divisive decisions.[4]

Shultz and Seitz returned to the issue the next day, reflecting on how Shultz's travel abroad cut him off from the flow of decision-making, leaving him vulnerable to maneuvers by the White House staff, the Pentagon and other agencies that did not share his views about handling the Kremlin and other matters. "When you are out of town for a stretch of time you start to lose the taste and feel of Washington," Seitz told Shultz. For instance, Shultz did not fully understand that Clark and Deaver were increasingly at odds and that Deaver's role in helping arrange the Dobrynin meeting with Reagan would likely infuriate Clark.

The two men considered the different, more effective way Shultz had played Middle East policy discussions and the pipeline sanctions, working the issues over time with the White House, Pentagon and other agencies and slowly trying to build a consensus. Seitz observed that a similar process on American-Soviet relations might not have achieved the same outcome, especially if Reagan was unwilling to override Pentagon opposition. But he said that Shultz had erred by acting impulsively after the snowbound dinner with Reagan. He told Shultz his actions had been "too rushed" and "too telescoped." Seitz continued, "The process is especially important in this

Administration because frankly the people at the White House as well as Bill Clark simply don't understand the issues. Clark doesn't get the subtleties or the nuance, so the process is extremely important."[5]

Shultz said he did not know how to solve the travel challenge. He noted that Ken Dam, the deputy secretary of state, was doing a fine job but could not substitute for the secretary. Dam, a lawyer who succeeded Walter Stoessel in the post in September 1982, had previously served as provost of the University of Chicago. "'Even the snow had something to do with it,' Shultz said. 'If it hadn't snowed, the President would probably have gone to Camp David and I would not have been invited there Saturday night.' . . . As the Secretary was changing into evening wear, I asked him how the meeting with Clark had gone. In a discouraged tone, he said, 'Oh, not so well.'"[6]

The intensity of opposition to Shultz's Kremlin initiative became vividly apparent on February 18 when Dam met with Clark and McFarlane. Dam reported to Shultz that Clark had told him Reagan was unenthusiastic about following up with Dobrynin. Even more startling, Dam said Clark asserted that the Dobrynin meeting "did not represent Reagan's real wishes—he was just appeasing Nancy." There seemed to be no way around the frustrations. Seitz dryly noted, "This is all very confusing—what's the real Ronald Reagan?" He ended the day's journal entry: "GPS is exhausted."[7] A few days later, Seitz reported, "GPS is walking on eggshells regarding his initiative with the President on the Soviet Union."[8] Shultz said as much himself at a State Department staff meeting, telling aides he was not sure if Reagan really wanted to move ahead.[9] Seitz observed, "I had the impression that GPS is slightly disillusioned with the President. He is not certain where he stands on some of these issues and is concerned about the force of the President's follow-through. Clark leaves his imprint on most questions."[10]

Shultz got some good news on the last day of February when Oleg Sokolov, second in command at the Soviet embassy, delivered a message from the Kremlin about the Pentecostals. It said that if the Pentecostals left the embassy and returned home to Siberia, their applications to emigrate would be reviewed favorably. The implication was that the Soviet authorities would not detain the Pentecostals when they exited the embassy. Although the message fell far short of a guarantee that the Pentecostals would be free to emigrate, Shultz considered it a promising sign and doubted the Kremlin would double-cross the United States by arresting them.[11]

Shultz's optimism was dented on March 8 when the president delivered a fiery speech to the National Association of Evangelicals in Orlando. In a passage that instantly generated headlines around the world, Reagan said, "In your discussions of the nuclear freeze proposals, I urge you to beware the temptation of pride—the temptation of blithely declaring yourselves above it all and label both sides equally at fault, to ignore the facts of history and the aggressive impulses of an evil empire, to simply call the arms race a giant misunderstanding and thereby remove yourself from the struggle between right and wrong and good and evil."[12] The obvious reference to the Soviet Union as "an evil empire" seemed in a flash to erase all the hopes raised for Shultz by his dinner with Reagan and the Reagan-Dobrynin meeting.

The next day, Shultz told Clark, "I desperately need a meeting with the president on the Soviet Union."[13] He got it on March 10, but not in the fashion he hoped for. It was a fiasco. Instead of an intimate meeting with Reagan and Clark where Shultz could seek Reagan's overt approval for constructive engagement with the Kremlin, the Oval Office was packed with White House aides opposed to any overtures to Moscow, including Clark, Meese and Pipes. Shultz angrily replayed the scene to Seitz when he got back to the State Department. Seitz recorded the moment in his journal:

> The President didn't like it, particularly because the idea had been to keep everything quiet about the channel with Dobrynin. The Secretary said he was irritated. The attitude of the people in the room was, "Once the Russians have changed, then maybe we can do something with them." GPS said that when the meeting was ready to break up, he had summarized by saying that what he understood from the meeting was that he should stop seeing Dobrynin and leave things as they are. Everyone in the room protested that this was not the correct interpretation, but the meeting broke up anyway and the Secretary left with everyone understanding that he was most annoyed. After GPS had told this story, he turned grumbling to his desk.
>
> "The trouble is the President wants to do what I want to do, but Clark is standing in the way. Clark put these people there as 'Soviet experts.' I started off saying I wanted to speak candidly but I don't even know who all these people are! I looked at Pipes and said, 'For example, sir, I don't even know who you are.' Clark then jumped in and said, 'This is Richard Pipes. He's an NSC member. He's on the payroll.' Then I said, 'Perhaps we should ask our Ambassador in Moscow for his opinion.'"[14]

Later that day, McFarlane told Larry Eagleburger he was outraged by the meeting and had been unaware that Clark was going to pack the room with aides opposed to Shultz's proposals. Eagleburger cautioned Shultz that even if Reagan agreed with his secretary of state, nothing would come of it if the president failed to tell aides and the government bureaucracy. Shultz, annoyed and frustrated by the day's events, complained that Reagan probably had not even understood what he was proposing because Shultz had not been able to explain his hope that his dialogue with Dobrynin about the Pentecostals could lead to their release from the embassy and approval to emigrate, a small but promising step toward broader discussions with the Kremlin. "They want to keep State on a tight rein," Shultz told Seitz. "It's like a sergeant I had in the Marine Corps who would say, 'Don't fall out until I tell you to fall out! Fall out!'" The discouraging day ended with a call from Clark, who seemed to think there had been nothing amiss about the meeting.[15]

The next day Shultz found an unexpected moment after a White House meeting on the Middle East to talk privately with the president about Soviet policy. He recalled, "I said I needed some direction on Soviet relations. I summarized the program. He basically said go ahead." Shultz instructed State Department aides to prepare a brief paper for Reagan providing a road map for how talks with the Kremlin on a variety of issues could unfold in a graduated way in the weeks ahead, including a possible Shultz meeting with Gromyko in Moscow followed by a Reagan-Gromyko meeting in Washington in the fall. He said, "The president is afraid—Clark even more so—that if they give a green light the State Department will run off and do things that will change the atmosphere when nothing is warranted. We need to be careful."[16]

Another reason to be careful was growing sentiment among some Reagan aides that all top national security officials, including the secretary of state, should be required to take periodic polygraph tests to ensure that they were not improperly disclosing classified information. Ostensibly, the point was to protect the security of secret documents, deliberations and decisions across agencies such as the State Department, Pentagon and White House, where polygraph tests were not routinely conducted. Implicitly, the recommendation was aimed at Shultz and other senior officials suspected of leaking information to journalists. For Shultz, whose well-known circumspection with journalists was disappointing to reporters, the pressure to polygraph was outrageous. "I won't do it," he told Seitz.[17]

The March 10 dysfunctional Oval Office meeting about Soviet policy did not pass unnoticed by Michael Deaver and James Baker, who attended the session. On March 12, Deaver phoned Shultz to tell him that he should get in touch anytime he wanted to see the president alone. Deaver said Reagan had told him before the March 10 meeting that too many people had been invited. The Deaver invitation was alluring. Shultz noted to Seitz after the call that it was, in effect, an invitation to go around Clark. Yet he thought it was a dangerous gambit—private access to the president, valuable as it might be, could make Clark and the White House national security staff even more antagonistic to Shultz. After sleeping on it, Shultz told Seitz the next day that he would keep Clark informed, but if Deaver offered the only way to get to see Reagan, he would work through Deaver.[18]

Meanwhile, Weinberger continued to irritate Shultz. The two men disagreed over how the United States could counter the increasingly pro-Soviet policies of Suriname, a small nation on the northeast coast of South America that was a self-governing territory of the Netherlands. Desi Bouterse, leader of a military coup that overthrew the elected government of Suriname in late 1982, was rounding up and killing critics of his regime and courting Cuba and the Soviet Union. Weinberger opposed a State Department plan that called for Dutch military intervention to restore civilian leadership in Suriname, with the US Navy blocking sea lanes from Cuba to prevent Fidel Castro from coming to Bouterse's aid. When the Dutch declined to intervene, the CIA came up with a bizarre plan to covertly inject South Korean commandos into Suriname to overthrow the regime. Senior Reagan administration officials also talked about enlisting Venezuelan assistance to train Surinamese forces that could remove Bouterse from power. That idea blew up after a public comment from Weinberger. When Shultz learned of Weinberger's remarks, he muttered, "Why can't people shut up?"[19]

Weinberger's reluctance to use the navy also troubled Shultz because it seemed grounded in the Pentagon's aversion to using military power after the Vietnam War. Shultz believed American military force could and should be applied at times in carefully calibrated ways to support American interests and diplomacy. In his view, "The Vietnam War had left one indisputable legacy: massive press, public and congressional anxiety that the United States—at all costs—avoid getting mired in 'another Vietnam.' News items datelined from Central America or the Caribbean raised the alarm that this or that country of the region was about to become our next quagmire. . . . So the American agonies subsumed under the terms Vietnam and Watergate had us tied up in knots."[20]

Shultz's frustration with the roadblocks he faced on Soviet policy, and Reagan's failure to cut though the resistance, started to break out in his public appearances. Grilled at a House hearing about administration efforts to counteract Soviet influence in Central America, he unwisely complained about religious leaders in El Salvador. Catholic priests in El Salvador, outraged by the killing of nuns by government-condoned death squads, were protesting about human rights abuses. Mary McGrory, a *Washington Post* columnist, shot back at Shultz in her column. "Secretary of State George Shultz' extraordinary outburst against 'churchmen who want to see Soviet influence in El Salvador improved' has provided another chapter in the continuing saga of the irascibilization of the administration's Mr. Calm. Imperturbability used to be Shultz' trademark, that and measured, thoughtful expression."[21]

In an interview with the *Washington Post*, Shultz responded to a reporter's observation that he sounded more and more like his sometimes gruff predecessor, Alexander Haig. "I don't feel that I've changed," he said. "I can get tired or needled, too, like anybody else. When you get hammered on day after day, you don't choose your words exactly right." When asked by the *Post* if he was happy in his job after nine months as secretary of state, Shultz brusquely replied, "I didn't come here to be happy."[22]

CHAPTER THIRTEEN

A Test of Loyalty

SHULTZ'S MOOD DID NOT improve a few days later when he first got word that Reagan was about to upend decades of American nuclear deterrence doctrine by announcing that the United States would try to build an impenetrable missile defense in space. Shultz immediately recognized that the idea was fanciful—technologically unrealistic, inevitably vulnerable to offensive weapon advances and incompatible with long-standing nuclear defense strategy. He fought hard but unsuccessfully to dissuade Reagan. Then, to the dismay of his State Department colleagues, he reversed course after Reagan unveiled the plan, enthusiastically backing the project and telling his aides to do the same or quit.

The crisp about-face reflected Shultz's strong belief in loyalty that dated back to his childhood and marine service and was evident when he lingered in the Nixon cabinet as Watergate swamped the White House. This time, the president's affront was not ethical or legal but rather a dumbfounding policy decision. In Shultz's view, public service at the highest level required challenging misguided presidential impulses. That was more than many of his colleagues would dare to do. But once the president decided, it was time to salute smartly and carry on, regardless of how much he might still disagree. In this case, his loyalty went unrewarded. Within days of the Reagan speech, Shultz confronted a new wave of resistance to his diplomatic leadership, leaving him more dispirited than ever. And yet he remained reluctant to force a showdown with Clark and demand that Reagan either back his secretary of state or get a new one.

Reagan had referred vaguely to the missile shield idea when the Shultzes and Reagans dined together at the White House in mid-February, but Shultz had not understood what the president had in mind or its revolutionary implications for cold war defense strategy. The idea of a space shield that could destroy hundreds of nuclear-tipped missiles streaking toward targets in the United States was the stuff of science fiction. In theory, the defense system would intercept a barrage of incoming missiles and nuclear warheads with a variety of futuristic weapons, including ground- and space-based lasers, electromagnetic pulses and kinetic devices. By the time Reagan took office, antimissile technology had advanced, but not anywhere near the vision that seized Reagan in 1983. Reagan's infatuation with the plan stemmed partly from a misinformed view that the technology could be perfected within a few years rather than decades, if at all. Edward Teller, one of the primary designers and advocates of America's first hydrogen bomb in 1952, a weapon exponentially more powerful than the atomic bombs dropped on Hiroshima and Nagasaki in 1945, helped sell the space defense scheme to Reagan.

The notion of making America invulnerable to nuclear attack, in effect rendering nuclear weapons obsolete, played powerfully to Reagan's visceral aversion to nuclear war and his desire to reduce the threat of a nuclear conflict. Reagan welcomed the utopian view that if the United States developed a shield and shared the technology with other nations, including the Soviet Union, which he wanted to do, there would be no need for nuclear weapons. "He believed it, I'm telling you, to the depth of his soul," Colin Powell recalled.[1]

Reagan decided to unveil the plan to the world during a nationally televised speech on March 23, 1983, that was intended to stoke public support for the defense budget. The plan would be called the Strategic Defense Initiative, or SDI. Critics immediately dubbed it "Star Wars," a reference to the enormously popular George Lucas fantasy movie series that debuted in 1977. Shultz first heard about the upcoming speech two days earlier. He was stunned. Work on the shield plan and the speech had been limited to a small group of administration officials, including the White House science adviser, George Keyworth. The secretary of state was not in the loop. Shultz doubted the plan was technologically feasible and immediately understood that it would overturn conventional nuclear deterrence theory based on the chilling notion that the best way to avoid a nuclear war was to be so heavily armed with nuclear weapons that an enemy would never initiate a nuclear conflict because it knew it could never prevail.

An ambitious missile shield would also violate the 1972 Anti-Ballistic Missile Treaty, which barred development of nationwide missile defense systems by the United States and Soviet Union. Each nation was initially limited to two missile defense systems, one to protect its capital city, the other to shield a land-based missile base. The accord also banned the development, testing or deployment of sea-, air- and space-based missile defense systems. As aides were informing Shultz about Reagan's plans on March 21, Richard Burt, one of the State Department's most knowledgeable nuclear experts, joined the meeting in Shultz's office. Burt was flabbergasted, Seitz noted in his journal that evening: "He said that not only is a world free of nuclear weapons a pipe dream, but a speech such as this by the president would unilaterally destroy the foundation of the [NATO] alliance."[2] He also worried that Reagan supported the shield as a way to drain support from the nuclear freeze movement that commanded growing public allegiance in the United States and abroad.[3]

Over the next two days, Shultz frantically tried to persuade Reagan to remove the shield plan from the speech or, at least, tone down the language and reduce expectations that a shield could be put in place anytime soon. The same day he learned about the upcoming speech, Shultz tried to persuade Reagan during a White House meeting to drop the idea. Shultz recalled: "I found great resistance to any change in the words for the speech. 'This paragraph is a revolution in our strategic doctrine,' I told President Reagan. He had Keyworth called in. I asked him, 'Can you be sure of an impenetrable shield? And what about cruise missiles? What about stealth bombers? Your language is sweeping. I'm not objecting to R and D, but this is a bombshell. What about the ABM Treaty? What about our allies and the strategic doctrine on which they depend? You don't say anything about those questions.' His answers were not at all satisfactory to me."[4] Reagan grew concerned enough about Shultz's objections that he called Shultz the next evening. Seitz recounted the conversation in his journal. Shultz told the president:

> "I think the wording (of the speech) is better in this current draft and some of the Qs and As are helpful. But I still have grave reservations, not about the R&D effort but about advancing this matter as something of such tremendous importance and scope. It implies we are changing our strategic doctrine. There is a host of unanswered technical questions. There is tremendous strength in offensive and defensive measures, but the former historically has the upper hand. I can't see being certain of one system defending against cruise missiles and submarines, etc. I can see the moral ground you want to stake out, but I don't want to see you put something forward so powerfully only to find technical flaws or major doctrinal weaknesses. . . . I have to say honestly that I am deeply troubled. Of course, I will support you. I'm sure you know that."
>
> The President responded for awhile stressing the overwhelming attractions of a purely defensive system. GPS answered, "I agree that if we got there we'd be in the catbird's seat. So, we must push R&D if for no other reason than because the Soviets are. But it can be destabilizing as to what the Soviets do, how they respond. They will assume we have a major scientific breakthrough. I don't know the implications of that." RR interrupted to say that this was the part that would make a news item and attract the networks. GPS said, "It's more than a news item—it's a sweeping proposal."[5]

As the day ended, Shultz thought he had made some progress in toning down the speech draft. He was ready to go home but was scheduled to meet with the undersecretary of state for economic affairs, Allen Wallis, who had been dean of the University of the Chicago business school when it hired Shultz. Shultz muttered to Seitz, "God, he comes in here and talks about things I'm not interested in—Concorde, Swiss Air, Pan Am—I don't give a shit!"[6]

That evening, Reagan noted in his diary: "On my desk was a draft of the speech on defense to be delivered tomorrow night on T.V. This was one hassled over by N.S.C., State & Defense. Finally I have a crack at it. I did a lot of re-writing. Much of it was to change bureaucratic into people talk."[7] Shultz's efforts to modify the speech resumed the next morning, now just hours before Reagan would address the nation from the Oval Office. Clark and McFarlane were growing impatient with Shultz's intervention. Several top Pentagon officials told Shultz that they, too, were alarmed by the space shield concept. That convinced Shultz that the whole idea was, in his words, "a White House contraption." He told aides, "The president was almost sold a bill of goods. They did it with their little hatchets. Clark told me last night he really didn't know much about this, and I wanted to say, 'buddy boy, you've got to get into the substance.'"[8]

As the hours passed, McFarlane and Clark gave conflicting reports to State Department officials about the draft of Reagan's speech. McFarlane assured them the draft was being toned down; Clark complained to Shultz that he had heard that Fred Ikle, the undersecretary of defense for policy, and Richard Perle had worked the phones overnight to tell officials that the Joint Chiefs of Staff did not support the space shield. Clark told Shultz, "They are liars." Shultz said they were wrong to misrepresent the views of the Joint Chiefs but were right to oppose the space shield. By early afternoon, Reagan had settled the matter, telling aides he would go ahead with the announcement, which came near the end of his address. He told the nation:

> After careful consultation with my advisers, including the Joint Chiefs of Staff, I believe there is a way. Let me share with you a vision of the future which offers hope. It is that we embark on a program to counter the awesome Soviet missile threat with measures that are defensive. Let us turn to the very strengths in technology that spawned our great industrial base and that have given us the quality of life we enjoy today.
>
> What if free people could live secure in the knowledge that their security did not rest upon the threat of instant U.S. retaliation to deter a Soviet attack, that we could intercept and destroy strategic ballistic missiles before they reached our own soil or that of our allies?
>
> I know this is a formidable, technical task, one that may not be accomplished before the end of the century. Yet, current technology has attained a level of sophistication where it's reasonable for us to begin this effort. It will take years, probably decades of efforts on many fronts. There will be failures and setbacks, just as there will be successes and breakthroughs. And as we proceed, we must remain constant in preserving the nuclear deterrent and maintaining a solid capability for flexible response. But isn't it worth every investment necessary to free the world from the threat of nuclear war? We know it is.
>
> I clearly recognize that defensive systems have limitations and raise certain problems and ambiguities. If paired with offensive systems, they can be viewed as fostering an aggressive policy, and no one wants that. But with these considerations firmly in mind, I call upon the scientific community in our country, those who gave us nuclear weapons, to turn their great talents now to the cause of mankind and world peace, to

give us the means of rendering these nuclear weapons impotent and obsolete.[9]

The *New York Times* summarized the Reagan initiative the next morning:

> President Reagan, defending his military program, proposed tonight to exploit advances in technology in coming decades so the United States can develop an effective defense against missiles launched by others.
>
> In effect, Mr. Reagan proposed to make obsolete the current United States policy of relying on massive retaliation by its ballistic missiles to counter the threat of a Soviet nuclear attack.[10]

The immediate reaction from American allies and nuclear policy experts was overwhelmingly negative. The common view was that Reagan was recklessly overturning the core defense principles of the nuclear era in naïve pursuit of a missile shield that was technologically unfeasible. Shultz, though deflated by the announcement and abrupt policy shift, decided to live with Reagan's fantasy. His initial strategy was to support the initiative in deference to Reagan and to try to sell the idea to American allies while working inside administration circles to see if SDI could eventually be considered a bargaining chip in arms talks with the Kremlin.

Secretaries of state, like other executive branch officials, cannot defy a presidential order or policy decision and expect to remain in office. Shultz clearly did not see the SDI decision as warranting his resignation. Still, his decision to fall in line behind the president on a plan that Shultz clearly knew was misguided reflected an ingrained instinct to be cautious in challenging presidents for whom he served and a habit of remaining loyal to supervisors and colleagues despite deep policy disagreements. These dynamics now left Shultz as secretary of state for a president pursuing a chimerical defense plan that was bound to unsettle allies, seemed likely to undermine arms control talks and would make the elimination of nuclear weapons an even more improbable goal.

Some State Department aides were startled by his willingness to mute his opposition to SDI and the vehemence of his allegiance to Reagan. Shultz snapped at Rick Burt when he challenged him about SDI. Burt recalled the exchange: "Rick, I've gotta remind you of something you know. We work for the President of the United States. The President of the United States wants to do this. If you don't want do it, you don't have to work for the President of the United States. But as long as you *are* working for the

President of the United States, you are going to support this policy. Is that clear?' And I had to meekly tell him yes."[11]

As the SDI announcement reverberated across the government and around the world, Shultz continued to struggle with his lack of access to Reagan on a host of foreign policy matters, including the Soviet Union, the Middle East and Central America. He vented about the White House staff two days after the SDI speech. "They are doing more things. They sit around in that morning meeting and make decisions or semi-decisions. I haven't been able to have private sessions with the President. There is always a crowd. I don't think a meeting with RR should be one-on-one. Clark has to be included. If he is excluded—such as the Dobrynin exercise—then the NSC doesn't like it. They've been fighting this Soviet business every step of the way."[12]

Recalling Deaver's recent offer to get Shultz into the Oval Office anytime he wished, Shultz said, "That's an offer I have left on the table. Clark arranged the meeting last Monday. That's a good sign. I've tried for routine if not regular meetings with RR, but Clark always seems to blame it on the schedulers. Apparently Clark and Deaver are barely speaking to each other." A call from Clark interrupted Shultz as he was talking about Deaver. Seitz noted the moment:

> Clark told GPS that he had arranged a meeting the next day with the President to discuss relations with the Soviets. It would be a small meeting. GPS said that Clark should be there. Clark said he would try to arrange to do this sort of thing a couple of times a week. Clark said he (Clark) had had a heart-to-heart with the President urging that RR needed to spend more time talking about foreign policy issues. According to Clark, RR had agreed to tell Deaver to put this kind of thing on the schedule. Clark also passed on an invitation to come to the WH to listen to a report on opinion poll findings about foreign policy. GPS was also invited to have lunch with RR along with Arthur Sulzberger [publisher of the *New York Times*]. When GPS hung up the phone, we all laughed that apparently his office was bugged by the NSC.[13]

The call was soon followed by an invitation from the Reagans to spend the weekend with them at Camp David. "Gee, I wonder what's happening," Shultz told Seitz sarcastically.[14] The positive signs continued the next day when Shultz and Reagan talked. Reagan seemed supportive of Shultz's plan to deepen engagement with the Kremlin on a variety of issues, encouraged by the news that Lidia Vashchenko, one of the Pentecostal leaders, was free to leave the Soviet Union. The Kremlin decision was a signal that Andropov was prepared to work with Reagan to ease tensions.

When Shultz returned to the State Department, he reflected on the state of play:

> You have to keep in mind the background context of all of this—power, the economy, China. Then we have to focus on the immediate steps. We have to create the background music which are essentially human rights issues and bilateral issues. The big ones are arms control and regional issues. Meeting with Gromyko in Moscow adds visible momentum. Then Gromyko would come here in October. I can see a summit in early 1984. Wirthlin [Richard Wirthlin, public opinion pollster and Reagan political adviser] says the President is surging domestically but is going downhill on foreign policy. Our instinct on INF has been right, as I told Clark. If the President agrees to the agenda, we then have to point out that it is almost April and we don't have a lot of time. We have to move this bull. We need a process that leads to speed. We are saying we are dealing with the Soviets. Others may disagree. So we have to decide. If the answer is yes, then we need to decide on a process. It has to be direct to the President with Clark. Mike Deaver said it ought to be just me and the President, but I said it had to be with Bill Clark as well. I must say, however, it's Deaver who got me this appointment. Anyway, we have to move in a low-key way, but we need to let the world know what's going on. We can call it "probing."[15]

The weekend at Camp David with the Reagans did not lend new urgency to Shultz's efforts to advance relations with the Kremlin. Unknown to Shultz, Reagan privately recorded his view that he fully supported Shultz's efforts.

> Learned in office George S. is upset—thinks NSC is undercutting him on plans he & I discussed for "quiet diplomacy" approach to the Soviets. They have let Lydia—the young hunger striker member of the family that's been living in the embassy basement in Moscow for 4 yrs. go. She is in Vienna as of today. We had a meeting later in the day with George & cleared things up I think. Some of the N.S.C. staff are too hard line & don't think any approach should be made to the Soviets. I think I'm hard-line & will never appease but I do want to try & let them see there is a better world if they'll show by deed they want to get along with the free world.[16]

As the weeks passed, Shultz became increasingly disappointed in Reagan's failure to follow through on his endorsement of Shultz's plan. Meetings between Shultz and Dobrynin continued but bogged down without producing tangible progress beyond the Pentecostal case. A few positive signs appeared in talks between Max Kampelman, the US ambassador to the Conference on Security and Cooperation in Europe, and his Soviet counterpart, Ambassador Sergei Kondrashev, including additional discussion about the Pentecostals and the imprisonment of Anatoly Shcharansky, an outspoken critic of the Kremlin. Kondrashev, who was actually a senior KGB officer, appeared to have a direct channel to Andropov and told Kampelman that their discussions should never be mentioned to other Soviet diplomats. After the Soviet ambassador to Spain learned of the Kampelman-Kondrashev talks and informed the Foreign Ministry, the conversations abruptly ended.[17]

By mid-May, Shultz seemed to be blocked again. He confided to Seitz, who recorded the scene:

> After the meeting, when we were alone in the office, GPS said to me, "There is a management crisis in foreign affairs here. It's easy not to accomplish anything. I can take trips and that's it. Clark is so frustrating to talk to. He doesn't move fast. He wanders. He makes deals. He talks to HAK [Henry Kissinger] a lot. They are two Svengalis trying to do things."
>
> I said to GPS that he seems stymied at every turn and there is no apparent way to break through. I said I knew he had one card that he had not as yet played. I knew also that he did not want to play it. The only other cure I could think of was for him to see the President regularly. I said I knew he had resisted this, but I can think of no other answer. Without decisions from the President everything just sloshes around and people can set up hurdles at will. Even with regular meetings, I said, the problem won't be resolved because the President doesn't pay continuing attention once he has made a decision. "You need regular meetings with the President so that you can keep his eye on the ball." GPS listened to this but did not respond directly. He did say, "It's the worst organization I've ever seen. It's worse than a university. . . . I have to put my foot down somewhat and say to the President, 'You hired me to do a job, but I can't do it.'"[18]

Remarkably, Shultz's power ebbed even further as hard-core opponents outmaneuvered him on Central America policy in the summer of 1983, gaining Reagan's approval for steps to increase American covert military and intelligence operations in the region without informing or consulting the secretary of state.

CHAPTER FOURTEEN

Hitting Bottom

SHULTZ'S DISSATISFACTION WAS COMPOUNDED by the administration's chaotic handling of Soviet and Cuban troublemaking in Central America. Concern about Soviet subversion in the region seized the CIA and Pentagon during the first months of the Reagan presidency and grew more intense over time. A few days before Christmas in 1982, Bill Casey abruptly pulled Shultz aside as they were leaving a meeting in the Roosevelt Room at the White House and delivered a curt lecture about Central America that troubled Shultz. "The American people are not behind our policy in Central America," Casey told Shultz. "Our support in Congress is fading. We are in danger of losing on what is by far the most important foreign policy problem confronting the nation. You shouldn't be traveling around Europe. You should be going around the United States sounding the alarm and generating support for tough policies on the most important problem on our agenda. Force is the only language the Communists understand."[1]

By summer 1983, Casey and like-minded colleagues such as Clark and Fred Ikle, the undersecretary of defense for policy, were determined to escalate the use of American force to help overthrow the leftist government of Nicaragua and support the pro-American government of El Salvador. They managed to get Reagan to approve their plans before Shultz learned about them. The end run staggered, humiliated and infuriated Shultz. After a year of mounting frustration, he finally confronted Reagan about the dysfunctional policy-making process that was hobbling the Reagan presidency.

The focal point of concern for Casey, Clark and others was Nicaragua, where leftist insurgents in 1979 had overthrown the dictatorial regime of Anastasio Somoza Debayle, whose family had governed the country with an iron grip for forty-three years. The rebels, known as the Sandinista National Liberation Front, openly courted support from Havana and Moscow, raising alarm in Washington that Nicaragua would join Cuba as American antagonists in the Western Hemisphere. Casey warned colleagues that Nicaragua was becoming a base for Soviet subversion in the region. If the United States did not respond, he said, Mexico would be next and the threat of Communism would come to America's southern border. Reagan officials feared that El Salvador, where a coalition of leftist groups, the Farabundo Martí National Liberation Front, was conducting a guerrilla campaign against an unelected government led by military officers, would also become a Communist base in the region.

With Casey citing a stream of CIA reports about the rising danger in Central America, and many officials determined to take action, the Reagan administration decided to counter the threat several ways. It would increase the number of American military advisers working with the Salvadoran military, support covert paramilitary forces against the Sandinistas and build up the American military presence in Honduras, which welcomed Washington's assistance and was ready to serve as an anchor for American activities in the region. The initial attempt to support paramilitary forces in Nicaragua relied on Argentina to train and direct the forces. When the plan collapsed, Washington took a more direct approach by providing money and military equipment to forces organized by anti-Sandinista leaders. Training would be done in Honduras and Panama, with the paramilitary units infiltrating into Nicaragua.

All this was unfolding as Shultz assumed command at the State Department. Though he shared the administration's concerns about Central America, he soon found that the White House, CIA and Pentagon were driving policy, with the State Department relegated to a secondary role. Clark, in particular, seemed to own Central America policy. Shultz's efforts to add a diplomacy track to the policy were initially rebuffed and, then once launched, directed by the White House rather than the State Department. Critical decisions about widening American military and intelligence activities in the region were made while he was traveling abroad and unable to attend White House meetings.

The situation was untenable for a secretary of state. Shultz knew it but could do little about it. His irritation about Central America escalated through the first six months of 1983, at times exceeding his exasperation about his constrained role in setting Soviet policy. After confronting Clark about Central America in mid-May, he fumed, "I don't know what role I have, if any. As unbureaucratic as I tend to be, it's time I put my foot down and say, 'If you want me to run foreign policy, get out of the way and don't touch my people.'"[2] Among other things, he was incensed that the White House was directing the work of Richard Stone, a former Democratic senator from Florida, who had been appointed as the president's special envoy for Central America.

On May 25, he vented directly to Reagan. "Mr. President, you have a fed up, frustrated secretary of state on your hands," he said. He went on to describe the conflicting lines of authority in setting Central America policy and the sidelining of the State Department. "I told the president he could have the best policies in the world, but he couldn't get them done with this organization," Shultz recalled. Reagan seemed surprised and dismayed by Shultz's account. Even though Shultz had stopped short of explicitly threatening to resign, the threat was implicit. Reagan well knew that the resignation of a second secretary of state would cripple his presidency. He agreed a clearer structure was needed and approved Shultz's request that the secretary of state should take the lead in managing diplomatic efforts in the region. Within hours, Reagan, Mike Deaver and Jim Baker called Shultz to reassure him.

Shultz told Deaver that Shultz's recommendations about senior personnel changes at the State Department were being blocked and, in some cases, undone by White House aides even after Reagan had approved them. The latest example involved Thomas Enders, the assistant secretary of state for Latin American affairs. Shultz, unhappy with Enders's performance, wanted to ease him out by making him ambassador to Spain. When Reagan called Shultz soon after Shultz's conversation with Deaver, the president said he thought Enders did not want the Madrid post. "Jesus Christ!" Shultz exclaimed as he hung up the phone. "Clark never gives up. He told the president that Enders wanted to go into private business. I told the president we had to give him a choice."[3]

Deaver called again that evening to report that the Reagans would be happy to have the Shultzes over for dinner anytime. Jim Baker reaffirmed the president's support for Shultz and said he would not renew Richard Stone's White House security pass. Shultz was gratified and amused by the flurry of calls. He knew his blunt complaints had shaken Reagan. Whether real changes would be made remained to be seen.[4] He did not have to wait long. While attending a Group of Seven economic summit meeting in Williamsburg, Virginia, Shultz learned that top intelligence and Pentagon officials had agreed, without consulting the State Department, to plant limpet mines on vessels in Nicaraguan ports, mine a major Nicaraguan river and send high-speed patrol boats into Nicaraguan waters to strike port facilities. He was furious. He instructed Ken Dam to ask the White House to put the decisions on hold. Seitz noted, "What is astonishing here—as well as indicative of the power of the national security advisor—is that while the president had made clear that GPS should run Central America policy, events such as personnel and covert action decisions were proceeding as if nothing had happened. Clark is still trying to direct things."[5]

After meeting with Clark in Williamsburg, Shultz told Seitz that everything that he thought he had cleared up with Reagan two days before seemed to have unraveled. During a break in the summit, Baker, Meese and Clark joined Shultz in his hotel suite to go over how decisions would be made about Central America. Shultz was not happy with the emerging plan, which watered down his authority. The other officials also pressed for the appointment of an ambassador to El Salvador whom Shultz thought was unqualified.[6] When Shultz got back to Washington after the summit, he was greeted with a "Managing the Central America Strategy" memo from Clark that essentially funneled all decisions through an interdepartmental group reporting to Clark. "I don't report to the NSC," Shultz grumbled. "I report to the president."[7] The next day, Deaver recounted to him Reagan's dismissive reaction to the Clark plan: "I don't want a memorandum like that. I'm not dealing with Al Haig."[8]

Shultz's effort to forge a closer relationship with the Reagans got a boost when the president and Nancy came to dinner at the Shultz's Bethesda home on June 5. Shultz, delayed at work, got home after the Reagans had arrived. They greeted him cheerfully on the front steps, looking as if they were the homeowners and hosts. A few days later, Nancy Reagan sent him a photo of the front-step tableau, with a warm, handwritten inscription: "Dear Obie and George—It was so nice of you to drop in. Wait a minute—

how did we get there first? Best regards, Nancy & Ron." During the dinner, Nancy left no doubt about her disdain for Bill Clark, and the president himself was dismissive of his national security adviser. "He's a good one to steer clear of," Reagan told Shultz.[9] Easily said, not easily done. A few days later Bud McFarlane reported to Larry Eagleburger that Clark was consulting with Henry Kissinger on a variety of topics, including relations with the Soviet Union. Kissinger informed Clark that Dobrynin had complained to him about Shultz, saying that too many aides were present when Shultz and Dobrynin met.[10]

On June 15, Shultz delivered a summation of his views about the Soviet Union to the Senate Foreign Relations Committee. The policy statement tried to bridge the widely divergent views within the administration, blending hard-line rhetoric with peaceful phrases. As he began speaking, he pointedly informed the committee that Reagan had read, edited and approved his lengthy opening statement. Unsurprisingly, the text was subject to varying interpretations, as coverage in the *Washington Post* and *New York Times* illustrated. The *Post* depicted Shultz's testimony as a reiteration of the administration's harsh policies. The *Times* portrayed it as a softer approach, opening the door to better relations. When the State Department public affairs office asked Shultz for guidance about how to interpret the testimony in light of the sharply differing accounts, he said to go with the version in the *Times*. In his mind, this was the key sentence of the testimony: "Strength and realism can deter war, but only direct dialogue and negotiation can open the path toward lasting peace."[11]

Though Shultz later looked back on the Senate appearance as a turning point in his struggle to prevail in administration Soviet policy debates, saying Reagan had "given him the authority he was looking for," his struggles were far from over.[12] In early July, Shultz learned that Andropov had sent a letter to Reagan saying the Kremlin favored "the elimination of the nuclear threat" and was committed to "the cause of peace." The language was Soviet boilerplate but it resonated with Reagan. He drafted a handwritten response, emphasizing that the United States was dedicated to abolishing nuclear weapons. He went on to say, "If we can agree on mutual, verifiable reductions in the numbers of nuclear weapons we both hold, could this not be a first step toward the elimination of all such weapons? What a blessing that would be for the people we both represent." He deleted the two sentences after Clark objected to the wording.[13] All this was news to Shultz.[14] He was pleased to hear that Reagan and Andropov were corresponding about reducing nuclear threats but aggravated that he had not been informed about the developments.

Shultz's impatience with the White House hit a new level when he discovered that White House aides were overriding his recommendations for ambassadorial posts so they could consider other candidates. In a testy call with John Herrington, the newly named head of the White House personnel office, Shultz snapped, "I consider this intolerable. I am trying to manage this department. People tell the president things with which I don't agree. . . . What are you going to do? Tell me whom I am going to work with? Who is going to be secretary of state? Who wants this job? Why does it take a phone call from me to eke out this information? Apparently there has been a meeting with the president that I didn't even know about. There has also been a meeting with Clark I didn't know about. I didn't even get to have a say. That's what really gets to me!"[15]

Shultz was particularly irked by two presidential appointments in his sphere: McFarlane as special negotiator for the Middle East, and Kissinger as chair of a bipartisan commission on Central America. The McFarlane role appeared to undercut Shultz's authority because McFarlane retained his title as deputy national security adviser and would continue to report to Clark. Though Kissinger would not be involved in active diplomacy about Central America, he and his commission would tread into territory normally handled by the secretary of state.

Larry Eagleburger and other Shultz colleagues at the State Department told Shultz the appointments were fueling a rising sense in Washington that Clark was taking control of foreign policy. The capital was abuzz with gossip that Clark was ascendant and Shultz losing power by the day. Senator Charles Percy, the Illinois Republican who chaired the Senate Foreign Relations Committee, told Powell Moore, who managed State Department liaison with Congress, that he was concerned about the derisive chatter. "Good, they'll drive me out of town," Shultz said. When Ken Dam told Shultz that no one would believe that McFarlane reported to the secretary of state on Mideast matters, Shultz magnanimously replied, "I can't destroy his negotiating effectiveness for the sake of my public image." Eagleburger warned that reporters would connect the seeming setbacks for Shultz, undermining his authority. "Perceptions have a great deal to do with your success in this town." Eagleburger said. When the others departed, Shultz told Seitz, "I have always tried to avoid reacting to the press. The point is just to do the job. But maybe they are trying to cut me down to size."[16]

While musing about his press coverage, Shultz absorbed another blow. Paul Nitze, the intermediate-range missile negotiator, had met with Reagan the day before without Shultz's knowledge.[17] More ominously, Eagleburger suspected that the Pentagon had outmaneuvered Shultz on Central America by obtaining Reagan's approval for new military and intelligence actions in Central America without consulting, or even informing, Shultz. He shared his concerns privately with Seitz, who noted in his journal at the end of the day, "GPS is feeling a little fatalistic and a little gloomy. Things are not shaping up well."[18] Just how badly they were shaping up became clear over the next few days with a series of front-page news stories about secret escalation plans in Central America, including navy and army exercises in the region and a possible blockade of Nicaraguan ports. Although there had been some preliminary discussions about the plans with Tony Motley, the new assistant secretary of state for Latin America, the proposed steps were ultimately routed to Reagan via a Pentagon–White House back channel that excluded the State Department. Shultz had not been consulted or informed about any of the decisions.

"Reagan Plans Rise in Military Moves in Latin America," the *New York Times* disclosed in its lead story on July 23: "President Reagan has approved a plan calling for a substantial increase in American military involvement in Central America and preparations for a possible limited military blockade of Nicaragua, senior administration officials said today. Military operations that the United States will soon conduct in Central America and the Caribbean are designed to lay the groundwork for the expanded American presence and the possible quarantine, the officials said."[19]

The next day, the *Times* reported, "Pentagon Seeking a Rise in Advisers in Salvador to 125": "The Defense Department has recommended to President Reagan that he raise the number of American military advisers in El Salvador to 125 next year, more than doubling the current total, senior Administration officials said today."[20]

On July 25, the *Times* disclosed, "U.S. Seeks Increase in Covert Activity in Latin America":

> The Reagan administration is preparing a major expansion of covert intelligence operations in Central America as part of a plan to increase American military activity in the region, senior Administration officials said today.
>
> The plans, which the officials said are being refined but have been approved in general by the White House, include stepped-up support for anti-Government insurgents in Nicaragua and a campaign of sabotage directed against Cuban installations in Nicaragua.
>
> The expanded program of paramilitary action, the officials said, would make the activities of the Central Intelligence Agency in Central America the most extensive covert operations mounted by the United States since the Vietnam War.[21]

On July 26, Reagan tried to blunt the blitz of alarming news coverage, declaring during a nationally televised news conference that the United States was "not seeking a larger presence" in Central America. He said that planned American military exercises were aimed at providing "a shield for democracy and development" in the region and that "we have no military plans for intervention" in the area.[22] The presidential spin was not convincing.

While Shultz was digesting all these surprises, he learned that Bud McFarlane had traveled to the Middle East the week before on a secret diplomatic mission without informing the secretary of state. State Department officials frantically tried to reconstruct what had happened, how the president had taken decisions based on partial information provided by the Pentagon and CIA, absent any involvement by the State Department. And how the White House could have dispatched McFarlane to the Middle East without consulting Shultz in advance. As they collected details, Seitz noted, "There is utter confusion everywhere. Apparently there has been a disastrous failure in coordination and discipline." In fact, the Pentagon and CIA had managed to bypass the normal decision-making process and get Reagan to sign off on a series of escalatory steps in Central America. Shultz was shocked. "There is complete disarray in the administration," he told his top aides on July 25. Then, alone with Seitz, he said, "Don't worry. I am going to raise holy unshirted hell!"[23]

As July 25 unfolded, Shultz made several visits to the White House. During the first, he and Clark met privately with Reagan. Clark told the president that all was going smoothly on Central America and that "everyone was on board." Shultz countered that that was simply not true. He reported afterward to Seitz that Reagan had not reacted to the conflicting accounts.[24] With a second meeting with Reagan planned for that afternoon, Shultz said, "I guess I'll have to do it with the bark off." Before Shultz headed back to the White House, Eagleburger confirmed that Reagan had made a series of decisions the week before absent consultation with his secretary of state and the State Department. "Apparently, GPS has been colossally blind-sided," Seitz noted.[25]

When Shultz got to the Oval Office, he found Reagan in the company of Clark, Meese, Baker and Vice President Bush. Shultz unloaded: "I can't be your secretary of state under these circumstances. . . . Either you want a Secretary of State who is sort of an errand boy—if that's what you want, that's not me—or you want somebody that you have some confidence in. And I remember back in Camp David when you and I met after you asked me to be Secretary of State and we talked about how this was going to work. And I have tried faithfully to work with the White House and not against the White House. And so I'm gone. I've got tenure. Goodbye."[26] To underscore his impatience, Shultz handed Reagan a list of potential successors, including Clark, Jeane Kirkpatrick and Henry Kissinger.[27] Reagan, clearly shaken by the resignation threat, assured Shultz that he wanted him to remain as secretary. "He wanted me to do the job," Shultz recalled. "He had no idea how these things had happened; he could understand how they affected me. I had made myself clear in front of everyone, but even so, I left the Oval Office without a feeling that a definitive change would be made."[28]

Once back at his State Department office, Shultz described the dramatic showdown to Eagleburger and Seitz. He told them that Reagan and the others "seemed astonished at my perceptions" and that "Clark was very aggrieved." A few hours later, Shultz and Clark dueled again over the phone. Clark told a disbelieving Shultz that Tony Motley had been consulted about the escalatory steps and accused Motley and his staff of peddling a story that the military maneuvers were being conducted without presidential approval. Shultz shot back, "I don't see how anyone could be putting out that story. The military never does anything like that without orders."[29]

As the startling day came to an end, John Hughes, the State Department spokesman, informed Shultz that *Time* magazine was working on a story about Clark that implied Shultz had no interest in Central America matters. "This unraveling of my image is a problem," Shultz said. "If they

want to paint me as a hapless, irrelevant person it will be hard to correct."
Shultz's secretary came into his office to let him know that he was invited
to an informal dinner with Reagan the following week, a sign that Reagan
knew he needed to reassure his secretary of state that his views would be
heard. Shultz's parting words to Seitz: "They just don't seem to understand.
And Bill Clark said some things that simply weren't true."[30] Reagan recorded his own reactions to the turbulent events of July 25 in a diary entry
that acknowledged Shultz's irritation but seemed remarkably oblivious to
its cause. "The press has been dishing up stories all describing a situation
in which Bill C. and George S. are battling for supremacy. It is totally false
but George thought he might be so tarnished that he was a liability to me.
I told him he had my confidence & that it would be a disaster for all of us
if he left."[31]

Over the next few days, Shultz and his inner circle pieced together the
decision-making on Central America. At a critical moment when State
representatives were still participating, the Pentagon had unexpectedly
stopped talking about its proposals for increased military actions in Central America. The abrupt disappearance of the proposals had baffled State
officials, but they surmised at the time that the Defense Department had
decided to withdraw its plan. Instead, unknown to State, the Pentagon sent
its plan directly to Clark and Reagan, who approved it. The brazen sub-
terfuge astonished Shultz and his colleagues. They were even angrier over
Clark's misleading accounts of his role and his false assertions that the State
Department had been fully involved. Reflecting on Clark's role, Shultz, recalling Al Haig's role as White House chief of staff before Nixon resigned,
said, "I dealt with Haig when I was at Treasury until I learned that Haig did
not have integrity. He was deceitful, so I stopped dealing with him. I think
I have the same problem now. Clark does not have integrity." Shultz told
Seitz, "This is the worst botched thing I have seen in government foreign
policy. It's all because of a headstrong attitude. It's bound to happen when
the NSC tries to run things. They just don't have the horses. The press is not
distorting what happened."[32]

Seeking relief, Shultz invited Seitz, Motley and John Hughes to dine
with him and O'Bie in a quiet corner at the Four Seasons Hotel in Georgetown. O'Bie confided to Seitz that Shultz was frazzled and awaking often
at 3:30 a.m. Shultz told his dinner guests that he was amazed by the Penta-

gon's contempt for congressional oversight. "I keep pointing out that Congress is provided for in the Constitution. What I find incomprehensible is their disrespect for the Constitution and constitutional procedure." Shultz also reported that Weinberger seemed puzzled by Shultz's outrage over the handling of the Central America decisions. At least Weinberger was not deceitful, in Shultz's view. Given the serial meltdown in administration policy making, Weinberger's personal conduct momentarily looked almost benign to Shultz: "He's completely honest. No double-dealing."[33]

The dinner interlude offered only a brief respite from the tumult. The next day, July 29, Hughes reported that the *Time* story in the works seemed likely to say that Clark was running foreign policy, not Shultz. "Clark has made a mess of this and will try to lay it off on us," Shultz said. "I won't accept that." In a call with Jim Baker, Shultz again expressed his dismay at the policy-making process: "I get the feeling I made no impact on you people the other day. It has gotten to a point where we can't work together. There is too much maneuvering. I can't trust what I'm told. Trust is the coin of the realm. When you lie and maneuver you are in bad shape. You know this town. . . . It's gotten to the point where one of us has got to be replaced."[34]

Hughes told Seitz that *New York Times* columnist James Reston had mused with him about a Reston call with Shultz in which Shultz had resurrected a piece of Reston advice from years earlier: keep a diary and know when it is time to go. Reston wanted to know if Shultz was implying he was about to quit. Late that afternoon, Nancy Reagan called Shultz, and they conferred privately. But before heading home, Shultz recounted the call to Seitz. The first lady had essentially decapitated Clark. "Nancy Reagan is furious," Shultz reported. "She thinks Clark ought to be fired. She thinks he doesn't have the president's best interests at heart, which I don't accept. But she is angry." Shultz added, "Clark is in a rage. I think our relations are irreparable." Seitz replied, "Your strength is patience. Let it emerge and choose your time."[35] Whether Shultz fully grasped the import of the first lady's call that day is unclear. In his memoir, with the benefit of hindsight and some positive spin, he said he understood that it was only a matter of time before Clark was cashiered. Seitz's contemporaneous journal suggests Shultz was a good deal less sure of himself and Clark's fate. "Oh, I suppose we could work together for another year or so but things won't be the same at all," he told Seitz.[36]

The package of stories in *Time* that appeared a few days later was a blow to Shultz, casting him as a dwindling figure in the Reagan firmament. But for a small audience—Nancy Reagan, Mike Deaver and Jim Baker—it was more damaging to Clark, depicting him as the driving force behind a dangerously confrontational escalation of American military intervention in Central America. Combined with the administration's strident handling of Soviet relations in general, the *Time* coverage added to a picture of Ronald Reagan as a reckless leader who might propel the nation into a volatile confrontation with the Kremlin. That was exactly the image that Nancy Reagan and her allies feared would undermine the Reagan presidency and tarnish his legacy. Clark later ruefully recalled that Alexander Haig had warned him, "Once you appear in this town on the cover of *Time* or *Newsweek*, count your days in the shop."[37]

The cover featured an illustration of Clark's face and the headline: "The Big Stick Approach":

> "We don't want war, but . . ."
> Maneuvering the Military
> Uproar over Covert Aid[38]

The main story, about Clark, was headlined "The Man with the President's Ear": "After a rocky start, Clark takes charge in the White House." Making clear in a publisher's note that Clark had cooperated extensively with *Time* reporters, including several interviews and a private dinner, the story stated:

> The ascendancy of William Patrick Clark in Washington has been swift and, to many, unsettling. . . .
>   Indeed, his management ability, infighting skills and close ties to Reagan have made him, in the judgment of many, the second most powerful man in the White House. Clark has encouraged the President to follow his raw, conservative instincts rather than the more pragmatic and politically savvy agendas suggested by White House Chief of Staff James Baker. This uncritical "let Reagan be Reagan" approach has resulted in a harder line and some political embarrassments.[39]

Time dismissed Shultz in a separate story under the headline "Disappearing Act at Foggy Bottom. The State Department's Influence Continues to Wane":

> Shultz has been losing influence to National Security Adviser William Clark and other hard-line presidential advisers. . . .

The loss of the State Department's authority is in part due to Shultz's own personality. Although he has enormous leverage over the Reaganauts, who can scarcely afford to lose another Secretary of State, he is temperamentally reluctant to argue his case in public, or even very strongly in private. Like the good Marine he used to be, he soldiers on. But both his reticence and his unwillingness to take firm policy positions leave the impression—and hence add to the reality—that he is not in control. The professionals who work with him can only hope that those who have usurped the department's role might overextend themselves, and thus let the pendulum of power swing back toward State.[40]

Reflecting on his situation in the wake of the *Time* stories and weeks of rising frustration, Shultz said, "I have had two hell-raising sessions with the president. The first one did bring order for a while but nothing really happened. What the press writes is usually correct fundamentally, despite distortions. Now we have a national security adviser with the bit in his teeth and lashing out in all directions. It makes the president look like an unstable war-monger." Weighing the prospect of having to testify to the Senate Foreign Relations Committee about Central America, he said, "Now the question is what to do. If I go testify, I have to defend the mess I didn't create. . . . One thing the press doesn't like about me is that I don't give them any news. It all goes to the White House, which is as it should be. They really haven't followed up on my Soviet testimony, though I was laying out the policy right there on the table." Turning introspective for a moment, he mused: "People are now goading at me to raise hell, to take charge. They don't like my nature. I'm 'too easy going,' although it is not always what it seems. If RR wants it to go this way, it is not my job to prevent it. But I must point out that it makes me less effective." At the end of the day, Shultz, Seitz and Ken Dam revisited the recent developments. Shultz said, "The path of least resistance is to shut up and see what happens. The trouble is, nothing will happen."[41]

At a White House meeting the next day with Republican congressional leaders, Weinberger astonished Shultz by arguing that the administration had withheld advance word from lawmakers about the military maneuvers in Central America for a number of reasons, including fear of leaks to the press. "I almost contradicted him, but I bit my tongue. I wanted to say the complaint about no consultation was legitimate, that we blew it, and that Democrats are now leading the charge."[42]

That evening, NBC News reported that Shultz would not serve in a second Reagan term and might not last until the end of the first term. "I have never said anything like that," Shultz sighed.[43] Before Shultz headed home, he took a call from Clark, who told him that the first lady was unhappy with Clark's performance. Shultz dryly observed, "She's hard to beat."[44] Hard, indeed. The next day, Vice President Bush phoned Shultz, telling him, "I'm on your side," and inviting Shultz to swing by for a drink. That evening Reagan called Shultz. The president said he wanted to schedule two private meetings a week with Shultz to discuss foreign policy matters and instructed Shultz to let Deaver know when to start adding the sessions to Reagan's calendar. When Shultz, wary of excluding Clark, suggested that the national security adviser ought to attend the meetings in a listening mode, Reagan replied, "Let's try it with just the two of us first."[45] Within a few days, Deaver sent Shultz a private note informing him that the president would meet with Shultz on Wednesdays and Fridays at 1:30 p.m.

The new arrangement did not immediately solve the problem of tangled lines of authority. As Bud McFarlane traveled about the Middle East in his new role as special envoy, while retaining his title as deputy national security adviser, he dealt directly with Clark and bypassed Shultz. "Maybe this is just because the White House has better telephone equipment," Shultz grumbled. He worried that the NSC's direct role in managing Mideast policy was likely to repeat the dysfunction caused by Clark's leading role on Central American affairs. Shultz sadly noted that Reagan seemed to believe that decisions about Central America had been taken in a methodical fashion.[46]

The next twist of the cold war—the Soviet interception of a South Korean commercial airliner that strayed into Soviet airspace—jolted Washington as Shultz returned from the Berkshires several weeks later, convulsing East-West relations and reshaping Shultz's role in the Reagan administration.

CHAPTER FIFTEEN

The Target Is Destroyed

THE SOVIET ATTACK ON Korean Airlines Flight 007 hit Washington like a bolt from the blue on September 1, 1983. Over the next frantic hours and days, Shultz seized control of American foreign policy. Emboldened by his showdown with Reagan over Central America policy, fed up with the foreign policy disputes and sensing that Reagan's impulse to improve relations with Moscow would give him cover, Shultz momentarily cast aside the hesitation that had defined much of his time as secretary of state. He secured Reagan's support for a tempered response, overcoming opposition from Weinberger, Clark and other officials who wanted to freeze relations with Moscow and cut off communication with the Kremlin. Although the Soviet attack temporarily spiked cold war tensions, and Shultz's rivals remained formidable opponents, the episode enhanced Shultz's clout. With a few months, his prospects improved even more when Reagan removed Clark as national security adviser.

Shultz had returned to work on August 29, refreshed from a two-week vacation at the family farm in Massachusetts. Arriving at the State Department before 7:00 a.m., he declared, "Well, we've returned to a peaceful world." He happily informed colleagues he had played four rounds of golf in a row and scored in the 70s each time. A computer had been installed behind his desk while he was away, a novelty at the time. "GPS is delighted with this," Seitz noted. "He said he looked forward to playing with it. I said he would never use it."[1] Shultz spent the next three days dealing with a variety of issues in the Middle East, Central America and Europe. Tensions in Lebanon remained especially high as the Israeli military occupation continued in parts of the country and a contingent of US Marines that had been sent to help keep the peace came under artillery fire at their base on the outskirts of Beirut.

Much of Washington was still on vacation, including the president and first lady, who were spending August at their California ranch. Nancy Reagan called Shultz from the ranch late in the morning to say she opposed the proposed nominee for ambassador to Belgium because she thought he was weak and his wife unwell. Shultz told her he was not the State Department preferred choice. Nancy reported that the president wanted to talk with Shultz and that he should place a secure call to him. When Shultz and Reagan connected, they talked briefly about arms control matters and a recent letter from Andropov that contained some new proposals. The relative tranquility ended abruptly as August expired and one of the most shocking events of the cold war played out in the night sky over the Soviet Far East.

For five hours and twenty-three minutes since a refueling stop in Anchorage, Korean Airlines (KAL) Flight 007 from New York to Seoul has drifted ever farther from the normal commercial flight vector across the North Pacific. It is now 360 miles off track, flying for the second time directly toward heavily defended Soviet airspace. Captain Chun Byung-in, a veteran South Korean military and commercial pilot, and his cockpit colleagues do not realize their Boeing 747, with 240 passengers and 29 crew members aboard, is dangerously lost, hunted by Soviet air defense forces activated to highest alert by the errant flight path of the aircraft. Soviet commanders suspect it is a military plane on a spy mission.

A flight attendant enters the 747's cockpit: "Captain, sir, would you like to have a meal?" "What? Meal?" Captain Chun asks, apparently awakened by the flight attendant. "Is it already time to eat?"

He is nearing the maximum work time that Korean Airline pilots are permitted to log each month and is completing a five–day, multi-time-zone flight marathon that has taken him from Seoul to Anchorage to New York to Toronto to

Anchorage. As the plane left Alaska, Chun had made one of two fateful mistakes. He had failed to switch the plane's autopilot system from the magnetic compass heading used at takeoff to the aircraft's inertial navigation system (INS), the automated device that guides modern airplanes to their chosen destination. Or he had made the switch too late in the flight for the INS to capture the desired flight track. Either way, the autopilot remained fixed on a constant compass heading that guided it inexorably toward the Soviet Pacific coast. Captain Chun and his cockpit colleagues have failed to detect the errant track as the deviation grows by the hour.

Most passengers, including Representative Larry McDonald, a Georgia Democrat and national chairman of the far-right John Birch Society, are dozing, reading or watching an in-flight movie, unaware their flight has strayed far off course. The reassuring hum of the 747's four powerful jet engines permeates the cabin as the plane streaks across the partly moonlit sky. Fifty-three of the passengers are Americans. Six miles away, a Soviet fighter pilot, Major Gennadi Osipovich, is stalking the Korean airliner in his Sukhoi-15 fighter jet. His call sign is 805. A Soviet ground controller, code-named Deputat, delivers new orders from General Aleksandr Kornukov, commander of the local Soviet air defense units: "The target is military. Upon violation of the state border, destroy the target. Arm the weapons."

The distinctive shape of the 747 jumbo jet, with its humpback upper deck, is known to air travelers and pilots around the world. As he closes in on Flight 007, Major Osipovich spots two rows of windows, which he recognizes as the hallmark of a Boeing jumbo commercial airliner. The plane's navigation lights are flashing, another indication that the plane is not on a clandestine mission. He nevertheless decides the intruder is no ordinary commercial flight. "I knew this was a civilian plane," he recalled years later, "but this meant nothing. It is easy to turn a civilian type of plane into one for military use." Major Osipovich and his commanders have decided it must be an enemy aircraft engaged in a deliberate, illegal violation of Soviet airspace.

The Soviet calculation is partly influenced by the concurrent flight of an American intelligence-gathering plane, an RC-135, on a surveillance mission in international airspace off the Kamchatka Peninsula to monitor the final flight phase of an expected Soviet long-range missile test. The American plane passed within eighty miles of Flight 007 earlier in the evening but by now has returned to its Alaskan base. At least some Soviet air defense officials fear the mysterious airplane now in their sights may be the American spy plane. Flight 007 brazenly flew over Kamchatka ninety minutes earlier. Other Soviet officers are not so sure.

As the plane nears Sakhalin Island, Soviet territory studded with defense bases, General Kornukov consults the commander of the Soviet Far Eastern Air Force, General Valeri Kamenski: "We must find out, maybe it is some civilian craft or God knows what," General Kamenski warns General Kornukov.

"What civilian?" General Kornukov caustically replies. "It has flown over Kamchatka. It came from the ocean without identification. I am giving the order to attack if it crosses the State border." General Kornukov instructs the ground controller to tell Major Osipovich to intercept the plane, rock his wings to signal that the aircraft must land and force it to head for Sokol, site of a Sakhalin military airfield.

The Soviet pilot's efforts to get the attention of the flight crew aboard Flight 007 are unsuccessful. He pulls up alongside the Korean plane and fires his cannon, shooting 520 rounds into the night sky. The shells do not contain tracers and are not visible as they streak by Flight 007. The Korean pilots apparently do not see the muzzle flashes of the Soviet jet as its cannon fires. Osipovich flashes his navigation lights, an international aviation signal to pilots of a nearby plane that they should follow the signaling plane. Again, the Korean crew does not respond. With time rapidly dwindling before the foreign aircraft reenters international airspace, Osipovich, who speaks only Russian, makes no effort to establish radio contact with Flight 007. "How can I talk with him?" he later said. "You must know the language."

With the plane about to exit Soviet airspace and head out over the Sea of Japan, Kornukov fears it will again escape. "Oh, fuck," he shouts at ground controllers. "He is already getting out into neutral waters. Engage afterburner immediately. Bring in the MiG-23 as well," he tells them, ordering a second warplane to attack. "While you are wasting time, it will fly right out," he complains. "Destroy the target," Kornukov orders.

By this time, Major Osipovich has pulled up behind the commercial jet and armed his weapons. The ground commander relays the order: "Launch!"

Seconds later, Major Osipovich replies: "I have executed the launch. The target is destroyed."

In fact, it is gravely damaged but not destroyed. Flight 007 staggers in the night sky six miles above Sakhalin Island as at least one of two missiles slams into the Boeing 747. "What's happened?" Captain Chun yells as he struggles to *control the giant plane. The plane heaves upward and rolls slightly rightward. It continues to climb for at least seventeen seconds, reaching a maximum altitude of 38,250 feet. The jet's four engines are still operating. Captain Chun does not seem to realize the problem is a missile strike, not a terrifying mechanical breakdown.*

One minute and forty-four seconds after the missile strike, the 747's electric power cuts out and the cockpit recording system shuts down. For another ten harrowing minutes, the plane plummets earthward. It hits the ocean at roughly six hundred miles per hour, killing anyone who somehow survived the heart-stopping descent.

"805, did you launch one missile?" the Soviet ground commander calmly asks Osipovich.

"Launched both," he replies matter-of-factly.

"Roger, well done."[2]

It was a few hours before dawn, Tokyo time, on September 1, 1983, midafternoon on August 31 in Washington. Labor Day weekend was fast approaching. President Reagan was vacationing at Rancho del Cielo, his seven-hundred-acre retreat atop the Santa Ynez Mountains overlooking Santa Barbara. Most of his top aides were enjoying the last days of a late-summer break at their own vacation destinations before returning to Washington. Within a few hours, one of the most brutal incidents of the cold war would shock the world and engulf Reagan and his national security team, including Shultz. How they responded would shape the course of American-Soviet relations for months to come, possibly throwing the cold war into a deep freeze or even igniting a military conflict between the two superpowers.

For the first time since becoming secretary of state a year earlier, Shultz took control of American foreign policy as the KAL 007 crisis played out. He designed and executed a nuanced response that held the Kremlin accountable while keeping open lines of communication. He moved quickly and decisively while several players, including Reagan, were out of position at vacation sites. It was a critical moment for Shultz in his struggle to move from being a muzzled minority voice in the highest councils of the administration to emerging by 1985 as the dominant figure and indispensable partner of the president in the fashioning of American foreign policy. "It was a vindication," Shultz said many years later, looking back at the jetliner episode. He defied the advice of hard-line colleagues, and the president supported him. Recalling the attack on the Korean airliner, Shultz said, "I knew where Reagan was. The bottom line when it came down to it: he thought the same as me."[3]

William Casey was the first senior American official to learn about the disappearance of the Korean airliner and the possibility that Soviet defense forces had blown it out of the sky. The initial intelligence was imprecise. Not long after the plane failed to appear as scheduled in Seoul, Korean Airlines reported that it had landed safely on Sakhalin Island. News agencies, starting with the Korean Broadcasting System, picked up the story, flashing word of a forced landing on Sakhalin around the world. An aide to Representative McDonald told reporters after a briefing at the Pentagon that "indications are" that Soviet forces had forced the jetliner to land. Korean Airlines said it would immediately start work to make arrangements to transfer the passengers to Seoul.

As the hours passed, Japanese and American intercepts of Soviet military communications, including the staccato conversations between Major Osipovich and his ground controllers, revealed that a Soviet missile strike had terminated the flight. Casey notified Clark that a Korean commercial airliner had disappeared over the Sea of Japan. Clark, stationed at a Santa Barbara seaside hotel not far from the Reagan ranch, phoned the president to let him know. It was 7:30 p.m. in California. Clark called again a few hours later to relay word from Casey that Soviet forces might have shot down the plane. "Bill, let's pray it's not true," Reagan told Clark. "If it is, let's be careful not to overreact to this. We have too much going on with the Soviets on arms control. We must not derail our progress. We cannot derail our negotiations."[4]

As more information poured in overnight, including some of the Soviet radio communications, it became clear that Soviet forces had shadowed the Korean airliner for hours, then attacked it, but details remained sketchy. The State Department operations center, staffed twenty-four hours a day and the nerve center for international crises communications, called Shultz at his home in Bethesda on September 1 at 6:30 a.m. to tell him a Korean passenger plane had probably been shot down by the Soviet Union the evening before. He hung up the phone, shaken by the news. This was not going to be a quiet early September day in Washington. He informed O'Bie that an international crisis was brewing and that their Labor Day weekend plans would be disrupted, dressed quickly and headed to the State Department headquarters just a few blocks from the Lincoln Memorial.

When Shultz got to the State Department, initial reports left unclear what exactly had happened to the airliner. Shultz spent several hours handling other issues. A few hours later, Edwin Meese called the presidential ranch, waking Reagan and informing him that the missing plane had almost certainly been downed by Soviet air defense forces. Instead of another vacation day horseback riding and relaxing with Nancy, the president confronted an unexpected calamity. "My God, have they gone mad?" Reagan said. "What the hell are they thinking of?"[5] Though Shultz and Reagan had not yet conferred about the attack, the secretary of state's reaction mirrored the president's. Both men were appalled and eager to denounce the attack and rally world opinion against the Kremlin. Yet they were anxious not to suspend relations with Moscow, interrupt nuclear arms control negotiations or cut off high-level communication between Soviet and American leaders as President Jimmy Carter had done after the 1979 Soviet invasion of Afghanistan.

The first order of business was to let the world know about the attack. In a pre-internet era when global communications were not instantaneous, news of the downing of Flight 007 had not yet flashed around the world. A few hours after Shultz arrived at his State Department office, the National Security Agency produced a partial transcript of the radio communications between Major Osipovich and his ground commanders. It eliminated any doubt about what had brought down the plane. Shultz and his colleagues successfully pressed the NSA to declassify the intercepts so Shultz could make the transcript public, overcoming concerns that the secret methods used to capture the transmissions would be compromised.

Despite the potential global reverberations of the Soviet attack, Reagan was not initially inclined to cut short his vacation. Larry Speakes, the White House press secretary, told the reporters who had traveled to Santa Barbara with the presidential party, "There are no plans for the president to return to Washington earlier than anticipated." With Reagan out of town, Shultz stepped to center stage. He prepared to break the news of the attack to the world at the State Department morning press briefing. The appearance would have the double benefit of pinning the blame on the Soviet Union and demonstrating that Shultz was managing the American response. As Seitz noted, "It would demonstrate that he was in charge."[6] Unlike Haig following the assassination attempt on Reagan, Shultz could do so without sounding like he was usurping presidential authority.

"People began to give me drafts of what I should say," Shultz recalled. "I found them all dangerously overdrawn, couched in an ominous tone that might suggest some form of U.S. military reaction or retaliation. I rejected the confrontational rhetoric." Just before 11:00 a.m., he walked into the State Department ground-floor pressroom, surprising reporters, who assumed the days leading to Labor Day weekend would be a languid news period. The appearance of the grim-looking secretary of state behind the lectern rather than the department spokesman instantly signaled that something significant was up. Shultz, usually impassive, made no effort to disguise his anger as he read a terse statement describing the stalking of Flight 007 and the attack, quoting from the NSA transcript: "The United States reacts with revulsion to this attack. Loss of life appears to be heavy. We can see no excuse whatsoever for this appalling act." Roger Mudd, the NBC News anchorman, described Shultz's performance as "controlled fury."[7]

When he returned to his office, Shultz called Reagan. It was their first conversation since the downing of KAL 007. "This has great implications," Shultz told Reagan. "We've got going an effort to think this through and what our follow-on activities should be." Shultz advised Reagan that there would be intense pressure to cancel a meeting that Shultz was scheduled to hold a few days later in Madrid with Andrei Gromyko, the Soviet foreign minister. Shultz said he thought he should go ahead with the meeting and use it bluntly to register American disgust at the incident and to demand a Soviet explanation and apology.

Later that afternoon, Reagan issued a statement through the White House castigating the Kremlin: "I speak for Americans and for the people everywhere who cherish civilized values in protesting the Soviet attack on an unarmed civilian passenger plane. Words can scarcely express our revulsion at this horrifying act of violence." By this time, Reagan had decided to upend his vacation and return to Washington. Shortly after noon, the Soviet embassy in Washington sent word to Shultz from Gromyko that Soviet defense forces had warned the airliner that it was flying through

Soviet airspace and that plane had likely crashed.[8] It was the first of many deceitful Soviet accounts about KAL 007.

Shultz's modulated policy response seemed timid to other senior national security officials. As word spread about the shoot-down, most favored a much more aggressive response. Weinberger and several White House national security aides called for suspending all contacts with the Kremlin, including the nuclear arms talks. They urged Shultz to cancel the Gromyko meeting. The macho mood in the capital was summed up by a desk clerk at the Four Seasons Hotel in Georgetown that evening as Shultz crossed the lobby on his way to dinner. He shouted, "Hey, Mr. Secretary, let 'em have it."[9] Shultz resisted the pressure, determined not to let the incident eliminate any hope of easing tensions with the Kremlin. Reagan, suppressing his own outrage, supported Shultz. Sticking to the Shultz approach was far from easy. Misleading Soviet statements about the incident angered American officials as the Kremlin tried to suggest that an American surveillance plane gathering intelligence off the Soviet coast had entered Soviet airspace, igniting the confrontation. Moscow also suggested that the Korean plane might have been on an intelligence mission itself.

Even as the Kremlin propaganda machine cranked out public denials and misleading information, Andropov was privately incensed at the defense commanders for attacking the Korean plane. He ordered Ambassador Dobrynin to cut short his vacation and return immediately to Washington. "Try to do your utmost to dampen this needless conflict bit by bit," he told Dobrynin. "Our military made a gross blunder by shooting down the airliner and it probably will take us a long time to get out of this mess." Dobrynin recalled: "Andropov cursed 'those blockheads of generals who care not a bit for grand questions of politics' and put our relations with the United States on the verge of a complete break. 'Just think of all the effort we have put in to improve them, and there they are making a mess of the whole thing.'"[10] Andropov was prepared to admit the attack was a mistake, Dobrynin said, but the defense minister, Dimitry Ustinov, objected and Andropov did not press the issue. Dobrynin speculated that Andropov's failing health—he was now on dialysis—might have played a role. As Dobrynin noted in his memoirs, the Kremlin was also not in the habit of admitting error. The Reagan administration had no inkling of Andropov's reaction. Even the most advanced American spy technology could not penetrate the inner councils of the Kremlin.

The next day, September 2, Reagan convened an early-evening meeting of top officials to go over what they knew about the Soviet attack and what to do about it. Weinberger pressed the president to call off the Shultz meeting with Gromyko and suspend arms talks. Treasury Secretary Donald Regan argued for biting economic sanctions. "I can't begin to tell you all the things Cap suggested," Shultz told colleagues.[11] Shultz's views were informed by an observation from Arthur Hartman, the American ambassador in Moscow, who noted that the United States should not be surprised by brutish Soviet behavior or act as if it were. Cold-blooded conduct was a Kremlin hallmark. Hartman pointed out that Jimmy Carter had seemed astonished by the Soviet invasion of Afghanistan, a reaction that made Carter appear to be naïve. Shultz borrowed the Hartman point at the White House meeting, contrasting the Reagan and Carter administrations' view of the Soviet Union. "I think Ronald Reagan bought the idea," he told Seitz following the meeting. Shultz said it was important to make the issue "the USSR versus the world."[12]

As Labor Day weekend began on Saturday, September 3, a chipper Shultz, buoyed by Reagan's support on the KAL 007 case, decided some recreation was in order despite the unfolding crisis. He called Mike Deaver at 8:00 a.m. to invite Reagan to join him that afternoon for a round of golf at the Burning Tree course in Bethesda. A few hours later Deaver reported that the president was game but Shultz would have to select a different golf club because Burning Tree did not admit women. They settled on the Chevy Chase Country Club. For Shultz, the outing promised to be a preview of an October weekend with Reagan at Augusta National Golf Club, the Georgia home of the Masters Tournament. As the hours passed on September 3 with meetings at the State Department and White House, Shultz and Reagan gave up on the golf outing in Chevy Chase.[13]

Reagan used his weekly Saturday-morning radio address to the nation to talk about the downing of KAL 007. The speech captured the essence of the administration response: strong verbal condemnation, emphasis on international rather than exclusively American outrage, coupled with relatively mild actions. Reagan told the American people, "This murder of innocent civilians is a serious international issue between the Soviet Union and civilized people everywhere who cherish individual rights and value human life. It is up to all of us, leaders and citizens of the world, to deal with the Soviets in a calm, controlled, but absolutely firm manner."[14] As if to underscore the measured American response, the Agriculture Department announced the same day the first sales of American grain to Moscow under a new five-year grain agreement.

The news drew immediate criticism from members of Congress. Leslie Gelb of the *Times* summarized the trade-offs for Reagan: "In the short run, the incident lends great weight to Mr. Reagan's portrayal of the Soviet Union as an 'evil empire.' It strengthens him politically on the Pentagon budget and Central America and diplomatically in marshaling support in Europe for deploying new missiles. But in the long run, the harder Mr. Reagan comes down on Moscow now, the more difficult it will be to improve relations later. By Presidential election time, he may need to show progress in reducing Soviet-American tensions and producing an arms control treaty."[15]

On Monday, September 5, as debate continued within the administration, Shultz successfully urged Reagan to reject a proposal to expel 269 suspected KGB agents operating under diplomatic cover in the United States. He told the president the Kremlin would retaliate by expelling American intelligence officers and diplomats based in the Soviet Union, making the KAL 007 case appear to be primarily an American-Soviet confrontation. Only a few days had passed since news of the Soviet attack, but Shultz was prevailing inside the administration at a critical cold war moment. "It was a vindication," Shultz said many years later, looking back at the jetliner episode.[16] Reagan asserted himself in Shultz's favor, cutting through the opposition within his administration, acting on the more temperate instincts he had revealed to Shultz at dinner during the February blizzard. Seitz could sense a change in Shultz's mood: "By and large my impression is that GPS is feeling pretty good. He is rested, confident and on top. He controlled the KAL incident and our reaction. . . . RR has made a number of gestures in his direction to demonstrate his regard. GPS is enjoying himself."[17]

That evening, Reagan delivered a nationally televised address about the downing of the Korean plane, calling the incident "the Korean airline massacre" and "an act of barbarism." He announced new limitations on cultural, scientific and diplomatic exchanges with the Soviet Union and declared that Washington would work with the thirteen nations that had citizens aboard the plane to seek reparations for the families of those killed.[18] Reagan said he was still planning to send Shultz to meet with Gromyko in Madrid later that week. As Seitz noted the next day, the speech "had a lot of bark but not much bite."[19]

Before departing for Madrid, Shultz talked with several aides concerning his philosophy of using American military strength to signal adversaries about the seriousness of Washington's interests in global trouble spots, including the Middle East and Central America. Though he did not refer directly to the marine drill sergeant's admonition to him in boot camp about pointing a rifle at someone, the lecture was implicit in his comments. Shultz told the aides that the administration had to be careful about sending the USS *New Jersey*, a battleship, to the eastern Mediterranean to demonstrate its resolve to support the Lebanese government and prevent Syrian-backed militia forces from overrunning the country. "We can't put ships in the eastern Mediterranean just to have their pictures taken."[20]

In midafternoon, Deaver phoned on a secure line with major news—Clark was being removed as national security adviser. He would go to the Department of the Interior, replacing Secretary James Watt, who had generated serial controversies with his antienvironmental agenda and insensitive comments about African Americans and Jews. Deaver told Shultz that Jeane Kirkpatrick, Bud McFarlane, Brent Scowcroft and Jim Baker were the leading candidates to succeed Clark. Shultz instructed Seitz and Charles Hill, another aide, to think about the pros and cons of each candidate, though he and his colleagues instantly knew that Kirkpatrick would be unacceptable to Shultz. Curiously, there was no sense of jubilation that Clark, who had done so much to limit Shultz's influence and his access to Reagan, would vacate the White House.

A meeting with Reagan that evening slightly deflated Shultz's expectations about working on a variety of issues with the Kremlin despite KAL 007. The president told him to stick strictly to human rights issues when talking with Gromyko. "Now our attitude is that we will continue with the arms control talks, but that's it. Nothing else."[21] Before the attack on the Korean plane, Shultz had hoped to use the Madrid meeting with Gromyko for a wide-ranging discussion of issues that would lead to a second Gromyko meeting in New York later in the month at the UN General Assembly. The ultimate goal was a Reagan-Andropov summit meeting in 1984.

Once in Madrid to see Gromyko and attend a multinational conference on East-West security issues, Shultz found America's European allies wary of confronting Moscow with more than a few mild sanctions, including suspending air travel to the Soviet Union for two weeks. He considered, but decided against, walking out of the conference when Gromyko addressed the gathering. Shultz's meeting with the Soviet foreign minister was at the American ambassador's residence in Madrid. He got there first and waited tensely in the study, telling Seitz, "It's hard for me to greet someone without smiling." Earlier in the day, O'Bie told Seitz how little Shultz looked forward to confrontational meetings because he far preferred to talk through problems.[22]

The showdown with Gromyko proved to be among the most acrimonious of the cold war. Rather than wait at the front entrance of the residence to greet Gromyko as he stepped from his limousine, Shultz sent Ambassador Hartman to welcome the foreign minister. The meeting room, the ambassador's dining room, was unadorned—no bottles of mineral water or other refreshments on the oval table, no flower arrangements. Shultz declined to shake hands with Gromyko. Jack Matlock, a national security council aide who accompanied Shultz to Madrid, described the encounter:

> When Shultz announced that he was prepared to discuss only the Korean airliner incident and started to set forth the American position, Gromyko exploded in fury and stood up as if to leave, literally throwing his glasses on the table. . . . Gromyko, pacing the floor, started a harangue that went on for a full twenty minutes. In his excitement he frequently interrupted Viktor Sukhodrev, his interpreter, in mid-sentence, so Shultz grasped only snippets of Gromyko's outburst.
>
> Shultz stood with a look of amazement on his face and interjected periodically that he was following President Reagan's instructions. Gromyko thundered that *he*, the foreign minister of the Soviet Union, was not subordinate to Reagan and did not take orders from him. Those of us who were present were glad that a table separated the two. Shultz was outwardly calm, but his cheeks were flushed with anger.[23]

Seitz, who waited down the hall during the meeting, could hear Shultz's angry voice booming through the doors. Shultz told reporters after the meeting that Gromyko's responses to him were "totally unacceptable." He added, "This is not the end of the matter." Back in the residence study, Shultz called Reagan. "The meeting was totally unsatisfactory," he told the president. "Gromyko couldn't bring himself to face any of the real questions. It became so outrageous that I just ended the meeting. I'm sorry I can't give a better report on the Russians, but that's no surprise." Before heading to bed after midnight, Shultz reflected on the Gromyko meeting. "I really don't think he was expecting anything so harsh from me. He just can't get it through his thick head."[24] The *New York Times* summed up the state of play: "As a result of the increasingly bitter exchanges between Soviet and American officials over the downing of the Korean airliner, relations between the two powers appear as bad as they have been in some time. There are not only substantive disagreements in almost every field but also a highly polemical character in the words used by the two sides, with Mr. Shultz and his aides seemingly personally insulted by Soviet statements about the airliner."[25]

Back in Washington a few days later, Shultz found himself at the vortex of an unexpected furor over whether he and other senior officials would be required to take lie detector tests. Clark, infuriated by leaks about a McFarlane visit to Beirut and White House discussions about shelling Lebanese militia forces in the hills outside Beirut, persuaded Reagan to order an investigation "by all legal means" to identify the source of the news reports.[26] Attorney General William French Smith launched the inquiry, but neither he nor Reagan consulted about the decision with cabinet members who would be affected, including Shultz and Weinberger. Jim Baker and Mike Deaver also knew nothing about the plan.

When Baker heard about it on his way to the Madison Hotel with Deaver for lunch with a Republican strategist, he ordered the driver to return immediately to the White House, where Reagan, Bush and Shultz were at lunch. Baker and Deaver burst into the small private dining room used by the president adjacent to the Oval Office. When Reagan confirmed he had ordered up lie detector tests, Baker told him, "With all due respect, sir, I'm not so sure you can polygraph a constitutional officer," referring to the vice president.[27] Shultz, offended by the idea, told Reagan that it implied the president had lost confidence in Shultz and that his usefulness as secretary of state was at an end. Baker recalled, "The President had been sold a bill of goods by Clark. He wasn't really focused. He's not a lawyer; he didn't understand. He was outraged at the leak, as a lot of people were, and he just said, 'I want it investigated.'"[28] Clark had a different perspective: "Of course the polygraph wasn't used, nor did I expect it to be, but we were so exasperated we didn't know what else to do. After the polygraph story was leaked, things did dry up. So they finally got the message."[29]

Before their lunch was interrupted by the leak affair, Reagan and Shultz had reviewed the state of relations with the Kremlin in the wake of the Korean airliner attack and Shultz's Madrid meeting with Gromyko. The downing of the plane, they agreed, had drained momentum from Shultz's hope of working with Andropov to stabilize superpower relations. Reagan, mindful of his reelection hopes in 1984, knew that steps to improve relations might be politically untenable to his Republican base. "We're in the process of concluding that Andropov is a tough son-of-a-bitch and won't give," Shultz said, "so we better settle down to a cold war. That means no arms control." Later that day, Shultz mused aloud to aides: "Our fledgling effort with the Soviets is the first victim. In the wake of all this we have to have a combination that is sophisticated and that shows condemnation and restraint and a continuation of the arms control process. But we may not be up to such a sophisticated approach. It will be a cold day before you persuade RR or me to see Gromyko. If it's bad politics in the United States, the president pays."[30]

He returned to the topic the next day, clearly trying to clarify his own thinking about how to deal with the Kremlin after another meeting with Reagan. "A lot hangs on the analysis of whether the Soviets are indeed getting more inflexible. Three weeks ago the president had a constructive attitude regarding the Soviets. He thought we were putting something together, and that affects the politics. The atmosphere is different now, particularly where the campaign turns hard right. We are precipitating that. . . . If we tell RR that the Soviets have turned tough, he's only too ready to believe it. And if you believe it, you kiss other initiatives goodbye."[31]

News of Clark's transfer to the Interior Department broke in mid-October. Shultz aides predicted the theme of press coverage would be "Shultz wins." Shultz confided to Seitz that Nancy Reagan must have played a role. "She despises Clark," he said. "Won't even talk to him."[32] Unlike the muted response by Shultz and his aides several weeks earlier when they first learned that Clark would be dislodged as national security adviser, the State Department contingent was gleeful. O'Bie Shultz, who happened to be at her husband's office, laughed that Clark was "too dumb for Interior." Shultz facetiously told John Hughes, the State Department spokesman, to tell reporters, "The nation has suffered a severe blow."[33] Shultz was pulled from a diplomatic reception that evening to take an urgent call from Deaver, who told him he was pushing for Baker to succeed Clark. "Everyone has an angle," Shultz observed afterward, noting that the Baker shift would open the chief of staff post for Deaver.[34] Shultz knew that his lunch with Reagan the next day might be critical as the president pondered whom to appoint.

The intrigue only increased the next day. Vice President Bush called Shultz in the morning. "I guess this will be the Baker lobby," Shultz said dryly as he picked up the phone. Before heading to the White House for lunch, Shultz outlined his thinking: "It comes down to two people: Baker and Bud. The VP and Deaver and probably Mrs. Reagan want Baker, and all the other people in the NSC system want Bud. . . . There is also a move afoot to postpone the decision until after I have consulted with Casey and Cap. The battle is going on so I'll make a friend and an enemy. We can get along with either Baker or McFarlane. I hope Jeane's name doesn't come up. I don't know if I should bring it up and then knock it down. I have a hard time believing Baker would give up campaign politics. There might also be a problem with the right wing. There is no negative fall-out from Bud."[35]

Reagan informed Shultz at lunch that he knew Kirkpatrick would not be the right choice. It was clear to Shultz by this time that Weinberger and Casey opposed Baker, fearing he was too moderate. Reagan's most startling comment at the lunch was not about Clark's successor but about possibly meeting with Andropov. After Shultz remarked that the absence of a dialogue with the Kremlin might be a concern to some American voters in 1984, Reagan raised the idea of meeting with Andropov to propose the elimination of nuclear weapons. The abolition of nuclear weapons was not a new thought for Reagan, but the notion of actually proposing it at a meeting with the Soviet leader was striking. Shultz was surprised and reminded the president that without nuclear weapons, the Soviet Union would not be a superpower.[36]

The pace of conversations about Clark's successor picked up after lunch when the president informed Shultz he would hold off making a decision. Nancy Reagan soon called to tell Shultz that her husband had selected Baker but pulled back after encountering fierce opposition in the West Wing. Shultz resisted her entreaties to organize Baker supporters. As

Shultz had surmised, Jim Baker and Mike Deaver had proposed that Baker replace Clark and Deaver succeed Baker as White House chief of staff. They thought they had Nancy Reagan's blessing. The plan blew up when the president informed Clark on the way to a National Security Council meeting where he planned to announce the appointments. Clark urged Reagan to reconsider until other officials had a chance to make their views known. Reagan agreed. As the meeting proceeded, Clark handed a note to his conservative allies warning them that Reagan intended to make Baker national security adviser and Deaver chief of staff. When the meeting ended, Clark, Weinberger, Casey and Meese cornered Reagan and told him they would not countenance Baker in the security post. They questioned Baker's knowledge of national security affairs and knew he would likely support Shultz in internal policy debates. Braced by the pushback, Reagan summoned Baker and Deaver to the Oval Office. "Fellas, I got a revolt on my hands," he told them.[37] Reagan left to spend the weekend at Camp David without announcing a decision.

Shultz and his State Department colleagues reviewed the field on Saturday morning. Shultz reiterated that he could work with anyone but Kirkpatrick. He reported archly that Weinberger opposed Scowcroft on grounds that he was insufficiently confrontational and tried to work out problems. "There is more going on," Shultz said. "Jim Baker is also leaving regardless of what happens to the NSC job. When Reagan called yesterday he raised the idea of Baker going to the UN. I think I'll call the president and say it is hard to lose Baker from the White House."[38] As Shultz was meeting with his aides, Weinberger and Casey appeared unexpectedly and huddled privately with Shultz. Weinberger suggested the best outcome, given the lack of consensus, would be for Clark to remain in the job. If not Clark, Weinberger said, he supported Kirkpatrick. Casey concurred and joined Weinberger in urging Shultz to support the president's notion of sending Baker to the UN. At the end of the weekend, Shultz strongly suspected that Reagan would appoint McFarlane. On Monday, after explaining his decision to Kirkpatrick, Reagan announced that McFarlane would replace Clark. Shultz was relieved. After meeting with McFarlane a few days later, Shultz said, "Bud is a matter-of-fact guy. This is a big job. He's been observing it for years. I said I would always brief him after my meetings with the president. I said he is our guy in the White House."[39]

In his memoirs, Shultz reflected on the difficulties generated by the National Security Council staff, pointing more to a structural flaw than to Clark and other personalities. "Time and again, I had seen White House and NDC staff members all too ready to take matters into their own hands, usurping power and authority that was not theirs and going off on their own. As one who had blown the whistle more than once, I became an obstacle in their eyes—someone to be eliminated or circumvented. Their answer seemed to proceed without my knowledge."[40] Shultz's unflattering portrait of Clark angered Clark and his friends. Clark fired back, calling the Shultz memoirs "a very negative, almost bitter book." He said, "I could never determine why. But we had a good working relationship."[41]

With McFarlane in place as national security adviser, some of the resistance to Shultz on the National Security Staff seemed likely to dissipate. Shultz's assertive handling of the KAL 007 incident had shown he could exercise a more muscular role in internal administration deliberations. But the path was not yet open for Shultz to direct a fundamental course correction in relations with the Kremlin. In the short term, the downing of the South Korean airliner had poisoned East-West relations, even if Shultz had prevented a frightening escalation in the cold war. Weinberger, Casey and Kirkpatrick were still standing in his way. Adding to the mixed picture, the administration was distracted by developments in Lebanon, where a contingent of marines was vulnerable to attack and the Lebanese civil war was intensifying by the day. A mini-crisis was also developing on the Caribbean island of Grenada, which seemed to be flirting with Cuba and the Soviet Union.

An election year was fast approaching, so the main potential advantage for Shultz was the prospect that Reagan would need to tack toward improving relations with the Soviet Union to reassure Americans that he was a peacemaker, not a president courting war with the Soviet Union.

CHAPTER SIXTEEN

Combating Terrorism

THE FIRST SERIES OF suicide terrorist attacks by Islamic fundamentalist extremists in 1983, the beginning of a wave that reached its zenith with the September 11, 2001, strikes on the World Trade Center in New York and the Pentagon, caught Shultz and the Reagan administration unprepared. The targets of the first attacks in Lebanon, the American embassy and a Beirut building housing hundreds of US Marines, were flimsily secured. Faced with a sinister new threat, the administration struggled to come up with an effective response, riven by disagreement over whether to retaliate and, if so, where and when. Tensions flared anew between Shultz, who favored a military response, and Weinberger, who did not. A mighty armada was assembled in the eastern Mediterranean, including at one point three US aircraft carriers, and multiple strike plans were devised, rehearsed and set to launch. But none were activated for weeks because of indecision in Washington.

In one extraordinary instance, Reagan ordered an air strike, but Weinberger called it off at the last minute. The decision, tantamount to insubordination, surprised the president, stunned colleagues and shocked Shultz, who was profoundly discouraged by Washington's feeble response to terrorism. Ignoring his customary impulse to shield policy conflicts from public view, he openly challenged the administration's hesitation in a series of appearances that exacerbated the divisions in the administration and drew a rebuke from Vice President Bush. It was a rare instance of open rebellion by Shultz.

Shultz and Reagan were enjoying a golfing break in Georgia in late October 1983 when terrorists struck the barracks in Lebanon. The golf outing with Donald Regan, the Treasury secretary, and former senator Nicholas Brady was first disrupted when an armed man crashed his truck through a gate at the Augusta National Golf Club, seized several hostages at the pro shop and demanded to speak to the president. The Secret Service immediately hustled Reagan, Shultz, Regan and Brady off the course at the 16th hole. The incident ended peacefully after Reagan tried unsuccessfully to speak to the intruder by phone. The trip was cut short on October 23 when word reached the president and his party at 2:30 a.m. Eastern time that terrorists had blown up the US Marine barracks in Beirut, killing scores of marines. Shultz headed directly to the State Department when Air Force One landed outside Washington. "He looked stunned and drawn," Seitz reported.[1] Not only had Shultz pushed for the marine deployment, but he was also a former marine himself. Shultz later called it his worst day as secretary of state.

The dimensions of the attack soon became clear—a Mercedes truck loaded with the equivalent of six tons of explosives had crashed through the few feeble barriers erected outside the barracks, plowed into the entrance hall and exploded, collapsing the building and killing 240 American servicemen, most of whom were marines. A similar, simultaneous attack at a French base nearby left fifty-nine French troops dead. Six months earlier, on April 19, a lone terrorist had driven a black pickup truck packed with explosives past a porous barricade at the American embassy on the Beirut waterfront and detonated the truck bomb. The center section of the horseshoe-shaped building collapsed. Sixty-three people were killed, including seventeen Americans. Robert Ames, the CIA's leading Middle East expert, was among the dead. A shadowy Muslim fundamentalist group, Islamic Jihad, claimed responsibility for the embassy attack. After learning of the terror strike, Reagan recorded in his diary: "Lord forgive me for the hatred I feel for the humans who can do such a cruel but cowardly deed."[2]

The attacks ominously suggested that a new era of suicide terrorist attacks by Muslim fundamentalist extremists was beginning. Shultz was reluctant to retreat but realized Washington's objectives in Lebanon were unclear to many Americans. "We've tried to state our objectives," he said, "but we need something shorter. We need both a general statement of purpose in the Middle East as well as the specifics regarding Lebanon. Why do we care about our stated objectives? Why fight and die? The main policy decision is that we are not going to pick up and leave. But we simply cannot replace the casualties and sit there."[3]

Terrorism was not a new phenomenon. It had become an all-too-familiar threat over the postwar decades, including hijacked commercial flights, operations of the Red Brigade in Italy, attacks by the Baader-Meinhof Gang and Red Army Faction in Germany, the Palestinian assault on Israeli athletes at the 1976 Olympics in Munich and numerous other bloody events. Not long before Shultz became secretary of state, Pope John Paul II was shot while greeting people in St. Peter's Square, and Egyptian president Anwar Sadat was assassinated while reviewing a military parade in Cairo. The new element was the appearance of suicide bombers, attackers at the wheel of cars and trucks packed with explosives who blew themselves up when they ignited their deadly cargo. The powerful car and truck bombs exponentially increased the destructive power of terror attacks.

Realizing that American diplomacy in the Middle East would be severely undermined by the April attack on the embassy, Reagan dispatched Shultz to the region a week after the bombing on his first visit to the area as secretary of state. His mission: salvage an American initiative to secure the withdrawal of Israeli, Syrian and PLO forces. Negotiations had stalled after four months of talks. Nearly two thousand US Marines had been sent to Lebanon in 1982 to ensure the peaceful withdrawal of PLO forces from Lebanon as the Israeli army closed in on Beirut. The marines briefly withdrew to ships offshore after the PLO evacuation was completed. They rushed back a few weeks later after Christian Phalange militia, unblocked by Israeli forces, raided Muslim refugee camps and slaughtered hundreds of Palestinians, including women and children. Shultz spent two weeks in the Middle East, starting in Egypt, then shuttled between Jerusalem and Beirut, with excursions to Damascus and Amman. Despite a nasty cold and high fever that kept him in bed for parts of several days, he managed to secure an imperfect agreement for Israeli withdrawal from Lebanon that was sealed on May 17. The deal proved fragile and eventually collapsed in 1984 after Syria refused to pull back from Lebanon.

In the months that followed Shultz's visit to the region, the marines faced increasing threats themselves as they tried to maintain a neutral presence as part of a multinational peacekeeping force that included French, Italian and British troops. The marines established a base and barracks near the Beirut airport on the outskirts of the city. Before long, they came under fire from Muslim militia forces based in the hills overlooking the airport and encampment. The shelling killed two marines in August and in September and wounded others. The next jolt to American peacemaking efforts came with the destruction of the barracks. Reagan recalled the moment he learned of the attack during his golf weekend in Georgia with Shultz and other companions:

> That night, our group had a pleasant dinner together. Nancy and I went to bed a little earlier than usual because we were tired after the early morning interruption the night before. At about 2:30 A.M., however, our phone rang again. Again it was Bud McFarlane: He said a suicide bomber had just driven a truckload of dynamite past our sentries and smashed into the marine barracks at the Beirut Airport. According to the first reports, at least one hundred marines had been killed.
>
> There was to be no more sleep for us that night. I got on the phone with the Pentagon to make sure that everything possible was being done to protect the remaining marines in Beirut, then met with George Shultz and Bud for several hours in the same living room where we'd spent much of the night before.[4]

Their first impulse was to retaliate. After quickly packing up before dawn on Sunday morning and heading to Air Force One, Reagan and Shultz were back in Washington by 8:30 a.m. Gathering in the White House Situation Room with his top advisers, Reagan said, "This is an obvious attempt to run us out of Lebanon. . . . The first thing I want to do is find out who did it and go after them with everything we've got."[5] Before the long day ended, Reagan signed National Security Decision Directive 109, holding Iran and Hezbollah responsible for the barracks bombing. Planning for a retaliatory strike immediately began at the Pentagon. "We wanted to put a cruise missile into the window of the Iranian ambassador in Damascus," recalled Richard Armitage, an assistant secretary of defense.[6]

Shultz thought it was critically important for the administration to reaffirm its commitment to rid Lebanon of foreign forces and to maintain a marine contingent in the country to show American resolve. Weinberger and others feared that a continued marine presence, even if better fortified and operating with more assertive rules of engagement, would make the United States a combatant in Lebanon and the marines a target for additional attacks. General P. X. Kelley, the marine commandant, was dubious about extending the marine presence but headed to Beirut to assess the military dynamics and threat level. Work began almost immediately at the CIA and Pentagon to identify retaliatory targets and attack plans to strike them.

McFarlane later recalled the incoming intelligence data:

> The CIA had tracked the source of the bombing to a Shia Muslim commando unit known as the Husayni Suicide Forces, led by Abu Haydar Musawi, a radical Shia Muslim who had broken away from the mainline Amal organization in 1982 and formed the radical Islamic Amal. This group was put under the command of the Iranian Revolutionary Guards in June 1983. If the Iranians did not plan and launch the attack, they were nonetheless witting conspirators in it. And the Iranians were allied with Syria. French observers in Beirut had watched the evacuation of an Iranian embassy office in West Beirut 10 minutes after the explosion occurred. In addition, Majid Kamal, an Iranian intelligence official who had guided the terrorist activities of pro-Iranian groups, was in Beirut at the time of the bombing. Seven intercepted Iranian messages since September showed Iranian officials in Tehran and Damascus urging their Lebanese colleagues to attack French and American targets. Specifically, the Iranian ambassador in Damascus stated on September 22 that he had instructed Abu Haydar Musawi to "undertake an extraordinary attack against the U.S. Marines."[7]

To blunt rising congressional concerns about the marine role, Shultz forcefully told lawmakers, "If we as Americans decide we do not want the role and influence of a great power, then I shudder to think what kind of world of anarchy and danger our children will inherit."[8] Reagan reinforced the message: "Let no terrorist question our will and no tyrant doubt our resolve. Americans have courage and determination, and we must not and will not be intimidated by anyone, anywhere."[9] A plausible target set was soon located in Baalbek, the primary city in the Syrian-controlled Bekaa Valley in eastern Lebanon. Revolutionary Guard units were stationed at the Sheikh Abdullah barracks and the Al Shams Hotel. By this time, the US Navy had assembled a formidable fleet in the eastern Mediterranean, including the aircraft carriers USS *Kennedy* and USS *Eisenhower*. The USS *Independence* would soon join them.

The *Eisenhower* was on port call in Naples when the barracks was hit. In the pre-cell-phone era, sailors enjoying liberty ashore spotted a US Navy SH-3 helicopter circling around the Bay of Naples with its sonar boom in a lowered position, a signal to return immediately to their ship. Sam Cox, a young navy intelligence officer who was enjoying a sunny afternoon in Sorrento, an hour's drive down the Amalfi coast from Naples, was one of the *Eisenhower* crew members who saw the helicopter. Two days later, he and the *Eisenhower* were steaming toward Lebanon, leaving several hundred sailors behind in Italy who had not made it back to the ship in time for its emergency sortie. "We'd just spent three months off Beirut providing cover to the Marines," Cox recalled, "and on our first port call since mid-July, someone had blasted the barracks to smithereens. Did they time the truck bombing for when the carrier was gone or was it just coincidence?"[10]

Soviet naval vessels in the area tracked the *Eisenhower* as it headed toward Beirut. A few weeks earlier American and Soviet warships had crossed within yards of each other as the commander of the *Eisenhower*, Vice Admiral Jerry Tuttle, ordered the aircraft carrier to run at high speed directly at the Soviet ships as they were refueling. Cox described the dangerous cold war gambit on the high seas: "As the ships steamed right at each other, neither side gave way in the game of chicken, although the Soviets were forced to break off their refueling. The IKE split the Soviet formation in two, with the *Slava* and *Mod Kashin* passing down the port side, while the oiler and the *Riga* passed down the starboard side. I've wondered what the Russians must have been thinking as the solitary U.S. carrier plowed right through the center of their refueling formation, with about 2,000 U.S. sailors on the flight deck, almost all with cameras taking pictures, flashbulbs popping in the deepening dusk, and many U.S. Sailors were waving."[11]

After the marine barracks bombing, Cox was soon drawn into planning for an air strike against the Sheik Abdullah barracks in Baalbek. A courier delivered the orders from Washington to the *Eisenhower*. "I thought they just did this in the movies," Cox recalled. "The courier was a full commander, in Service Dress Blue, and he arrived with a briefcase, literally chained to his wrist." Cox was selected to be the primary intelligence planner for the mission:

> My first reaction looking at the target photo was, "Gee, I'd like to go there someday," as my eye was drawn to the spectacular Roman temple

ruins atop an acropolis overlooking the city, which I also noted could serve as a great radar-offset aim point to improve the accuracy of our bombs. Only a small handful of people in the air wing were initially read into the plan. We were actually provided very little information on what exactly went on at the barracks, but we assumed since we had been given the target by Washington, that it was likely that the suicide bomber that hit the Marine Barracks had been trained there. The planners also presumed that because of the time that had passed since the attack any guilty parties were long since gone from the facility.[12]

The doubts about whether any terrorists were still at the barracks echoed similar questions that Shultz, Weinberger and others were considering while Reagan and Shultz were traveling in Asia. Weinberger and top commanders at the Pentagon feared an air strike would kill civilians rather than terrorists, increase hostility toward the United States, expose the marines to greater risk and put navy pilots in danger for little gain. Shultz, while aware that terrorists had probably abandoned the barracks, thought American military action was necessary to demonstrate that the United States would not tolerate attacks on its forces in Lebanon. Shultz's outlook was informed partly by his inspection of the wreckage of the American embassy in Beirut when he visited Lebanon just days after the attack. "You have to see. Sometimes seeing makes a big impact. It was a terrible thing to see. The place was ripped apart. Morey Draper, who was the ambassador, had been on the top floor, and by just a stroke of luck, he didn't get killed."[13]

Beyond Lebanon, Shultz saw terrorism as a rising threat to the United States and its interests abroad. He connected the attacks in Lebanon to the massacre of Israeli athletes in Munich, the hijacking of commercial airliners by terrorists and other incidents. "There was a difference of opinion in appraising the seriousness of the problem. I thought it was a very serious problem and would get worse, and some people didn't think so. They sort of saw it as a one-off event." Looking back on the early terrorist incidents, he said, "I think we in the United States, and in the Western world generally, have been very slow to recognize the seriousness and nature of the terrorist threat."[14] "I wasn't advocating some sort of giant war. I was advocating very sharply focused preventive measures. And I was supportive—very much supportive—of the general Reagan stance. We believed in strength, and in order for your strength to be real, people have to feel you might use it. I think we could have done more in retaliation against these terrorist attacks, and that's in part because when the terrorists attack you and there's no consequence, it encourages them. There have to be consequences. There has to be accountability."[15]

McFarlane found Weinberger obstinate about Lebanon:

> I believe that as a result of the bombing, Cap Weinberger adopted an absolute commitment to getting us out of Lebanon as soon as possible. And in it, he was no doubt backed by the Joint Chiefs, who didn't want to lose any more troops, and didn't want to take a proper military role in support of the diplomacy the President had approved for the Middle East. After the Joint Chiefs sent back their response to the NSDDs, I met with Weinberger in an effort to harmonize the political and military dimensions of the situation, but without much success. Not only was Weinberger against the State Department's Middle East policy, he was against George Shultz personally, and that made winning him over virtually impossible.[16]

Weinberger recalled that he was "very skeptical about the effectiveness of putting a few regiments or a few battalions or joining international forces, particularly in the Mideast, where they would go in without any kind of proper rules of engagement and where they would be basically unable to do anything to protect themselves. So we had disputes there."[17] Shultz understood Weinberger's concerns but was undeterred by them. "I suppose if you're the secretary of defense, you feel a direct responsibility for people, and when they go into something that's even remotely like combat, you know that people can get killed or wounded, and that's something you obviously worry about. But I worried about it, too."[18]

As the debate rolled on in Washington, Cox and his navy colleagues moved ahead with strike preparations. He recalled: "From a physical aspect, the barracks was a great target. A large (but not too large) building situated on the outskirts of Baalbek, surrounded by a fairly wide sand strip with only some minor civilian encroachment at one corner, and damage to that could be mitigated by using a proper bombing run-in heading. The target even looked like a big bullseye, and with the distinctive radar significant terrain (the acropolis) it would not be hard to find in the dark."[19]

Before dawn on an early November morning, crews on the *Eisenhower* and the *Kennedy* armed A-6 twinjet attack aircraft with live bombs and pilots were strapped into the cockpits, jet engines roaring. As Cox recalled, everyone was "awaiting the final go order for the first strike by the U.S.

Navy since the Vietnam War era. The order never came." The drill was soon repeated for another target, Cox said:

> The new target was near a small Lebanese village called An Nabi Chit. Proving that all men are still sixth grade boys at heart, even those who fly multi-million dollar combat jet aircraft, this immediately provoked an extended round of coming up with alternative permutations of the village name. The final winner proved to be both a challenge and a prophesy; Can't Hit Shit. We were given even less information about the significance of the buildings near An Nabi Chit, but we assumed that it was where those responsible for the Beirut USMC Barracks Bombing had taken refuge after clearing out of Baalbek. An Nabi Chit was actually a much tougher target; smaller, harder-to-find, tucked into rough, mountainous terrain right up against the Syrian border, uncomfortably close to multiple Syrian mobile SA-6 radar-guided surface-to-air missile (SAM) batteries immediately across the border. Once again, final approval for the strike never came. When the launch time passed and no orders came, the jets were shut down, and the aircrew went back to sleep.[20]

The available historical record leaves unclear whether the two aborted attacks were approved in Washington and called off or were rehearsals for an American strike yet to be authorized by Reagan. After the first week in November, retaliatory plans were put on hold while Reagan traveled to Japan and South Korea. He departed on November 8 and returned to the White House on November 15. Officials did not want Middle East events to distract from news coverage of the Asian trip.

Israeli planes attacked targets in the An Nabi Chit area on November 16, setting afire several buildings and an ammunition dump. Lebanese police reported that thirty people were killed. The *Washington Post* reported that Israeli officials said the attack was conducted after Israel determined that the United States was not going to retaliate on its own for the terror bombing of the marine barracks.[21] Israel did not give Washington advance notification about the attack.

A third American attack plan, this time developed in coordination with France, called for American and French planes to strike targets in Baalbek on November 18. This time, the decision to launch the air strike was firm. Reagan approved the attack at a national security meeting after his return from Asia. McFarlane recalled, "On November 14, I convened an NSPG meeting to address this matter. The President gave his approval for a retaliatory strike to be conducted on November 16. It was a direct, unambiguous decision."[22] The target set was identified, and the case for and against striking the targets was robustly discussed. Public statements about the attack were drafted, and messages alerting American allies about the strike were prepared for transmission to foreign leaders. The public announcement drafted for Reagan said, in part:

> On the basis of the solid evidence developed, we have taken steps to discourage further attacks by these international criminals. About one hour ago, at ____ EST, aircraft from the carrier USS Eisenhower attacked a headquarters and training complex in the Bekaa Valley used by the group. The strike was successful. All aircraft have been recovered safely.
>
> I deeply regret that this action was necessary. We took every conceivable precaution to limit damage to innocent civilians and to avoid armed confrontation with third parties. We are prepared to let the matter rest here, although I caution those states responsible for supporting this form of terrorism that we have increased our vigilance and heightened our readiness.[23]

Cox described the renewed preparations and launch moment for the attack:

> Strike aircraft on the Eisenhower, Kennedy, Independence and the French carrier Foch, were armed, manned and waiting for the launch order. The original Baalbek strike plan had mutated to a four carrier, multi-national, multi-target extravaganza. All that was needed was the "final" launch order from higher authority. The jets waited, and waited, and waited. Eventually the French started calling on the radio, asking something like, "You are going? No?" Finally it got to the point where we either had to launch or cancel the strike, and still no orders either way had been received. The French radioed their apologies and launched their strike without us, hitting the same Baalbek Barracks that had been our original target. The damage inflicted by the much smaller French Super Etendard fighter-bombers was far less than we would have done with A-6's. But they hit the target. Immediately after the strike, the Foch headed for home.[24]

McFarlane, Shultz and others were stunned to learn that the American planes had never left the carrier decks. McFarlane recounted his view of what happened:

> On the afternoon of November 15, Admiral Jerry Tuttle, commander of the Sixth Fleet, reported through the European command that he was ready to strike and asked for authority to conduct the attack at first

light the following day. But he never received it. Shortly after I arrived at the White House at 6 a.m. on the morning of the 16th, Cap Weinberger called. "Bud," he said, "I had a request [to strike], but I denied it." I was dumbfounded. "I don't understand, Cap," I said. "What went wrong?" Weinberger launched into a long series of obfuscations about misunderstandings with the French and all the things that could have gone wrong with an attack. "I just don't think it was the right thing to do," he said.[25]

McFarlane went on:

It was outrageous. Weinberger had directly violated a presidential order. Whatever his feelings about our role in Lebanon, whatever his disagreements with our policy, the fact was that a presidential decision had been made and an order given and that should have been that. In a private corporation, someone who defied authority as Weinberger just had would have been fired on the spot. But Weinberger knew Ronald Reagan better than most of us, and that knowledge of his old friend had probably given him the confidence to behave as he had.

I said as firmly as I could, "The President isn't going to be able to understand this, Cap. You were there. You saw how strongly he felt about this." "I'll be glad to talk to him," Weinberger replied without turning a hair. "But I thought it was the wrong thing to do." I went into the national security brief and told the President what had happened. "I don't understand," Reagan said. "Why didn't they do it?" "There's no excuse for it, Mr. President," I said. "You approved this operation, and Cap decided not to carry it out. The credibility of the United States in Damascus just went to zero. There's no justification. The Secretary of Defense was wrong, and you ought to make clear to him how you feel about it."

"Gosh, that's really disappointing," Reagan replied evasively. "That's terrible. We should have blown the daylights out of them. I just don't understand." He went on in that vein for some minutes, but it was more for my benefit than anything else. It was clear he wasn't going to call Cap. It was more than he could bring himself to do, to embarrass an old friend. But in the end, this inability on Reagan's part to act decisively on matters that involved his friends was destructive to our Middle East policy, and damaging to other foreign policy initiatives as well. As far as I know, he never did take Weinberger to task for his insubordinate behavior. Weinberger, for his part, had won a decisive battle in his now all-out effort to pull us out of Lebanon.[26]

Not surprisingly, Weinberger's recollection about the aborted attack was quite different. He recalled:

While I am dealing with myths and canards, let me try to set at rest another. The NSC staff people, always eager for combat at all times, circulated a report that I had been "ordered" to participate with the French in a joint attack on Syria's position in the Bekka Valley, but I had refused at the last minute to carry out that order. This is, of course, absurd; because, on the face of it, if I had been ordered by the President to do anything and refused, I would not have been around for several more years.

The facts are that I received a telephone call from Charles Hernu, the French Minister of Defense, on the morning of November 16, telling me French planes were going to attack Syrian positions in about two to three hours. I had received no orders or notifications from the President or anyone prior to that phone call from Paris. I thanked my friend Charles Hernu, wished him and his pilots good luck, and said, "Unfortunately it is a bit too late for us to join you in this one." Of such a chimerical collection of threads are woven lies of whole cloth. This is another instance when McFarlane's "recollections," well known to be "flexible," differed sharply from those of other participants.[27]

Reagan's memory supported Weinberger's contention that he had not over-turned a presidential order without Reagan's consent, but Reagan's account nevertheless implied that he had ordered a strike. Several Reagan aides suggested Reagan's version did not directly address the actual sequence of events and was based either on a memory lapse or a desire to shield Wein-berger from criticism and deflect accusations that Reagan had failed to con-front Weinberger for insubordination. Reagan said, "Our intelligence ex-perts found it difficult to establish conclusively who was responsible for the attack on the barracks. Although several air strikes were planned against the possible culprits, I canceled them because our experts said they were not absolutely sure they were the right targets. I didn't want to kill innocent people. While our intelligence people resumed their efforts to confirm that we had the right targets, Israeli and French forces, convinced they had suf-ficient information, raided the same Shiite Muslim redoubts in the moun-tains that we had considered attacking."[28]

Further declassification of Reagan administration documents may even-tually provide a definitive account of why and how the attack plan was can-celed. There seems no doubt that Weinberger made the operational decision to call off the attack, but it remains unclear whether the decision was a bla-tant refusal to carry out a presidential order or a reasonable last-second de-termination that the mission was ill-advised and might be ineffective. James Baker, speaking generally about Reagan administration decision-making dynamics, not specifically about this incident, said, "Decisions would be made by the president and Cap just wouldn't implement them."[29] Sadly, the on-again, off-again series of air strike plans ended in early December with an ineffectual American attack that left one pilot dead, another captured and detained by Syria, while inflicting little damage on terrorist groups in Lebanon. Ironically, Weinberger also attempted to stop the attack, which would have been the right decision, but he intervened too late.

As the months passed, Shultz remained adamant about the need for military retaliation after terrorist attacks. He was one of just a handful of Reagan administration officials who kept pressing for military action. "He always had a proclivity for perhaps thinking about using military force preemptively," Colin Powell said. "I think it came from his military experience as a Marine. I never quite understood why he found this always as such an attractive option. What he was really saying was: 'Diplomacy without force is not useful.' Okay, I'll buy that. Diplomacy should have force behind it, but let's not use it just because it's there. But he always had that instinct, and I think it sometimes got us in trouble."[30]

In April 1984, Shultz addressed the issue in an appearance at the Trilateral Commission: "Certainly we must take security precautions to protect our people and our facilities; certainly we must strengthen our intelligence capabilities to alert ourselves to the threats. But it is increasingly doubtful that a purely passive strategy can even begin to cope with the problem."[31] Shultz returned to the topic in October 1984 at the Park Avenue Synagogue in New York. Defying objections from Vice President Bush, who considered the speech belligerent, Shultz declared, "We may never have the kind of evidence that can stand up in an American court of law. But we cannot allow ourselves to become the Hamlet of nations, worrying endlessly over whether and how to respond."[32]

Speaking just days after Reagan insisted that the United States could not attack terrorists unless it was certain it was targeting people who had conducted terror strikes against the United States, Shultz argued that Washington faced "a choice between doing nothing or employing military force. . . . We can expect more terrorism directed at our strategic interests around the world in the years ahead," he said. "To combat it we must be willing to use military force." The next day, Bush openly questioned the Shultz strategy. During a campaign swing in Ohio, he said, "I think you

have got to pinpoint the source of the attack. We are not going to go out
and bomb innocent civilians or something of that nature. I don't think we
ever get to the point where you kill 100 innocent women and children just
to kill one terrorist."[33] Shultz knew that Reagan had read and approved
the Park Avenue Synagogue speech. "The vice president didn't like it at all.
Fortunately, I'd cleared it with the president and he liked it. If you want one
person on your side, he's the right guy."[34]

Weinberger countered a month later with his own set of principles for
the use of military force, outlined in a speech at the National Press Club.
The list seemed quite reasonable for the use of American forces in a major
foreign engagement, including the need for clear objectives, the use of overwhelming force and broad congressional and public support. The lessons of
Vietnam permeated the Weinberger doctrine. Shultz agreed with much of
the list if applied to conventional war fighting but found it underwhelming
as a policy for combating terrorism. Noting that a journalist derisively referred to the Weinberg principles as the "Capgun doctrine," Shultz called it
"a counsel of inaction bordering on paralysis."[35]

CHAPTER SEVENTEEN

Reelection and Renewed Hope

APART FROM SHULTZ'S FRUSTRATIONS with the administration's response to the terrorist attacks, the last months of 1983 and much of 1984 tested his patience and resolve. His leverage in the administration was growing, but he still found himself constrained by acidic policy debates and a president unwilling to give Shultz a decisive mandate to tone down the cold war. Shultz spent much of his time dealing with policy skirmishes on a variety of international issues, at times wondering again if he should resign, all the time hoping a Reagan second term would give new impetus to diplomacy with the Kremlin.

While the White House was pondering how to respond to the Beirut attacks, Reagan decided to intervene militarily in Grenada, a small Caribbean island nation that appeared to be drifting politically leftward. Shultz picked up a large briefing book on Grenada, mispronouncing the name of the island as he opened it. Corrected by Seitz, Shultz impishly started singing a spontaneous variation of "Let's Call the Whole Thing Off," a Gershwin duet that plays with differing pronunciations of the word "potato." Shultz loved the tune, famously performed by Ella Fitzgerald and Louis Armstrong. The secretary of state sang out, "You say Grenada and I say Grenada, you say potato and I say potato . . . Let's call the whole thing off."[1]

The American invasion began the night of October 24, 1983. The public rationale for intervening was to evacuate several hundred Americans enrolled in medical school on the island. The deeper reason was a desire to push back against Cuban inroads on Grenada and to demonstrate to the world that the United States was prepared to engage militarily again after a long hiatus following defeat in Vietnam in 1975. The navy and marine forces that landed on Grenada ran into greater resistance than expected from Cuban troops, requiring the dispatch of troops from the 82nd Airborne to reinforce American forces. As a military engagement, the American invasion—employing a sledgehammer to swat a fly—was a bizarre exercise for a global superpower and an improbable way for Washington to show the world it was once again ready to initiate combat operations to advance its interests. The Grenada campaign, brief as it was, exposed serious flaws in operational coordination among the armed services. Commanders, wary of press coverage after the countless reports from Vietnam that contradicted rosy Pentagon depictions, tightly restricted American media access to Grenada as the invasion unfolded.

Shultz's communication with the Kremlin resumed on October 28 during a lunch with Ambassador Dobrynin, seven weeks after the tense Madrid meeting with Gromyko. Dobrynin told Shultz that Soviet leaders thought the Reagan administration overreacted to the KAL 007 attack and that Washington looked as though it was spoiling for a confrontation and was no longer interested in problem solving. Shultz countered that Soviet behavior was the issue, not American policy, including unfulfilled Kremlin promises to address some human rights issues, among them possibly freeing Anatoly Shcharansky, a dissident who had been imprisoned in 1977. "We do not have a policy of confrontation," Shultz told Dobrynin. "We don't foresee situations where we aren't at least competitive, but that doesn't mean we can't have discussions on important problems. We are ready for it if it can be fruitful and broad gauged. It can't simply be arms control. It has to be in a constructive atmosphere."[2]

Although Shultz did not tell Dobrynin, he was worried about the American handling of negotiations on limiting long-range nuclear weapons. "We don't have a bargaining position," he told colleagues. "We only have a position. Nothing to bargain. We seem to have no concept of give and take. We don't discuss it that way now. We just change numbers. If the president agrees to a concept, then we can get directions from the top." Rick Burt, the assistant secretary of state for European and Canadian affairs, noted that Washington wanted to constrain Moscow without constraining itself. He told Shultz that the Reagan administration had cloaked this by saying it wanted to deal on destabilizing systems that happen to be Soviet. He said that Washington was negotiating its limits but without knowing what to limit.[3]

While Reagan was traveling in Asia, an elaborate NATO war game exercise was unfurling in Western Europe that seized the attention of Soviet defense forces and rapidly developed into a serious war scare in the Kremlin. The exercise, code-named "Able Archer 83," involved a series of escalatory steps toward a war between Warsaw Pact forces and NATO. It reached a peak on November 8 when NATO simulated the launch of nuclear weapons against Soviet and Warsaw Pact targets. Imprecise Soviet intelligence about the war game stirred alarm in Moscow that the United States and its NATO allies might be planning a surprise nuclear attack under the cover of a military exercise. Soviet leaders ordered defense forces on high alert. American intelligence reports on the Soviet reaction failed to recognize the mounting concern in Moscow and potential for a monumental misunderstanding that could start a nuclear war. Reagan and Shultz were unaware of the danger. When Reagan later learned about the near crisis, he called it "really scary." A subsequent investigation of the events by a White House intelligence panel found the NATO exercise "may have inadvertently placed our relations with the Soviet Union on a hair trigger."[4]

A few weeks after the exercise, a real change in NATO's military hardware unfolded in West Germany. The first battery of American Pershing 2 missiles arrived on November 24, several years after the Soviet Union had positioned its own intermediate-range missiles with nuclear warheads within striking distance of Western Europe. Delivery of the American weapons generated a good deal of media coverage, but the significance of the moment was not fully appreciated at the time. After years of planning and serious doubts that West Germany would ultimately accept placement of the weapons on its soil, not to mention massive antinuclear public demonstrations in Western Europe, the United States was putting a new generation of nuclear-tipped missiles on the doorstep of the Soviet Union. Helmut Kohl, the West German chancellor, had resisted relentless pressure to block delivery of the missiles. Ten days earlier, American cruise missiles that could carry nuclear warheads had started arriving in Britain despite the spectacle a few months earlier of tens of thousands of antinuclear demonstrators forming a human chain stretching fourteen miles across the English countryside. Shultz thought the deployment of the Pershing 2 missiles was "the turning point" in the Reagan administration's handling of the cold war. He said it forced the Kremlin "to face up to the fact that the alliance had cohesion and strength."[5]

The import of all this was not lost on the Kremlin. Within hours, the Soviet Union announced it was breaking off negotiations over intermediate-range nuclear weapons in Europe. Reagan said he was disappointed with the decision but predicted that the talks would resume. Whether the presence of the Pershing missiles would eventually drive Moscow to seek a deal to remove them and spur the Kremlin to seek a general warming of relations was uncertain. But the combination of the emergence of a new military threat so close to the Soviet Union and continuing stagnation of the Soviet economy seemed likely to focus the attention of Soviet leaders on how to balance security interests with a need to manage domestic discontent over a dismal standard of living. Shultz thought it was a pivotal cold war moment that showed the Kremlin that a negotiated resolution of East-West tensions was its only viable option. He pressed Reagan to pick up the pace of diplomacy.

Shortly before Thanksgiving, Reagan approved Shultz's request to pursue intensified talks with Dobrynin aimed at getting a dialogue with the Kremlin back on track. The hope was to reopen discussions about Shcharansky, the Middle East and other matters frozen since the downing of the Korean airliner. "We were moving into something substantive with the Soviets but then it all went awry with the KAL and Madrid," he said. "We can't just talk about dialogue. We have to have substance to it. We need specifics in it. Otherwise, things don't move."[6]

Shultz sounded off again about Weinberger after a meeting on the Middle East at which the defense secretary proposed stationing marines on a navy ship off the Lebanese coast. "Jesus Christ," Shultz complained, "Cap can't even see the nose in front of his face. He wants to put Marines on the ship. That makes no sense at all. McFarlane and the president are on board. We can't wait around about a strategy on Lebanon. We've just got to move this thing."[7] He was also concerned about widespread hostility toward Israel abroad. "It is amazing there is so much anti-Israel sentiment in the world, especially in Europe," he told colleagues. "It is a latent anti-Semitism."[8] He mused, "The Middle East is so tough. Sometimes I just want to get out of there."[9] He grew so disillusioned with developments in the Middle East, especially the unraveling of his own efforts to broker a peace deal in Lebanon, that he once again thought seriously about resigning. The failure of American efforts to pacify Lebanon stirred renewed press coverage about whether Shultz might decline to serve in a second Reagan term.

In early December, Shultz seemed to toy briefly with the idea that he might someday be a presidential prospect. When informed that a "Shultz for President" committee had been established by a few Republicans, he surprised aides by rejecting a draft press statement that called the notion "absurd." Instead, he proposed telling reporters, if they asked, that "I have no intention of running."[10] The committee seemed to lose interest once Reagan announced he would run for reelection, but the episode offered a momentary glimpse of nascent ambition that Shultz held in check as he served alongside Reagan.

As the holidays approached, and with them the opening of an election year, Shultz knew that campaign calculations would influence foreign policy making in 1984. He assumed Reagan would seek reelection. Democratic presidential contenders would inevitably pounce on Reagan's belligerent rhetoric about the Kremlin to argue that he had aggravated tensions and put the United States at greater risk of a military conflict with the Soviet Union. Public opinion surveys in 1983 showed Americans were strongly anti-Communist but wary of foreign military entanglements, including the Reagan administration's interventions in Lebanon and Central America. Reagan would need to counteract his aggressive image by presenting himself as a man of peace. The political calculus, combined with Clark's exit as national security adviser, seemed propitious for Shultz. "The Soviet deep-freeze is not hard for the president to handle, but the interplay of politics is such that we can't get on a constructive track unless we do it soon," he told aides.[11]

Looking ahead to an East-West security conference in Stockholm in late January, including a possible Shultz-Gromyko meeting there, the White House started work early in 1984 on a Reagan speech about the state of American-Soviet relations. Shultz thought aloud with aides about how he could most effectively steer the speech in a positive direction. "We have to lay some wood," he said. "What do I have to get the president to agree to? The framework. We can do it through meetings and then an NSC, and I can take one view and Cap another and Bud tries to meld it together and we get fudged. The other way is direct to the president."[12] He knew working directly with Reagan would be best.

After Reagan raised the prospect of abolishing nuclear weapons again in mid-December, Shultz instructed aides to prepare a background paper for the president. "This is his impulse. It is a sensitive reflection of popular opinion. The president has noticed that no one pays any attention to this [idea] anymore. I told him I would study the proposition. If we put it forward seriously, what would we be proposing specifically? In the end, it may collapse of its own weight. It's a gigantic build-down. I want a preliminary cut at this by somebody. The president believes in this. That is the way to go. If not, then we have to demonstrate why not." When Rick Burt noted that elimination of nuclear weapons would need to be done gradually, Shultz said, "That could be, but let's not think about that way. Give the man what he wants."[13]

As Shultz and his team mulled the next steps with Moscow, they considered opening a back channel to Andropov that bypassed Gromyko and the Soviet foreign ministry. The KGB had recently reached out to the CIA station chief in Moscow about establishing a private Kremlin–White House channel. There had also been some private discussions between Max Kampelman and his Soviet counterpart, an overture that had evaporated after the Soviet foreign ministry learned about it. Shultz and his aides settled on Brent Scowcroft, Vice President Bush's closest national security aide, as best suited for secret diplomacy. Jack Matlock, the White House Soviet specialist, advised that the Kremlin might be most receptive to a back-channel approach if it involved any initiative that was not part of the normal diplomatic dialogue between Washington and Moscow.[14]

After a holiday break in California, including a day golfing with Reagan in Palm Springs, Shultz met with Dobrynin. The Soviet ambassador reported that Moscow was willing to open private discussions with the Reagan administration if Reagan and Shultz were prepared to talk about substantive matters. As drafts of a presidential address about American-Soviet relations started to circulate within the government, Shultz ironically complained it was too conciliatory. "It's not supposed to take on the Soviets, but it should be determined, both about realism and willingness to talk as well as a determination to be strong." He was also unhappy that the State Department had failed to produce the paper he had requested in December about a world without nuclear weapons. "The president is traveling on a fast track," he told Rick Burt and Jonathan Howe, the director of the department's bureau of political-military affairs, "so if you don't like it, you better give him something that he can pay attention to. Every meeting I go to, the president talks about abolishing nuclear weapons. I can't get it through your head that the man is serious. We either have to tell him he is barking up the wrong tree or reply to his interest."[15]

On January 16, Reagan delivered the address about Soviet policy, trying to reassure Americans he was committed to improving relations as the presidential election campaign began. "We must and will engage the Soviets in a dialogue as serious and constructive as possible, a dialogue that will serve to promote peace in the troubled regions of the world, reduce the level of arms and build a constructive working relationship," Reagan said. "Neither we nor the Soviet Union can wish away the differences between our two societies and our philosophies, but we should always remember that we do have common interests. And the foremost among them is to avoid war and reduce the level of arms. There is no rational alternative but to steer a course which I would call credible deterrence and peaceful competition. And if we do so, we might find areas in which we could engage in constructive cooperation."[16]

Near the end of the address, Reagan brought the fraught relationship down to a human level, giving a fictitious example of American and Russian couples that met one day by chance. He had penned the passage himself in long hand as he reviewed the draft of the speech. Like the 1981 letter that he insisted be sent to Brezhnev, the thought was idealistic, simplistic and a striking departure from normal diplomatic discourse, but it reflected the president's emotional belief that a safer world could be achieved someday. Unlike Haig, who had scoffed at the Brezhnev letter as naïve, Shultz embraced Reagan's vision. Reagan told the American people:

> Just suppose with me for a moment that an Ivan and an Anya could find themselves, oh, say, in a waiting room or sharing a shelter from the rain

or a storm with a Jim and Sally. And there was no language barrier to keep them from getting acquainted.

Would they then debate the differences between their respective Governments? Or would they find themselves comparing notes about their children and what each other did for a living? Before they parted company, they would probably have touched on ambitions and hobbies and what they wanted for the children and problems of making ends meet.

And as they went their separate ways, maybe Anya would be saying to Ivan: "Wasn't she nice. She also teaches music." And Jim would be telling Sally what Ivan did or didn't like about his boss. They might even have decided they were all going to get together for dinner some evening soon.

Above all they would have proven that people don't make wars. People want to raise their children in a world without fear and without war. They want to have some of the good things over and above bare subsistence that make life worth living. They want to work at some craft, trade or profession that gives them satisfaction and a sense of worth. Their common interests cross all borders.[17]

While the speech seemed a genuine effort to reset relationships with the Kremlin after the rocky days following the downing of the Korean airliner, the political objectives were also obvious as the presidential election year opened. The White House unsubtly made the point clear by giving reporters advance excerpts from the speech the day before, just as the leading contenders for the Democratic presidential nomination, Senators Walter Mondale and Gary Hart, were debating in New Hampshire.

The *New York Times* noted the timing:

> By striking a tone of moderation toward the Soviet Union and urging a new effort for arms talks at a time when Soviet-American relations are extremely tense, President Reagan is apparently seeking to recast his image and take the offensive against both American political rivals and the Kremlin.
>
> As the election year begins, Reagan strategists grudgingly acknowledge that Mr. Reagan faces a widespread impression here and in Western Europe that he has not tried hard enough to get arms agreements and that his policies and harsh criticism of the Soviet Union have produced a cold war mood of confrontation with Moscow.[18]

A few days later, Shultz traveled to Stockholm for the East-West security conference where Gromyko and he would address delegates from thirty-five nations and meet privately. Shultz tried to set the tone as he arrived. The

New York Times reported:

> Secretary of State George P. Shultz said today that he was prepared to discuss all the issues between the United States and the Soviet Union "in a constructive spirit" when he meets with Foreign Minister Andrei A. Gromyko next week in Stockholm.
>
> But when asked if he thought the chill in Soviet-American relations would end, he said, "It takes two to thaw."[19]

Moscow had walked out of talks in November as the placement of new intermediate-range American missiles and cruise missiles began in Western Europe, so Shultz's agenda with Gromyko included the stalled negotiations. Gromyko delivered a bombastic speech at the security conference that irritated Shultz. His face was flushed and he was physically agitated as he met afterward with aides. "It was slanderous," he said. "I should have walked out." His anger dissipated later in the day during his private meeting with Gromyko, which proved surprisingly civil and constructive. He reported to Reagan that the meeting had gone on for five hours instead of the scheduled two. He described it as "careful and low-key" and said the tone was "good." He told Reagan, "If we manage it carefully, we'll see some improvements that are helpful to us and to them."[20] A few days later, after meeting with Shultz at the White House, Reagan said the Shultz-Gromyko meeting "did not resolve our differences, but had reduced world tensions."[21]

On the eve of the State of the Union address, Shultz was braced by two passing episodes involving work in the Reagan presidency. First, the White House neglected to include O'Bie on the list of people invited to attend the address. He noted to Seitz that the Nixon White House had not been so rude. Then Don Rumsfeld stopped by the State Department to tell Shultz he was disgusted with the deliberations about American policy in Lebanon, particularly Weinberger's intransigence and insistence that the marines be transferred offshore. Rumsfeld told Seitz, "The next time you have a nice guy to work for like Shultz, put him at DOD or the White House. Not here. There's no power here. Tea and crumpets."[22] Shultz expressed his own view soon afterward. "Cap makes me so angry," he said. "He just wants to get the Marines out as if they were the only issue."[23] He added about the Pentagon attitude not long after: "They remind me of librarians—they want all the books on the shelf and don't want anyone to take them out."[24]

Reagan used the State of the Union address at the end of January as an opening argument for his reelection even though he had yet to declare his candidacy. Picking up the foreign policy themes he had enunciated two weeks earlier, Reagan stressed his desire to ease tensions with the Soviet Union. Addressing his remarks to the Soviet people rather than their government, he said, "People of the Soviet Union, there is only one sane policy for your country and mine to preserve our civilization in this modern age: A nuclear war cannot be won and must never be fought. The only value in our two nations possessing nuclear weapons is to make sure they will never be used. But then, would it not be better to do away with them entirely? . . . If your Government wants peace, there will be peace. We can come together in faith and friendship to build a safer and far better world for our children and our children's children. And the whole world will rejoice. That is my message to you."[25]

As the political situation in Lebanon deteriorated, Shultz found himself increasingly isolated in arguing for preservation of the May 17, 1983, peace plan Washington had supported for months. It called for the withdrawal of Israeli and Syrian forces from Lebanon. While traveling in Latin America in early February, Shultz could see his position would not prevail. He told Seitz one evening in Barbados that he was thinking about resigning. He lamented the absence of firmness in the face of terrorism and Washington's desire to abandon the Lebanon agreement he had helped negotiate. Seitz urged Shultz to carry on.[26] O'Bie told Seitz she would not object if her husband resigned; indeed, she said she would welcome it, even if it were a pity to exit at a time of disappointment.[27]

Back in Washington, Shultz continued to complain about the wobbly American policy in Lebanon. He was especially disillusioned with Vice President Bush, who was pushing for withdrawal from Lebanon. "The thing to say is that they [marines] are there now and will stay. There will be a schedule. The vice president last week was leading the charge to get them all out rapidly. Now the Congress and Senate are echoing this. Cap will push this behind the scenes. DOD will try to get the Marines out without putting new elements in. It's a rout. . . . I'm going to the Bahamas," he snapped, referring to his vacation plans. "I don't give a damn what's happening."[28]

Washington learned on February 10 that Andropov had died the day before. Discussions immediately commenced about the policy implications and who should attend the funeral. Shultz saw the death as a possible opening to progress on arms control and other issues. "Turmoil in the Soviet leadership doesn't necessarily rule out constructive developments," he said. White House aides proposed that Reagan lead the American delegation. Shultz opposed the idea, and Reagan soon killed it by telling Shultz he thought it was ridiculous, given that he had never met Andropov, that Andropov had run the KGB and that the Soviet Union had shot down the Korean plane while Andropov was the Kremlin leader. "I don't want to honor that prick," Reagan said.[29]

CBS News reported that evening that Reagan would not go to Moscow but a representative would carry a Reagan proposal that he hold a summit meeting within the next few months with Andropov's successor, who had yet to be publicly identified. The report mystified Shultz. "If that's a decision, it was done without any consultation with me," he said.[30] Reagan soon told Shultz there was no summit proposal. Efforts to determine how the idea had made its way to reporters proved futile, leaving Shultz and Reagan wondering if it had been planted by State Department officials who wanted to accelerate talks with the Kremlin. Konstantin Chernenko, a veteran Soviet official and member of the Politburo, was named to succeed Andropov on February 13. In failing health himself at age seventy-three, Chernenko was viewed as a transitional figure likely to give way before too long to a younger figure, most likely Mikhail Gorbachev. The assumption in Washington was that Chernenko would be a cautious caretaker, aligned closely with hard-line colleagues like Gromyko.

Meantime, the internal battle over Lebanon policy reached a decisive point. Shultz returned from a lunch with Weinberger, McFarlane and Rumsfeld, among others, with notes that McFarlane and Rumsfeld had scribbled about Weinberger and slipped to Shultz during the discussion. McFarlane's note said, "This kind of undisciplined comment deserves a private session with the president. It's outrageous." Rumsfeld wrote, "Is our nation so great and large that we need two secretaries of state? P.S. I don't know how you retain your poise. It's bloody outrageous." Seitz stapled the notes in his notebook for safekeeping.[31] With everything pointing toward a collapse of the American peace plan and withdrawal of most marines from Lebanon, Shultz vented to aides: "An act of terror tipped the Congress," he said. "We have to say you are ready to go after terror. It's not enough to put up barriers around the White House. Cap is saying the Marines will be out by the end of the month. There will be 100 left for the embassy and residence and another 80 or so trainers. That's about one-fifth of what we expected."[32]

A new round of press reports questioning Shultz's influence left him depressed. The coverage was soon followed by rumors that he would resign. All this was reminiscent of the downbeat coverage the previous summer. *Time* magazine reported:

> Critics are now saying with increasing sharpness that Shultz has not lived up to expectations. His methodical approach to problems has at times seemed merely flat-footed and unimaginative. He has never taken charge of Central America policy, choosing instead to focus almost single-mindedly on the Middle East, especially Lebanon. While he is by no means wholly to blame for the failure of U.S. policy there, his refusal to admit mistakes and change course let a bad situation get much worse. . . .
>
> Throughout his career, Shultz has been known for his perfect corporate cool, his poker-faced steadiness. But last Wednesday, as he read a defensive statement about Lebanon to reporters, his face was ashen and puffy, his voice trembled. He stuck by the now irrelevant May 17 agreement. He referred to "the explosive flow of current events" as if it were an imposition, something beyond the call of duty for a Secretary of State. Next day, his 38th wedding anniversary, Shultz took off with his wife for the Bahamas, seeking some needed rest far from that explosive flow.[33]

During a news conference on February 24, Reagan swatted away the resignation rumor: "I have seen that talk and I think it's disgraceful, frankly. And I hope he doesn't have any thoughts about leaving us at this point."[34] Reagan's remarks did not end the rumors. Rowland Evans and Robert Novak, whose joint syndicated column frequently echoed Pentagon complaints about Shultz, continued to report that he would soon leave the administration. Weinberger denied to Shultz that he was cooperating with the columnists and assured Shultz that he was not telling people that Shultz should exit. Shultz worried that people would believe the rumors, undermining his authority. "They will think if there is smoke, there is fire," he said.[35] He sighed, "There isn't any joy in anything these days. Doesn't anything good happen? I'm sick of it."[36]

Hoping to capitalize on the leadership change at the Kremlin, Shultz pressed Reagan to approve a fast-track decision-making process on Soviet affairs. He was encouraged by Reagan's response and satisfied that his direct access to the president was proving helpful, even if McFarlane sometimes bristled at being bypassed.[37] "Most people think we should make a real try with the new Soviet leadership," he said. "If so, we have to show we are serious and ready to negotiate. I'll want to draw people out and get some running room. If there were a mutual desire, we could do something, but the Soviets are as worried as we are about how to posture. Is the best way to do things one at a time to encourage the atmosphere? Should we try to do something more major? The first didn't work last summer. KAL stopped it. But really Andropov stopped it before the KAL."[38]

Shultz's impulse to accelerate diplomacy with the Kremlin seemed to hit a wall at a meeting of top officials chaired by Reagan. Weinberger was particularly resistant. Shultz reported sarcastically to colleagues, "What I got out of the meeting there is a desire to move forward on most things as long as the Soviets agree to our positions completely. At least that's what Cap wants. The president wants to move if we can get decisions to him. Cap wants everything to move through the interagency group. . . . Movement on arms control will be very hard. Cap wants no changes in our position or in the channel we use. He simply wants the Soviets to come back to the table. I'm not sure this is what the president wants." Weinberger also objected to sending Scowcroft to Moscow as a special emissary. Larry Eagleburger, soon to step down as deputy secretary of state, was discouraged. "Hopeless! Hopeless!" he muttered. Seitz noted in his journal, "Now I can't see any reason for GPS to serve in a second administration."[39]

When Shultz arrived at his office the next morning, he seemed more optimistic. He told Seitz in confidence that Reagan had proposed inviting the Kremlin leadership to the 1984 Summer Olympics in Los Angeles and spending some time with Chernenko at the Reagan ranch in Santa Barbara.[40] More good news came a few days later when McFarlane reported that Reagan had approved some adjustments in the American negotiating position on long-range nuclear weapons and the intermediate-range missile talks. The president also signed off on a letter to Chernenko that held out some hope for better relations.[41]

As he prepared for a meeting with Dobrynin, Shultz listed the steps that Reagan was prepared to take. "We are ready to talk about START [Strategic Arms Reduction Treaty], but not in this channel," he said, meaning the administration hoped to open a private channel with the Kremlin to test some new START proposals. He reported that Reagan was open to revising the American bargaining stance about reducing conventional forces in Europe. He saw potential progress on a chemical weapons treaty; a technical upgrade of the hotline to Moscow, the special communications channel reserved for urgent talks during an escalating crisis; and the opening of new consulates, including a Soviet office in New York and an American consulate in Kiev. The list extended to agricultural, environmental, health and cultural matters. All in all, it was an ambitious agenda. As Tom Simons observed, there was plenty to talk about, much of it on issues that the Kremlin favored discussing, so the Kremlin would have to decide it really wanted to engage the Reagan administration in serious talks across an array of topics.[42]

Dobrynin responded cautiously to the agenda. He told Shultz that Gorbachev was likely to be elevated to serve as second in command at the Kremlin. The Soviet ambassador suggested that Chernenko would be dependent on Gromyko for managing relations with Washington, signaling that significant policy changes were unlikely. He also indicated that the Scowcroft mission was unwelcome because the Kremlin preferred to work through established channels.[43] In fact, Gromyko, wary of any back channel that might bypass him, rebuffed the Scowcroft initiative a few days later. It was quickly abandoned when Gromyko directed Scowcroft to meet with a deputy foreign minister. Meantime, the Pentagon, adamantly opposed to Shultz's initiatives, pressed Reagan to resist new diplomatic efforts with Moscow. Knowing that interagency policy making was slow and vulnerable to delaying tactics, Shultz said, "If someone wants to stop something, he can bring the whole process to a halt. In this administration, we have a veto-oriented decision process."[44]

Prospects for renewed engagement with the Kremlin sagged when the Soviet Union announced it would boycott the Olympic Games in Los Angeles. The decision mirrored Jimmy Carter's decision not to send an American team to the Moscow Olympics in 1980 after the Soviet invasion of Afghanistan. The Soviet decision aborted the idea of inviting Chernenko to Los Angeles and the Reagan ranch. When Reagan proposed sending an invitation despite the boycott, Shultz and other aides strongly advised against it. The plan was dropped. The chill with Moscow deepened when the Kremlin confined Andrei Sakharov's wife, Yelena Bonner, to the Sakharov apartment in Gorky, where the physicist and designer of Moscow's first hydrogen bomb had been exiled in 1980 after criticizing Soviet leaders.

As Shultz dealt with these setbacks, Walter Mondale rolled through the Democratic presidential primaries once Gary Hart's candidacy faded after some early success. Mondale's attacks on Reagan's record as president concentrated on domestic issues but repeatedly chastised Reagan for escalating tensions with the Soviet Union and failing to reach any new arms control agreements with the Kremlin. In his acceptance speech on the last night of the Democratic convention in San Francisco on July 19, Mondale berated Reagan for mishandling relations with the Kremlin:

> We know the deep differences with the Soviets. And America condemns their repression of dissidents and Jews, their suppression of Solidarity, their invasion of Afghanistan, their meddling around the world. But the truth is that between us, we have the capacity to destroy the planet. Every President since the bomb has gone off has understood that. Every other President talked with the Soviets and negotiated arms control: Why has this Administration failed? Why haven't they tried? Why can't they understand the cry of Americans and human beings for sense and sanity in control of these God-awful weapons? Why? Why?
>
> Why can't we meet in summit conferences with the Soviet Union at least once a year? Why can't we reach agreements to save this Earth? The truth is, we can.[45]

Reagan gave new ammunition to Mondale on August 11 when, unaware he was on a hot microphone while preparing to give his weekly Saturday radio address, he jokingly told aides, "My fellow Americans, I'm pleased to tell you today that I've signed legislation that will outlaw Russia forever. We begin bombing in five minutes." Reagan blamed the press for the resulting international flap. "I gave the press an opening to display their irresponsibility which they did," he noted in his diary. "The networks had a line open & recorded it and of course made it public—hence an international incident."[46]

As the perturbations continued in Washington and Moscow, Shultz began to hear from a variety of American diplomats that Soviet officials they encountered were privately inquiring if a Gromyko visit to Washington in September might be possible after he attended the annual UN General

Assembly meeting in New York. Until the Soviet invasion of Afghanistan in 1979, Gromyko had routinely added an autumn stop in Washington to meet with the secretary of state and often with the president. Jimmy Carter suspended the visits to protest the Soviet action in Afghanistan, and Reagan had shown no interest in resuming them. Shultz reported to Reagan in August: "At four different places in Europe, US diplomats have been approached by Soviet representatives who say virtually the same thing. We interpret the comments to mean that if Gromyko is invited to Washington as he used to be, he would accept." Shultz called the Soviet signaling an indication that the Kremlin was eager to put relations on a more productive track. "The Soviets blinked," he later said.[47] Reagan immediately approved. The meeting was set for September 28 in the Oval Office, with a working lunch to follow at the White House.

Reagan's admirers like to argue that he effectively used his first term to strengthen America's military forces and rattle the Soviet Union with his aggressive rhetoric and the launch of the space-based missile defense program. Certainly, Reagan's hard approach alarmed the Kremlin and motivated it to seek a less combustible relationship. But nearing the end of four years as president, Reagan did not have a single significant diplomatic achievement with Moscow to go with his combative strategy. The conundrum of Reagan's first term was vividly evident at a contentious meeting of top officials at the White House on September 18. The subject was whether the administration should agree to a Soviet proposal to open talks in Vienna about the militarization of space, including topics such as anti-satellite weapons (ASATs). The discussion also touched on how Reagan should handle his upcoming meeting with Gromyko.

"We should try to move the ball along now," Shultz said, according to minutes of the meeting. "To do so, we need to make reasonably concrete proposals." Weinberger shot back, "Now is very inappropriate for any proposals. There is no interagency position on ASAT or defensive systems." Casey and General P. X. Kelley, the commandant of the Marine Corps, agreed with Weinberger. Shultz impatiently responded: "The idea of waiting for the interagency group to agree is a non-starter. The IG never agrees. If we wait for it to agree, nothing will go to the president. The IG is not a fourth branch of government. We can't give it a veto power." Clearly irritated, he vented about the entire Reagan first term: "The idea of general palaver now and specifics later is unreal. We have been around four years. What have we been doing?"[48]

Reagan, like Shultz, did not want to get sidetracked by specific negotiation positions. "Maybe we need a general discussion to clear the air, telling them these are the reasons why we fear your actions. We are not going to seek advantage, but we will keep our defenses up." He argued for exploring in a general way how to get agreement. The meeting, like so much of the administration's debates about Soviet policy, ended without a clear mandate to Shultz to pursue diplomatic solutions.[49] Ken Dam, who attended the meeting in his role as deputy secretary of state, was appalled by the discussion. He noted: "It was clear that the President wanted to take some steps in the meeting with Gromyko and particularly to hold out some prospect of real movement on our arms control position. But except for the Secretary of State, all of the agencies appeared implacably against anything significant." Dam reported that as the meeting neared an end, Bob Gates, the deputy CIA director, handed him a note saying that "the president was out in front of all of his advisers."[50]

Reagan and Shultz devoted a great deal of additional time preparing for the Gromyko meeting. Reagan ultimately drafted his own talking points. He told Shultz, "George, I've looked over your talking points, and they are very good. But I've been thinking about this all weekend up at Camp David, and I've written my own talking points, and I'm very satisfied with them. You can look them over if you want."[51] They reflected his earnest desire to tamp down cold war tensions, reduce American and Soviet nuclear arsenals, defuse regional conflicts and address Soviet human rights abuses. His reasoning about raising human rights, which Soviet leaders vehemently rejected as unacceptable interference in their internal affairs, offered a revealing glimpse of Reagan's idealized view of America:

> Ours is a nation of immigrants. We are made up of the bloodlines of all the world and our people retain a loyalty to the countries of their origin. A man does not forget his mother because he has taken a wife. We also have a governmental system responsive to public opinion. It is easier for us to arrive at agreements with you if segments of our society are not upset by what they feel is a violation of human rights in the land of their ancestry. May I point to your handling of the matter of the Pentecostal families in our embassy. We have not, nor will we indicate in any way that this was anything other than a generous action by your gov-

ernment. Your handling of that matter made such things as the grain agreement easier for us to achieve.[52]

Reagan also returned to a theme he often cited in public and private—that after World War II, when the United States had a monopoly on nuclear weapons and unchallenged global military superiority, it had generously come to the aid of its erstwhile enemies and acted with restraint. His hand-written draft, discovered years later in a desk drawer, was the work of a man who genuinely thought he could reason with Kremlin leaders and convince them that America's intentions were honorable and peaceful. Naïve as it may have been, it was a far gentler message than the one his administration had conveyed for nearly all of his first term.

The importance of the Gromyko meeting for Reagan was evident in the extended diary entry he recorded that evening:

> The big day—Andrei Gromyko. Meeting held in Oval office. Five waves of photographers—1st time that many. I opened with my monologue and made the point that perhaps both of us felt the other was a threat then explained by the record we had more reason to feel that way than they did. His opener was about 30 min's. then we went into dialogue. I had taken notes on his pitch and rebutted with fact & figure a number of his points. I kept emphasizing that we were the two nations that could destroy or save the world. I figured they nurse a grudge that we don't respect them as a super-power. All in all 3 hrs. including lunch were I believe well spent. Everyone at our end thinks he's going home with a pretty clear view of where we stand.[53]

Shultz was bemused by Gromyko's encounter with Nancy Reagan during the interval between the meeting and lunch:

> I said to Nancy, "How about coming to the stand-around time? You're the hostess." She thought that was a good idea, so she did. Gromyko was a smart guy. He saw Nancy Reagan and made a beeline for her. There was nobody else in the room as far as he was concerned, and they talked. All of a sudden, he said to her, "Does your husband want peace?" Nancy bristled and said, "Of course my husband wants peace." Gromyko said, "Well then, every night before he goes to sleep, whisper in his ear 'Peace.' Gromyko was taller than Nancy so she put her hands on his shoulders and pulled him down so he had to bend his knees and she said, 'I'll whisper it in your ear, 'Peace.'"[54]

While the meeting resolved nothing, as expected, it reopened Soviet-American face-to-face communication at the highest level, putting Shultz on track to talk further with Gromyko in Geneva in early January 1985, assuming Reagan was elected to a second term. "All in all, President Reagan and I felt that a great deal of progress had been made. We had engaged in a rigorous give-and-take on nearly every global and bilateral issue. The discussions had been direct and nonconfrontational."[55] The *New York Times* reported: "Today's talks brought to a conclusion an unusual week of foreign policy activity that marked an interlude in President Reagan's reelection campaign. At the same time, White House officials have made no secret of their goal of using the meetings with Mr. Gromyko and others this week to enhance the President's ratings as a leader concerned about reducing world tensions."[56]

Walter Mondale was not impressed. "The American people have seen the pictures and read the captions," he declared. "But when it comes to war and peace that's not nearly enough. For four years he has pursued an arms race in the name of arms control and has nothing to show for it."[57] When Reagan and Mondale engaged foreign policy issues on October 21 in their third nationally televised presidential debate, the Democratic nominee excoriated Reagan for his handling of East-West relations, suggesting at one point that Reagan did not even understand arms control issues and his own Strategic Defense Initiative. "Who's in charge, who's handling these matters?" he scoffed. "Your definition of military strength is to throw money at the Defense Department," Mondale said. "When you pay $500 for a $5 hammer, you're not buying strength."[58]

The *New York Times* reported:

> Mr. Mondale leaped on a suggestion by Mr. Reagan that space-based antimissile systems could be shared with the Soviet Union under some future treaties.
> "The idea that we would share this with the Soviet Union is, in my mind, a total nonstarter," Mr. Mondale said. He then condemned the entire program. "Why don't we stop this madness now and draw a line to keep the heavens free of war?" Mr. Mondale asked.[59]

Mondale's criticism did not stick. Reagan crushed him on election day, winning 58.8 percent of the popular vote to Mondale's meager 40.6 percent. Reagan carried every state but Mondale's home state of Minnesota. Although cold war issues did not play a central role in the campaign, the victory left Reagan free to deal as he wished with the Kremlin. Shultz clearly understood the outcome could strengthen his hand in the administration if Reagan remained on a negotiating track with the Kremlin.

But just getting to the Geneva meeting with a unified administration strategy and team proved challenging. The internal strife that had beset the administration since Reagan's 1981 inauguration flared anew now that high-level talks were resuming with the Kremlin. First came a fight over who would set nuclear arms control strategy. Nominally, the secretary of state did, but Shultz's fitful effort to run arms control policy over the past few years made clear that opening a new round of talks with the Kremlin would require greater coherence and clearer leadership.

That was painfully evident when Ken Adelman, who had taken over as director of the Arms Control and Disarmament Agency in 1983 despite Shultz's misgivings, defied Shultz by publicly calling for a radical shift in arms control strategy. Instead of spending years trying to negotiate complex arm accords, Adelman told the *Wall Street Journal*, Washington and Moscow should make independent but reciprocal cuts in their arsenals. Shultz was infuriated that Adelman had ignored his request to limit discussion of the idea to internal channels. Shultz urged Reagan to name Paul Nitze as arms control policy coordinator. Ed Rowny, the chief negotiator at the strategic arms talks, bitterly opposed the idea. Weinberger and Casey were unenthusiastic. Just at the moment when Reagan was overwhelmingly reelected and the Kremlin was keen to explore diplomatic opportunities, the Reagan team was as disjointed as ever.

Sensing that Reagan's second term would replicate the Soviet policy meltdowns of the first, Bud McFarlane made a valiant effort to get Reagan to quell the feuding. "The problems between George Shultz and Cap Weinberger had not improved over time," McFarlane recalled. "If anything, despite my efforts and those of their subordinates at creating harmony, they persisted."[60] After repeatedly witnessing the tension between the men, McFarlane said, "It became clear that Weinberger was acting not out of reasoned policy differences, but instinctively; he was not giving anti-policy speeches, he was giving anti-Shultz speeches." McFarlane, who thought Weinberger was miscast as defense secretary and never really mastered Pentagon policy issues, attributed Weinberger's hostility to a desire to be secretary of state. "Weinberger lusted to replace Shultz, no doubt believing that as the president's conservative conscience, he was the man best suited to formulating and running foreign policy.[61]

Returning to Washington from California with Reagan on Air Force One on November 11, McFarlane bluntly described the constant bickering between Shultz and Weinberger: "I must tell you, Mr. President," he said, "that I fear that nothing can get accomplished if you don't recognize that you face paralysis within your administration owing to the largely personal animus that exists between Cap and George." If Reagan was unwilling to build his team around one or the other, instead of keeping both, McFarlane predicted, "you're going to have discord and you're going to have to be the arbiter and be much more active."[62] McFarlane's intervention, along with some separate comments to Reagan by Shultz, got Reagan's attention. On November 14 the president noted in his diary: "We have trouble. Cap and Bill Casey have views contrary to Sec. Shultz's on S. Am., the middle East and our arms negotiations. It's so out of hand George sounds like he wants out. I can't let that happen. Actually George is carrying out my policy. I'm going to meet Cap & Bill & lay it out to them. Won't be fun but has to be done."[63]

Back in Washington, McFarlane discussed the issue privately with Shultz, who said he would bring it up himself again with Reagan at their next meeting with McFarlane on November 16. When they convened in the Oval Office, Shultz said, "To succeed, we have to have a team: right now, there isn't one. Cap Weinberger, Bill Casey, Jeane Kirkpatrick and I just don't see things the same way." He denounced the constant leaks, end runs, failures to follow through on decisions and other maneuvers. "I have always been able to develop a team wherever I have worked. Here I have been unable to do so. I can't produce a team for you. I'm frustrated and ready to step aside so you can put somebody else at State who can get along with them. You will see no results without a team."[64]

Shultz recalled, "We were smack in the middle of what was ever more clearly shaping up to be the endgame of the cold war."[65] While that was an overstatement at the time, there seemed little doubt that the administration would squander a promising opportunity if Shultz showed up in Geneva without a unified American strategy. After consulting Bush about the infighting, Reagan asked Weinberger and Casey to meet him at the White House on November 17 before he departed for Thanksgiving break in California. "Tomorrow morning I'm meeting with Cap W & Bill Casey to iron out (if I can) some difficulties involving George S," Reagan noted in his diary on November 16. White House records show the meeting lasted fifty-three minutes, but no record of the conversation was made.[66]

"I had stirred things up, and that was to the good, but I had no illusions that the battle would end," Shultz recalled.[67] Hoping a neutral, intimate setting might help, he secured Reagan's support for a weekly lunch with Weinberger, Casey and McFarlane in the Old Family Dining Room located in the residential quarters at the White House. The first lunch on December 1 quickly disintegrated into an argument. "Cap was impossible: he was not even willing to have us reiterate to the Soviets our own START and INF positions. He took up most of the time, elaborating endlessly on his positions, setting up straw men and knocking them down. When I spoke, he half closed his eyes. Nothing was accomplished."[68]

Some of the differences about how to handle Shultz's upcoming meeting with Gromyko were resolved in late December when Shultz, Weinberger and McFarlane met with Reagan for nearly two hours at Sunnylands, the expansive Palm Springs estate of Walter Annenberg, the founder of *TV Guide*. Reagan's pre-Thanksgiving exhortation to Weinberger and Casey to cease feuding with Shultz may have helped diminish the friction between Shultz and Weinberger in Palm Springs. The discussion yielded agreement on negotiation instructions for Shultz that were spelled out in a National Security Decision Directive on January 1, 1985. The overarching goal was to gain agreement from Gromyko to restructure and energize nuclear arms talks. The directive called for "a sustained, formal negotiation process with the Soviet Union on offensive nuclear arms which would permit us to pursue our goal of achieving deep reductions in U.S. and Soviet arsenals." The directive stipulated that strategic nuclear weapons talks and negotiations about intermediate-range nuclear missiles be substantively separate, and procedurally distinct, if possible. It endorsed negotiations on defensive systems, including space weapons. Reflecting Reagan and Weinberger's commitment to the development of a space-based missile shield, the directive stated that the Strategic Defense Initiative should be protected during arms talks.[69]

"I finally had the negotiating room I needed," Shultz recalled.[70] In his first session with Gromyko, Shultz outlined the American plan for negotiations over three primary issues: space-based systems, strategic weapons and intermediate-range forces. The two sides jousted over the course of two days, eventually agreeing to launch new negotiations on nuclear weapons and space arms. "I think this is an opportunity for a new beginning," Shultz told Reagan in a call from Geneva. "There is a wide difference of opinion on important topics, and the negotiations will be long and tumultuous. It will require patience, but we have an agreement."[71] Reagan was pleased. "Word from Geneva continues to be good.'. . . . I was in the family theatre briefing for tomorrow nites press conf. when I was called upstairs to take a call from George S. on the secure phone. The meetings in Geneva are over & the Soviets have agreed to enter negotiations on nuclear weapons etc. Within the month a time & place will be agreed upon."[72] A day later Reagan noted, "George S. is back & things are better than I'd thought & I thought they were pretty good."[73]

Reagan remained upbeat about the meeting and prospects for relations with Moscow at his opening news conference in 1985, the first since his reelection. The *New York Times* reported:

> President Reagan said today that he hoped the agreement with the Soviet Union on holding arms talks would produce "a new dialogue" and better relations between the two countries.
> Mr. Reagan said he hoped the improved climate brought on by arms talks would also lead to warmer relations on other issues, such as trade and handling of regional conflicts.[74]

A few weeks later in his second inaugural address, delivered inside the Capitol Rotunda because of the frigid Washington weather, Reagan emphasized his desire to work with Soviet leaders. While reminding Americans that he had strengthened American military forces, he declared:

> There is only one way safely and legitimately to reduce the cost of national security, and that is to reduce the need for it. And this we are trying to do in negotiations with the Soviet Union. We are not just discussing limits on a further increase of nuclear weapons. We seek, instead, to reduce their number. We seek the total elimination one day of nuclear weapons from the face of the Earth.
> Now, for decades, we and the Soviets have lived under the threat of mutual assured destruction; if either resorted to the use of nuclear weapons, the other could retaliate and destroy the one who had started it. Is there either logic or morality in believing that if one side threatens to kill tens of millions of our people, our only recourse is to threaten killing tens of millions of theirs?

I have approved a research program to find, if we can, a security shield that would destroy nuclear missiles before they reach their target. It wouldn't kill people, it would destroy weapons. It wouldn't militarize space, it would help demilitarize the arsenals of Earth. It would render nuclear weapons obsolete. We will meet with the Soviets, hoping that we can agree on a way to rid the world of the threat of nuclear destruction.[75]

The shift toward better relations with Moscow was accelerating as Reagan began his second term. Hard-edged disagreements within the administration remained, but Shultz and the president were aligned on the core objectives, and the policy-making process was bending toward Shultz. The question was whether the Kremlin could respond in kind.

CHAPTER EIGHTEEN

Sea Change in the Kremlin

THE ANSWER CAME QUICKLY with the elevation of Mikhail Gorbachev as Soviet leader in March 1985. Shultz immediately recognized that Gorbachev could be the key to modulating the cold war. Though worn down by the years of conflict with his opponents and his frustration with Reagan's indecisiveness, Shultz rallied as the opportunities with Gorbachev drew into view. Discarding another impulse to resign, he navigated through continuing resistance from Weinberger, Casey and others, skillfully guiding Reagan toward a meeting with Gorbachev, Reagan's first summit with a Soviet leader. As Reagan himself sensed the peacemaking possibilities, he gave Shultz increased latitude. Over time, Shultz edged ever closer to becoming the indispensable man, the secretary of state he had always wanted to be—the president's partner in winding down the cold war.

Kremlin watchers in Moscow suspected Chernenko had died as soon as Radio Mayak, one of the Soviet Union's main stations, switched from normal programming to solemn classical music shortly after 1:00 a.m. on March 11, 1985. Further evidence came when several Politburo members traveling abroad abruptly cut short their trips to head back to Moscow. The Kremlin confirmed the news a few hours later, simultaneously announcing that Mikhail Gorbachev would succeed Chernenko. The ascent of Gorbachev, age fifty-four, signaled that a new generation of leaders would be taking power in Moscow. Although Gorbachev's intentions, and the strength of his position within the Kremlin, were opaque to Western leaders and intelligence agencies, Soviet officials who knew him well understood that he represented a sea change in the governance of their nation and empire. His faith in Communism was strong, but he recognized that the Soviet Union was a declining power in all but military dimensions. He knew the Soviet economy, stifled by decades of central planning and state control, was anemic. He was well aware that the standard of living across the USSR, especially shortages of food and consumer goods, left his country increasingly far behind the United States and other capitalist countries. While loyal to the Communist Party, which he now headed, he recognized the party was crippled by stale dogma and resistant to change.

On global issues, Gorbachev saw that ever-increasing defense expenditures to support an endless arms race with the United States were not sustainable and that the nuclear balance of terror with the United States was senseless. His intention as Soviet leader was to reform and refresh the Soviet Communist Party and the Soviet Union itself, not to dismantle them. To that end, he planned to pursue policies of renovation, not revolution, encouraging greater openness and transparency (glasnost), political restructuring (perestroika) and a fresh approach to Kremlin foreign policy.

Much of this was as yet unknown outside a small group of Gorbachev allies in Moscow, but the Politburo's swift decision to promote Gorbachev within hours of Chernenko's death indicated that even the Kremlin's sclerotic establishment knew the nation needed a younger, dynamic leader. When word of Chernenko's death reached Shultz, his first impulse was that this time—the third Kremlin leadership transition in less than three years—Reagan should go to Moscow to attend the funeral. Reagan disagreed: "Awakened at 4 A.M. to be told Chernenko is dead. My mind turned to whether I should attend the funeral. My gut instinct said no. Got to the office at 9. George S. had some argument that I should—he lost. I don't think his heart was really in it. George B. is in Geneva—he'll go & George S. will join him leaving tonight."[1]

As Shultz prepared to leave for Moscow, the CIA and State Department doubted that Gorbachev's appointment would lead to significant change in Moscow's foreign or domestic policies. The day after Gorbachev took power, the consensus among National Security Council staff members was that the transfer of power in the Kremlin augured no change in Soviet policy. "In spite of the fact that we have a new face," a secret memo said, "we will be dealing with a quintessential Communist Party man, whose ability to exercise his own individual political predilections is severely constrained by the control mechanism built into the Soviet system." The memo went on: "The very fact of a new face, however, tempts many Americans—most importantly, members of Congress—to believe that a new General Secretary has similar latitude for individual decision-making as does an American President. From this assumption comes the further assumption that it is within Gorbachev's power to change radically the character of Soviet policy toward the West."[2]

The *New York Times* captured the uncertain mood in a story from Moscow:

> For all the fervor, style and obvious achievement he has displayed in reaching the highest position in the Soviet power structure, Mr. Gorbachev and the generation he represents remain an untested and largely unknown political force.
> These are people who were reared after the war and after the Stalinist terrors, who grew up in a state more secure in its power and potential, men who got better educations than their predecessors and had more contact with the outside world.
> Yet these are also men who have made their careers in a Communist Party that has changed from an idealistic elite into an entrenched, privileged and self-perpetuating bureaucracy intolerant of too much independence or nonconformism among its members.[3]

A few hours after the Chernenko funeral in Red Square, Shultz and Bush met with Gorbachev and several Kremlin aides for eighty-five minutes in St. Catherine's Hall, an ornate room in the Grand Kremlin Palace. Bush handed Gorbachev a letter from Reagan inviting him to visit Washington at his earliest convenience. The letter said, in part, "As you assume your new responsibilities, I would like to take this opportunity to underscore my hope that we can in the months and years ahead develop a more stable and constructive relationship between our two countries."[4]

Gorbachev, an energetic, balding, compact man with a conspicuous red birthmark high on his forehead, opened by outlining his views on international relations. With Bush taking the lead for the Americans, Shultz observed Gorbachev closely during the encounter. It did not take long for him to see that Gorbachev was far more intellectually agile, informed and open-minded than his predecessors, or for that matter, any senior Soviet official Shultz had met. "Gorbachev had an extensive set of typed notes that he shuffled around and at first looked at from time to time," Shultz recalled. "He soon put them aside completely. He was articulate and spontaneous. He seemed to be thinking out loud. Maybe he was. . . . Gorbachev's free-flowing monologue showed a mind working at high intensity, even at the end of a long, hard day. He displayed a breadth of view and vigor, I thought, but his basic positions were ones we had heard before."[5]

While Gorbachev's tour d'horizon did not depart from familiar Soviet policies, his fluency in global relations impressed Shultz, who knew that Gorbachev's Communist Party career dealt primarily with domestic affairs, including agriculture. Gorbachev told Shultz and Bush that the Kremlin entertained no expansionist ambitions, was determined to avoid a military conflict with the United States and would leave it to history to judge whether Communism or capitalism was the better system. He stressed the importance of bringing the nuclear arms race under control before technological advances produced irreversible developments such as space-based weapons, clearly a reference to Reagan's missile shield plans.

When his turn came to address Gorbachev at the meeting, Shultz told him:

> President Reagan told me to look you squarely in the eyes and tell you: "Ronald Reagan believes that this is a very special moment in the history of mankind." You are starting your term as general secretary. Ronald Reagan is starting his second term as president. Negotiations are beginning in Geneva. Over the past year we have found solutions to some problems, though not to the great problems, and if it is at all possible, we must establish a more constructive relationship between the United States and the USSR. President Reagan knows that he personally must work on this hard, and he is ready to do so. He expects the negotiators in Geneva to discuss the details, and there are many of them, but only people like those present in this room and the president can resolve the main issues. President Reagan is ready to work with you and in his letter is inviting you to visit the United States at the earliest convenient time.[6]

Shortly after the meeting, Shultz told Bush and other colleagues, "In Gorbachev we have an entirely different kind of leader in the Soviet Union than we have experienced before." Shultz thought that Gorbachev "was quicker, fresher, more engaging, and more wide ranging in his interests and knowledge. The content of our meeting was tough and his manner was aggressive, but the spirit was different. He was comfortable with himself and with others, joking with Gromyko in a way that emerged from a genuine confidence in his base of knowledge and in his political abilities. . . . He performs like a man who has been in charge for a while, not like a man who is just taking charge."[7]

Shultz summed up his reaction to Gorbachev in a conversation with Brian Mulroney, the Canadian prime minister, who had also come to Moscow for the funeral. When Mulroney asked Shultz when he expected to see "serious change" start in the Soviet Union, Shultz replied, "today."[8] Shultz's view of the new Soviet leader dovetailed with Margaret Thatcher's impression of Gorbachev. After spending time with Gorbachev during his visit to Britain at the end of 1984, Thatcher memorably told the BBC, "I am cautiously optimistic. I like Mr. Gorbachev. We can do business together."[9] After three years of toiling with little success to ease tensions between Washington and Moscow, Shultz now appeared to have an interlocutor in the Kremlin capable of moving relations to a new plane. First impressions were unreliable, but as he had told Gorbachev, the nearly simultaneous start of Reagan's second term and Gorbachev's rise to power presented a rare moment to alter the course of the cold war.

As he jetted back to Washington, Shultz could not help wondering if he could consolidate the gains he had made inside the administration to move American policy in the directions he favored. He also wondered if Gorbachev could move the Soviet Union. He knew that the administration's initial response to Gorbachev would help shape how the new Soviet leader handled his job and old guard colleagues remaining on the Politburo, including Gromyko. To make progress, Washington would need to encourage cooperation, not rebuff it.

Back in Washington a few days later, Bush and Shultz told Dobrynin in separate encounters that Gorbachev had impressed them. When Dobrynin noted to Bush that Reagan's hard public rhetoric about the Soviet Union seemed to belie his interest in working with the Kremlin, Bush told him not to be distracted by Reagan's statements. "Reagan is still Reagan," he said.[10] On March 24, Reagan received a positive letter from Gorbachev responding to the letter Bush had given the Soviet leader in Moscow. Gorbachev welcomed the invitation to arrange a summit meeting, even if new accords were not signed at the gathering. Gorbachev demurred on setting a date.

Shultz pointed out to Reagan that the letter was "notable for its non-polemical tone."[11]

The same day, an incident in East Germany abruptly undercut the new sense of optimism about relations with Moscow. McFarlane awakened Reagan to inform him that a Soviet sentry had shot and killed Major Arthur D. Nicholson Jr., an army officer attached to an American military liaison office in Potsdam, as Nicholson was conducting reconnaissance of Soviet forces in the area. Nicholson's role in East Germany, including monitoring Soviet forces, was permitted under one of a series of agreements in 1946 and 1947 to coordinate activities by foreign forces in the four occupation zones established in Germany by the United States, Britain, France and the Soviet Union after the war. Moscow quickly accused Nicholson of "espionage activities" and, as in the downing of the Korean airliner two years earlier, offered no apology for the attack. "It was cold-blooded murder," Shultz recalled.[12]

The incident instantly ignited a new round of debate in the Reagan administration over how to respond and whether to scuttle the encouraging initial overtures to Gorbachev. Hoping to defuse the mini-crisis, Shultz summoned Dobrynin to the State Department, where he demanded an apology, restitution for the Nicholson family and new safeguards to protect the security of the American liaison operation in Potsdam. Dobrynin agreed that Soviet and American commanders should meet to review ground rules. Cap Weinberger objected, calling the plan a "love and kisses" session,[13] and refused to dispatch any American officers to a meeting until an apology was received. Shultz argued that it would be acceptable if an apology was made at the meeting and that it was critically important not to let the incident throw relations into a new tailspin.

Weinberger's anger escalated in early April after he watched a jovial and smiling Dobrynin field questions about the attack in a televised interview. He called Reagan, who watched the broadcast and was also upset.[14] The internal strains were evident at the end of April when officials met over breakfast to discuss whether Malcolm Baldrige, the commerce secretary, should travel to Moscow on a trade mission. Weinberger, Casey and Donald Regan opposed the idea. Shultz and McFarlane favored going. "The scene was bizarre," Shultz recalled. "Here was the president ready to lead the charge to engage with the Soviets. At the same time, his secretary of defense and director of central intelligence were leading their own charge in exactly the opposite direction."[15]

As the wrangling continued over how to respond to the Nicholson killing, Reagan was consumed by a public furor over his decision to accept an invitation from Helmut Kohl to visit a World War II military cemetery outside Bitburg, West Germany. The notion of an American president honoring soldiers of the Third Reich seemed heretical, and it became even more politically explosive when word came that the cemetery included graves of members of the Waffen SS, among the most brutal of Nazi forces. Reagan refused to back down but did add a stop at the remnant of the Bergen-Belsen concentration camp. The tempest raged for days before, during and after Reagan's early May visit to West Germany.

On May 14, Shultz met with Gromyko in Vienna, the first extensive discussion with a Kremlin leader since the leadership transition in Moscow two months earlier. Shultz and Gromyko came to the meeting with the usual lists of talking points and policy positions, but the real point was to see if a Reagan-Gorbachev summit would be possible. The two men, and their supporting casts, spent six hours going over their briefs without a single word about the summit option. Shultz deliberately avoided the topic, determined that the United States not seem to be overly eager to arrange a meeting. As the marathon session ended, an aide whispered to Shultz that Gromyko wished to see him privately. As Shultz and Gromyko huddled in a corner of the room, Gromyko asked if there was anything else that Shultz wanted to discuss. "No," Shultz answered. "I've gone through everything." Gromyko than asked, "What about the summit?" They spent the next few minutes talking about possible venues. Reagan wanted Gorbachev to come to Washington. Gromyko rejected the idea. The conversation turned to Geneva, perhaps by the end of the year. "The meeting had been sterile and peculiar—but at the final moment productive," Shultz recalled.[16]

The two men talked further the next evening after a dinner marking the thirtieth anniversary of the Austrian State Treaty that established Austria as an independent, neutral nation after World War II. Gromyko seemed much more enthusiastic about setting Soviet-American relations on a more positive course. Shultz surmised: "He had been sent to tell me that the Soviets wanted a summit and to make it appear, if possible, that the United States was the petitioner. Gorbachev had reduced him to an errand boy."[17]

Shultz did not realize how accurate the putdown was. Even though Gromyko had nominated Gorbachev to be Communist Party general secretary and urged Politburo members to elect him at the decisive meeting following Chernenko's death, Gorbachev considered him dogmatic and tiresome. He also did not forget that Gromyko had criticized Gorbachev's performance during his visit to Britain in late 1984. Gromyko, in turn, privately complained about Gorbachev.[18]

Shultz himself was weary from the internal battles and the meandering state of Soviet relations, even with the hopeful signs from Gorbachev. He ran into resistance to a summit when he got back to Washington on May 17. McFarlane told him Reagan was not inclined to travel abroad to meet Gorbachev, reflecting the sequencing of cold war summit meetings that called for the United States to host the next one. Reagan himself seemed cool to a meeting. He told Shultz they should "think about it some more, play hard to get." Shultz pushed back. "Many key people in your administration do not want a summit," he said. "You have to make up your mind. You have to step up to the plate. And when it comes to the divisions in your administration over the issue, you can't split the difference."[19] To make his impatience clear, he told Reagan he planned to step down as secretary in late summer. "He's tired and wants to bow out before the summer is over," Reagan noted in his diary on May 17. "I told him that I had never envisioned being here without him but didn't have the heart to lean on him if he really wants to go. I'm afraid he really wants to go."[20]

A few days later, Shultz returned to the Oval Office with the outline for a summit meeting in November in Geneva. Reagan approved. After further communications with the Kremlin, a date was set: November 19–20. The decision reassured Shultz, and he dropped the threat to resign. In late June, Casey sent Reagan a CIA assessment of Gorbachev's first one hundred days as Kremlin leader, describing it as "good airplane reading" and noting that it offered "a good picture of Gorbachev's style, objectives and operating methods." The paper, titled "Gorbachev: The New Broom," opened by saying, "Gorbachev has demonstrated in his first 100 days that he is the most aggressive and activist Soviet leader since Khrushchev." The CIA found that "Gorbachev is gambling that an attack on corruption and inefficiency, not radical reform, will turn the domestic situation around." In regard to Soviet foreign policy, the agency stated, "Gorbachev's impact on foreign policy has so far been mostly stylistic. He has revealed no urgent agenda to match his determination to accelerate economic growth at home."[21]

Just days after Casey forwarded the report, Gorbachev appointed a new foreign minister, a dramatic and pivotal change that help set Kremlin foreign policy on a new, more productive trajectory. On July 2, the Kremlin announced that Gromyko had stepped aside after twenty-eight years to become president of the Soviet Union, a largely ceremonial post. To replace him, Gorbachev surprisingly selected Eduard Shevardnadze, the Communist Party chief of the Soviet republic of Georgia. Shevardnadze's appointment, and his simultaneous elevation to voting member of the Politburo, came eight months before nonvoting Politburo membership for another rising party star, Boris Yeltsin, the Moscow-area party boss. Yeltsin, who previously directed construction activity in the Soviet Union, had served as the party leader of Sverdlovsk Province, an industrial region in the Ural Mountains where the last czar, Nicholas II, and members of the imperial family were detained and executed following the Bolshevik seizure of power in Russia in 1917. The new appointments consolidated Gorbachev's power as he added allies and ousted rivals such as Grigory Romanov, the Leningrad party boss, and Victor Grishin, who preceded Yeltsin as head of the Moscow party committee.

The Shevardnadze announcement startled Western diplomats and journalists in Moscow accustomed to Kremlin promotions coming from a familiar roster of aged officials. It even caught top Soviet officials by surprise, including veteran Soviet diplomats who assumed one of their colleagues would be chosen, possibly Ambassador Dobrynin. Ambassador Hartman in Moscow cabled his initial assessment to Shultz: "Appointing a neophyte like Shevardnadze to be Foreign Minister will make it easier for Gorbachev and the party apparat to step into what has been for almost thirty years the preserve of Andrei Gromyko. . . . You will have an opportunity to size up this handsome, southern activist who has a lot of success behind him but unknown views on foreign policy."[22]

Jack Matlock, the senior Soviet specialist at the National Security Council, told his colleagues, "Gorbachev has pulled off a brilliant tactical move which puts him in direct charge of foreign policy. . . . Like Gorbachev, he [Shevardnadze] seems to have a flair for PR, and may be adept at projecting an attractive image to foreign audiences, in sharp contrast to the dour

Gromyko." Matlock added, "I expect to see no major changes in the Soviet policy toward the U.S. in the *immediate* future."[23]

The *New York Times* offered a Shevardnadze snapshot:

> Mr. Shevardnadze, 57 years old, made his mark in the freewheeling southern republic as a warrior against corruption and as an economic innovator. A career party worker, he spent several years as Georgian Interior Minister, presumably charged with routing out the rampant corruption for which Georgia has been legendary.
>
> In 1972, when the longtime Georgian leader, Vasily P. Mzhavanadze, was ousted by Mr. Brezhnev in a major scandal, Mr. Shevardnadze took charge. He led a purge of the Georgian party and undertook measures to strengthen the republic's economy. Georgia supplies subtropical produce such as tea and fruit.
>
> Mr. Shevardnadze, who became a candidate member of the Politburo in 1978, is a dapper man with wavy white hair and well-tailored suits. He has established a reputation in Georgia as a man tough on corruption but flexible in economic matters. The republic allows farmers larger private plots than the rest of the Soviet Union, and was a pioneer in decentralizing its agriculture.[24]

In reality, as later learned, Gorbachev and Shevardnadze were kindred spirits. They were born and raised in rural villages far from the center of power in Moscow—Gorbachev in the southern Russian agricultural region around the city of Stavropol, Shevardnadze in Georgia, a mountainous land on the Black Sea with its own distinctive identity, history, culture and language. Gorbachev's farming family had been victims of Stalin's tyranny, famine and the Nazi occupation of the region. Shevardnadze's father, Ambrosi, survived time in one of Stalin's Gulag labor camps. A distant cousin, Dimitri Shevardnadze, a painter, art collector and member of Georgia's cultural elite, was executed during Stalin's Great Terror, as were the parents of Shevardnadze's wife, Nanuli.

Both Gorbachev and Shevardnadze grew up wary of Communist Party autocracy even as they joined the party and rose to leadership posts. They met at regional party gatherings and became friends, comparing notes about misguided and failed Soviet policies. The friendship deepened when the men moved to Moscow and served together initially as nonvoting members of the Politburo. Neither man was invested in cold war doctrines and the hidebound mores of Soviet-American relations. In that sense, they were like Reagan and Shultz, who were foreign policy novices when they came to office and grew up distant from the hothouse politics of their capital cities.

Shultz knew little about the Gorbachev-Shevardnadze history as he prepared for his first encounter with Shevardnadze in late July. The setting would be a meeting of the Organization for Security and Cooperation in Europe (OSCE) marking the tenth anniversary of the signing of the Helsinki Final Act. The agreement was endorsed by thirty-five nations, including the United States, Canada, the Soviet Union and every European nation except Albania. It covered a broad range of political and economic issues and included a section affirming the importance of human rights, a free press, unfettered emigration and reunification of families separated by postwar borders. When signed in 1975, the accord seemed more aspirational than practical, but over time it proved to be a useful mechanism for pressing Moscow on human rights issues such as its suppression of dissidents, emigration restrictions and refusal to allow a small number of Soviet citizens married to Americans to be united with their spouses.

When Shultz learned that Shevardnadze would be accompanied by his wife, Nanuli, he invited O'Bie to join him, thinking there might be an opportunity for the two couples to get together and for the two wives to spend some time touring Helsinki together. After six stiff, chilly meetings with Gromyko, Shultz was eager to forge a more congenial relationship with Shevardnadze, if possible. "We're going to have plenty of arguments with this guy," he recalled telling O'Bie, "but let's make friends with him. We don't have to have personal animosity. Let's try to fix it so we don't have that problem."[25] The effort reflected his belief that a human touch could help resolve seemingly intractable conflicts and that cold war divisions might be ameliorated if American and Soviet leaders could build some rapport and make their encounters less frosty.

He found the ideal partner in Shevardnadze. Georgians by nature are a warm and spirited people who relish convivial gatherings of family and friends over dinners fueled with tangy Georgian cuisine and homegrown wines. Shevardnadze shared those traits, which masked a ruthless streak that had helped propel him through Communist Party ranks. Shultz established a different tone with the new Soviet foreign minister the moment Shultz walked into Finlandia Hall, the site of the OSCE meeting. Delegations were seated alphabetically, front row to rear in the large auditorium, using French as the operative language. That put the United States, États-Unis, in the front row, and the Soviet Union, Union soviétique, near the back. As Shultz and the American delegation entered the hall, Shultz placed his papers at the United States table and then mounted the steps toward the Soviet team. A hush fell over the hall as delegates realized Shultz was making his way to welcome Shevardnadze. Flashbulbs lit up as the two men shook hands.

When Shultz's turn came to address the delegations, he delivered a blistering critique of Soviet human rights abuses, detailing a litany of individual cases: Jews denied permission to emigrate, Soviet spouses of Americans prevented from being reunited and dissidents jailed, exiled or forcibly placed in psychiatric institutions. During a break, Shevardnadze asked him, "Did you have to deliver such a tough speech?" Shultz replied, "I just stated facts, and I look forward to discussing this subject privately with you."[26]

The two men, accompanied by a few aides, met for three hours the next day at the American ambassador's residence overlooking the Gulf of Finland. At Shultz's suggestion, approved by Shevardnadze, simultaneous translation was employed for the first time in Shultz's dealings with a Soviet official. The faster pace, compared to consecutive translation, allowed the men to cover more ground. Just days in his new job, Shevardnadze wanted to set aside the talking points prepared for him in Moscow but decided he might inadvertently wander off message, so he dutifully read the script. Ambassador Dobrynin hovered nearby, monitoring the performance. "I was a member of the Politburo," Shevardnadze recalled years later, "and there was an unwritten rule that all the Politburo members would read whatever they needed to say. And of course I was aware that I was speaking with Secretary Shultz, but first of all I was concerned about how my meeting with Shultz would be regarded back in the Politburo. That's why I presented this style of communication."[27]

Jack Matlock, who attended the meeting as a White House aide, said, "We were in for a pleasant surprise. A white-haired, cheery man with a ready and winning smile came into the room, shook hands with the Americans, and began telling his aides in his accented Russian, 'I'm new at this. Be sure to correct me if I goof.' With a chuckle, he got down to business."[28] Matlock recalled:

> There were no histrionics, no long lectures, no recriminations. The substance of Soviet policy had not yet changed, but the mode of presenta-

tion was totally different. Instead of indulging in oratory as if he were addressing an audience of thousands, as Gromyko had, Shevardnadze spoke in a voice so soft that one had to strain to keep from missing a word or phrase. As the meeting ended, he turned to his staff and asked, "Okay, fellows, how did I do? How many bloopers did you count?" Before they could reassure him, he laughed and said, "Hold on, tell me when we get out of the room," shook hands all around, and departed. "Don't tell me that's a *Soviet* foreign minister!" exclaimed one of the American participants when Shevardnadze had departed. "We're in a whole new ball game!" And so we were.[29]

Yet the old ball game persisted in Washington as administration hard-liners tried to undermine the upcoming summit. Several officials tried to downplay the planned Reagan-Gorbachev meeting by dropping the word "summit" when talking publicly about the event and just calling it a meeting, thinking the word choice would lower expectations. McFarlane, summarizing the prevailing view of Gorbachev in early September, told a meeting of top officials, "Gorbachev is proclaimed as something new, a new force, yet there is nothing new about their approach to building arms, human rights, Afghanistan, sinking economy, declining mortality. Gorbachev has heavy debts in the military and KGB."[30] The CIA concurred, warning the same month that Gorbachev was trying to lure the United States back to a "détente atmosphere on East-West relations and pick its fruits."[31]

A long, simmering debate escalated about whether the ABM Treaty barred the testing of proposed elements of Reagan's space-based missile shield. The Kremlin insisted that the treaty prohibited any testing. Weinberger and his Pentagon colleagues argued that a clause in the treaty left open a loophole that permitted testing of technologies based on "other physical principles" than ones known when the treaty was signed in 1972. Testing of the new technologies envisioned for the Reagan system, proponents contended, was permissible. Shultz also grew impatient with McFarlane, who seemed to Shultz overly eager to open his own diplomatic channel with the Kremlin. Shultz's anger spiked after McFarlane, in an appearance on *Meet the Press*, said the ABM Treaty permitted research, testing and development of new defense weapons systems. "He had, in effect, declared publicly that the U.S. was unilaterally changing its long held position on the treaty. No such decision had been made! And there would now be hell to pay. I was appalled and angry at this arrogation of power."[32]

In an effort to overcome the endless internal strife, Shultz told Reagan in mid-September, "I believe we should take a much more positive and commanding attitude toward Geneva than is at present apparent to the public. We sought the meeting, and we got it. We have important objectives."[33] To underscore the point, Shultz added, "We should stop poor-mouthing this gigantic event and take it on as the important challenge and opportunity it really is. This is not the opening game of the little-league season. This is THE SUPER BOWL."[34] Shultz warned Reagan that the Pentagon was concerned about softening Washington's approach to Moscow. "Met with Geo. Shultz about the summit," Reagan noted. "I sense he and Bud feel that 'Defense' is going to be uncooperative & not want to settle anything with the Soviets. I can't quite agree on that. One thing I do know is I wont [sic] trade our S.D.I. off for some Soviet offer of weapons reductions."[35]

At the end of September, Shevardnadze unveiled a new Soviet arms control proposal in his first appearance at the United Nations. It called for a 50 percent reduction in strategic weapons. The Soviet definition of weapons used in the proposal sharply tilted the plan in the Kremlin's favor, making it instantly unacceptable to the United States, but the idea of slashing nuclear arsenals resonated with Reagan's desire to make deep cuts. "I regarded the proposal a breakthrough of principle, even though the specifics were not remotely acceptable," Shultz said. "It was a victory for the president's policy of seeking significant reductions in offensive nuclear arms. The Soviet preoccupation with our SDI program was obviously a prime motivation for their desire to reach an agreement with us. Radical cuts in arms would be possible, but they would require tough negotiating."[36] "I went back to the idea I had earlier discussed with the president: strategically significant reductions by the Soviet Union would have an effect on how the United States would go forward with eventual deployment of strategic defenses. Cap Weinberger, Richard Perle and others at the Pentagon were totally opposed to this approach. They wanted to proceed forward with SDI at full speed no matter what. To them the ABM Treaty was an obstacle to be sidestepped. I was clear in my mind that we had to abide by the ABM Treaty."[37]

In a private meeting with Shultz in New York, Shevardnadze said that Gorbachev hoped the Geneva summit meeting would make clear to the world that the United States and Soviet Union agreed "on the inadmissibility of nuclear war."[38] Shultz reported to Reagan that he had told Shevardnadze "that we now need to get on with the process of radical reductions in offensive arms."[39] Shevardnadze traveled to Washington after his UN appearance for additional meetings with Shultz and an appointment with Reagan on September 27. Reagan was impatient with his preparatory homework: "An NSC briefing for my visit tomorrow with Soviet Foreign Minister Shevardnadze. I'm getting d—n sick of cramming like a school kid. Sometimes they tell me more than I need to know."[40]

Both Shultz and Reagan found Shevardnadze refreshingly affable. Shultz said he "came across as a real human being. Ronald Reagan started telling jokes to Eduard Shevardnadze—jokes about Communists—and Shevardnadze laughed. What a change!"[41] Shevardnadze recalled, "Reagan was very much a lover of jokes."[42] Reagan noted, "He's a personable fellow but we had our differences. My goal was to send him back to Gorbachev with a message that I really meant "arms reductions" and I wasn't interested in any detente nonsense. For the 1st time they talked of *real* verification procedures."[43]

A breakthrough with the Kremlin seemed imminent. The meeting in Geneva would prove whether the hope would turn into a mirage or a turning point.

CHAPTER NINETEEN

The Fireside Summit

SUMMIT PREPARATIONS ACCELERATED IN October. Shultz and Shevardnadze met again in New York when the United Nations marked its fortieth anniversary. In advance of their meeting, Shultz presented Reagan with draft language for a communiqué that Reagan and Gorbachev could jointly issue after their Geneva summit. This was customary for cold war summitry—the two sides, in effect, outlined the likely outcome of meetings before they took place, using the drafting of communiqués as a vehicle for partly predetermining the ground to be covered during talks and agreements or disagreements that would result. Typically, negotiation over the wording would intensify during the summits, as the two sides defined the points they were prepared to make jointly. In the case of Reagan-Gorbachev, Weinberger strenuously objected to the State Department draft, echoing a top aide who dismissively referred to diplomats who were pressing for the joint statement as "eager détente beavers."[1] To quiet the dispute, Reagan decreed there be no further work on an advance communiqué and that a joint account of the Geneva meeting be negotiated during the summit, giving the American and Soviet delegations a chance to see what Reagan and Gorbachev could accomplish absent an advance script.

The decision put greater pressure on Shultz to prepare the groundwork for the summit when he traveled to Moscow with McFarlane in early November, just two weeks before the Geneva meeting. It would be the first visit by a secretary of state to Moscow in seven years other than to attend the funeral of a Kremlin chief. With a new Soviet leader and foreign minister heading into their first summit meeting, the American government was not sure what to expect, whether decades of stale policy positions would be rehearsed or whether Gorbachev would set Kremlin foreign policy on a new course. In the months after taking office, Gorbachev repeatedly talked about "new thinking" in Kremlin foreign policy involving the easing of cold war tensions, reductions in nuclear arms and the opening of doors with the West. But his specific intentions were not entirely clear to his Kremlin colleagues, much less foreign governments. Washington certainly was largely unaware that Gorbachev thought the Soviet Union was falling ever farther behind its capitalist rivals technologically and economically and that the Kremlin's defense expenditures were unsustainable in a society with shabby living standards and few consumer goods.

The Gorbachev who welcomed Shultz and McFarlane to his businesslike Central Committee office, rather than in one of the Kremlin's grand rooms, was combative and less congenial than the man who had met with Bush and Shultz right after the Chernenko funeral. Several factors accounted for the change. Though Gorbachev was steadily solidifying his power in the Kremlin, he was obliged to clear his talking points for Shultz with the Politburo before the meeting and to report back after it. He surely wanted to show strength in his first sustained encounter with a high-level American official. And he knew that Dobrynin, who attended the meeting, would evaluate Gorbachev's performance when recounting the session with Soviet colleagues.

"Gorbachev, I could see, was in a feisty mood," Shultz recalled. "He went immediately on the offensive, declaring that 'disinformation' in the United States about the Soviet Union made it impossible to build a healthy relationship."[2] Gorbachev aggressively challenged American policy on a host of issues, including nuclear weapons and opposition to the Soviet occupation of Afghanistan, and rejected the idea that American pressure would win concessions from Moscow. He impatiently dismissed suggestions that the Soviet Union was technologically lagging behind the United States and that Washington could pressure Moscow to accept American development of a space-based missile shield. At one point, he even alluded to Cap Weinberger in a way that suggested he knew not only that Weinberger was hawkish on relations with the Kremlin but that Weinberger and Shultz had a strained history in Washington and at Bechtel.[3]

Gorbachev's take on the American economy surprised Shultz, who recalled, "Gorbachev then took off on the military-industrial complex. 'If you need help in employing 18 million people, let us know; maybe we can buy something to keep them busy,' he said sarcastically. I thought Dobrynin was egging him on and was surprised that Dobrynin, who should have known better, had apparently been feeding him so much nonsense."[4] The verbal volleying continued for more than an hour, Gorbachev and Shultz unyielding in their accusations about the conduct of the other side. It was faster, livelier than Shultz's meetings with Gromyko but established positions did not seem to be budging. Gorbachev was especially adamant in his opposition to the Strategic Defense Initiative and any interpretation of the ABM Treaty that would permit work on a space-based missile defense system. Shultz gave no ground on that or any other issue.

The mood changed when Shultz started talking about the dawn of the information age that he said was already altering industry, finance, communications, weapons technology and the lives of millions of people the way the Industrial Revolution had reshaped societies. His aides had urged Shultz not to turn professorial with Gorbachev, arguing that ominous warnings about the fate of closed societies in an information age was not an appropriate topic for a meeting with a Soviet leader. Shultz ignored the advice and delivered a brief lecture as though he were instructing students at the University of Chicago business school. It was a prescient presentation, summarizing Shultz's prophetic analysis:

> Science and technology are moving quickly, and this affects everything, including military weaponry, but it also affects how we produce things and how we live. We have left the era of the industrial age and have moved into what we might think of as the information age, in which we will have to think about new ways of working, new ways of making decisions. Society is beginning to reorganize itself in profound ways. Closed and compartmented societies cannot take advantage of the information age. People must be free to express themselves, move around, emigrate and travel if they want to, challenge accepted ways without fear. Otherwise, they can't take advantage of the opportunities available. The Soviet economy will have to be radically changed to adapt to the new era.[5]

Gorbachev listened intently and seemed delighted by the presentation, jokingly telling Shultz he should move to Moscow to run Gosplan, the Soviet agency charged with centrally managing the nation's economy. "You have more ideas than they do," he said. All in all, the two-hour encounter was bracing for both men, a first skirmish of cold war combatants eager to demonstrate toughness and resolve while simultaneously edging the Washington-Moscow relationship toward more spontaneous and open dialogue. Shultz summed up his reaction:

> I was pleased with my day. I had a toe-to-toe encounter with Gorbachev. I liked it. He probably got some matters off his chest with me that would not come up again with the president. I hoped he learned something from my comments. He didn't take offense when I interrupted; I think he even enjoyed it. He talked a lot, but he also listened. SDI obviously hit a raw nerve. That was good: SDI had brought them to the table. And I was glad to see that we had succeeded in getting human rights on Gorbachev's mind. "What's the headline? What's the headline?" Bernie Kalb [the State Department spokesman] asked me as we were getting ready to leave. "Stalemate on Eve of Summit," I said with a laugh. Gorbachev had been acting, posturing, I felt, trying to show how tough he was.[6]

After talking to Shultz on a secure line, Reagan noted, "Geo. S. called from Moscow on scramble phone—6 more hours of talks—4 of them with Gorbachev. Apparently not much progress. Gorbachev is adamant that we must cave in on SDI—well this will be the case of an irresistible force meeting an unmovable object."[7] Dobrynin offered a similar assessment. "Gorbachev's attempts were of no avail to search out areas of agreement for the summit with Shultz, who talked in his characteristic generalities, making noncommittal declarations about the importance of the summit in itself. He also did not fail to raise the subject of human rights, which Gorbachev simply declined to discuss again. It certainly gave Gorbachev a more realistic view of what to expect. Later Gorbachev told me he liked Shultz's general ideas about economic problems, upon which they touched during the conversation and which were increasingly attracting his interest. On that subject he willingly would talk with Shultz in the future."[8]

Domestic political considerations played a part in Gorbachev's performance. Shortly after Shultz's visit, the Kremlin leadership, including a bevy of top generals, gathered atop Lenin's Tomb to watch the annual military parade in Red Square marking the anniversary of the Bolshevik Revolution. As the *New York Times* noted, the military high command "may be wondering why Mr. Gorbachev is heading for the summit meeting if all he stands to get there is a lecture on human rights and regional conflicts, and no concession on the American space-based missile defense program. Mr. Gorbachev's bravado may be his response."[9] When Gorbachev met with the Politburo after the meeting, he complained that Shultz had come to Moscow unprepared to negotiate about specific issues. As a result, the Politburo gave "him a free hand to have a more informal talk with the president," Dobrynin recalled."[10] After Shultz returned to Washington, Dobrynin told him that Gorbachev was unlikely to be as combative in his meeting with Reagan and wanted the summit to be a success. The comment surprised Shultz, who took it as an oblique apology for the way Gorbachev had handled their meeting. Shultz also took it as a sign that the Geneva meeting might prove more productive than he expected.

Reagan received numerous briefings in the weeks leading up to the summit, more than he welcomed, as the White House staff and national security apparatus assembled memos and intelligence data about Gorbachev and the Kremlin policies on a multitude of issues. After a CIA briefing about the Soviet Union on November 13, Reagan noted in his diary, "Their presentations on the people of Russia were great & confirmed things I had heard from unconfirmed sources. The Soviet U. is an ec. Basket case & among other things there is a rapidly spreading return to religion."[11]

Reagan was also hearing about the Soviet Union from an unusual source, Suzanne Massie, the author of *Land of the Firebird: The Beauty of Old Russia.* Massie's unconventional role puzzled the Reagan staff, and her interest in serving as ambassador in Moscow concerned them, but she added new dimensions to Reagan's understanding of Russian history and culture. Over time, her access to Reagan grew and he would sometimes send her to the State Department to share her thoughts with Shultz. Her influence is difficult to pinpoint but seems generally to have helped give Reagan and Shultz a more nuanced sense of pre-Soviet Russian history and the contours of Russian culture. When she later became more assertive about serving as an informal emissary or go-between with the Kremlin, White House officials discouraged Reagan from relying on her for diplomatic overtures.[12]

As the summit date approached, American officials played down expectations, leading to a series of pessimistic news stories under headlines such as "Hectic Prelude: Both Sides Anticipate Some Tough Summit Talk,"[13] and "Slim Chance Seen for Arms Agenda at Summit Talks."[14] Even on the eve of the summit, there was no containing the divisions within the administration. The morning that Reagan, Shultz and other officials boarded Air Force One for the flight to Geneva, the *New York Times* and the *Washington Post* carried front-page stories about a Weinberger letter to the president warning against compromises on arms issues at the summit. Weinberger specifically urged Reagan not to support a "restrictive" interpretation of the 1972 ABM Treaty and not to commit to observing all facets of the 1979 SALT II nuclear arms accord. The accord was signed by President Carter but never ratified by the Senate. The Reagan administration had said it would not undermine the treaty as long as the Soviet Union abided by it as well.[15]

The leak of the Weinberger letter outraged Shultz and McFarlane. The national security adviser called it an effort to sabotage the summit. Beyond the policy issues involved, Weinberger may have been annoyed that he was not included in the delegation of American officials going to Geneva. Reagan did not seem upset by the newspaper reports. "The press is excited about a leak of a letter to me from Cap on why I shouldn't be trapped into endorsing a continued observance of SALT II. It is a great distortion & is not as the press would have it an in house battle. I agree with Cap & wanted his factual accounting in writing."[16]

The first US-Soviet summit in six years opened on an unusually frigid November morning with Gorbachev's ten o'clock arrival at Fleur d'Eau, an estate on Lake Geneva with a stunning view of the Alps and featuring a large chateau and a smaller pool house. The Swiss government made it available as a neutral site for the first day of meetings. The magnitude of the moment was clear to all involved, including the small army of journalists from around the world—3,614, to be exact—who had gathered in Geneva to cover the meeting. Camera crews were dispersed outside the summit venues to record every public movement of Reagan and Gorbachev.

The two leaders recognized the import of their rendezvous. "This was the day. Mr. G and I met," Reagan recorded in his diary.[17] The Kremlin had dispatched a band of propagandists to Geneva to give journalists a steady stream of pro-Soviet commentary. White House officials noted the Kremlin gambit and decided to match the Soviet maneuver at the next summit. "We viewed the Geneva meeting realistically, without grand expectations, yet hoped to lay the foundations for a serious dialogue in the future," Gorbachev recalled.[18] The long interval since the last summit meeting—Jimmy Carter's 1979 meeting with Leonid Brezhnev in Vienna to sign the SALT II Treaty—lent added drama to the Geneva meeting.

Reagan, the host for the first round of talks, had arrived at the chateau several minutes before Gorbachev, decked in a dark overcoat and white scarf. After debating with his aides whether to put back on the overcoat and scarf when he stepped out the door to greet Gorbachev, Reagan emerged from the house coatless and hatless. He spryly descended a short set of stairs to the street to greet Gorbachev, who disembarked from his limousine in a heavy gray topcoat, plaid wool scarf and brown fedora. The men smiled broadly as they shook hands by the curb, and Reagan guided Gorbachev up the stairs to a landing outside the front door, where they stopped briefly, facing the television cameras and photojournalists. Gorbachev pointed to Reagan's light attire, joking that he hoped the president would not come down with a cold. The side-by-side image made Reagan look like the younger man even though he was twenty years older than Gorbachev. Gorbachev shed his overcoat when greeting Reagan the next morning at an estate the Soviet Union used to host the second day of meetings.

After the gaggle of American and Soviet officials greeted each other, Reagan and Gorbachev and their interpreters stepped into a side room for a private opening conversation expected to last twenty minutes. After forty minutes, Don Regan told James Kuhn, the president's personal aide, to ask Shultz if the meeting should be interrupted so the day could stay on schedule. Kuhn thought Reagan and Gorbachev should not be interrupted but conveyed the question to Shultz. "If you're dumb enough to do that, you shouldn't be in your job," Shultz snapped at Kuhn. "I just got clobbered by Shultz," Kuhn unhappily recalled.[19] Reagan and Gorbachev ended up talking for seventy-five minutes. The two leaders emerged smiling. The initial conversation was a predictable exchange of cold war perceptions, Reagan citing human rights abuses in the Soviet Union, Gorbachev alluding to the power of the military-industrial complex in the United States. Looking back later at the discussion, Gorbachev said he was "amazed at the extremely ideological stands" each man took, with Gorbachev talking like the "No. 1 Communist" and Reagan like the "No. 1 Imperialist."[20]

Yet Reagan sensed the first inklings of a rapport between the men after he told Gorbachev: "You and I were born in small towns about which nobody's ever heard and no one ever expected anything of either of us. There are all these people sitting in the next room. They have given us 15 minutes to meet in this one-on-one and we can do that and we can go out there and spend the next three days doing what they have written for us to do. They've programmed us—they've written your talking points, they've written my talking points. We can do that, or we can stay here as long as we want and get to know each other and we can create history and do some things that the world will remember in a positive way."[21]

A warming atmosphere was not evident immediately after the Reagan-Gorbachev private conversation when the two delegations got seated at a large rectangular table in a conference room to begin the first round of group discussions. Reagan and Gorbachev vigorously debated a variety of issues, including the Soviet role in Afghanistan, Reagan's Strategic Defense Initiative and even Soviet-American cooperation during World War II. Reagan mistakenly accused Moscow of refusing to refuel American bombers at Soviet airfields after they had attacked targets in Germany and lacked sufficient fuel to make it back to Britain. When Gorbachev suggested that the Kremlin might agree to withdraw its military forces from Afghanistan—a startling statement—Shultz recognized the significance, but neither he nor Reagan tried to draw out Gorbachev on the comment.

In midafternoon, Reagan invited Gorbachev to walk with him down a winding gravel path to the pool house by the lake. The day before, while touring the estate, the president and Nancy Reagan agreed with the White House team that had previously scouted the grounds that the pool house, an intimate space with comfortable arm chairs and a fireplace, would provide a good setting for informal conversation. "It was fascinating to watch Reagan survey the villa and grounds," Shultz said. "He immediately understood the intimate attraction of the pool house. Reagan, the actor, was examining the movie set."[22] As Reagan and Gorbachev made their way toward the lake, Reagan genially told Gorbachev that contrary to what the Soviet leader had heard about his Hollywood career, Reagan had not acted only in grade-B films. Gorbachev graciously replied that he had seen *King's Row*, one of Reagan's movies, and liked it very much.[23]

The setting proved ideal. Though the conversation dwelled on difficult issues, including updated American arms control proposals that Reagan handed Gorbachev as the meeting began, the rapport between the two men grew as the minutes passed. As they walked back to the chateau in the fading afternoon light, Reagan invited Gorbachev to visit Washington in 1986. Gorbachev accepted on the spot and asked Reagan to come to Moscow the following year. Reagan immediately agreed. The spontaneous exchange instantly settled one of the main objectives that the Americans had set for the summit and had assumed would require intricate negotiations with the Soviet delegation. "I scored one we've worried about—that the meetings should be on an ongoing basis," Reagan privately boasted. "He accepted my invite to U.S. next year & I'm invited to U.S.S.R. in '87. That in itself could make the meeting a success."[24]

As the day progressed, Gorbachev sensed a developing rapport as well, though he thought it was due as much to the global responsibilities the two men shared as to their personalities. "As it seems to me now," he recalled later, "something important happened to each of us on that day, in spite of everything. I think there had been two factors at work—responsibility and intuition. I did not have this impression after lunch, and in the evening we were still clinging to our antagonistic positions. But the 'human factor' had quietly come into action. We both sensed that we just maintain contact and try to avoid a break. Somewhere in the backs of our minds a glimmer of hope emerged that we could still come to an agreement."[25]

Camaraderie was notably absent as Nancy Reagan and Raisa Gorbachev spent time together during the day. "From the moment we met, she talked and talked and *talked*—so much that I could barely get a word in, edge-wise or otherwise," Nancy Reagan reported. The tension was inevitable, given their different backgrounds and personalities. Raisa Gorbachev was intensely intellectual. While quite stylish by Soviet standards, and youthful compared to the wives of previous Soviet leaders, she did not match up well with the American first lady and her glitzy social world in Hollywood and Washington. Raisa Gorbachev lectured Nancy Reagan about Marxism and Leninism. At an afternoon tea, Raisa complained about the chair she was given and a replacement. "I couldn't believe it," Nancy Reagan said. "I had met first ladies, princesses and queens, but I had never seen anybody act in this way."[26]

The first day of the summit ended with a dinner hosted by the Gorbachevs in the Villa Rose, an ornate nineteenth-century home located in the otherwise utilitarian Soviet mission compound in Geneva. When shot glasses were filled with vodka to wash down a first course of caviar, Shevardnadze wryly remarked that he had to come all the way to Geneva to get vodka. The joke was a reference to a Gorbachev crackdown on alcohol consumption that had limited vodka supply in the Soviet Union, infuriating consumers. Gorbachev joined the laughter, a sign of his relaxed relationship with Shevardnadze. The notion of Gromyko joking about vodka shortages with Brezhnev, Andropov or Chernenko in the presence of an American president was inconceivable. Gorbachev warmly welcomed the Reagans with a toast that surprisingly included a line from the Bible and a description of a cartoon showing the two leaders standing on opposite sides of an abyss. In the cartoon, Reagan calls out to Gorbachev, "Gorby, I am prepared to go my part of the way." To which Gorbachev replies, "Come ahead." Reagan's toast was equally convivial.[27] Shultz watched the unfolding scene with quiet satisfaction and a sense that Reagan and Gorbachev were beginning to establish a constructive relationship. "The personality factor was important," Shultz later said. "They got along well."[28]

As talks continued the next day at the Soviet compound, a chill seemed to return to the proceedings. The two men met alone again with interpreters first. Reagan resumed his offensive about Soviet human rights abuses and Gorbachev ridiculed the United States for racial tensions, economic inequities and unemployment. "I explained I wasn't telling him how to run his country," Reagan recorded in his diary. "I was asking for his help; that I had a better chance of getting support at home for things we'd agreed to if he would ease some of the restrictions on emigration, etc." In a plenary session of the two delegations, Reagan and Gorbachev argued heatedly over nuclear weapons proposals and Reagan's missile shield. If nothing else, Shultz surmised, Reagan made clear his visceral commitment to SDI and the reality that he would not give up his vision at a negotiating table. Reagan recalled, "I took off on arms control then he fired back about S.D.I. creating an arms race in space & the stuff really hit the fan. He was really belligerent & d—n it I stood firm."[29]

As the afternoon session wound down, Reagan and Gorbachev retired to a smaller room, where they traded stories while American and Soviet of-

ficials started work on a joint communiqué that could be made public when
the summit ended the next day. Because advance drafting had halted several weeks earlier at Reagan's instruction, the two sides would need to work
quickly so the statement could be given to reporters early the next morning.
After Reagan left the Soviet compound, Shultz encouraged Gorbachev to
describe points of agreement over the two days of talks, apart from the
planned summits in Washington in 1986 and Moscow in 1987. Gorbachev
mentioned the discussion about 50 percent cuts in strategic nuclear arms,
a goal the two sides were now exploring, the prospect of an accord on intermediate-range nuclear forces and cultural and educational exchanges.
Based on the Gorbachev list, Shultz figured that Roz Ridgway and her
colleagues could quickly come to terms on a communiqué with their Soviet
counterparts.

As a second Reagan-Gorbachev dinner was ending, this one hosted by
the Reagans at Maison de Saussure, an eighteenth-century gray stone chateau where the Reagans were staying, Ridgway sent word to Shultz that
Soviet officials were balking at the communiqué content. Even though their
lead drafters had heard Gorbachev review the summit with Shultz, they
were refusing to include the items Gorbachev had mentioned. Shultz returned to the dinner table after talking by phone with Ridgway and complained openly to Gorbachev in the presence of Georgi Kornienko, the
deputy foreign minister who was directing the Soviet drafting team. The
scene offended Kornienko and Gorbachev, but the remonstration produced
the desired result. A joint statement was finished by early morning. When
Shultz ran into Kornienko the next day, he told him he thought the communiqué had "turned out well and was the product of a lot of give-and-
take." Kornienko's response: "Yes, and we did all the giving."[30]

The most significant and memorable statement in the joint document
was about the prospect of nuclear war. Surprisingly, it got little attention
at the time. It said, "The sides, having discussed key security issues, and
conscious of the special responsibility of the USSR and the U.S. for maintaining peace, have agreed that a nuclear war cannot be won and must never
be fought." While it may have struck journalists at the time as a restatement
of cold war wishful thinking, it actually reflected a renewed and deepened
determination by Reagan and Gorbachev to assure that a global nuclear
war was unthinkable. For Reagan especially, it was a clarion declaration of

his long-standing goal of removing nuclear war as an option for American and Soviet leaders. It also reflected Shultz's commitment to do away with nuclear threats.

Otherwise, the summit results seemed tepid. The main immediate achievement was the scheduling of future summits in Washington and Moscow. There were modest agreements on measures to improve safety along North Pacific commercial air routes, a response to the 1983 downing of the Korean airliner, and scientific, educational and sports exchanges. The rest of the communiqué was devoted largely to topics on which Washington and Moscow agreed further discussion was warranted, including nuclear arms issues. The *Washington Post* summarized the Geneva news:

> After six years of open bitterness and hostility between their two nations, President Reagan and Soviet leader Mikhail Gorbachev appeared together on a stage here today to express a joint determination to curb the arms race and to "improve U.S.-Soviet relations and the international situation as a whole."
>
> But the two leaders, concluding three days of summitry marked by outward appearances of warm personal contact between them, were unable to elaborate any new specific steps they will take to limit or reduce their nuclear arsenals. Instead, they celebrated the reaching of accords on cultural and other bilateral matters, and emphasized their new agreement on the need for a fresh start in East-West relations.[31]

But for Shultz, the meeting marked a critical inflection point in relations with the Kremlin. As he put it, "The fresh start that the president wanted had become a reality in Geneva, not least because the two leaders had come to like and respect each other. They had agreed; they had disagreed. We had heated moments; we had light moments. We had come in order to get to know each other as people by working hard on the issues, and we did, as did the two leaders, who spent almost five of the fifteen hours of official meetings talking together privately."[32]

Reagan stopped in Brussels on the way home to brief NATO allies about the talks and then went directly to the Capitol after landing in Washington to tell a joint gathering of the House and Senate about the summit. He received an enthusiastic welcome. Democrats and Republicans gave him a sustained standing ovation as he began his remarks in the House chamber: "I called for a fresh start, and we made that start. I can't claim that we had a meeting of the minds on such fundamentals as ideology or national purpose, but we understand each other better, and that's a key to peace. I gained a better perspective; I feel he did, too. It was a constructive meeting; so constructive, in fact, that I look forward to welcoming Mr. Gorbachev to the United States next year. And I have accepted his invitation to go to Moscow the following year. We arranged that out in the parking lot. I found Mr. Gorbachev to be an energetic defender of Soviet policy. He was an eloquent speaker and a good listener."[33]

Seated in the House well alongside cabinet colleagues, Shultz knew the summit had been a pivotal moment for him. It set the Reagan presidency on a course that enhanced his influence. Divisions within the administration over Soviet policy were too deep to be healed by a single summit meeting, but momentum now favored Shultz. Lou Cannon, the *Washington Post*'s astute White House correspondent and chronicler of Reagan as California governor and president, observed: "The dominant view among the president's advisers yesterday was that he had started down a course at Geneva which will not be easily reversed. By agreeing to the series of summits with Gorbachev and pledging to push for agreements in the interim, these advisers said, Reagan had staked the course of his second-term presidency on bargaining with the Soviets instead of confronting them."[34]

CHAPTER TWENTY

Battles That Never End

THE MOMENTUM GENERATED BY the Geneva summit stalled in the weeks that followed. Dissension about Soviet policy reignited in the Reagan administration over a series of specific issues, and negotiations about reducing strategic and intermediate-range nuclear weapons bogged down. McFarlane, frustrated by the never-ending Shultz-Weinberger battles and his own run-ins with Donald Regan, resigned in early December. His successor, Admiral John Poindexter, struggled to manage the policy-making process and became ensnared in the arms-for-hostages dealing with Iran that exploded into the Iran-Contra scandal. As a result of the turmoil, the Reagan-Gorbachev commitment to meet again in 1986 seemed moribund as Moscow and Washington jousted over various matters. Shultz once again grew frustrated over the caustic internal debates.

It took two unrelated events—the catastrophic nuclear accident in late April at the Chernobyl Nuclear Power Plant in Ukraine and the KGB entrapment and detention of an American reporter in Moscow in late September—to end the impasse and bring Reagan and Gorbachev back together for an impromptu summit in Iceland in October. The snap summit, which seemed by all initial accounts to fizzle, actually vaulted American-Soviet relations to a new plane that opened the way to ending the cold war.

The euphoric greeting Reagan received in Congress the night he returned from Geneva soon gave way to renewed disagreement about the Soviet threat. The Pentagon and CIA churned out new reports warning of enhanced Soviet military might and predicting that Gorbachev could not fundamentally alter Soviet domestic or foreign policy. A Kremlin decision in February 1986 to release Anatoly Shcharansky from prison after nine years and let him move to Israel, brokered by Senator Edward Kennedy, did not impress the skeptics, nor did a startling Gorbachev proposal in early 1986 to eliminate nuclear weapons and ballistic missiles by the year 2000 in a three-stage process.

Hard-liners viewed the initiative primarily as a propaganda ploy. No doubt, it offered obvious public relations benefits for the Kremlin. But Shultz saw the broader significance. Despite flaws in the proposal that advantaged Moscow, he welcomed the ambitious goal of abolishing nuclear weapons and thought the blockbuster proposal echoed Reagan's own call for eliminating the weapons. He and his aides quickly cobbled together a set of talking points for Shultz to use in a meeting with Reagan just hours after the State Department received a Gorbachev letter to Reagan outlining the Soviet proposal. Shultz told Reagan, "This is our first indication that the Soviets are interested in a staged program toward zero. We should not simply reject their proposal, since it contains certain steps which we earlier set forth."[1]

In late February, Reagan responded to the Gorbachev proposal in a restrained letter that called the initiative "a significant and positive step forward" while making clear that numerous issues would have to be resolved to get Washington and Moscow to a point where Gorbachev's ambitious agenda could be realized.[2] Gorbachev, impatient with Washington's tepid response, complained to Reagan in an April 2 letter about American efforts "to portray our initiatives as propaganda."[3] Dobrynin, recently promoted to a senior Community Party Central Committee post, paid a last visit to the White House as Soviet ambassador on April 8. The meeting with Reagan, Shultz and other American officials was cordial, but no date was set for the 1986 Gorbachev visit to Washington promised at the Geneva summit.

The ingrained distrust between Washington and Moscow was illustrated by a small request Dobrynin made as he and Shultz stood on the secretary of state's office balcony overlooking the Lincoln Memorial. Saying he had admired the view during his many encounters with secretaries of state over the past twenty-five years, Dobrynin asked if he might get a photo of the panoramic vista, which stretched down the mall to the Washington Monument and the Capitol in the distance. Shultz instructed aides to arrange the photograph. When it was delivered, security officials raised concerns about sending it to the Kremlin, fearing it would help Soviet missile forces target Washington. Shultz sent it to Dobrynin anyway.[4]

As the debate continued over how to deal with Gorbachev, Shultz lamented the moldy thinking by his administration rivals: "I would describe how the Soviets were moving in our direction and point to steps we should take to keep that positive movement going. Cap Weinberger would then say we were falling for Soviet propaganda. CIA director Bill Casey, or his deputy, Bob Gates, would say that CIA intelligence analysis revealed that Gorbachev had done nothing new, only talked a different line. And most of those present would try to stimulate the president's fear that any U.S. diplomatic engagement with Moscow would jeopardize the future of SDI."[5]

Shultz's view was informed by his interaction with Shevardnadze and Gorbachev and his firsthand impressions of the Soviet Union. Unlike his colleagues, Shultz did not see the Soviet Union as a mighty antagonist inherently bent on dominating the world. The Soviet threat described by his colleagues, Shultz said, "did not match the reality I saw." He went on: "The Soviet leadership, and Soviet society, seemed increasingly in disarray, and the USSR's strength—outside the field of nuclear weapons—was highly questionable. Their society was demoralized and their economy unresponsive."[6] Surveying various fronts in the cold war, Shultz believed that Moscow was losing ground in the Middle East, Africa, Central America and Asia and retained sway over Eastern Europe only through military force. "My conclusion is radically different from that of Casey and Weinberger," he recalled. He told them, "The Soviets have lost the ideological battle. Their idea is receding; ours is moving forward."[7]

Anyone who spent time in the Soviet Union during Gorbachev's first months as Soviet leader could see the internal political and economic rot that Shultz perceived. As the months passed, it became clear that Gorbachev was much more than a younger version of his predecessors and that he was determined to upend ossified Communist policies and practices that were crippling the Soviet Union. The first concrete evidence of his reform agenda, apart from his often dense and extended speeches, was the appearance of dissenting views in a number of publications, including unfettered reporting about the brutal Soviet occupation of Afghanistan and the death of Soviet soldiers there. Long-suppressed literature and films started appearing in bookstores and in movie theaters, some powerfully denouncing Stalinism. Gorbachev was questioning the basic tenets of authoritarian rule, acknowledging the economic weaknesses produced by rigid central planners, the agricultural shortcomings of collective farming and the consequences of media censorship.

If Gorbachev needed further evidence of defects in the Soviet system, he got it on April 26 when technicians managing the No. 4 reactor at the Chernobyl Nuclear Power Plant in Ukraine mishandled a safety test that quickly cascaded into a catastrophic chain reaction and explosion. The eruption of the reactor instantly spewed highly radioactive debris into the air around the plant. Prevailing winds soon carried hazardous particles across portions of Ukraine, Belarus, Poland and Sweden. The accident, and lethally incompetent reaction to it by Chernobyl plant managers and government and Communist Party leaders in Ukraine and Moscow, quickly became a microcosm of Soviet misgovernance. The first impulse of the authorities was to play down the magnitude of the disaster and to deny the Soviet people, and the world, critical information about the accident and the threat it presented. The Kremlin waited three days before disclosing the accident. It finally did so in a short, anodyne statement: "An accident has occurred at the Chernobyl nuclear power plant as one of the reactors was damaged. Measures are being taken to eliminate the consequences of the accident. Aid is being given to those affected. A Government commission has been set up."[8]

The bland wording masked the horrific reality at the damaged reactor and surrounding area. The top of the reactor had literally blown apart, and massive amounts of radioactive materials were ejected into the air. The chain reaction and fire continued for days, as courageous but doomed firefighters tried to extinguish the nuclear fuel, most of them unaware that they were absorbing lethal levels of radiation. An afternoon soccer match at a field near the ruined reactor proceeded, the athletes ignorant of the hazardous conditions. Residents of Pripyat, the nearest town, home mostly to workers at the nuclear plant, were not evacuated for thirty-six hours. In Moscow, the scale of the disaster was either not fully understood or deliberately suppressed, even among top government leaders. By the time of the terse government announcement, radiation sensors in Sweden and other countries along the path of the radioactive plume were detecting abnormally high levels of radiation in the atmosphere. Government officials in these countries checked possible sources within their borders, found none, and immediately suspected the Soviet Union was the source.

Reagan and Shultz first learned of the accident on April 28 aboard Air Force One on the way to Indonesia. Shultz, recalling his talk with Gorbachev about the implications of the advent of the information age, speculated that Gorbachev would quickly make information about the accident available in the Soviet Union. He was wrong. Gorbachev did not address the nation about the reactor calamity until May 15, nearly three weeks after the explosion. As Air Force One made its way across the Pacific, Shultz drafted a short letter for Reagan to send to Gorbachev, offering the assistance of American reactor experts and doctors trained to treat radiation victims. Admiral Poindexter, the new national security adviser, wanted to convene an NSC group to consider how to respond to the accident, but Shultz secured Reagan's approval and the letter was quickly transmitted.

As the true dimensions of the nuclear accident became apparent, Gorbachev and Reagan recognized its far-reaching implications. Both men saw it as a frightening warning of the destructive power of a nuclear war. The death and sickness caused by the accident was just a small sample of the casualties that would result from the detonation of just a few nuclear warheads, much less the thousands that Washington and Moscow planned to unleash in a nuclear war. The accident reinforced their view that a nuclear conflict must be avoided. Chernobyl was also undeniable evidence of the failure of the Soviet system. After struggling for several weeks to get a full account of the accident and its consequences, Gorbachev assembled enough information to see that it had exposed the bankruptcy of the Soviet state. Chernobyl, he recalled, was "graphic evidence, not only of how obsolete our technology was, but also of the failure of the old system."[9] "Everything that had been built up over the years converged in this drama: the concealing or hushing up of accidents and other bad news, irresponsibility and careless-ness, slipshod work, wholesale drunkenness. This was one more convincing argument in favor of radical reforms.[10]

The accident gave impetus to the growing view in the White House and Kremlin that deep reductions in nuclear arsenals were necessary. The chal-lenge was finding a mutually acceptable formula to cut strategic and inter-mediate-range weapons while leaving Washington some latitude to pursue Reagan's missile shield vision. In Washington itself, major differences re-mained about whether any limits on the development of the shield should be negotiable with Moscow. Over the summer of 1986, Shultz faced stiff Pentagon resistance to the slightest sign of flexibility about SDI, including a Soviet suggestion that testing of new technologies be limited to the lab-oratory for ten years. The definition of laboratory was imprecise, but realis-tically it seemed unlikely that the exotic technologies imagined by Reagan could move beyond nascent testing for at least a decade. In that case, testing could actually be confined to laboratories. Still, Weinberger rejected the idea, and Reagan himself was unwilling to compromise.

But Weinberger surprised Shultz by suggesting that the United States could agree to eliminate all ballistic missiles. In the end, Reagan and Wein-berger came around slightly and agreed with Shultz and other officials on a proposal to limit research, development and testing of antimissile tech-nologies for five years consistent with the AMB Treaty. If Washington or Moscow decided to move ahead with deployment of new missile defenses, it would commit to negotiate a plan to share the technology with the other side and to eliminate offensive ballistic missiles. The proposal was transmit-ted to Gorbachev on July 25.

The proposal represented a rare instance of comity among the feuding factions in the administration, but the cooperation did not last long. A few days later, officials sympathetic to South Africa's government outmaneu-vered Shultz and the State Department in the drafting of a presidential speech about South Africa that failed to strongly condemn apartheid rule. Shultz was incensed by the maneuver, and his sense was that the Reagan national security team was still incapable of sustaining a coherent and con-sistent foreign policy. On August 5, he submitted a new resignation letter, fed up with the policy combat, including running conflicts about the Krem-lin. "I was sick and tired of fighting the same battles on Soviet matters over and over again," he recalled. Reagan refused to accept Shultz's resignation. Instead, Don Regan, the White House chief of staff, tried to mollify Shultz by telling him national security decision-making would be streamlined. Shultz gave Regan a blunt rundown of his complaints: "The environment is a very frustrating one to work in. I find it difficult to pull together a team in the national security field. The situation is debilitating. I am constantly under attack. I get no sense of support. I feel I'm out there operating on my own."[11]

With the president vacationing at his California ranch, Shultz headed to his family retreat in the Berkshires for a late August break and chance to ponder whether to carry on as secretary of state. The decision was made for him by the onrush of unexpected events, starting with the arrest and detention of Nicholas Daniloff, the *U.S. News & World Report* bureau chief in Moscow. On August 30, Daniloff met a Soviet source he trusted at a rendezvous in a Moscow park. The source handed Daniloff a package containing some provincial newspaper clippings requested by Daniloff and two maps of Afghanistan marked "top secret." Moments later, after the men separated and Daniloff was walking back to his Moscow apartment, a white van pulled up near him and six plainclothes agents stepped out. One pinned Daniloff against the van and handcuffed him while another agent filmed the arrest and a third photographed it. The incident quickly escalated into a nasty crisis in Soviet-American relations, with Shultz playing a leading role as he tried to broker a resolution that would free Daniloff and Gennadi Zakharov, a Soviet diplomat arrested by the FBI in New York a week before Daniloff was seized. It seemed clear that the KGB had arrested Daniloff in retaliation for the FBI action and that Moscow would use Daniloff as trade bait to make a deal to free Zakharov, who faced espionage charges in New York.

The KGB ensnared Daniloff, a veteran Moscow correspondent and fluent Russian speaker, in an elaborate trap. American and Western reporters in Moscow were under constant surveillance by the KGB through listening devices implanted in office and apartment walls, wiretaps and shadowing by KGB agents as the reporters moved about Moscow and other Soviet locations open to Western journalists. Efforts to try to draw reporters into compromising relationships were common. Members of the small journalist community in Moscow often compared notes about entrapment schemes reporters faced. A British correspondent described being approached one evening by an attractive young woman at a hotel bar in a provincial Soviet city. When the reporter, a man, showed no interest, the next evening a handsome young man took the bar seat next to him. Periodically, the KGB would activate a trap that led to the expulsion of an American journalist. In 1977, Robert Toth of the *Los Angeles Times* was detained by the KGB after he was handed an essay on parapsychology by a scientist who said he was doing investigations in the field. Toth was questioned by the KGB for five days, facing possible charges of possessing state secrets, before he was allowed to leave the Soviet Union.

The Daniloff trap was enhanced by the clumsy conduct of the CIA station chief in Moscow, as Shultz discovered to his dismay as the affair unfolded. The KGB operation started months before Daniloff's arrest. After meeting with Father Roman Potemkin, a Russian Orthodox priest he did not know, Daniloff arrived at work in late January 1985 to find a package left at the *U.S. News* bureau by Father Potemkin. Inside the package, he found an envelope addressed to the American ambassador, Arthur Hartman. Daniloff hesitated to deliver the envelope, then handed it over to American diplomats at the US embassy during a meeting in a secure room. Acting as an intermediary between a Russian source and the US government was a risky step for a reporter. While it might seem a patriotic act on one level, it could also easily create the impression that the journalist was working for the American government. News organizations, by and large, discouraged their reporters from acting as intermediaries and strictly prohibited them from working directly or indirectly for the US government. In 1981, a *Washington Post* reporter had delivered documents to the embassy that turned out to contain highly sensitive data about Soviet missiles. Ben Bradlee, executive editor of the *Post* at the time, pulled the reporter from Moscow.

After Daniloff's January 1985 meeting at the embassy, a CIA officer in Moscow tried to reach Father Potemkin by phone. The call—whether it was with Father Potemkin or someone else is unclear—was recorded by the KGB and played back to Daniloff in 1986 while he was held at Lefortovo Prison in Moscow. In the recording, the CIA station chief referred to Daniloff, reinforcing the impression that Daniloff was somehow associated with the CIA, which was not the case. The call, coupled with the "top secret" maps in Daniloff's hands when he was arrested, had the makings of espionage evidence that the KGB could use against Daniloff.

It quickly became clear to Shultz and his State Department colleagues that the KGB could produce enough "evidence" to frame Daniloff for espionage, a crime that could carry life imprisonment or the death penalty. Shultz worked feverishly with Shevardnadze to resolve the affair. The two men met multiple times in New York, Washington and again in New York as the days passed, searching for a resolution. Hoping to maintain the cooperative relationship established at their previous meetings, Shultz emphasized his respect for Shevardnadze when the Soviet foreign minister came to the State Department on September 18. Shultz recalled:

> I had long since learned in negotiations that personal confidence and a personal touch can be helpful. I decided to break with precedent. I went to the Treaty Room, near my office, to meet Shevardnadze as he arrived. I watched him get off the elevator and walk through the series of stately rooms on his way to the central area used for signing ceremonies and other special events. The last time we met, he had been pink cheeked and confident; now he seemed peaked, thin, and nervous. I peeled him off from his entourage and took him to my private office. "We have a lot of sensitive matters to talk about," I said, "and we will just have to try to work our way through them as human beings. I want you to know that I value our personal relationship and that while you are here, you will be treated with courtesy and respect, whatever the strains of U.S.-Soviet relations."[12]

The talks were difficult. Shevardnadze insisted that the Kremlin had proof that Daniloff was a CIA operative, dismissing a personal message from Reagan to Gorbachev to the contrary. "I can give you my personal assurance that Mr. Daniloff has no connection whatever with the U.S. Government," Reagan told Gorbachev in a letter on September 4. "If you have been informed otherwise, you have been misinformed."[13] Reagan was incensed when he got word that the Kremlin planned to charge Daniloff with espionage despite his assurance to Gorbachev. He called Gorbachev's handling of the matter "arrogant." "I'm mad as h—l," he wrote in his diary.[14] Reagan angrily denounced the detention of Daniloff in an Oval Office meeting with Shevardnadze. Eventually, Shultz and Shevardnadze found a route out of the crisis. The first step called for transferring Daniloff and Zakharov from captivity to the custody of their respective diplomatic missions in Moscow and New York on September 12. While liberated from a KGB prison cell,

Daniloff was confined to the American embassy building in Moscow and barred from leaving the Soviet Union. Zakharov, released by the FBI, still faced trial in New York.

After several false starts and resistance within the Reagan administration to any deal that might be perceived as caving to the Kremlin, Shultz secured Reagan's assent to a complex, carefully choreographed denouement. On September 28, Daniloff was allowed to exit the American embassy and catch a Lufthansa flight to Frankfurt. He traveled on to Washington the next day. Twenty-four hours after Daniloff's release, under the agreement, Zakharov would plead nolo contendere, or no contest, to the charges against him and the United States would expel him. On day three, the United States would announce that Yuri Orlov, an imprisoned Soviet dissident, and his wife, could leave the Soviet Union. A last-minute snag almost upended the arrangement when the Justice Department insisted that Zakharov stand trial. The White House intervened, Zakharov was allowed to plead no contest and the remaining elements of the deal proceeded.

Critics quickly accused the White House and Shultz of trading Daniloff for a Soviet spy, a charge Reagan and Shultz denied but was essentially correct. William Safire wrote in the *New York Times*:

> Equivalency is the Russian propaganda game; we should have no part of it. Mr. Gorbachev is trying to create a value—a captured spy—out of nothing, to balance the man we caught red-handed. We cannot tacitly accept this while formally rejecting it. . . .
> As long as Mr. Daniloff remains in his cell, sitting on the cot with him is arms control, summitry, obscene grain subsidies, cultural exchanges, the works. The hostage is the gun Mr. Gorbachev holds to Mr. Reagan's head, precluding all civilized dealing.[15]

Shultz later defended the deal by explaining that critics at the time did not know that the espionage charges against Daniloff, while false, would be difficult to overcome because of the CIA's involvement in the case.

Safire's harsh critique about the Daniloff case was roughly in sync with a National Intelligence Estimate about Gorbachev's overall diplomatic strategy delivered to Reagan as the Daniloff affair was unfolding. The estimate, which could be read as a rebuke of Shultz's peacemaking efforts, depicted Gorbachev's moves to ease East-West relations as a deceptive maneuver to buy time for the Soviet economy to rebound, eventually allowing the Kremlin to expand its global influence. The assessment argued that Gorbachev was offering nuclear force reductions and the prospect of additional summit meetings to induce Washington to curtail development of a missile shield and weaken its anti-Soviet policies.[16]

As Shultz and Shevardnadze were wrestling with the Daniloff affair, Gorbachev tossed a wild card into the deliberations—a proposal for a snap summit meeting in London or Reykjavik, Iceland. After a summer of Kremlin discontent over the lack of movement in relations with Washington, and the failure to set a date for a 1986 summit in Washington, Gorbachev decided to shake up the stalled diplomacy and, in Gorbachev's view, "unblock the strategic talks in Geneva, which were in danger of becoming an empty rite."[17] Shevardnadze delivered the summit proposal to Reagan while in Washington trying to untangle the Daniloff case. Reagan liked the idea, favored Reykjavik as the site but insisted that the Daniloff case be resolved before he would agree to the summit proposal. Once Daniloff was airborne and on his way to Frankfurt, Washington and Moscow quickly agreed to proceed with the Reykjavik meeting on October 10–12. They announced the plan on September 29 as the plane ferrying Daniloff from Frankfurt touched down at Dulles Airport outside Washington.

The impromptu summit in the secluded Icelandic capital proved to be the most dramatic and fateful cold war meeting of American and Soviet leaders. For a few extraordinary hours Reagan, with Shultz at his side, talked with Gorbachev and Shevardnadze about previously unthinkable reductions in long-range nuclear weapons. They even momentarily considered the elimination of all nuclear weapons. Reagan's vision of abolishing nuclear arms was on the table for the taking. He rejected it, with Shultz's support, to protect his imagined missile shield. Yet the summit, which initially seemed a dismal failure, improbably opened the way to an agreement to eliminate intermediate-range nuclear missiles and helped reset Soviet-American relations on a trajectory toward ending the cold war.

Reagan and Shultz did not know what to expect from Gorbachev in Reykjavik. Shultz saw it as an opportunity. "We should take a positive, self-confident and commanding approach to the meeting," he told Reagan. "The American people are all for it so we should not seem to be playing it down or disparaging its chances for solid progress."[18] Absent the usual months of preparatory time and advance negotiation among top American and Soviet officials, the meeting seemed primarily intended to lay the groundwork for a Gorbachev visit to Washington, most likely now in 1987. Gorbachev's letter to Reagan proposing the Iceland meeting suggested the meeting "would not be a detailed one."[19] Stephen Sestanovich, a senior National Security Council aide, advised, "We go into Reykjavik next week with very little knowledge of how Gorbachev intends to use the meeting."[20] While American preparations touched on the full spectrum of arms control, human rights and other issues, Reagan was not armed with new proposals as he headed to Iceland.

Gorbachev had a very different plan in mind. Impatient to break the nuclear arms control deadlock with Washington, he assembled a far-ranging set of proposals, rejecting incremental options suggested by aides. After nearly eighteen months as Soviet leader, he had a clear-eyed view of his country's vulnerabilities, especially its feeble economy. His audacious goal of reforming the Soviet Union depended partly on controlling defense spending and improving the standard of living. The implications for relations with Washington were obvious: reduce overall tensions, negotiate arms control accords that would take pressure off military spending and block the American development of new missile defense technologies that the Soviet Union could not match or afford.

He was direct in making the case to his Politburo colleagues. "Our goal is to prevent the next round of arms race. If we do not do this, the threat to us will only grow. And if we do not compromise on some questions, even very important ones, we will lose the main point: we will be pulled into an arms race beyond our power, and we will lose this race, for we are presently at the limit of our capabilities. . . . If the new round begins, the pressure on our economy will be inconceivable."[21] Anatoly Chernyaev, Gorbachev's national security adviser, recalled that Gorbachev wanted "to sweep Reagan off his feet with our bold, even risky approach to the central problems of world politics."[22]

The setting and conditions at Reykjavik abetted Gorbachev's summit goals. Hofdi House, the seaside site of the talks, was a small, simple building that lacked the opulent spaces and decor that would have come with a meeting in London or another European location. By mid-October, daylight was short in Iceland and the weather chilly. Instead of plenary meetings attended by numerous American and Soviet officials, Reagan and Gorbachev

Figure 26. Ronald and Nancy Reagan come to dinner at the Shultz's Bethesda home on June 5, 1983. The Reagans, having arrived before Shultz, inscribed this photo, "Wait a minute – how did we get there first?" Source: Ronald Reagan Presidential Library.

Figure 27. Shultz on a secure phone line from Augusta National Golf Club, during the Grenada crisis, October 22, 1983. Source: Bill Fitzpatrick, White House Photo Office.

Figure 28. Shultz meets with President Reagan and Deputy National Security Advisor Bud McFarlane, late at night in the Eisenhower Cabin at Augusta National Golf Club, to discuss the crisis in Grenada, October 22, 1983. Source: Ronald Reagan Presidential Library.

Figure 29. President Reagan with (left to right) Defense Secretary Caspar Weinberger; Vice President Bush; United States Ambassador to West Germany Arthur Burns; Shultz; Assistant Secretary of State for European and Canadian Affairs Rick Burt; and National Security Advisor Bud McFarlane in the Oval Office, November 15, 1984. Source: Ronald Reagan Presidential Library.

Figure 30. Shultz and Defense Secretary Caspar Weinberger at the White House, January 1, 1985. Source: Diana Walker, Getty Images.

Figure 31. Shultz and Soviet Foreign Minister Andrei Gromyko at the Soviet mission in Geneva, January 7, 1985. "Time flies when you're having fun," Shultz noted wryly in his memoir. Source: L. Bianco, Geneva.

Figure 32. Shultz with Israeli Prime Minister Shimon Peres and Foreign Minister Yitzhak Shamir at Yad Vashem, the World Holocaust Remembrance Center, Jerusalem, May 10, 1985. Source: George Pratt Shultz papers, Hoover Institution Library & Archives.

Figure 33. In Moscow, Shultz meets with Soviet General Secretary Mikhail Gorbachev, Soviet Minister of Foreign Affairs Eduard Shevardnadze, and Soviet Ambassador to the United States Anatoly Dobrynin. November 4, 1985. Source: George Pratt Shultz papers, Hoover Institution Library & Archives.

Figure 34. President Reagan meeting about the Philippines with (left to right) White House Chief of Staff Don Regan; Defense Secretary Caspar Weinberger; Vice President Bush; Shultz; and National Security Advisor John Poindexter, February 25, 1986. Source: Ronald Reagan Presidential Library.

Figure 35. President Reagan and Shultz talk with Soviet General Secretary Mikhail Gorbachev and Foreign Minister Eduard Shevardnadze in Hofdi House, the seaside site of the October 10–12, 1986, Reykjavik Summit. Source: George Pratt Shultz papers, Hoover Institution Library & Archives.

Figure 36. Shultz is sworn-in to testify before the joint Senate-House Iran-Contra Committee in Washington, DC, July 23, 1987. Source: Paul Hosefros, *The New York Times*.

Figure 37. Shultz and Gorbachev discuss the ABM treaty and Soviet-US relations in Moscow, with Paul Nitze in the background, October 23, 1987. Source: George Pratt Shultz papers, Hoover Institution Library & Archives.

Figure 38. Shultz with (left to right) Soviet Ambassador to the United States Yuri Dubinin; Soviet General Secretary Mikhail Gorbachev; Central Committee official Anatoly Dobyrnin; Pavel Palazhchenko (translator); and Foreign Minister Eduard Shevardnadze in Moscow, February 1988. Source: Hoover Institution Archives.

Figure 39. Shultz with Soviet Foreign Minister Eduard Shevardnadze, with Assistant Secretary of State for European and Canadian Affairs Rozanne L. Ridgway in the background, location unidentified. Source: George Pratt Shultz papers, Hoover Institution Library & Archives.

Figure 40. Reagan and Shultz, with British Prime Minister Margaret Thatcher, at a NATO meeting in Brussels, March 2, 1988. Source: George Pratt Shultz papers, Hoover Institution Library & Archives.

Figure 41. Shultz tours Kiev, April 1988. Source: George Pratt Shultz papers, Hoover Institution Library & Archives.

Figure 42. Shultz shares a laugh with First Lady Nancy Reagan in the Oval Office, August 1988. Source: George Pratt Shultz papers, Hoover Institution Library & Archives.

Figure 43. Shultz bids farewell to the State Department staff, January 19, 1989. Source: George Pratt Shultz papers, Hoover Institution Library & Archives.

Figure 44. Shultz receives the Medal of Freedom from President Reagan, January 19, 1989. Source: George Pratt Shultz papers, Hoover Institution Library & Archives.

Figure 45. George and Charlotte Shultz, date unknown. Source: George P. Shultz Personal Photo Album.

Figure 46. Jiang Zemin, President of the People's Republic of China, is greeted by George Shultz in San Francisco, October 28, 2002, George Pratt Shultz papers, Hoover Institution Library & Archives. Ronald Reagan Presidential Library.

Figure 47. George and Charlotte Shultz with President George W. Bush at the Shultz home on the Stanford campus, April 21, 2006. In the background, left to right: Stanford President John Hennessy; Stanford Board of Trustees Chair Burt McMurtry; Stanford Professor of Economics and Hoover Institution Senior Fellow John Taylor; Vice Chair of the Hoover Institution Board of Overseers and limited partner of Sequoia Capital Thomas F. Stephenson. Source: George Pratt Shultz papers, Hoover Institution Library & Archives.

Figure 48. President Barack Obama discusses nuclear non-proliferation in the Oval Office with (left to right) former Defense Secretary William Perry; former Senator Sam Nunn; Shultz; and former Secretary of State Henry Kissinger, May 19, 2009. Source: George Pratt Shultz papers, Hoover Institution Library & Archives.

Figure 49. Shultz and former Secretary of State Madeleine Albright, with Elizabeth Holmes seated behind and between them, testify before the Senate Armed Services Committee, January 29, 2015. Photographer: Jay Mallin. Source: George Pratt Shultz papers, Hoover Institution Library & Archives.

Figure 50. As former US Secretary of State Henry Kissinger looks on, Shultz, age 94, pushes away protesters shouting "Arrest Henry Kissinger for war crimes" during Senate Armed Services Committee testimony, January 29, 2015. *Tampa Bay Times*: Photo by Win McNamee/Getty Images.

talked around a small rectangular table in a compact room, accompanied by Shultz and Shevardnadze, two translators and an American and a Soviet note taker. The atmosphere was informal and the conversation spontaneous. The environment seemed suited for freewheeling discussion. As Shultz later said, the potential for unfettered talk unsettled traditionalists. "That's what alarmed people so much about Reykjavik. You get two leaders there without being controlled by their respective bureaucracies."[23]

In multiple sessions over two days and a long night of detail work by American and Soviet aides, Reagan and Gorbachev blasted through the conventional boundaries of summit meetings. They seriously considered sweeping nuclear arms control options. Gorbachev opened by offering a 50 percent cut in strategic, or long-range weapons, including land-based intercontinental missiles, bombers and submarine-based missiles. He proposed the elimination of American and Soviet intermediate-range missiles in Europe and western regions of the Soviet Union. He also outlined a variation of the recent American suggestion about managing the development of new missile defense weapons, proposing that the development and testing of new technologies be limited to laboratory work along with an agreement not to withdraw from the ABM Treaty for ten years. Reagan and Gorbachev sparred over the proposals at their first session. During a break, Paul Nitze said, "This is the best Soviet proposal we have received in twenty-five years."[24]

Reagan countered after lunch with the recent American offer to eliminate offensive ballistic missiles over the next ten years, as well as making a 50 percent reduction in strategic offensive arms. The two leaders discussed intermediate-range missile options. Common ground on offensive weapons seemed in sight, but neither side was willing to adjust its missile defense position. When Reagan repeated his promise to share any new missile defense technologies with the Kremlin, Gorbachev dismissed the offer as a fantasy, noting that the United States was unwilling to share oil-drilling technology or even milking machines. "He and I had at it all afternoon," Reagan recalled.[25] Before recessing for the day, Reagan and Gorbachev instructed their colleagues to work together overnight on narrowing differences on the arms issues. A working group on human rights issues was also assembled, capitalizing on Gorbachev's new willingness to address the matter with the Americans—another sign that he was eager to reach agreements.

It was an eventful night. The Soviet and American teams spent more than ten hours in discussions at Hofdi House. At one point, several American officials placed a board on top of a bathtub to create a makeshift desk. Marshal Sergei Akhromeyev, the Soviet Union's top military officer, led the Soviet arms control group and proved to be surprisingly cooperative. During a break at 2:00 a.m., Nitze, leader of the American group, and his colleagues drove across Reykjavik to their hotel to consult with Shultz, awakening the secretary of state.[26] His suite was chilly. "I put a sweater on over my pajamas and over that a bathrobe," Shultz recalled.[27] Nitze reported considerable progress in the talks but complained that some members of the American negotiating group opposed some of the arms reductions under consideration.[28] Shultz told him, "This is your working group and you're the boss. It's not a meeting in which everyone has a veto."[29] The Americans returned to Hofdi House and the negotiations at 3:00 a.m.

The Soviet team had new instructions of their own after waking up Gorbachev to consult with him. The breakthrough came by dawn: agreement in principle to a 50 percent reduction in strategic nuclear arsenals with equal numerical end levels on warheads and delivery systems. Numerical equality was critical because simply making 50 percent across-the-board reductions would leave the Soviet Union with more weapons because its arsenal of some weapons systems was larger. The agreement included another major Soviet concession: counting each strategic Soviet and American bomber as one weapon regardless of how many gravity bombs and short-range missiles the bomber carried. "A terrific night's work," Shultz exclaimed when Nitze filled him in on the talks.[30]

A second set of American and Soviet working groups dealing with other issues also made progress overnight. Shultz was pleasantly surprised that Soviet officials had agreed to make human rights issues a legitimate topic for discussion, abandoning the long-standing position that Soviet domestic affairs were off-limits. When Reagan, Shultz, Gorbachev and Shevardnadze reconvened, and unexpectedly extended the meeting into the afternoon, they knew extraordinary accords were possible. "George and I couldn't believe what was happening," Reagan said. "We were getting amazing agreements. As the day went on I felt something momentous was happening."[31]

Remarkably, Reagan and Gorbachev vaulted beyond nuclear arms reductions, spontaneously agreeing to abolish nuclear weapons. Reagan raised the prospect: "Do we have in mind—and I think it would be very good—that by the end of the two five-year periods all nuclear explosive devices would be eliminated, including bombs, battlefield weapons, cruise missiles, submarine weapons, intermediate-range system and so on? It would be fine with me if we eliminated all nuclear weapons."

Gorbachev: "We could say that, list all the weapons."

Shultz jumped in: "Then let's do it."

Reagan: "If we agree by the end of the end of the ten-year period all nuclear weapons are to be eliminated, we can turn this agreement over to our delegations in Geneva so they can prepare a treaty which you can sign during your visit to the U.S."

Gorbachev: "Well, all right. Here we have a chance for an agreement."[32]

But Gorbachev wanted to know if Reagan would also agree to adhere to the ABM Treaty for ten years and limit the development of new missile defense technologies to laboratory testing for a decade, concessions Reagan again refused to accept. The gap between the American offer about new missile defense technologies and Gorbachev's demand seemed bridgeable, were Reagan willing. The United States had proposed to restrict testing for five years in accordance with its interpretation of the ABM Treaty. Accepting Gorbachev's stipulation about laboratory testing would not have meant abandoning his vision. Rather, it would have consigned the project to a design and testing phase that seemed likely anyway, given the steps necessary to produce innovative defensive weapons. Realistically, a Reagan-Gorbachev agreement to abolish nuclear weapons would have ignited ferocious opposition in Washington and Moscow and probably would never have been approved. But Reagan's reason for turning away from the agreement in Reykjavik was based on his blind faith in a missile shield.

Shultz could have recognized this reality and appreciated that his intent to use SDI as leverage with the Kremlin had worked and yielded Soviet concessions that seemed unimaginable just weeks before. Instead, he locked arms with Reagan. When Reagan slipped a note across the table to Shultz asking, "Am I wrong?" Shultz whispered to the president, "No, you are right." In a futile effort to overcome the differences, Shevardnadze said, "Let me speak emotionally, because I feel we have come very close to accomplishing this historic task. And when future generations read the record of our talks, they will not forgive us if we let this opportunity slip by."[33]

From there, the conversation quickly dissolved into recriminations about who was to blame for the collapse. As Reagan and Gorbachev exited Hofdi House into the early autumn darkness, Reagan's grim expression captured the disappointment. As Reagan settled into his limousine, Gorbachev made a final attempt to salvage the summit. "There is still time Mr. President," he said to Reagan. "We could go back inside to the bargaining table. I don't know what more I could have done." "You could have said yes," Reagan replied. With that, the summit ended.[34]

Reagan quickly headed for the airport, hoping to get back to the White House in time for dinner with Nancy. Speaking to reporters briefly at Keflavik Air Base before boarding Air Force One, Reagan said, "We came to Iceland to advance the cause of peace and, though we put on the table the most far-reaching arms control proposal in history, the General Secretary rejected it." Shultz stayed behind to describe the talks to hundreds of journalists assembled in Reykjavik. He looked grim and emotionally drained. "We are deeply disappointed by this outcome," he said. "The president's performance was magnificent and I have never been so proud of my president as I have been in these sessions and particularly this afternoon. . . . In the end, with great reluctance, the president, having worked so hard creatively and constructively for these potentially tremendous achievements, simply had to refuse to compromise the security of the U.S., of our allies and freedom by abandoning the shield that was held in front of freedom."[35]

Looking back at his downbeat news conference years later, Shultz said, "Sometimes people asked me why I looked tired and disappointed, and I said, 'Well, because I was tired and disappointed.' But I should have taken a deep breath and thought more carefully about it and projected a different image. I don't think I did a good job in the press conference. Because I said how I felt, and I said what happened."[36] Shultz argued in retrospect that keeping SDI alive was essential to force the Kremlin to deliver on the arms reductions Gorbachev had accepted at the summit. "Without SDI as an ongoing propellant, these concessions could wither away over the next ten years," he said.[37] Perhaps, but the Soviet Union might just as easily have determined that any defensive system devised by the United States could be defeated by advances in offensive weapons and the use of decoy warheads. In fact, many American defense experts at the time contended that a missile defense system, no matter how technologically advanced, could be overcome by Moscow's offensive weapons.

Gorbachev held his own news conference across town shortly after Shultz. As he entered the hall, he was inclined to condemn Reagan, just as he had assured the Politburo he would do if the talks failed. But as he surveyed the hundreds of journalists from around the world, he changed course. "When I came into the room, the merciless, often cynical and cheeky journalists stood up in silence. I sensed the anxiety in the air. I suddenly felt emotional, even shaken. The people standing in front of me seemed to represent mankind waiting for its fate to be decided."[38]

The *New York Times* ran a two-line banner headline across the top of its front page: "Reagan-Gorbachev Talks End in Stalemate as U.S. Rejects Demand to Curb 'Star Wars.'" The news story reported:

> President Reagan and Mikhail S. Gorbachev ended two days of talks here today with no agreement on arms control and no date for a full-fledged summit meeting in the United States.
> While officials said that the two leaders had succeeded in developing tentative understandings on most arms control issues, a possible accord foundered over Soviet insistence that the United States scrap its space-based missile-defense plans.[39]

Because neither Shultz nor Gorbachev gave a comprehensive account of the two days of talks, initial media coverage about the near agreement to abolish nuclear weapons was fragmentary, leaving American allies mystified whether Reagan had actually agreed, even momentarily, to the elimination of nuclear arms. Margaret Thatcher was appalled at what she heard and raced to Washington to admonish Reagan and Shultz. Republicans, including Richard Nixon and Henry Kissinger, castigated Reagan and Shultz. So did Democratic leaders, including Senator Sam Nunn.

A few weeks after Reykjavik, Shultz updated his assessment about nuclear arms negotiations in an appearance at the University of Chicago. He described the summit as "a turning point in our strategy for deterring war and preserving peace."[40] But he pointedly did not reaffirm his or Reagan's desire to abolish nuclear weapons. After Reagan instructed the Joint Chiefs to study how the United States could transition to a world without offensive ballistic missiles, the Pentagon brass essentially balked. The generals reported back that the cost of substituting other offensive weapons would be prohibitive. Asked many years later if the Reykjavik summit could have ended differently, Shultz wondered how the conversation might have played out had he asked a basic question: "What exactly do you mean by laboratory?" He added, "Is space a laboratory? When you say the word 'laboratory,' you think of a little room and people in white coats. But maybe we could have found out how to define laboratory in a way that would have been acceptable, but I didn't think of that and we didn't do that."[41]

For all the uproar over Reykjavik, and the sense of disunion left by the failed talks, the meeting moved the cold war into a new and gentler phase. Despite continuing disagreements between Washington and Moscow, Reagan and Gorbachev together crossed a critical threshold in talking about eliminating offensive ballistic missiles and even all their nuclear weapons. The two delegations that negotiated through the night productively reviewed human rights and regional issues. Agreement came into view on aspects of an accord to pull American intermediate-range missiles out of Western Europe and Soviet medium-range missiles out of striking distance of Western Europe. When Gorbachev in late February 1987 decoupled the INF issues from other nuclear arms, the groundwork at Reykjavik made it possible to move relatively quickly to agreement on a treaty and planning for a Gorbachev visit to Washington in December 1987.

Shultz summed up his view of Reykjavik in his State Department memoir: "I took the criticism of Reykjavik seriously. Yet contrary to public perception, the accomplishments were immense. The Soviet agreement that human rights belonged on the regular agenda of U.S.-Soviet relations was astonishing. I thought that we had in fact arrived at an enormous turning point. I recognized full well that the nuclear age could not be abolished or undone; it was a permanent reality. But we could at least glimpse a world with far diminished danger from possible nuclear devastation. A better world was possible."[42]

CHAPTER TWENTY-ONE

Implosion of a Presidency

SHOCKING NEWS ABOUT SECRET arms-for-hostage deals rocked Washington three weeks after the Reykjavik meeting. The first hint came with a White House announcement on November 2, 1986, that David Jacobsen, an American held hostage in Lebanon by Iranian-directed Islamic forces, had been released. As Shultz read a draft White House statement about the development, he noted that it referred to freed "hostages," with the "s" crossed out. That told him that the White House had expected Jacobsen would not be alone. Shultz suspected that the news meant that clandestine White House efforts to free captive Americans in the Middle East by sending arms via Israel to Iran might be responsible. He had first heard about the possibility in mid-1985 and opposed it.

More news followed quickly after the David Jacobsen development. On November 3, a Lebanese weekly newspaper, *Al Shiraa*, reported that Bud McFarlane, by then no longer the White House national security adviser, had visited Teheran two months earlier on a secret White House mission aimed at gaining the release of American hostages in exchange for American missiles and other military hardware. McFarlane had come bearing a Bible signed by Reagan and a cake baked in the shape of a key meant to signify the opening of a new era in relations with Iran. It was stunning, improbable news, quickly picked up by news organizations around the world.

Within a few weeks, the dimensions of the story expanded exponentially with word that some Iranian payments for American arms had been

secretly diverted to the Contra forces in Nicaragua that Washington hoped
would topple the Sandinista regime. The funding was in clear violation of
a congressional cutoff of aid to the Contras. Overnight, the affair, quickly
dubbed the Iran-Contra scandal, engulfed the White House. Reagan soon
established a commission, headed by former senator John Tower, a Texas
Republican, to examine the affair and the role of the National Security
Council. Separate congressional investigations began. On December 19,
a panel of three federal appeals court judges in Washington, acting at the
request of the Justice Department, appointed Lawrence Walsh as independent counsel to conduct a criminal investigation of the Iran-Contra activities. Walsh, a Republican, had served as a federal district court judge and as
deputy attorney general during Dwight Eisenhower's second term.

Even before the investigations began, Shultz realized that Reagan faced
an explosive crisis similar to Watergate that might upend his presidency.
The fiasco staggered Shultz. It exposed his own failure to stop the arms-for-
hostage dealing at several critical moments when he heard about pieces of
it, objected to it but stopped short of forcefully intervening. He had deliberately kept his distance, telling the White House officials who managed
the arms shipments to Iran that he did not want to know the details. The
scandal also forced Shultz to face up to Reagan's weaknesses as president,
for the affair, at its core, was a colossal blunder. Even as the affair unraveled in public view in late 1986, Reagan insisted arms had not been traded
for hostages, a surreal case of magical thinking. As Shultz confronted the
issue, he struggled mightily to remain loyal to Reagan while simultaneously
protecting his own reputation and legacy. In doing so, he barely escaped
indictment by Lawrence Walsh for obstruction of justice.

The sudden crisis had been a long time in the making, born of two
international flashpoints that the Reagan administration struggled to
manage: the Middle East and Central America. The 1979 Iranian revolution
ousted Shah Mohammad Reza Pahlavi, an autocratic but ardent American
ally installed by the CIA in a 1953 coup. His imperial rule was supplanted
by a tyrannical anti-American theocracy led by Ayatollah Ruhollah
Khomeini that was determined to assert Iranian power in the region. The
US-Iran skirmish opened on November 4, 1979, when a mob of young

Iranians overran the American embassy in Teheran and seized fifty-two Americans as hostages. Their prolonged detention and a failed April 1980 American rescue mission grievously damaged Jimmy Carter's reelection bid. On January 20, 1981, after 444 days in captivity, the hostages were freed moments before Reagan was sworn in as president. In the years that followed, the Khomeini regime supported Shiite proxy groups in Lebanon and elsewhere in the Middle East that killed or kidnapped Americans.

Although Reagan administration policy clearly barred making concessions to hostage takers, Reagan yearned to free them. He also bought the untenable proposition that by selling arms to Iran he could establish a less adversarial relationship with the ayatollahs and turn Iran into a moderating Shiite influence in the region. That, in turn, would benefit Israel and prevent the Soviet Union from expanding its influence in the region. Israel, for its part, offered to sell American arms in its arsenal to Iran to secure the release of hostages. While the Middle Eastern plot was taking shape, the American officials who favored it—including William Casey, Bud McFarlane and navy lieutenant colonel Oliver North, a National Security Council staff member—grew increasingly concerned about Soviet and Cuban inroads in Central America. When congressional Democrats moved to curtail and then cut off American support to paramilitary forces trying to overthrow the Nicaraguan government, these men first looked to Israel and South Africa as potential sources of money for the Contras. Over time, the Middle East and Central America vectors converged. The result was an elaborate plot in which Israel sold American weapons to Iran in exchange for hostages, and profits from the arms sales were funneled to the Contras. Reagan enthusiastically endorsed the arms sales but was not informed about the diversion of money to the Contras.

Shultz's first inkling about irregular activity came in mid-April 1984 during administration debates about Central America policy and possible third-country aid to the Contras. Shultz wanted to maintain American assistance to the guerrilla forces, but not by funneling foreign money to them. He preferred to persuade Congress to extend American aid, if possible. When Casey suggested enlisting South Africa's help in April 1984, Shultz was appalled. "We can't abandon the Contras," Shultz said. "There are 15,000 of them. Bill Casey called me saying they had gotten a good response from South Africa, but I went through the roof saying it was about as stupid as the mining [of Nicaraguan harbors]. That has to be turned off." He noted that David Kimche, former deputy director of Mossad, the Israeli spy agency and the current director-general of the foreign ministry, seemed interested in helping secure funding. Kimche was well connected in Iran. "We'll have to figure out how to keep them going after the cutoff," Shultz continued, referring to the Contras. "We need to think about it. There aren't any subtle thinkers around here, certainly not Casey."[1]

McFarlane did not share Shultz's concerns about third-country help and pushed for Israeli involvement. Kimche came to New York to meet with Adnan Khashoggi about an Israeli-Saudi arrangement involving a barter arms deal. Khashoggi was a wealthy Saudi arms dealer who often acted as the middleman for the sale of American military equipment to Saudi Arabia. As the first steps toward some kind of external funding for the Contras were taken, Shultz fretted about the CIA role. "I have the feeling the CIA is out of control again," he said.[2] In an effort to salvage congressional support for the Contras, Shultz arranged to meet with House leaders in a closed session to talk about American interests in Central America and the effective role he thought the Contras could play if they received funding. Casey wanted to join Shultz at the meeting and insisted on attending despite Shultz's objections as the two men talked on the phone. "GPS slammed the phone back onto the cradle," Seitz reported. Shultz muttered, "Some people have their own agendas."[3]

On June 25, 1984, when Reagan, Shultz, Bush and others conferred about outside support for the Contras, Shultz told the group that James Baker, the White House chief of staff, believed "that if we go out and try to get money from third countries, it is an impeachable offense."[4] The initial indication for Shultz of abnormal arrangements with Iran materialized a year later when Sam Lewis, the American ambassador in Israel, reported that an American scholar was in Israel boasting that he was on a secret White House mission involving Israel and Iran.[5] Other clues appeared for Shultz as the months passed, pointing to the possibility of Israel transferring arms to Iran in exchange for hostages.

The arms-for-hostages operation came up formally in a July 13, 1985, McFarlane memo to Shultz, who was in Australia at the time. The national security adviser described an Israeli proposal, outlined by David Kimche and supported by Israeli prime minister Shimon Peres, to ship American arms to Iran to encourage a political dialogue and dislodge hostages from captivity. To get the dialogue started, McFarlane said, Iran wanted one hundred American antitank missiles. Shultz told McFarlane to "make a tentative show of interest without commitment." He went on: "I do not think we should be turning our backs on the prospect of gaining the release of the other seven hostages and perhaps developing an ability to renew ties with Iran under a more sensible regime, especially when presented to us through the prime minister of Israel." Shultz neither opposed nor supported the missile transfer—he did not address the question. He advised McFarlane to manage the initiative personally. Reflecting later on his response to McFarlane, Shultz said, "I was uneasy about my response, but I well knew the pressures from the president to follow up on any possibility of gaining the release of our hostages. I felt that Bud would in fact go ahead no matter what I said and that I was better off to stay in close touch with him and thereby retain some influence over what happened."[6]

Eight days later, McFarlane outlined the Israeli proposal at a White House meeting. Shultz, apparently reluctant to reiterate his earlier equivocation, objected to the arms transfer, arguing that it brazenly violated the administration's firm stance against trading guns for hostages or making any concessions to terrorists. Weinberger agreed. The meeting ended inconclusively, but two days later Reagan told McFarlane to move ahead with the plan. On August 20, Israel shipped 96 antitank missiles to Iran and another 408 two weeks later. One American hostage, Benjamin Weir, was soon freed. Upping the ante, Iran requested a shipment of more powerful weapons, medium-range surface-to-air HAWK missiles. When Israel could not deliver the larger weapons directly to Iran and efforts to ship them via a third country failed, Oliver North enlisted the help of the CIA. In late November, a CIA-operated air cargo company delivered eighteen HAWK missiles to Iran, the first installment of eighty missiles Iran had ordered.

Reagan enthusiastically supported the effort, acting on a humanitarian conviction that the United States should do everything possible to gain the release of the hostages. In doing so, he persuaded himself that the United States was not trading arms for hostages but instead was engaged in a noble attempt to save the lives of his countrymen. His well-intentioned but willful blindness was one of the more remarkable instances of presidential self-delusion in modern times, until the presidency of Donald Trump. It mirrored

Reagan's misplaced faith in the SDI. Both were driven by a naïve belief that outlandish actions in defense of America and Americans were justified, even if technologically fanciful or in conflict with American policy. In the case of the arms-for-hostage deals, Reagan's stubborn insistence that no such trade-off existed also makes one wonder if he was already suffering from early stages of Alzheimer's disease.

Once news of the deal broke into the open just days after the Reykjavik summit, Shultz's attempts to dent the Reagan illusion grew frantic—and perilous for him. His challenge was threefold: convince Reagan that McFarlane, Poindexter, Casey and North had misled him; end the arms-for-hostage strategy; and help Reagan survive the firestorm. Reagan did not want to hear that he had approved an arms-for-hostage strategy. On November 6, three days after the Lebanese newspaper report about the McFarlane mission to Teheran, Reagan declared that news coverage of the trip had "no foundation" and denied that the United States was exchanging arms with Iran for the release of hostages.

Shultz tried repeatedly to convince Reagan that his administration was trading arms for hostages and brazenly violating its own policies for dealing with terrorists. Reagan repeatedly rejected his appeals and grew increasingly impatient with Shultz. As the tension escalated, Shultz ruminated about his own failure to act more decisively in 1985 and 1986 as evidence of the operation caught his attention. "I felt I should have asked more, demanded more, done more, but I did not see how," he recalled. "Did I have myself to blame for the aggrandizement of the NSC staff? I agonized. Ever since my first days as secretary of state, I had sought to make the national security adviser my channel to the White House and, on day-to-day matters, to the president."[7]

On one level, he was right. Secretaries of state cannot operate independent of the White House and the national security adviser. The notable exceptions were Henry Kissinger, who served simultaneously for a time as secretary and national security adviser for Nixon, and James A. Baker III, whose close friendship with George H. W. Bush afforded him rare latitude. Shultz lacked that kind of easy relationship with Reagan. But on another level, Shultz was wrong. The weakness of the National Security Council staff was obvious from the day Shultz started work, and the conduct of Reagan's serial national security advisers often did not help: Richard Allen,

William Clark, Robert McFarlane and John Poindexter. Shultz's instinctive deference to the national security adviser hobbled him throughout the Reagan presidency, leading to years of paralysis on Soviet policy and the Iran-Contra fiasco. Shultz's faith in the orderly making of foreign policy, a reflection of his broader faith in the orderly management of organizations, left him vulnerable to the disorderly activities of zealots with access to the president. His willingness to rely on the White House national security staff after repeated setbacks caused by the incompetence and ideological rigidity of the staff does not make for a persuasive defense of his failure to act more decisively to stop the Iran-Contra affair before it reached critical mass.

Shultz's assertion at the time that he was unaware of many incremental developments in the arms-for-hostage operation, a defense repeated in his memoirs, does not conform with detailed notes kept by Charles Hill, who had succeeded Raymond Seitz as Shultz's executive assistant in 1985. The memory lapse can be explained by the dizzying demands that descend daily on a secretary of state and Hill's failure to capture all the relevant information about Shultz's awareness of the Iran-Contra activities when he reviewed his notes for Shultz to help prepare Shultz's congressional testimony. But Shultz's selective memory also evoked Richard Nixon's 1982 warning to William Clark and Reagan that Shultz had "a wonderful ability to, when things look iffy or are going wrong, he'll contend he never heard about the issue and was never briefed and was not a part."

Abraham Sofaer, the State Department's legal counsel at the time and former federal judge, made a similar observation years later. While not suggesting that Shultz was trying to dodge responsibility, Sofaer recalled: "He opposed it, clearly and definitively, but he sort of distanced himself from it. He has that way sometimes when he sees there's something that he probably can't do much about and doesn't take it very seriously. He sometimes will say to himself, 'I'm not going to spend my good will with the President on this or whatever.'"[8] The Tower Commission found that both Shultz and Weinberger "distanced themselves from the march of events" and "protected the records as to their own positions on the issues."[9]

Shultz's defective memory, compounded by Hill's handling of his notes, nearly proved disastrous for Shultz when Lawrence Walsh discovered that Shultz had withheld relevant information about the Iran-Contra affair in his 1987 congressional testimony, delivered under oath. Walsh weighed charging Shultz with obstruction of justice but ultimately found that "Shultz's testimony was incorrect, but it could not be proven that it was willfully false."[10] Walsh later said, "I had to admit that I had no urge to prosecute the one voice of courage and reason among Reagan's senior foreign policy advisors—the one person who had urged him to get the whole truth out to the public promptly."[11] Walsh did indict other administration officials, including Weinberger and McFarlane. The independent counsel report found that "there is strong evidence that Hill intended to mislead." But Walsh gave Hill a pass because he was not a central player: "It would not be appropriate to prosecute Hill, a subordinate to Shultz who had delivered that testimony and was not the subject of a prosecution himself."[12] Shultz, in his State Department memoir, excused Hill's incomplete handling of the notes, saying Walsh's staff spent "far more time" going through Hill's notes than Hill himself due to his "ongoing operational duties."[13] In the final days of his presidency in 1992, George H. W. Bush pardoned Weinberger, McFarlane and several other officials prosecuted by Walsh. Of all the senior officials involved in the affair, including Shultz, only McFarlane fully acknowledged and accepted blame for his role.

Shultz's faith in Reagan was shaken by the scandal. The president's refusal to acknowledge the reality of exchanging arms for hostages was dumbfounding. Reagan clearly was driven by a desire to liberate Americans cruelly held captive. White House aides played on that impulse by bringing family members of some hostages to the Oval Office to meet with the president and appeal for his help. The aides then exploited Reagan's sympathy. Yet even when Shultz confronted Reagan with the inescapable facts about the affair and the deceit of top aides, Reagan would not accept the truth. "Reagan was a romantic," said Sofaer, who delved deeply into the affair to reconstruct the State Department's role and Shultz's involvement. "Ollie North and Poindexter were well aware of Reagan's human vulnerability, and they brought the hostage families into the White House. I remember being in the White House one day and seeing one of these families being traipsed into Reagan's office to basically confront the president, to tell the president how much they were suffering."[14]

In a nationally televised address on November 13, 1986, that was meant to quiet the furor over the affair, Reagan said he had authorized a small shipment of arms to Iran but was not bartering arms for hostages. "We did not—repeat—did not trade weapons or anything else for hostages, nor will we." After the speech, Shultz tried to make sense of Reagan's blind spot. "The president's speech convinced me that Ronald Reagan still truly did not believe that what had happened had, in fact, happened. To him the reality was different. I had seen him like this before on other issues. He would go over the 'script' of an event, past or present, in his mind, and once the script was mastered, that was the truth—no fact, no argument, no plea for reconsideration, could change his mind."[15]

Dismayed by Reagan's attitude but determined to try to free Reagan from the quicksand enveloping the presidency, Shultz kept pushing to cut off the arms deals with Iran and reassert American policy against making concessions to hostage takers. On November 16, he made a fateful appearance on *Face the Nation*, the CBS News Sunday-morning interview program. When Lesley Stahl, host of the show, repeatedly pressed Shultz to state whether any further arms shipments would be made to Iran, he replied, "Under the circumstances of Iran's war with Iraq, its pursuit of terrorism, its association with those holding our hostages, I would certainly say, as far as I'm concerned, no." Stahl then asked if Shultz was speaking for the entire administration. "No," he answered.[16] It was a stunning moment—the secretary of state acknowledging that he could not speak for the US government. The remark instantly ignited speculation that Shultz was breaking with the White House and would soon resign or be fired. He headed for Chicago the next day, unsure if he would have a job by the time he returned to Washington that evening.

He barely survived. The White House announced that Shultz did speak for the administration and that Reagan had "no desire" and "no plans" to send further arms to Iran. Yet Reagan continued to defend the operation privately as justified to save American lives and strengthen America's influence in the oil-rich Middle East. Meanwhile, Poindexter and North kept working on plans for new arms shipments. Sensing that Shultz's persistence was annoying Reagan, Casey urged the president to select a new secretary of state. On November 23, Casey wrote to Reagan: "The public pouting of George Shultz and the failure of the State Department to support what we did inflated the uproar on this matter. If we all stand together and speak out I believe we can put this behind us quickly. You need a new pitcher. A leader instead of a bureaucrat. I urge you to bring in someone like Jeane Kirkpatrick or Paul Laxalt, who you may recall I recommended for State in 1980. You need this to give your foreign policy a new style and thrust and get the Carterite bureaucracy in State under your control. Otherwise, you will not be doing justice to yourself or to your presidency. Time is short."[17] Paul Laxalt, a Reagan friend and informal adviser, was a Republican senator from Nevada. Reagan tossed the letter in a White House fireplace, presidential aide A. B. Culvahouse later reported.[18]

The same day Casey sent his letter, he joined Bush, Shultz, Weinberger and others at the White House for a National Security Planning Group meeting with Reagan to hear from Attorney General Ed Meese. Reagan had commissioned Meese to investigate the arms-for-hostage operation. Shultz recalled that Poindexter dominated the meeting, informing the group that the White House planned to dispatch an emissary to foreign capitals to defend the American conduct. Reagan brushed aside Shultz's objections. As Shultz recalled the scene, "Ronald Reagan pounded the table. 'We are right,' he said. 'We had to take the opportunity! And we were successful. History will never forgive us if we don't do this! And no one is to talk about it!'"[19]

That evening, as Shultz lamented the latest developments, Poindexter called from the White House. His tone was entirely different—mild, even meek. He assured Shultz and several State Department colleagues that they could run Iran policy and he would be happy to turn his attention to other national security issues he had neglected. The change in tone pleased but puzzled Shultz. Two days later he learned the reason behind the turnabout. Meese aides had discovered the secret payments to the Contras. When top officials gathered again at the White House, Meese told the group that ten to thirty million dollars had been sent to the Contras. Reagan had not approved the diversion or even known about it. As a result, Poindexter was out and North reassigned. On November 26, three weeks after the first news reports about McFarlane's trip to Teheran, Shultz and Reagan stilled the rancor that had agitated their relationship and agreed Shultz should stay on as secretary of state through the end of the Reagan presidency.[20]

Astonishingly, even after all this, Reagan still resisted efforts to shut down back-channel communications with Iran. Poindexter and North were gone, but Casey and others tried to keep the discredited dialogue with Iran alive. After meeting with Reagan, Bush and Don Regan on December 15, Shultz told Bush, "Bill Casey is bad news." In Shultz's view, "Casey had grossly distorted the proper conduct of government."[21] He swore he would do everything within his power to prevent Casey from pursuing the Iranians. Forty-five minutes later, Shultz learned that Casey had been hospitalized with a malignant brain tumor. Robert Gates, Casey's deputy, was named acting CIA director. Casey never returned to the agency. He resigned as CIA director in early 1987 and died on May 6, 1987.

As a very eventful 1986 ended, Shultz was eager to reengage with the Kremlin to see if the melodramatic but inconclusive Reykjavik meeting might lead to new diplomatic opportunities. His relationship with Reagan looked stable again after the tumult of the Iran-Contra revelations, but other fallout from the affair was just beginning as a joint congressional committee geared up to investigate the scandal and Walsh started hiring staff for his inquiry. Reagan, battered by the turmoil and mounting public doubts about his leadership, seemed subdued to Shultz when they met over the holidays at Walter Annenberg's expansive Palm Springs estate. "He looked healthy, but hurt," Shultz recalled. "He was tentative and deferential, humbled. I had never seen him like that before. On our New Year's Eve golf outing, I rode on the cart with him. We bantered. He told a joke or two. But we had no real discussion of substance. Whether at a party, on the golf course, or in a policy discussion, the president just didn't seem ready to engage."[22]

Reagan eventually did face up to his own errors, spurred by the harsh criticism of the Tower Commission, which published its report at the end of February 1987. In a nationally televised address on March 4, 1987, Reagan said:

> A few months ago I told the American people I did not trade arms for hostages. My heart and my best intentions still tell me that's true, but the facts and the evidence tell me it is not. As the Tower board reported, what began as a strategic opening to Iran deteriorated, in its implementation, into trading arms for hostages. This runs counter to my own beliefs, to administration policy, and to the original strategy we had in mind. There are reasons why it happened, but no excuses. It was a mistake. I undertook the original Iran initiative in order to develop relations with those who might assume leadership in a post-Khomeini government. It's clear from the Board's report, however, that I let my personal concern for the hostages spill over into the geopolitical strategy of reaching out to Iran. I asked so many questions about the hostages'

welfare that I didn't ask enough about the specifics of the total Iran plan.[23]

Rallying from the downcast days at the end of 1986, Reagan told the nation: "You know, by the time you reach my age, you've made plenty of mistakes. And if you've lived your life properly—so, you learn. You put things in perspective. You pull your energies together. You change. You go forward. My fellow Americans, I have a great deal that I want to accomplish with you and for you over the next two years. And the Lord willing, that's exactly what I intend to do."[24]

CHAPTER TWENTY-TWO

Back on Track

A MONTH AFTER THE Reagan mea culpa, Shultz made his way to Moscow for his first encounter with Gorbachev and Shevardnadze since Reykjavik. Change was in the air in Moscow as Gorbachev pushed ahead with his reforms. Some of the positive fallout from the Reykjavik meeting was evident as Shultz prepared to accentuate Soviet human rights abuses while in Moscow in ways that would have been unimaginable before. But objections to the warming relationship with the Kremlin persisted in Washington, and a security crisis at the American embassy in Moscow nearly upended Shultz's diplomatic efforts. Unknown to Shultz, Gorbachev faced political turmoil inside the Kremlin.

Diplomatic communications with the Kremlin before Shultz headed to Moscow suggested Gorbachev might be prepared to move ahead on some of the issues left unresolved in Iceland, including terms for a possible treaty limiting or eliminating intermediate-range nuclear missiles. Shultz's Moscow schedule reflected the easing of repression and censorship under Gorbachev. Shultz would attend a Seder with Soviet Jews who wanted to leave the Soviet Union and had openly criticized the Kremlin. He would also do an interview on Soviet television that the Kremlin promised would air in full.

Four months earlier, Gorbachev had underscored his tolerance for dissent by inviting Andrei Sakharov and his wife, Yelena Bonner, to return to Moscow after almost seven years of internal exile in the industrial city of Gorky. The Brezhnev Kremlin had silenced Sakharov for questioning Soviet rule. Sakharov, a physicist, helped design Moscow's first hydrogen bomb and was repeatedly honored by the Kremlin until he started speaking out against human rights abuses and undemocratic rule in the Soviet Union. He was awarded the Nobel Peace Prize in 1975 for his courageous activism.

Reports about Soviet penetration of the American embassy in Moscow created a furor in Washington in the weeks before the Shultz trip. Two marines posted at the embassy to ensure that classified materials were kept secure had reportedly been seduced by female KGB agents. They let Soviet agents into the embassy building at night to rummage through secure files. The reports later turned out to be grossly exaggerated—there had been no KGB access to embassy files—but at the time security issues rippled destructively through the embassy and back in Washington. Construction of a new embassy complex on adjacent land was riddled with security problems. As news of the marine breakdown escalated, pressure built in Washington to cancel the Shultz trip. On the eve of his departure, the Senate overwhelmingly approved a resolution calling on the administration to cancel the trip.

The security flare-up fed concerns in the administration that Gorbachev could not be trusted and that Reagan should resist any temptation to give ground on nuclear arms issues or other matters. Weinberger was especially adamant that Reagan and Shultz not make any concessions about the development and testing of new missile defense technologies. "Cap Weinberger had opened a presentation at a Situation Room meeting by saying, 'Max Kampelman and the Communists want to . . . ' I hit the roof, and so did Max."[1] Weinberger grew so alarmed over the Moscow embassy issues that he suggested Shultz refuse to go to Moscow and instead meet with Shevardnadze in Geneva.

Frank Carlucci, the new national security adviser, was also wary of Gorbachev. He advised Reagan in early April: "At Reykjavik, Gorbachev was unable to catch you in a prelaid trap because you neither gave in on SDI nor accepted the outcome as a political failure." Looking ahead to next steps in dealing with the Soviet leader as the political fallout from the Iran-Contra affair was tapering at home, Carlucci said, "We remain unsure what course Gorbachev is on. We know he still wants to kill SDI, deflect your administration from broader policies that challenge the USSR and get to some sort of 'détente on the cheap.'" Taking a shot at Shultz, he added, "George Shultz must go to Moscow with his seatbelt securely fastened to your policy."[2]

Richard Nixon, still seeking to have a say on America's handling of the Soviet Union, seconded Carlucci's caution in an unpublicized meeting with Reagan, Carlucci and Howard Baker, the new White House chief of staff. The group, notably absent Shultz, assembled in the residential quarters of the White House in late April. Nixon registered his concerns about an intermediate-range missile accord, then attacked Shultz. "I got in one shot at Shultz, which I thought was quite effective," Nixon noted in a memo for his records. "I said he had been a great Secretary of the Treasury, a great Secretary of Labor and a great director of OMB, and said he did an outstanding job of negotiating with Meany for a period. But I said negotiating with Meany was much different from negotiating with Gorbachev." Nixon added to the memo that he thought Reagan himself was not up to the task of dealing with the Soviet leader. Reporting that he found Reagan looking "far older, more tired and less vigorous in person than in public," Nixon wrote, "There is no way he can ever be allowed to participate in private meetings with Gorbachev."[3]

Meantime, Gorbachev signaled that he wanted to strike an intermediate-range missile deal by the end of the year, a message that was quietly relayed to Washington. In the end, Reagan instructed Shultz to go to Moscow but curtailed his negotiating latitude.[4] "While the president supported me in going forward with the trip," he recalled, "he had sided with Cap Weinberger in giving me almost no room to maneuver, even drawing back here and there from positions we had taken in Reykjavik."[5] A late-spring dusting of snow greeted Shultz in Moscow on April 13. In an initial morning meeting with Shevardnadze, the foreign minster insisted that the panic about security breaches at the American embassy was unwarranted: "Mr. Secretary, you are being deceived," he told Shultz.[6] As it turned out, he was right, though the truth about the overblown marine scare did not come out until months later. In a sign that the progress made in Reykjavik was enduring, Shultz and Shevardnadze dispassionately discussed a wide array of issues, including human rights abuses in the Soviet Union.

When Nanuli Shevardnadze joined the men for an informal lunch, Shultz staged a musical performance that shattered diplomatic convention and would have been unthinkable in previous encounters between a secretary of state and Soviet foreign minister. Knowing the Shevardnadzes' affection for their homeland, Shultz had arranged to have the American song "Georgia on My Mind," memorably recorded by Ray Charles, translated into Russian. Shultz handed a copy of the translation to the Shevardnadzes, then sang the song himself in English. Four American diplomats who spoke Russian followed, singing the tune in Russian. The Shevardnadzes were delighted. The human connection that Shultz had initiated in Helsinki nearly two years earlier was deepening.

That evening, a small group of Russian Jews assembled for a Seder at Spaso House, the residence of the American ambassador. The *New York Times* reported: "Many who were at the seder had been in prison or Siberian exile for calling on Washington to put pressure on Soviet authorities to relax the emigration restrictions affecting all Soviet citizens. Mr. Shultz, an Episcopalian, wore a white yarmulke as he went to every table, shook every hand and exchanged a few words with practically everyone. He seemed in awe of these tough, cheerful, resolute men and women bearing names familiar to him from the lists he presents at every meeting with high Soviet officials."[7] Shultz told the guests, "You are on our minds, you are in our hearts." He later recalled, "The event moved me deeply."[8] While Gorbachev did not try to prevent the Seder, he complained about it to Shultz the next day,

When Shultz and Shevardnadze met again that evening, Shultz laid out a new argument for improving human rights in the Soviet Union that he had developed in the months since Reykjavik. He said, in essence, that as the industrial age gave way to the information age, open societies would thrive economically and closed societies would be unable to keep pace. If the Soviet Union suppressed free thinking and dissent and stifled the movement of peoples between nations, it would inevitably fall farther and farther behind the West. Shevardnadze listened attentively.

Gorbachev welcomed Shultz to St. Catherine's Hall in the Kremlin on April 4, a far more elegant and spacious chamber than their last Moscow meeting at Gorbachev's more workmanlike Central Committee office. Gorbachev quickly focused the discussion on intermediate-range missiles, announcing that he was ready to eliminate all of the Soviet weapons within range of Western Europe if the United States would withdraw its Pershing missiles from Western Europe. It was a bold proposal, more ambitious than the Reagan administration had expected. Gorbachev pressed Shultz to agree on the spot. "Some of our allies may prefer a finite number," Shultz said. "I will take this offer back to them. I owe you an answer." Gorbachev was impatient. He told Shultz, "You are just on an intelligence mission. What kind of leader are you? Why can't you make a decision?"[9]

Shultz used a break in the formal discussions to renew the conversation about global economic issues he had opened with Gorbachev in his last Moscow visit and alluded to with Shevardnadze just hours earlier. Shultz, once again acting more like a professor of economics than a diplomat, walked Gorbachev through an analysis of global economic trends pointing toward a future world in which resources, ideas and goods flowed freely among nations that understood the transformative power of new technologies and communication networks. He said, "We have entered a world in which the truly important capital is human capital, what people know, how freely they exchange information and knowledge, and the intellectually creative product that emerges." Gorbachev seemed engaged and interested. "We should have more of this kind of talk," he told Shultz.[10] When Gorbachev reported to the Politburo on the Shultz visit, he said, "Shultz is special."[11]

As the break ended, Marshal Akhromeyev, who had played a positive role at Reykjavik, joined the meeting along with other Soviet and American officials. The talk returned to arms control issues, with discussion about cutting long-range nuclear forces, limiting the underground testing of nuclear weapons and creating methods to inspect and verify compliance with any arms control agreements. Gorbachev said he was ready to pull Soviet forces out of Afghanistan, but Washington was putting "sticks in the spokes" with its continuing support of insurgent Afghan forces.[12] Nothing was settled, but the talks were productive. They left Shultz exhausted and exhilarated, sensing that an INF agreement was within reach and that the next summit might happen by the end of the year. Remarkably, Shultz's interview with Valentin Zorin, a Soviet journalist, was aired in full, as the Kremlin had promised. But his last words about the Soviet occupation of Afghanistan, while shown, were not translated: "It is a very devastating war, and they do not want you there. They want peace with you, but they do not want you occupying their country."[13]

Before heading home, Shultz and his wife made the short drive in a spring snowstorm to Peredelkino, a rustic village of simple homes, or dachas, outside Moscow, to meet with writers, poets and other literary and artistic figures long muzzled by the Kremlin. Shultz found "the wooded, muddy scene was reminiscent of Appalachia."[14] One of the men present, Anatoly Rybakov, was the author of an anti-Stalinist novel, *Children of the Arbat*, which the Kremlin banned from publication until 1987. While in Peredelkino, Shultz visited the grave of Boris Pasternak, author of *Doctor Zhivago* and winner of the Nobel Prize in Literature in 1958. The Kremlin viewed the book as anti-Soviet and prevented publication in the Soviet Union, but the manuscript was smuggled to Italy and published to acclaim in the West.

News coverage of the Shultz visit was positive. The *New York Times* reported: "Secretary of State George P. Shultz said today that a treaty eliminating medium-range nuclear missiles in Europe was within reach, despite continued differences over how to verify an accord and what limits to set on short-range missiles. The cautiously optimistic assessment at a news conference in Moscow seemed to be shared by the Soviet Foreign Minister, Eduard A. Shevardnadze, who said there was a 'rather good prospect' of a summit meeting in Washington this year to sign an accord."[15] Shultz stopped in Brussels to brief NATO allies, many of whom were alarmed by the drift of Washington's arms talks with Moscow, fearing American defense of Western Europe might be eroded. From there, he traveled directly to the Reagan ranch in California to report on his talks. Reagan was pleased to hear how productive the meeting had been. "My three days in Moscow had been extraordinary in content, in promise and in tone," Shultz said.[16]

On May 28, Gorbachev got an unexpected opportunity to assert his authority over the Soviet military high command when Mathias Rust, a nineteen-year-old German aviator, guided his single-engine plane unimpeded through Soviet air defenses for four hundred miles from Helsinki and gently settled the aircraft onto the cobblestones of Red Square. The sight of the small plane circling the Kremlin and landing in front of St. Basil's Cathedral was so improbable that Kremlin guards and tourists in Red Square assumed it must be an approved flight. Even seasoned Western journalists in Moscow doubted initial accounts and did not venture to Red

Square to see for themselves until hours later as the plane was being loaded onto a truck and hauled away. Rust announced to the few bystanders who gathered around him that he was on a mission of peace. Gorbachev, on a visit to East Berlin, rushed home to deal with the embarrassing defense breakdown. He promptly fired the defense minister and air defense chief, appointing successors more sympathetic to his policies.

The Rust flight was the talk of Washington, an embarrassing bookend for the Kremlin to the downing of KAL 007 four years earlier. But the upbeat mood generated by Shultz's April visit to Moscow dissipated over the spring and summer as Washington and Moscow haggled over terms of an INF agreement. The Reagan administration was distracted by congressional hearings on the Iran-Contra affair, including appearances by Oliver North, John Poindexter and others involved in directing the activities. Shultz himself was consumed by preparations for his testimony, which spanned two days in July.

He also wrestled with Frank Carlucci over management of national security policy. Carlucci was a Washington heavyweight who had served in a host of top government jobs in Republican and Democratic administrations, including deputy secretary of defense in Reagan's first term and CIA deputy director under Jimmy Carter. Shultz knew and liked Carlucci from the days when they had worked on domestic issues in the Nixon administration. At the time, Carlucci was director of the Office of Economic Opportunity. Shultz took offense at Carlucci's insistence that the White House national security staff supervise the development of foreign and defense policy, contending that it was just such White House conduct that had spawned the Iran-Contra operations.

Carlucci refused to back down and secured Reagan's approval of National Security Decision Directive 276, which put the national security adviser in charge of managing the interagency policy-making process. After hearing repeated complaints from Shultz, an annoyed Carlucci told him, "I did not return to government in order to be an executive secretary."[17] Carlucci recalled, "George was traumatized by the NSC and he wanted to reduce the NSC in effect to an executive secretariat. He didn't want me to see ambassadors, he didn't want me to travel, he didn't want to me to chair meetings."[18] The feud was intense but lacked the personal hostility that characterized Shultz's relations with Carlucci's predecessors as national security adviser and the constant policy combat between Shultz and Weinberger and Shultz and William Casey.

On June 12, Reagan delivered one of the most memorable lines of the cold war during a visit to West Berlin. Standing before the Brandenburg Gate and the Berlin Wall that the Kremlin and its East German partners erected in 1961, Reagan intoned, "Mr. Gorbachev, tear down this wall." Shultz and other Reagan aides had tried to dissuade him from making the statement, fearing it would spike cold war tensions and undermine Gorbachev's effort to improve relations with Washington. Twenty-four years earlier, during the first visit to the divided city by an American president since the end of World War II, John Kennedy had electrified hundreds of thousands of West Berliners by telling them, "Ich bin ein Berliner," "I am a Berliner."

In late October, Weinberger notified Reagan that he would resign as defense secretary to help care for his ailing wife. Reagan soon appointed Carlucci defense secretary, a step applauded by Shultz. After five years of unremitting policy combat with Weinberger, Shultz would be dealing with a more congenial line-up of fellow national security officials, including Carlucci and General Colin Powell, who would succeed Carlucci as national security adviser. It was a critical transition, giving Shultz, for the first time, a set of senior colleagues not intent on opposing the secretary of state.

While Washington was absorbed with the congressional inquest on Iran-Contra, Gorbachev announced that the Kremlin was ready to eliminate all intermediate-range nuclear missiles. This solidified the spirit of accommodation that Shultz had sensed during his April talks with Gorbachev. The way now seemed clear to pin down the details of an INF Treaty and to set a date for Gorbachev to come to Washington in late fall. Shevardnadze flew to Washington in mid-September to review INF and other matters with Shultz and Reagan. As the three-day visit began, Shevardnadze and Shultz signed an agreement to expand direct communication links between the American and Soviet governments to limit the risk of nuclear war. Reagan presided over the signing ceremony in the Rose Garden. The accord established a second link, modeled on the "hot line" between the White House and the Kremlin created in August 1963 in the wake of the Cuban Missile Crisis.

While in Washington, Shevardnadze confidentially told Shultz that the Kremlin had taken a final decision to withdraw Soviet forces from Afghanistan and would do so within a year. It was a momentous decision that would end nearly a decade of Soviet occupation that had convulsed Afghanistan and inspired growing, if muted, opposition within the Soviet Union. The decision would remove a major impediment to improved relations with Washington, which had long overtly and covertly supported anti-Soviet and antigovernment Islamic forces in Afghanistan known as the Mujahideen fighters. Shevardnadze asked for American help to prevent Afghanistan from veering toward Islamic extremism after Soviet forces left. When the topic of Afghanistan came up later in the day at a group meeting of American and Soviet officials, Shultz did not mention the Kremlin decision. The result was an awkward moment as the two sides wrangled over Afghanistan, unaware that Soviet troops would soon be leaving. "I'm sitting there saying to myself, 'Why are we having this discussion?'" Shultz recalled. "And I looked over to Shevardnadze once and I could see he was having the same thought, but it was going on and we just sort of let it go on."[19]

On September 17, Reagan announced the progress made by Shultz and Shevardnadze toward an INF accord: "I'm pleased to note that agreement in principle was reached to conclude an I.N.F. treaty. They'll meet again in Moscow next month to continue their efforts and to work out the details of a summit between me and General Secretary Gorbachev later this fall."[20] A month later, Shultz and Carlucci headed to Moscow, expecting to settle remaining differences with Gorbachev on an INF Treaty and to set a summit date in Washington. Reagan was keen to invite Gorbachev to see some of the United States and to come to his California ranch for Thanksgiving dinner. With the Soviet capital enveloped in a thick fog, the American delegation traveled overnight by train from Helsinki, arriving in Moscow early on the morning of October 22.

Unknown to the Americans, Boris Yeltsin, the Moscow area Communist Party boss and nonvoting Politburo member, had harshly criticized Gorbachev the day before at a Central Committee meeting. After unexpectedly asking to address the assembled Communist Party leaders, Yeltsin stepped to the lectern, collected himself for a moment and then declared that Gorbachev's reforms had proven to be empty promises. He accused the Politburo of "glorifying" Gorbachev and warned that a "cult of personality" was developing around him.[21] It was a startling scene—a fellow reformer, a Gorbachev protégé brought to Moscow from the provincial city of Sverdlovsk as a Gorbachev ally, openly castigating Gorbachev before the Communist Party elite. The outburst had been building for weeks, as an emotionally unstable Yeltsin grew increasingly impatient with the pace of change and Gorbachev's refusal to meet with him.

Gorbachev, angered by the verbal assault, invited Central Committee members to respond, unleashing a torrent of vitriolic denunciations of Yeltsin. The uproar left Yeltsin temporarily crushed, personally and politically. He was soon expelled from the Politburo and forced to issue a humiliating apology in *Pravda*, the Communist Party flagship newspaper. The incident also wounded Gorbachev, who was already facing growing resistance from Communist Party conservatives concerned that his reforms were too aggressive. Word of the showdown quickly spread among Communist Party members.

Though Shultz was unaware of the donnybrook, he detected a change in Gorbachev during their meeting. The Soviet leader was unusually testy, complaining about a lack of progress on limiting long-range nuclear weapons and new missile defense technologies. He told Shultz and Carlucci he was not ready to set a summit date. "The agenda does not seem to measure up to what would be necessary at a summit," he said. "People will not understand if the two leaders keep meeting and have nothing to show for it, especially since both agreed and said publicly that strategic arms were the key."[22] Gorbachev pressed Shultz for restraints on SDI, essentially holding other issues and potential agreements hostage to American concessions about the development and testing of new antimissile weapons. Gorbachev's unexpected aversion to a summit surprised the Americans. Only later did they learn that it was likely driven by the Yeltsin outburst and conservative opposition in the Kremlin. Shultz was disappointed by the delay but not inclined to offer concessions to lure Gorbachev to Washington. After the meeting, he told aides that he thought Gorbachev seemed different: "Today he no longer looks to me like a boxer who has never been hit," Shultz said. "This boxer has been hit."[23] It was a shrewd assessment.

Shultz informed Reagan of the impasse in a brief account of the meeting before leaving Moscow: "It's not peaches and cream."[24] "George reported on meeting with Gorbachev who sort of pounded the table at one point over a State Dept. paper he thought was critical of him," Reagan noted in his diary.

"George pounded the table back & the air cleared. We still believe he wants a summit but is playing a game thinking I want a summit so bad I'll pay the price regarding S.D.I. He's wrong."[25] Among the discouraging headlines was this from the *New York Times*: "Gorbachev, Demanding Change on 'Star Wars,' Bars Summit Talk Now." The news story from Moscow stated:

> Mikhail S. Gorbachev refused today to set a date for a summit meeting with President Reagan, unexpectedly insisting that differences over the development of space-based defensive weapons must be resolved first.
> The Soviet leader told Secretary of State George P. Shultz in a five-hour meeting that although negotiators from the two sides had resolved most remaining obstacles to a treaty abolishing medium- and short-er-range nuclear missiles and had made progress toward reducing lon-ger-range weapons, that was not enough to justify the promised meeting later this year.[26]

Gorbachev quickly reconsidered. By the time Shultz got back to Washington, Jack Matlock, the new American ambassador in Moscow, relayed word from the Kremlin that Shultz's meeting with Gorbachev had not gone "as planned" and that Gorbachev would like to come to Washington after all. He would send Shevardnadze there in three days to work out a summit date and agenda.[27] "Gorbachev just blinked," Shultz told Reagan.[28]

Events moved quickly after that. Shevardnadze flew to Washington on October 30, carrying a Gorbachev letter proposing early December for a Washington summit that would feature the signing of an INF Treaty and further negotiations about strategic arms and missile defenses. Three weeks later Shultz and Shevardnadze met in Geneva, coming to final agreement on the terms of the INF Treaty, including a set of exacting inspection and verification procedures that would give each nation the opportunity to assure that the other was complying with the treaty. Marshal Akhrome-yev, who worked alongside Shevardnadze, again proved to be very helpful in fine-tuning the terms of the accord. He jokingly told Shultz he might have to seek asylum in Switzerland. The Geneva discussions established a schedule for the Gorbachev visit. There would not be time for him to travel around the United States, but his three days in Washington would include several meetings with Reagan; gatherings with Americans from an array of fields, including politics, business and the arts; and lots of pageantry.

Shortly before Thanksgiving, Shultz prepared what he called a "non-pa-per" for Reagan about dealing with Gorbachev. Picking up a theme that

Carlucci had mentioned in a memo several months earlier, Shultz said that "it is increasingly clear that the Soviet Union is going to be seen by history as Ronald Reagan's 'China,'" a reference to Richard Nixon's unexpected diplomatic overtures to China, a nation Nixon had long reviled as a Communist dictatorship. Shultz explained that just as China had changed because of fear of the Soviet Union, a fear Nixon had exploited, the Soviet Union was now changing because of a fear of China's domestic reforms, Eastern European restlessness and concern about "falling permanently behind the U.S." While saying that "the road ahead is going to be rocky," Shultz made clear to Reagan that he thought relations with Moscow had reached a pivotal point that could fundamentally alter international relations. He wrote: "We have entered one of those rare historical periods when significant planned change is possible in relations between states. We are at a crossroads where East and West could transform the nature of their postwar relationship with a more constructive form of competition."[29]

As the summit approached, Robert Gates, the CIA deputy director, pulled together his thoughts about Gorbachev in a gloomy paper that contradicted Shultz's optimistic appraisal. It was as if the hard-liners around Reagan, even as their number and influence were declining, were making a last stand in hopes of preventing Reagan and Shultz from truly believing that East-West relations could be transformed. Drawing on his years as a leading CIA analyst of the Soviet Union, Gates discounted the numerous reforms initiated by Gorbachev, warning Reagan not to be seduced by the Soviet leader. The Gates memo opened by asserting that Gorbachev wanted "to establish a new and far-reaching détente," invoking a term and reference to an earlier period of American-Soviet relations that Reagan had consistently denounced as a failure in American foreign policy. Gates said, "The Soviets know that détente in the early 1970s contributed significantly to downward pressure on Western defense budgets, nearly halted military modernization, weakened resolve to counter Soviet advances in the Third World, and opened to the USSR new opportunities for Western technology and economic relations."[30]

He also argued, "A less visible but enduring element of foreign policy—even under Gorbachev—is the continuing extraordinary scope and sweep of Soviet military modernization and weapons research and development." Gates's conclusion was that "there clearly are great changes underway inside the Soviet Union and in Soviet diplomacy. Yet it is hard to detect fundamental changes, currently or in prospect, in the way the Soviets govern at home or in their principal objectives abroad." He ended with a reminder to Reagan of past disappointments: "Westerners for centuries have hoped repeatedly that Russian economic modernization and political reform—even revolution—signaled an end to despotism and the beginning of Westernization. Repeatedly since 1917, the West has hoped that domestic changes in the USSR would lead to changes in Communist coercive rule at home and aggressiveness abroad. These hopes, dashed time and again, have been revived by Gorbachev's domestic agenda, innovative foreign policy and personal style." For the coming summit, Gates advised, "amid the inevitable media extravaganza of the Summit, a sober—even somber—reminder of the enduring features of the regime and the still long competition and struggle ahead will be needed." While Gates's take on Gorbachev seemed excessively bleak at the time, his warnings about Russia proved all too true in the decades that followed Gorbachev's departure and the rise of Vladimir Putin as Russian leader.[31]

Paradoxically, just a few days after the memo reached Reagan, Gates and several administration colleagues dined in Washington with Vladimir Kryuchkov, chief of the KGB's foreign operations. It was the first time during the cold war that two such high-ranking American and Soviet spymasters had met. The two men debated and bantered, warily comparing notes, as Gates sipped a martini and Kryuchkov nursed a glass of Chivas Regal scotch at Maison Blanche, a high-end Georgetown restaurant. "The conversation was generally one of mutual barbs and debating points, punctuated by substantive discussions," Gates recalled.[32] As the dinner ended, Gates dryly observed that he hoped the encounter would not be harmful to either of their careers. Gates did not know at the time that Kryuchkov was intimately familiar with CIA secrets from reports provided by Aldrich Ames, a senior CIA official who was a KGB mole inside the agency.[33]

Though the Washington summit was in many ways an improvised affair, organized in little more than a month after Gorbachev agreed to attend, it proved to be a cold war pivot point. The summit centerpiece, the INF Treaty, was itself a breakthrough agreement that eliminated an entire class of nuclear weapons after several decades of Soviet-American arms accords that limited the growth of nuclear arsenals but did not cut them. The treaty mandated the elimination of 1,846 Soviet nuclear weapons and 846 American nuclear weapons within three years. Although that was just a small fraction of their nuclear arsenals, the treaty still marked a watershed moment. Even more than the signing of the INF Treaty, the spirit of the summit dramatically showed that the bitter enmity of the cold war was giving way to a new era. There was no surer sign of that than the welcoming crowds that lined Washington streets to get a glimpse of Gorbachev as his motorcades traveled through the capital.

Both Gorbachev and Reagan urgently needed a successful summit for domestic political reasons. The *New York Times* reported that Gorbachev "needs success in Washington to propel his program of domestic change and to quiet critics, ranging from Kremlin colleagues to collective farmers and factory workers, who have been buffeted by his policies but have yet to see tangible benefits."[34] For Reagan, the summit represented a chance to escape the lingering downdraft of the Iran-Contra affair as he headed into the last year of his presidency and an opportunity to claim success for his handling of the Soviet Union. Gorbachev was in a chipper mood when he landed outside Washington. "He was a man who had come up for air and was off and running," Shultz noted after his initial encounter with Gorbachev as the summit opened.[35]

The summit began at 10:00 a.m. on December 8 as Gorbachev's armored Soviet ZiL limousine pulled up in front of the South Portico of the White House. Ronald and Nancy Reagan greeted Gorbachev and his wife, Raisa. The two couples stood at attention during a trumpet fanfare and a twenty-one-gun salute. Reagan and Gorbachev then headed to the Oval Office for an initial conversation that quickly veered into an argument over human rights conditions in the Soviet Union and United States. "Mr. President, you are not a prosecutor and I am not on trial here," Gorbachev told Reagan. "Like you, I represent a great country and therefore expect our dialogue to be conducted on a basis of reciprocity and equality. Otherwise there simply will be no dialogue."[36] After lunching separately—Gorbachev at the Soviet embassy—the two leaders reconvened to sign the INF Treaty. As the Marine Corps band played American and Soviet marches in the White House foyer, dozens of American officials, congressional leaders and Soviet officials gathered in the East Room to witness the signing on a simple wooden table once used by Abraham Lincoln. Reagan opened the ceremony:

Welcome to the White House. This ceremony and the treaty we are signing today are both excellent examples of the rewards of patience. It was over six years ago, November 18, 1981, that I first proposed what could come to be called the zero option. It was a simple proposal, one might say disarmingly simple. (Laughter.) Unlike treaties of the past, it didn't simply codify the status quo or a new arms buildup. It didn't simply talk of controlling an arms race. For the first time in history, the language of "arms control" was replaced by "arms reduction"—in this case, the complete elimination of an entire class of U.S. and Soviet nuclear missiles.[37]

Quoting a Russian maxim that Reagan had repeatedly cited since learning about it months earlier from Suzanne Massie, Reagan said, "doveryai, no proveryai—trust, but verify." Gorbachev jovially interjected, "You repeat that at every meeting." A burst of laughter rippled across the East Room. The exchange, televised around the world, captured the developing bonhomie between Reagan and Gorbachev. Gorbachev spoke next:

Mr. President, ladies and gentlemen, comrades. Succeeding generations will hand down their verdict on the importance of the event which we are about to witness, but I will venture to say that what we are going to do, the signing of the first ever agreement eliminating nuclear weapons, has a universal significance for mankind, both from the standpoint of world politics and from the standpoint of humanism. For everyone, and above all for our two great powers, the treaty whose text is on the table offers a big chance, at last, to get onto the road leading away from the threat of catastrophe. . . . May December 8, 1987, become a date that will be inscribed in the history books—a date that will mark the watershed separating the era of a mounting risk of nuclear war from the era of a demilitarization of human life.[38]

Following the signing ceremony, Reagan and Gorbachev walked across the White House to the Cabinet Room for their next discussion, this time in a space packed with American and Soviet officials. The setting was not conducive to a productive conversation. Reagan looked tired and unengaged and struggled to keep pace with Gorbachev on policy issues. After about forty minutes, Reagan recounted a dismissive story about the Soviet Union that was clearly inappropriate for the occasion. The anecdote, which was doubtless apocryphal, involved an American scholar who visited Moscow. On his way to the departure airport in the United States, he asked his taxi driver, who was finishing his education, what he planned to do when he graduated. The man said he did not know. Upon arrival in Moscow, the scholar asked his Russian taxi driver the same question. The answer: They haven't told me yet.[39] After that miscue, which Gorbachev graciously deflected, Shultz moved quickly to end the meeting, telling everyone that working groups on various issues were waiting to get started. Shultz, Howard Baker and Colin Powell, by now the national security adviser, were all aghast at Reagan's performance.

Once back in the Oval Office with the president, Shultz bluntly critiqued Reagan's handling of the Cabinet Room session. Reagan acknowledged he had bungled the meeting. Baker, Powell and Shultz decided after talking to Reagan that they needed to prepare a new set of talking points for the president so he could keep pace with Gorbachev at their next encounters during the summit. Was Reagan's stumbling behavior with Gorbachev another early sign of the Alzheimer's disease that would engulf him within a few years? Impossible to know. Colin Powell saw Reagan's conduct as consistent with habits acquired as an actor. "I've often told people, 'You've got to remember: He's an actor. He needs to have a script.' And so it was always important if not to give him a script, then set the scene and tell him, you know, the importance of the subject or the lack of importance and what he needs to do. George was good at understanding this."[40]

The state dinner at the White House that evening was a glittering affair. A sense of exuberance, even euphoria, permeated the room as Reagan and Gorbachev delivered warm toasts. Shultz was seated at the same table as Marshal Akhromeyev. Each encounter with Akhromeyev deepened Shultz's respect for a man who had risen to the pinnacle of the Soviet military yet seemed to live by a code of honor that the marine in Shultz admired. During the dinner, Akhromeyev told Shultz: "I am the Marshal of the Soviet Union and have had many honors in my career, but I have never been as proud of anything as when I was a sergeant fighting for my country at Leningrad—until now. My country is in trouble, and I am fighting alongside Mikhail Sergeyevich to save it. That is why we made such a lopsided deal on INF, and that is why we want to get along with you. We want to restructure ourselves and to be part of the modern world. We cannot continue to be isolated." Shultz knew from his own visit to the Leningrad Cemetery years earlier how costly and important the defense of the city was for Russians. That Akhromeyev would compare his work with Gorbachev to his role at Leningrad deeply impressed Shultz.[41]

By the end of the day, the optimism of the summit was inescapable. R. W. Apple Jr., a veteran *New York Times* correspondent, painted the picture aptly in a front-page news analysis:

> Even for this city, which long ago mislaid its sense of wonder, this was a thrilling day, bathed in a glow of satisfaction at what has been achieved and of optimism about what may lie just ahead.
>
> Often Washington looks on the dark side, especially where the Soviet Union is concerned, but there were few in the capital who failed to feel a frisson of excitement as Mikhail S. Gorbachev stepped from his limousine and grasped Ronald Reagan's hand, few in the country who were immune to the drama of television pictures of the two leaders in profile with the red Soviet flag whipping in the wind behind them.
>
> Influenced by concessions from Moscow, by his wife's concern for his place in history, perhaps even by a sense of his own mortality prompted by an assassin's bullets and by serious illnesses, Mr. Reagan approaches the end of his second term, in the words of one of his closest confidantes, in the certain belief that "what he does with Gorbachev will make or break him."[42]

On the final day of the summit, after hosting Vice President Bush for breakfast at the Russian embassy, Gorbachev headed to the White House for a last meeting with Reagan. As the Gorbachev-Bush motorcade rolled by the corner of Connecticut Avenue and K Street, it came to a stop and Gorbachev bounded out of his limousine to greet people who had assembled at the intersection in hopes of seeing his car pass by. As Secret Service agents scrambled to catch up with Gorbachev, he stepped to the sidewalk, working the crowd like a veteran American political candidate. He seemed to relish the spontaneous encounter, as did the people he greeted. The scene all but shouted to the world that the cold war was ending.

Shultz hosted a gala lunch for Gorbachev at the State Department. He used the occasion to reiterate his long-term vision of a world transformed by new technologies, a theme he had outlined twice before for Gorbachev during visits to Moscow. Forecasting changes that would later be called "globalization," Shultz said, "In five to ten years, our world will be vastly different from the one we know today, and from the postwar world of the past 40 years, which has conditioned so much of our thinking. . . . The material substances of daily life are being transformed. The speed of human transactions is accelerating. Scientific, economic and political matters are now global in dimension. And through all these changes, runs the thread of knowledge: its discovery, its rapid transmission as information, and the education needed to use it. . . . The recognition that openness to ideas, information and contacts is the key to future success."[43]

Although strategic arms negotiations during the summit did not yield an agreement, they did close the gap between Washington and Moscow when Gorbachev softened his resistance to SDI. As the *New York Times* reported, "The United States and the Soviet Union were able to end the summit meeting on a positive note not only because they had made some real progress but also because they sidestepped their central disagreement on the issue of testing space-based defensive weapons. At this meeting, unlike the one last year in Reykjavik, Iceland, the two sides did not try to resolve the critical issue of what 'Star Wars' testing is allowed under the 1972 Antiballistic Missile Treaty. They simply deferred the resolution of that central matter for the time being. The two sides did move closer to an eventual agreement reducing long range arms in a few ways. They agreed on a limit of 4,900 warheads on missiles, a compromise between a U.S. proposal for a limit of 4,800 and an informal Soviet offer of 5,100."[44]

Before boarding his Aeroflot plane for the long flight back to Moscow, Gorbachev lingered for nearly two hours at a news conference that was broadcast across the world, including in the Soviet Union. Shultz monitored the event on television at the State Department before going to the Soviet embassy to accompany the Gorbachev motorcade to Andrews Air Force base and see Gorbachev off. "I was placed in a holding room" at the embassy, he recalled. "Before long, in bounced Gorbachev. 'George, I understand you watched my press conference,' he said, and invited my comment. 'You went on much too long,' I said with friendly candor. He clapped me on the back. 'Well,' I said, 'at least there's one guy around here who tells you what he thinks.' He laughed, in high spirits."[45]

Moments after the Soviet plane climbed into the night sky, Shultz's air force plane took off for Brussels, where Shultz would go over the summit developments with NATO allies. In his memoir, Shultz attributed the summit success "to the persistent effort of Ronald Reagan to stick by his basic objectives, to maintain our strength and the cohesion of our alliances, and to be willing to recognize an opportunity for a good deal and a changed situation when he saw one."[46] He might have said the same about himself. Absent Shultz's pivotal role, and patience in riding out the internal turmoil of the Reagan administration, there might well have never been a Reagan-Gorbachev summit meeting in Washington. After a long day of meetings in Brussels, Shultz retired to his hotel, as he recalled, "exhausted but quietly triumphant."[47]

CHAPTER TWENTY-THREE

Encore in Moscow

THE POSITIVE MOMENTUM OF the summit carried over into 1988, propelled in part by good working relations between Shultz, Carlucci at the Pentagon and Powell at the White House. With Weinberger and Casey gone, and the NSC staff now directed by Powell, the friction that had plagued the administration largely dissipated. Shultz reached the apex of his influence as the Reagan presidency headed into its final year and Reagan visited Moscow for a summit that radiated friendship. It was an extraordinary denouement for a president who had come to office seven years earlier as America's foremost Kremlin adversary. Though Shultz was overshadowed at the summit by Reagan, and his involvement little noted in media coverage, the event was the capstone of his seven-year effort to remake relations with the Soviet Union.

Some prominent Shultz critics were not stilled by the obvious improvement in Washington-Moscow relations. If anything, they were alarmed by it. Richard Nixon and Henry Kissinger complained publicly about the embrace of Gorbachev. Kissinger declared in a *Washington Post* essay: "The most conservative U.S. administration of the postwar era is preoccupied—almost obsessed—with arms control and personal appeals to the Soviet leadership."[1] Shultz, long irritated by Kissinger's sniping, dispatched an uncharacteristically cranky letter to Kissinger after reading the *Post* article:

"It is one thing to criticize the administration if you disagree with it; it is something else to attack us for failing to do what we in fact are doing. The dialogue which you say has not occurred has in fact taken place at all our key meetings with Gorbachev, and in depth. Incidentally, I don't sense any Gorbachev euphoria around here. It is all in a day's work."[2]

The Senate in April ratified the INF treaty, 93–5. Negotiations over strategic weapons continued, but an agreement increasingly seemed out of reach during the remaining months of the Reagan presidency. Shultz focused on finding mutually agreeable terms for the Soviet pullout from Afghanistan. The Kremlin wanted assurances from the United States that it would cease support of the Islamic fighters as Soviet forces exited. After several contentious discussions between Shultz and Shevardnadze, Washington and Moscow essentially agreed to disagree about a future American role. The United States reserved its right to resupply the fighters. Shultz flew to Geneva in mid-April to sign a four-nation Afghan peace agreement. The Soviet-installed regime in Afghanistan along with Pakistan signed as principals; the Soviet Union and the United States signed as guarantors.

Shultz and Powell traveled to Moscow in late April to prepare for a Reagan visit at the end of May. Reagan jokingly asked Shultz why he was always running off to Moscow.[3] The glow of the Washington summit five months earlier was still evident as Shultz met with Gorbachev and Shevardnadze, though Gorbachev was by this time facing increased opposition at home to his reform agenda. A recently published essay in the newspaper *Sovetskaya Rossiya* that belittled Gorbachev's policies was the talk of Moscow, indeed of the Soviet Union. The author, Nina Andreyeva, was an obscure chemistry teacher in Leningrad. Clearly, the article had been commissioned and prominently published by high-level Gorbachev opponents. It represented an open challenge to his leadership from conservative Communist Party forces who feared he was weakening and might ultimately undermine the Soviet system.

Shultz was aware of the article and used some of his time with Gorbachev to reinforce the idea that cooperation with the West and liberalization of the Soviet Union would enhance, not reduce, Soviet economic vitality. He was pleased to hear Gorbachev embrace a progressive vision. Shultz recalled: "Gorbachev then launched into what I regarded as truly remarkable statements for the Communist boss of the Soviet Union. 'The

Soviet Union does not pretend to have the final truth. We do not impose our way of life on other peoples. We've told you we want to cooperate, we want dialogue, we want to find answers together with the United States.'" Referring to Shultz's earlier presentations about global trends and technological advances, Gorbachev said, "If the trends continue as you outlined, our two countries have a lot of reason to cooperate."[4]

From Moscow, Shultz journeyed to the Soviet republics of Ukraine and Georgia, realizing a longtime desire to see other parts of the Soviet Union. While in Kiev, the Ukrainian capital, he toured the World War II memorial at Babi Yar, where Nazi occupiers in 1941 massacred thousands of Jews and Ukrainians. Shultz pointedly honored the Jewish victims, not a topic emphasized by the memorial. In Tbilisi, the Georgian capital, he and O'Bie attended services at the Georgia Orthodox cathedral. By doing so, he highlighted American support of religious freedom and religion itself, a theme that resonated with Georgians, many of whom remained devoted believers in the officially secular Communist nation.

Shultz's hopes for the upcoming summit were ambitious, especially in light of the failure to come to agreement on the terms of a strategic nuclear weapons treaty. Two weeks before Reagan traveled to Moscow, Shultz advised: "The temptation may be to look backward at all that has been achieved. The challenge will be to use the meeting to prepare the ground for further progress. We want the Moscow summit to be remembered as the place where our dialogue caught its second wind, not as its highwater mark."[5] When Shultz repeated the "second wind" formulation a few days later at a meeting with Reagan, the president endorsed the phrase and joked that he hated an actor who stole another actor's lines.[6]

Reagan arrived late for the meeting because he had been talking with Irina Ratushinskaya, a Soviet poet who had been imprisoned for three and a half years, including a year in solitary confinement, for speaking out against the Kremlin. She was released shortly before the 1985 Geneva summit, an early sign that Gorbachev might address Soviet human rights abuses. Reagan recalled that Ratushinskaya had managed to smuggle a letter to him from prison, signed by her and nine fellow inmates. He told Shultz and the other officials at the meeting that the inmates had crammed a remarkable amount of writing on the tiny sheet of paper that eventually made its way to the president.[7]

Reagan's late-May visit to Moscow, the first by an American president since Richard Nixon's 1974 Kremlin rendezvous with Leonid Brezhnev, reflected the arc of Reagan's Soviet odyssey from anti-Communist crusader to Kremlin friend. The tableaus during the visit were memorable: Gorbachev warmly welcoming Reagan to St. Catherine's Hall in the Kremlin. A beaming Reagan walking across Red Square. Reagan addressing—and impressing—skeptical students at Moscow State University. The Reagans mingling with Russians on a Moscow street. As Nancy Reagan observed, "If someone had told me when Ronnie and I were first married that we would eventually travel to Moscow as president and first lady, and would be the honored guests of the Soviet leadership, I would have suggested that he get his head examined."[8]

The summit was conveniently timed for Gorbachev as he prepared for one of the most important events since assuming power in 1985, the Nineteenth Party Conference of the Soviet Communist Party. The meeting, scheduled for late June, would assemble party leaders from across the nation and, if all went well, inject new energy in his reforms. After publication of the Nina Andreyeva letter, Gorbachev and his Kremlin allies knew opposition to his leadership was rising dangerously, led by Yegor Ligachev, a Politburo member and formidable opponent. To overcome the resistance, Gorbachev decided to strike at the party itself and use the conference to reduce the party's central role in managing the Soviet Union. The Reagan visit could fortify Gorbachev by showing that he was effectively dealing with the United States. Still, the summit was something of a sideshow for him as the party conference grew near. Anatoly Chernyaev, Gorbachev's national security adviser, reflected the relative importance when he noted that he and Gorbachev "took a break" from conference preparation for the Reagan visit.[9]

The Reagans and Shultzes arrived in Moscow on Sunday afternoon May 29 after pausing for three days in Helsinki to deal with jet lag. As Air Force One descended toward Vnukovo Airport over the outskirts of the Soviet capital, Reagan noted the absence of vehicles on the roads, a reflection of the Soviet Union's chronic shortage of consumer goods, including cars. For a first stop in Moscow, Nancy Reagan had proposed a visit with Yuri and Tatayana Zieman, a Jewish couple who had unsuccessfully sought permission for more than a decade to move to Israel. Soviet officials were horrified by the idea. Making the Zieman apartment Reagan's first stop in Moscow, they warned, would insult Gorbachev. When the Soviet objections were ignored, the Kremlin dispatched Alexsandr Bessmertnykh, the deputy foreign minister, to Helsinki to make plain to the Americans that the visit would undermine the summit and guarantee that the Ziemans would never emigrate. As a sweetener, Bessmertnykh said the couple would be allowed to leave in due course if the Reagans dropped the idea.

Colin Powell broke the news to Nancy Reagan. He recalled the scene with the president and first lady at the Helsinki hotel where the Reagans were staying:

> Nancy's right across from me. The President's over there. I said, "Mrs. Reagan, we have a problem. If you insist on this, one, it won't happen. They won't let you get there. Two, it will probably be very detrimental to the success of the summit and might blow it up. Three, if you were even to try this and it became public, this couple would never leave the Soviet Union. So we can't do this." She starts to cry. What are we going to do? So I said, "But there is one good point in this. I've gotten a deal from the Russians that if you don't push this—if you just drop it now—they will be released in a few months' time. They can't do it now, but that's the deal." She replied, "Well, all right." A couple of months later, they were released.[10]

Bypassing the Zieman apartment in one of Moscow's many shabby, nondescript apartment buildings, the Reagans went directly to the Kremlin. Gorbachev greeted the president in St. Catherine's Hall in the Grand Kremlin Palace for an initial conversation, attended only by translators and note takers. Gorbachev and Reagan agreed that relations between their countries had greatly improved since their first meeting in Geneva two and half years earlier, and they pledged to continue easing tensions. Gorbachev surprised Reagan by handing him wording for a joint statement that would formally record their commitment to improved relations. He explained that the language would build on the joint statement the men had made in Geneva that a nuclear war could not be won and must never be fought. Gorbachev handed Reagan an English translation of the proposal: "Proceeding from their understanding of the realities that have taken shape in the world today, the two leaders believe that no problem in dispute can be resolved, nor should it be resolved, by military means. They regard peaceful coexistence as a universal principle of international relations. Equality of all states, non-interference in internal affairs and freedom of socio-political choice must be recognized as the inalienable and mandatory standards of international relations."[11] The sentiment seemed innocuous but was lifted from the cold war lexicon of previous Kremlin leaders, especially the notion of "peaceful coexistence." Seemingly unaware that his own administration had long since rejected the term because the Kremlin liked to invoke it while ignoring it, Reagan said he liked it and would run it by his colleagues.

Reagan then renewed his concerns about human rights abuses in the Soviet Union and handed Gorbachev a list of dissidents and refuseniks he hoped the Kremlin would review. Although Gorbachev pushed back about racial inequities in the United States, he did not entirely rebuff Reagan's entreaties and even made some conciliatory comments on human rights. Sensing an opening, Reagan raised an issue—a "personal dream," he said— that he would publicly deny discussing with Gorbachev: religious freedom. The topic was not among the talking points prepared by Reagan aides but was one Suzanne Massie had stressed when talking with Reagan in March. Notes of the Reagan-Gorbachev meeting recount Reagan's concern about the sensitivity of the issue: "He had been reluctant to raise it with Gorbachev, but he was going to do it now anyway. He wanted no hint that anything had been negotiated, where we had insisted on something the Soviets had to do. If word got out that this was even being discussed, the president would deny he had said anything about it."[12]

Over the decades, Reagan had often ridiculed the Soviet Union's suppression of the Russian Orthodox Church and the Communist Party's embrace of atheism. Now, facing Gorbachev in the inner sanctum of the Kremlin, Reagan made the case for religious freedom in the Soviet Union. He told Gorbachev that he was doing so because they were friends and because Gorbachev could do something that would change the image of his country. For several minutes, the two leaders debated the limits of religious freedom in the Soviet Union. Gorbachev informed Reagan that he had been baptized and asserted that recent steps to unshackle the Russian Orthodox Church were eradicating religious intolerance. Reagan assured Gorbachev that the restoration of full religious freedom would make Gorbachev "a hero" and that "much of the feeling against his country would disappear like water in hot sun."[13]

To nail his argument, Reagan, as he often did, turned to a story. The American note taker recorded Reagan's account: "The president said he had a letter from the widow of a young World War II soldier. He was lying in a shell hole at midnight, awaiting an order to attack. He had never been a believer, because he had been told God did not exist. But as he looked up at the stars he voiced a prayer hoping that, if he died in battle, God would accept him. That piece of paper was found on the body of a young Russian soldier who was killed in that battle."[14]

Clearly tiring of the Reagan sermon, Gorbachev noted that time was running out for their first meeting and shifted topics to a Gorbachev proposal for a joint Soviet-American mission to Mars. Reagan agreed the idea should be studied, adding that the topic of space exploration was "in the direction of heaven." With Nancy Reagan and Raisa Gorbachev waiting nearby, the meeting ended with Reagan affirming that he and Gorbachev should set diplomatic protocol aside, as they had been doing since Geneva, and call one another Mikhail and Ron. He then made one last, awkward attempt to promote religion. Reagan said he had long yearned to serve his atheist son the perfect gourmet dinner and asked him if he believed there was a cook. Gorbachev graciously said the only possible answer was "yes."[15]

When Reagan informed Shultz, Carlucci and Powell about Gorbachev's proposed statement invoking "peaceful coexistence," they gently pushed back, reminding Reagan that the term evoked the era of détente. Shultz suspected that conservative Kremlin colleagues, especially Andrei Gromyko, the former foreign minister, had drafted the proposed language and pressed Gorbachev to endorse it. At a meeting with Shevardnadze later that day, Shultz politely resisted the Gorbachev suggestion, telling Shevardnadze that "it would be preferable to describe the relationship in operational terms, rather than to put things the way they had in the 1970s."[16]

Once ensconced at Spaso House after the president's initial meeting with Gorbachev, the Reagans told their Secret Service detail they wanted to override security concerns about seeing Moscow and insisted that they have a chance to mingle with some Russians. The presidential motorcade delivered them to the Arbat, a commercial street in the historic center of Moscow that Reagan's son, Ron, had seen during a visit to Moscow with a dance group the year before and advised his father to see. The outing resembled Gorbachev's improvisational interaction with Washingtonians.

The Reagans strolled along the street while Muscovites, astonished to see the president of the United States, tried to greet the visitors. The security detail quickly formed a tight rim around the Reagans, who watched with dismay as Soviet security forces roughly shoved Russians aside. "I've never seen such brutal manhandling as they did on their own people who were in no way getting out of hand," Reagan noted in his diary that evening.[17]

On Monday morning, Reagan returned to St. Catherine's Hall for a meeting with Gorbachev and senior American and Soviet officials. Gorbachev reiterated his hope that Reagan would endorse the peaceful coexistence statement. With numerous other officials in the room, Reagan let the issue pass without comment, and most of the two-hour discussion was devoted to nuclear weapons issues, particularly space-based weapons, which still concerned the Kremlin. Major differences remained. Nevertheless, Reagan again sensed a growing rapport with Gorbachev. "There is no question in my mind but that a certain chemistry does exist between us," he noted.[18] At one point, Shultz corrected Gorbachev about a class of weapon the two sides had discussed at Reykjavik, informing the Soviet leader that Air Launched Cruise Missiles (ALCMs) were the system in question, not Sea Launched Cruise Missiles (SLCMs). Gorbachev amiably accepted Shultz's intervention, telling officials assembled at the large conference table that there was a saying in Russian: "He who has a hurt, keeps talking about it." Looking at Reagan, he added with a smile, "So here was another for the president's collection of proverbs."[19]

The next stop for Reagan and Shultz, accompanied by Nancy Reagan, was the white-walled compound of the Danilov Monastery in Moscow, where the president again emphasized his wish to see religious freedom in the Soviet Union. The monastery, an ancient center of the Russian Orthodox Church, was turned into a factory site during Soviet rule and had recently been given back to the church. Because Reagan would be meeting later in the day with Father Gleb Yakunin, a fierce critic of the Kremlin and its suppression of the church, the patriarch of the Russian Orthodox Church would not host the monastery visit. Reagan invoked the words of Alexander Solzhenitsyn in calling for a renewal of religious faith in the Soviet Union: "When you travel the byroads of central Russia, you begin to understand the secret of the pacifying Russian countryside," Reagan read from Solzhenitsyn: "It is the churches. They lift their bell towers—graceful, shapely, all different—high over mundane timber and thatch." Solzhenitsyn, the winner of the 1970 Nobel Prize in Literature, was forced into exile in 1974 and lived in Vermont at the time of the Reagan visit.[20]

The Reagans and Shultz returned to Spaso House to host a reception for nearly one hundred dissidents and refuseniks, including the Ziemans. Though the gathering was an irritant to the Kremlin, the KGB worked with American security to bus guests through a security corridor from the American embassy, where the guests assembled, to Spaso House. Reagan warmly welcomed the group, reaffirming his commitment to secure their freedom to emigrate. As he spoke, several small children wandered among the thirteen tables, giving the event what Ambassador Matlock called a "homey touch."[21] The *New York Times* caught the spirit of the gathering in a front-page story that opened with Reagan greeting Abe Stolar, an American citizen born in Illinois, brought to Moscow as a child and barred from leaving ever since. "President Reagan walked up to Abe Stolar with a smile, shook his hand warmly, and said: 'I've just spoken to Mikhail Gorbachev about you. I told him we came from the same state and were born at the same time.' Then the two men from Illinois—one seeing the Soviet Union for the first time, the other trying to leave it for the last time—sat down together to chat in the ballroom of the United States Ambassador's residence."[22]

Gorbachev, nettled by Reagan's pronouncements about human rights during the day and the American meeting with dissidents, responded at a state dinner that evening in the Kremlin's Faceted Chamber. Standing before a wall of multicolored frescoes as waiters delivered fresh caviar puffs, fish soup and loin of veal and filled glasses with Georgian wine and Armenian brandy, Gorbachev's impatience with Reagan's lectures was clear. He said that widening exchanges with the United States "should be done without interfering in domestic affairs, without sermonizing or imposing one's views and ways, without turning family or personal problems into a pretext for confrontation between states."[23]

The third day of the summit opened with another Reagan-Gorbachev meeting devoted largely to Gorbachev's domestic reforms. Gorbachev made clear that his desire to make the Soviet Union more democratic was aimed at "developing socialism," not eliminating it. The meandering conversation touched on issues such as the proper role of large corporations or, in the Soviet context, large industrial enterprises long run by the state. As the hour ended, Reagan and Gorbachev agreed that their primary mission should be to eradicate the distrust between their two nations and remove the possibility of military conflict.

As the meeting wound down, Gorbachev invited Reagan to join him for a walk in Red Square. Shultz was not present but played a critical role in orchestrating the outing. Overriding White House staff concerns that photos of the president standing in front of Lenin's Tomb would be politically damaging at home, Shultz encouraged Reagan to ask Gorbachev if they could tour the expansive plaza outside the Kremlin.[24] Anticipating the outing, security forces had cleared the square except for a few small clusters of Soviet citizens who had undoubtedly been screened, if not preselected, by the Kremlin. The two leaders walked through the towering walls of Spassky Gate into the square, the brightly colored onion domes of St. Basil's Cathedral before them, Lenin's Tomb coming into view to their left. The day was sunny and warm. After briefly engaging with people in two clusters, they approached a third. A mother handed her small child to Gorbachev, who cradled the toddler in his right arm. "Shake hands with Grandfather Reagan," he said. A smiling Reagan reached out to touch the child. Reagan told another group, "We decided to talk to each other instead of about each other."[25]

As the two leaders turned back toward the Kremlin, Sam Donaldson, a tenacious ABC News correspondent well known for catching presidents off guard with impertinent, shouted questions, asked Reagan, "Do you still think you're in an evil empire, Mr. President?" Reagan instantly replied, "No, I was talking about another time and another era." In what was surely one of the most surreal images of the cold war, navy lieutenant commander Woody Lee stood just feet away, his wrist manacled to the briefcase—colloquially called the "football"—containing the nuclear codes that Reagan would use to order a nuclear attack on the Soviet Union.[26]

Two of the summit's most interesting events followed the walk in Red Square. The first was a Reagan lunch with Soviet writers, poets and other cultural luminaries at the Central House of Writers. Invoking the work of long-suppressed writers such as Anna Akhmatova and Nikolai Gumilev that he had probably not read and whose names he struggled to pronounce, Reagan nevertheless impressed the group with his charm, self-confidence and plainspoken defense of freedom of expression. The second event was an appearance at Moscow State University, the Soviet Union's elite university and alma mater of Mikhail and Raisa Gorbachev. Reagan addressed six hundred students and faculty members at a podium situated under a massive white marble bust of Lenin that the White House advance team worried would provide an unseemly Bolshevik backdrop. They had tried unsuccessfully to have it moved. Reagan gamely delivered his remarks in Lenin's shadow. Shultz, seated along the side of the hall, could see the skeptical audience slowly engage with Reagan as the hour passed, laughing at his corny jokes and anecdotes while paying close attention to his description of the coming information age, a topic not widely recognized yet in the Soviet Union. Shultz had repeatedly stressed the significance of new technologies in his meetings with Gorbachev and had urged Reagan to pick up the theme in his remarks at the university. He wondered if Gorbachev, undoubtedly watching the event on television, would see the connection to his presentations to the Soviet leader.[27]

At one point, Reagan alluded to a scene in *Butch Cassidy and the Sundance Kid*, an American film featuring two of Hollywood's biggest stars at the time, Paul Newman and Robert Redford. A Moscow movie theater had recently started showing the movie with Russian dubbing, but his extended reference to the film and its celebration of friendship and faith clearly puzzled the students. Reagan nimbly fielded audience questions for twenty minutes after finishing his speech. The audience gave him a standing ovation. The day ended with a dinner at Spaso House hosted by the Reagans and attended by the Gorbachevs and other Kremlin leaders. Andrei Sakharov, the nuclear physicist and Kremlin critic freed from internal exile by Gorbachev in 1986, was among the guests, as were George and O'Bie Shultz.

While Reagan was busy with various meetings, Raisa Gorbachev and Nancy Reagan were touring Moscow, seeming intent to show at least a modicum of mutual respect after previous chilly encounters. The *New York Times* reported: "When they met beneath the gilded bronze chandeliers in St. George's Hall, they smiled with brittle cordiality. When they listened to their husbands' dueling proverbs, their stolid expressions melted into laughter. By the time they emerged from the towering Assumption Cathedral, Nancy Reagan and Raisa Gorbachev were holding hands. Was this the gesture that stilled a thousand tongues? By the evening of Mrs. Reagan's first day in Moscow, that seemed at least possible."[28]

The fourth and final day of the summit showcased the formal exchange of INF Treaty ratification documents. As Reagan and Gorbachev prepared for the ceremony, Gorbachev made another attempt to secure Reagan's approval for the peaceful coexistence statement he had introduced on the first day of the summit. Inclusion of the wording in the joint statement obviously mattered to Kremlin cold warriors such as Andrei Gromyko. "Why is 'peaceful coexistence' a bad term?" Gorbachev snappishly asked Reagan. "Why are you against it? What are you against here? You told me last Sunday you were for it." He handed Reagan another copy of the statement. Reagan wavered, still drawn to the statement despite strong objections from Shultz, Carlucci and others. Shultz and Carlucci, seated on either side of Reagan, slipped notes to Reagan advising him not to agree. "This is no time to start writing" a joint statement, Shultz interjected to buy time.[29]

As the Americans fidgeted, Gorbachev suggested a break so each side could talk privately. After the Americans consulted, Reagan walked over to the Soviet group and told Gorbachev, "I'm very reluctant to put this in. I don't want to do it." Gorbachev replied, "Well, Mr. President, I don't understand why you are not for peace." Tension spiked in the room. After a pause, Gorbachev retreated. He put his arm around Reagan. "Mr. President, we had a great time." The two men walked off together toward St. Vladimir's Hall to exchange the ratification papers.[30] In retrospect, it appears that Gorbachev did his best to win approval for a statement that he did not consider essential and backed off after demonstrating to Gromyko and others that he had tried.

While Reagan and Gorbachev were meeting, Nancy Reagan and Raisa Gorbachev were sightseeing together in Leningrad. On the last evening of the summit, the Reagans and Gorbachevs attended a special performance of seven dances at the Bolshoi Ballet, seated in the royal box originally designed in the nineteenth century for use by the imperial Russian family. From there they made the short drive to a government guesthouse on the outskirts of Moscow for an intimate dinner with George and O'Bie Shultz and Eduard and Nanuli Shevardnadze. It was a jovial evening punctuated by frequent laughter as Reagan and Gorbachev swapped jokes. One featured Gorbachev, for a change of pace, taking the wheel of his armored limousine with his driver seated in the back. When they were pulled over by police for speeding, the policeman who inspected the speeding car told his fellow officer he had not issued a ticket because there was a "very important person in the car." When asked who, the officer said, "I don't know who the fellow in the back was, but his driver was Gorbachev." Another joke involved a gathering crowd in Red Square. As the number of people steadily increased, Gorbachev repeatedly told aides, "So what. Let them gather." When Gorbachev remained nonchalant as the number hit fifty thousand, the concerned aide told him, "They're all eating with chopsticks."

Gorbachev started to recount an apocryphal story that Reagan loved to recall and that Shultz would frequently tell while secretary of state and long after leaving office: After waiting in line for hours in hopes of buying a bottle of vodka, an irritated Russian announces he is going to the Kremlin to kill Gorbachev. When he returns a few hours later and is asked if he succeeded, the man reports, "No, the line there was even longer."[31] During the dinner, Gorbachev talked expansively about the coming of democracy to the Soviet Union, including genuine elections and term limits for national leaders. "That'll be the day!" Nanuli Shevardnadze exclaimed, and everyone laughed, Shultz recalled. "She was really outspoken and smart," he said. Shultz thought the "liveliness of the conversation and easy conviviality of the evening" made for a historic moment of friendship between the cold war superpowers. He told Reagan afterward that the "evening was a fitting climax to your four summits with General Secretary Gorbachev. O'Bie and I were honored to take part."[32]

Reagan thoroughly enjoyed the evening and told his security detail to stop in Red Square on the way back to Spaso House so Nancy could see the dramatic plaza. "It was a nice ride out in the wooded countryside to a really lovely home & a good time was had by all," he noted. "On the way back we drove through Red Square so Nancy could see it. Naturally the press was on hand & wanted photos. Believe it or not there were hundreds of people behind a rope there to see & wave at us. I don't know how they find out where we'll be. It was almost midnight."[33] Before departing the next day, Reagan spoke briefly at Vnukovo II Airport. The anti-Communist warrior of yesteryear had vanished, supplanted by a peacemaker. "Mr. General Secretary, I think you understand that we're not just grateful to you and Mrs. Gorbachev, but want you to know we think of you as friends. And in that spirit, we would ask one further favor of you. Tell the people of the Soviet Union of the deep feelings of friendship felt by us and by the people of our country toward them. Tell them, too, Nancy and I are grateful for their waves and smiles, and tell them we will remember all of our days their faces—the faces of hope—hope for a new era in human history, an era of peace between our nations and our peoples."[34]

The Moscow summit, the fourth meeting between Reagan and Gorbachev, was expected to be their last, but Gorbachev had other ideas. On November 12, four days after George H. W. Bush was elected president, handily defeating Michael Dukakis, the Democratic nominee, the Kremlin sent word to Shultz that Gorbachev had decided to come to New York early the next month to address the United Nations. He hoped Reagan and President-Elect Bush could come to New York to meet with him. Shultz welcomed the idea, though slightly miffed that the day after the election Bush had notified Shultz that he would be naming James Baker as his secretary of state that morning. "I thought this move was a little abrupt," he recalled.[35] Reagan and Bush readily agreed to meet Gorbachev in New York.

Gorbachev's December 7 appearance at the UN was the first by a Kremlin leader since Nikita Khrushchev's combustible 1960 visit. Khrushchev famously erupted in anger, brandishing his shoe in disgust, after a Philippine delegate criticized the Soviet Union. By contrast, Gorbachev's visit was a tranquil tour de force. The delegates from more than one hundred nations welcomed him with a standing ovation as he entered the General Assembly hall. After three and a half years as Soviet leader, he used his UN debut to make abundantly clear that he was directing a sea change in Soviet foreign relations. He described to the delegates a vision of a new world order governed by "the principle of freedom of choice." In doing so, he effectively discarded decades of aggressive Kremlin policy, including the Brezhnev Doctrine under which Soviet military forces had intervened in Hungary in 1954, Czechoslovakia in 1968 and threatened to do so in Poland in 1986 to overcome democratic uprisings against Communist regimes. Gorbachev also announced he was making large voluntary reductions in Soviet conventional military forces that would cut half a million troops over the next two years, including six divisions based in Eastern Europe. Gorbachev graciously took note of Shultz in his remarks. "We acknowledge and value the contribution of President Ronald Reagan and the members of his administration, above all Mr. George Shultz. All this is capital that has been invested in a joint undertaking of historic importance."[36] Shultz was pleased by the unexpected reference.

As Gorbachev was speaking, his Kremlin colleagues were reviewing initial damage assessments from a severe earthquake that had convulsed Soviet Armenia just hours before Gorbachev stepped to the UN rostrum. The 6.9-magnitude earthquake shattered buildings across Armenia. Though the extent of casualties was unclear in the first hours, the damage looked catastrophic. Gorbachev decided to cut short his time in New York so he could return to Moscow to direct recovery efforts. (The death toll from the quake ultimately topped sixty thousand people.) Before departing, he went to Governor's Island, a speck of land in New York Harbor, to meet with Reagan, Bush and Shultz.

The lunch was cordial, and Gorbachev clearly seemed intent on making a smooth transition from Reagan to Bush in Washington's relationship with the Kremlin. Don Oberdorfer, the veteran *Washington Post* diplomatic correspondent, later described the conversation:

> Over the elegantly set luncheon table, Gorbachev directed some of his remarks specifically at Bush. "I know what people are telling you now that you've won the election: you've got to go slow, you've got to be careful, you've got to review. That you can't trust us, that we're doing this all for show." But Gorbachev went on, in remarks that some of the Americans at the table would remember vividly for a long time, "You'll see soon enough that I'm not doing this for show and I'm not doing this to undermine you or to surprise you or to take advantage of you. I'm playing real politics. I'm doing this because I need to. I'm doing this because there's a revolution taking place in my country. I started it. And they all applauded me when I started it in 1986 and now they don't like it so much, but it's going to be a revolution, nonetheless."[37]

Shultz recalled his final encounter with Gorbachev as secretary of state: "The lunch conversation itself was free flowing. There were two highlights for me. In an exchange between Bush and Gorbachev involving investment, Bush said, 'We're a nation of investors, and an investor wants to know what conditions are like today. But an investor is even more interested in the prospective situation. So, Mr. General Secretary, what is it going to be like in the Soviet Union three or four or five years from now?' Gorbachev replied without missing a beat, 'Mr. Vice President, even Jesus Christ couldn't answer that question!' He laughed."[38]

Shultz also noted that Gorbachev had all but told the UN that the Kremlin was shutting down a large radar installation in Siberia that the United States had long claimed violated the ABM Treaty limit on missile defense radars. Gorbachev told Reagan, Bush and Shultz that he had put an end to the problem "to make things easier for the new president." He added, "Shultz has spent so much time on Krasnoyarsk that I have transferred it from the military to the scientists." Shultz interjected, "I listened carefully to your address and, concerning Krasnoyarsk, the word you used, in my translation, was 'dismantle.'" Gorbachev replied with a smile, "I bet you wrote that down. I can confirm the translation. Another victory for the secretary."[39]

"At the end of the luncheon," Shultz recalled. "President Reagan said to Gorbachev, 'This is my last meeting with you, and I raise a glass to what you have accomplished, what we have accomplished together, and to what you and George Bush will accomplish together after January 20.' 'I can join in that toast, and will the vice president do so as well?' asked Gorbachev. 'Yes, I do,' George Bush said. 'Good, then that is our first agreement,' Gorbachev said jovially."[40] The fellowship was genuine but misleading. President-Elect Bush was not prepared to receive a seamless handoff from Reagan. His incoming national security adviser, Brent Scowcroft, was urging Bush to proceed cautiously with Gorbachev, concerned that Reagan and Shultz had moved too far, too fast, with the Soviet leader. His views were supported by skeptical CIA reports questioning Gorbachev's intentions and the prospects for sustainable reform of the Soviet Union. James Baker, Bush's closest adviser and his choice to succeed Shultz as secretary of state, shared the doubts.

Robert Gates had reiterated his warning about Gorbachev's true intentions a few weeks before the presidential election in a public appearance: "Enduring characteristics of Soviet governance at home and policy abroad make it clear that—while the changes underway offer opportunities for the United States and for a relaxation of tensions—Gorbachev intends improved Soviet economic performance, greater political vitality at home, and more dynamic diplomacy to make the USSR a more competitive and stronger adversary in the years ahead. We must not mislead ourselves into believing otherwise." Gates's analysis about Gorbachev seemed overly wary, but his accompanying warning that powerful forces of resistance within the

Soviet Union might thwart Gorbachev, even imperil his leadership, proved prophetic.[41]

Bush's diffidence was evident in his body language at the Governor's Island meeting. Several times Bush looked disengaged and drifted apart from Reagan and Gorbachev. Reagan noted it. "What's the matter with George?" he asked Shultz. "He acted like he didn't want to be there," Shultz recalled. "I was very upset. They felt Reagan and I were all wrong in the way we were approaching the Soviet Union, that it couldn't change and wouldn't change. They couldn't have been more wrong. They really were wrong, deeply, deeply wrong. But Brent had this idea and he persuaded Bush to do a review, so everything was put on hold."[42]

In a farewell address to the nation on January 11, 1989, Reagan summed up his outlook on Gorbachev:

> My view is that President Gorbachev is different from previous Soviet leaders. I think he knows some of the things wrong with his society and is trying to fix them. We wish him well. And we'll continue to work to make sure that the Soviet Union that eventually emerges from this process is a less threatening one. What it all boils down to is this: I want the new closeness to continue. And it will, as long as we make it clear that we will continue to act in a certain way as long as they continue to act in a helpful manner. If and when they don't, at first pull your punches. If they persist, pull the plug. It's still trust but verify. It's still play, but cut the cards. It's still watch closely. And don't be afraid to see what you see.[43]

In his last acts as secretary of state in January, Shultz returned to New York to witness the signing of agreements by Angola, South Africa and Cuba that assured the withdrawal of Cuban troops from Angola and independence for Namibia, a nation ruled by South Africa. Shultz and Chester Crocker, the assistant secretary for Africa, had labored diligently for years to produce this outcome, ending years of Cuban military involvement in Angola that was supported by the Kremlin. Shultz also made a last visit to Paris as secretary to attend an international conference where some 150 nations renewed their vows never to use poison gas and encouraged completion of a treaty prohibiting the production of chemical weapons. It was his last encounter with Shevardnadze.

As the Reagan presidency neared an end, Reagan presented Shultz with the Medal of Freedom, the nation's highest civilian honor. State Department employees packed the State Department lobby to bid Shultz farewell on his final day at work, cheering him and O'Bie as they exited the building to the sounds of the Marine Band playing "California, Here I Come." Looking back on his roller-coaster ride with Reagan, Shultz was clear-eyed about Reagan's flaws but admired the pragmatism that ultimately defined Reagan's foreign policy. In his memoir, Shultz said:

> He had frustrated me with his unwillingness to come to grips with the debilitating acrimony among his national security advisers, with over-reliance on his immediate staff, with a sometimes wishful approach to an issue or program. He could rearrange facts to make a good story better, and he could allow himself to be deceived, sometimes almost knowingly. He and his administration paid the price, most dearly in the Iran-Contra affair.
>
> In truth, Ronald Reagan knew far more about the big picture and the matters of salient importance than most people—perhaps especially some of his immediate staff—give him credit for or appreciated. He had blind spots and a tendency to avoid tedious detail. But the job of those around him was to protect him from those weaknesses and to build on his strengths. Some of them did just the opposite. . . .[44]
>
> Ronald Reagan was not at the end of his presidency what he was when he started out: he was not a man who would stay labeled or stay put. He was ever changing, on the move, ever evolving in new and surprising ways. He was a doer, a pragmatist, and man who enjoyed hard physical work, as in the ranch work he loved to do.
>
> He believed in being strong enough to defend one's interests, but he viewed that strength as a means, not an end in itself. He was ready to negotiate with his adversaries. In that readiness, he was sharply different from most of his conservative supporters, who advocated strength for America but who did not want to use that strength as a basis for the inevitable give-and-take of the negotiating process.[45]

On January 20, 1989, as Bush took the oath of office to become the nation's forty-third president, George and O'Bie watched the inaugural ceremony on the one television still hooked up at their Bethesda home as movers loaded their belongings into a large van. The world George Bush was inheriting that morning was far different from the world that Alexander Haig had handed to George Shultz seven years earlier. It was a heady moment. The cold war was dissolving, though the demise of the Soviet Union and collapse of its empire in just a few years did not seem likely. China was rising from the wreckage of the Mao era and beginning to become an international economic powerhouse. White colonial rule in Africa was giving way to independent states, with South Africa on the verge of a transfer of power from white to black leaders. American influence around the world was expanding, fueled not so much by its military might as the model of its technology; its culture, including movies, soft drinks and jeans; and, most of all, its democratic ideals. Shultz said:

> The years of the Reagan presidency were, in the sweep of history, a turning point, building on the ideas and institutions put in place in the critical period right after World War II. For the bigger part of the century, the world had witnessed a titanic struggle between two visions of the future. Both were revolutionary: one based on freedom and flexibility, the other based on central power and control. When our country's military strength was built up to a point where our Soviet rivals recognized they could not match us, when they perceived that we might actually use our strength to repel aggression, and as their own system indisputably failed the Soviet people even as it abused them—then came the turning point.[46]

That afternoon, private citizen George Shultz boarded a commercial airliner for the first time in seven years, destination San Francisco.

Shultz's last encounter with Reagan came in February 1996 as Reagan was slipping ever deeper into the memory abyss of Alzheimer's disease. He traveled to the Reagan home in the Bel Air neighborhood of Los Angeles, where he and Reagan and Nancy Reagan sipped tea and talked politics for an hour. At one point, Reagan left briefly, accompanied by a nurse. As the former president returned, he stopped short of the room and said to the nurse, "Who is that man talking to Nancy on the couch? I know him. He is a very famous man."[47]

Epilogue

"I'M STILL IN THE game!" George Shultz exulted at his ninetieth birthday party in 2010. He certainly was. At an age when people fortunate enough still to be in good health usually kick back to enjoy retirement, and Shultz could easily have indulged his love of golf, he was productively engaged on multiple fronts. Worried about climate change, he was working with scientists to look for clean energy innovations. Concerned about the high cost and inequities of the American health care system, he was consulting with demographers, economists and biomedical specialists about feasible reforms. As he juggled these projects, he invested countless hours on the cause that most inspired him—abolishing nuclear weapons.

More than two decades after stepping down as secretary of state and returning to his California base, Shultz acted like someone half his age. Those who knew him well could see that his tireless efforts to solve national and global problems were the natural continuation of his commitment to public service. It extended until the day he died on February 6, 2021, at age one hundred. His office and home were meccas for national and international leaders, including President George W. Bush, who headed to the Shultz residence at Stanford on April 22, 2006, when protesters blocked the way to a campus auditorium where he was scheduled to speak. When Mikhail Gorbachev came to campus as Soviet leader in 1990, and again in 1992 as a private citizen, Shultz welcomed him to Stanford.

The ecumenical range of his work, some of it breaking with Republican orthodoxy, reflected the wide range of his interests and his government service. Soon after leaving Washington in early 1989, Shultz assembled a small staff to assist in writing a book about his years as secretary of state. The resulting volume, *Turmoil and Triumph: My Years as Secretary of State*, was a densely packed eleven-hundred-page opus that chronicled every aspect of American foreign policy on his watch. Washington cognoscenti hoping for a juicy, score-settling account were largely disappointed. Michiko Kakutani described the book in her 1993 *New York Times* book review as "long-winded and often tedious narrative that makes inclusiveness, not historical illumination, a goal."[1]

The main piece of news in the book was Shultz's assertion that Vice President Bush had misled the public and investigators about his role in the Iran-Contra affair by saying he was not informed as the plot unfolded. Shultz reported that he had warned Bush that the arms-for-hostage deal "would never stand up in public" and that Bush had attended at least one meeting where exchanging arms for hostages was discussed and raised no objection. The book's treatment of Reagan was flattering for the most part, with occasional gentle jabs. The sober tone was consistent with its author's workplace demeanor. When the book was published, Shultz showed little interest in driving sales by emphasizing insider anecdotes, instead offering interviewers bland primers on policy matters or commentary about global events in the news at the time rather than talking about his book.

After the book's publication in 1993, Shultz turned his attention to a variety of international and domestic issues, criticizing America's long-running "War on Drugs" for its emphasis on interdicting drug smuggling rather than addressing the underlying socioeconomic and biological causes of drug addiction. He supported George W. Bush's 2000 presidential campaign and firmly endorsed the 2003 American invasion of Iraq.

Shultz was devastated when pancreatic cancer killed O'Bie on September 5, 1995. Friends rallied to support him during melancholic months that made them worry about his own health. Fortunately, Charlotte Mailliard Swig, a twice-married San Francisco socialite and philanthropist, stepped into the void. Vivacious and high-spirited, she brought Shultz into her social orbit. They married in 1997 and soon became one of San Francisco's most prominent couples, hosting and attending parties, stepping out at the annual opening-night, black-tie galas at the San Francisco Opera and San Francisco Symphony. Those who knew O'Bie marveled that after years of happy marriage to a quiet, unassuming woman, Shultz seemed equally happy with an exuberant extrovert. Their mutual affection was evident at a festive Lunar New Year parade in San Francisco's Chinatown one year when Charlotte, featured guest on a float, passed by the reviewing stand. Shultz jumped to his feet in the grandstand as she appeared below. Smiling broadly, he tipped his hat to her as she joyfully waved back.

From time to time, Shultz participated in informal diplomatic talks with foreign leaders that were conducted in coordination with the White House. These back-channel activities, known as Track II diplomacy, allowed former senior American officials, including Shultz and Henry Kissinger, to explore ideas discreetly with foreign leaders that the president or secretary of state did not want to put forward as official American proposals. Shultz traveled to Beijing and Moscow on such missions. On July 13, 2007, Shultz met in Moscow with Russian president Vladimir Putin as part of a Track II delegation. The discussion touched on a range of issues, including the location of NATO conventional military forces in Europe, strategic nuclear weapons and ballistic missile defenses.[2] In 2014, Shultz agreed with a former State Department colleague who warned that Putin seemed intent on dominating neighboring European nations that had once been incorporated into the Soviet Union as Soviet republics.[3] Had he lived to see the 2022 Russian invasion of Ukraine, Shultz would undoubtedly have supported American and NATO efforts to provide Ukraine with conventional arms to defend itself against Russian aggression.

Shultz leaped back into the global spotlight in January 2007 when his appeal to abolish nuclear weapons appeared in a *Wall Street Journal* opinion piece coauthored by Henry Kissinger, William Perry and Sam Nunn. The article jolted the defense world. Two esteemed former Republican secretaries of state, Shultz and Kissinger, and two respected Democrats, Perry, a former defense secretary, and Nunn, who had chaired the Senate Armed Services Committee, improbably embraced a cause long championed by peace activists. Nuclear-era presidents from Truman to George W. Bush had broadly endorsed the goal, but their rhetorical support was belied by American defense strategies and arsenals anchored by nuclear weapons. The four men, in collaboration with Sidney Drell, a Stanford physicist and longtime arms control advocate, feared that nuclear dangers were rising, compounded by the possibility that terrorists could acquire or fabricate a nuclear weapon. Their credibility as proven defenders of American security gave weight to their argument. For Shultz, the roots of the op-ed article stretched back to the 1986 Reagan-Gorbachev summit meeting in Reykjavik, where the two leaders fleetingly talked about abolishing nuclear weapons. In fact, the impetus for the article came from a 2006 conference that Shultz and Drell organized at the Hoover Institution to mark the twentieth anniversary of the Reykjavik meeting. In Shultz's view, the op-ed essay honored not only the memory of Reykjavik but also Ronald Reagan's longtime desire to rid the world of nuclear weapons.

To the surprise of Shultz, Kissinger, Perry, Nunn and Drell, the call to end the nuclear weapons era generated wide support. Barack Obama embraced it and made it the centerpiece of his first major foreign policy speech as president in 2009. On April 5, addressing thousands of people assembled in Prague's Hradcany Square, he declared: "So today, I state clearly and with conviction America's commitment to seek the peace and security of a world without nuclear weapons. I'm not naïve. The goal will not be reached quickly—perhaps not in my lifetime. It will take patience and persistence. But now, we, too, must ignore the voices who tell us that the world cannot change. We have to insist, 'Yes, we can.'"[4]

Obama underscored his commitment later that year by chairing a UN Security Council meeting in New York devoted to nuclear disarmament. Shultz and his fellow advocates sat in the Security Council chamber as the council voted unanimously in favor of abolishing nuclear weapons. For Shultz the moment, and his role in inspiring it, was a reaffirmation of his stature as a global statesman. He savored the scene.

The initiative faded after several years, the victim of entrenched defense interests in Washington. Shultz remained committed to the goal and continued to push for it despite the obstacles. Throughout his nineties, he took every opportunity offered—university, high school, even junior high school speaking invitations—to warn about nuclear threats. Meantime, he authored or coauthored books about leadership, energy and environmental policy, health care, Social Security and a small volume recalling important diplomatic milestones in the last years of the cold war.

Every summer he made his way to the Bohemian Grove for several days to mingle amid the redwoods with fellow Bohemian Club members, often hosting former world leaders as his guests. With Charlotte at his side, he hosted countless dinner parties at his campus home, many of them extravaganzas choreographed by Charlotte. The parties featured roving mariachi bands, synchronized swimmers, elaborate multicourse menus and an endless supply of fine wines. When Henry Kissinger joined the party, as he often did on his way to the Bohemian Grove, Charlotte would plant a gigantic Mexican sombrero on his head and hand him two maracas as the band belted out a tune. Kissinger gamely played along. "What could I do?" he murmured to a fellow guest one July evening as they headed to the dinner table.[5]

The dinner crowd was invariably elderly, with a notable exception, Elizabeth Holmes, a twenty-something blonde who favored black turtlenecks. She had devised a novel blood-testing technology after dropping out of Stanford. The technology, as she described it, made it possible to use just a drop of blood to test nearly instantly for a variety of factors. It promised to transform health care by providing quick, easy blood tests instead of the need to draw several vials of blood and ship them to a lab for analysis. Impressed by the promise, Shultz lavished attention on Holmes and her newly established company, Theranos. He helped her assemble an eminent board of directors and raise money from Rupert Murdoch and other wealthy investors. Like Shultz, none of the board members had expertise in biomedical matters. Holmes quickly became the darling of Silicon Valley, appearing on the cover of *Fortune* and *Forbes*. Shultz repeatedly told friends that Holmes was brilliant. Over time, his associates grew alarmed, fearing that his enthusiasm was colored by personal affection for Holmes. He talked by phone with her almost every day and invited her to join Shultz family Christmas dinners. She encouraged his attention by leaning in close to him when they were seated together on sofas.

When doubts began to arise about the efficacy of Theranos blood-testing technology, Shultz ascribed it to efforts by established test companies to undercut Theranos. He seemed unwilling to believe his own eyes on one occasion when he went to a Theranos lab for a demonstration test, had his finger pricked and was then invited into another room where Theranos technicians drew blood from his arm. "That should have been the giveaway that Theranos was overselling its testing system," a Shultz colleague said. "He didn't want to believe it."[6] Shultz was so taken with Theranos that he encouraged his grandson, Tyler Shultz, to work there as a summer intern and as a full-time employee after he graduated from Stanford in 2013. Before long, Tyler began to suspect that the technology was flawed and that Holmes and the company were misleading the public and investors about its efficacy. He saw that test results were being manipulated to make Theranos technology look more accurate than it was. He noted that other laboratory workers realized the testing devices fell far short of the performance advertised by Holmes and her fellow executives. Shultz dismissed the concerns when Tyler described them to him.

Shultz's response to Tyler reached a flashpoint after Tyler took his concerns to John Carreyrou, a *Wall Street Journal* reporter.[7] Holmes, suspecting that Tyler was a source for a damning story by Carreyrou, sicced her lawyers on Tyler. Understandably rattled by the pursuit, which included surveillance of him by Theranos gumshoes, Tyler sought help from his grandfather. Instead of hugging his grandson and disowning Holmes, Shultz equivocated. He tried unsuccessfully to mediate between Tyler and Holmes. When that effort failed, he still refused to cut ties with Holmes, declining to sign and send a letter drafted by his staff that notified her he was resigning from the Theranos board. "I'm over 90 years old, I've seen a lot in my time, I've been right almost every time and I know I'm right about this," he told Tyler.[8] Carreyrou described Shultz's tragic dealings with Tyler in a heartbreaking 2016 *Wall Street Journal* story.[9]

Tyler felt betrayed by his grandfather. "He had chosen Elizabeth over me," Tyler later said.[10] Looking back on this bitter period on a podcast episode he hosted, Tyler imagined three reasons his grandfather had supported Holmes. "One is that you were corrupt and have invested so much money in Theranos that you were willing to make ethical compromises in order to see a return on your investment. The second is that you are in love with Elizabeth. So no matter how many times she lies to you, no matter how many patients she injures, and no matter how badly she harms your family, you will put her above everything else. The last possibility is that you have completely lost your mental edge and despite an abundance of data showing that she was a criminal, you somehow are incapable of connecting these very, very big dots."[11]

Personal financial gain was likely a motive. Though Shultz had become wealthy during his years at Bechtel, his holdings in Theranos stock skyrocketed in value before Holmes and the company imploded. Between the 2,750,000 shares that Holmes had given him, and 200,000 additional shares he purchased, his Theranos stock at peak valuation of $17 a share was worth more than $50 million.[12] Carreyrou reported in a podcast that Shultz had set aside 500,000 shares, worth $8.5 million, in a trust for his great-grandchildren.[13] Another factor, unmentioned by Tyler, clearly played a role—Shultz's steadfast loyalty. His sense that honorable people supported their friends through troubled times was evident in his continuing allegiance to Nixon as the Watergate scandal devoured the president and later by Shultz's fealty to Reagan during the Iran-Contra affair. Holmes's transgressions were glaring, but he would not disown her. After Theranos began to unravel, he declined to criticize her in an interview for this biography.

Shultz's performance left his family broken. Saddened friends and associates attributed the conduct to his advanced age. The Theranos saga played out while he was in his nineties. Months after Theranos disintegrated and Holmes was indicted in 2018 on criminal charges involving the defrauding of investors and deception of patients and doctors, Shultz tried to mend relations with Tyler and rebuild family ties. Carefully choosing his words, he said:

> The members of our family work to be loyal and supportive to one another and to the best of America's values. Most have inspired others to listen to their better angels; and some have shown tremendous courage and integrity when faced with difficult decisions or situations. Tyler's handling of the troubling practices he identified at Theranos is an example. He did not shrink from what he saw as his responsibility to the truth and patient safety, even when he felt personally threatened. I have learned—from my experiences beginning in World War II, in private industry, and in the various public service positions I have been privileged to fill—that the people in the field are closest to the issues and are the best sources of wisdom whenever a problem arises. That was certainly the case here. Tyler navigated a very complex situation in ways that made me proud. He has been an example for the entire family, for which all of us are grateful. I want to recognize and congratulate Tyler for his great moral character.[14]

The comments helped, but the task of rebuilding relations with Tyler remained unfinished business when Shultz died. As Tyler said some months before, "It's only been very recently that my relationship with my grandfather has started to heal. He's still never apologized for anything. But for me, having us occupy the same world is enough."[15]

As the shock of the Theranos affair lingered, Shultz did his best to remain actively engaged with public policy debates. In early 2017, he and fellow Republican James Baker called for a carbon tax to help combat global warming. "We suggest a solution that rests on four pillars," they said. "First, creating a gradually increasing carbon tax. Second, returning the tax proceeds to the American people in the form of dividends. Third, establishing border carbon adjustments that protect American competitiveness and encourage other countries to follow suit. And fourth, rolling back government regulations once such a system is in place."[16] Some years earlier, Shultz had also parted company with many Republicans by opposing a California referendum that would have suspended a 2006 law requiring the state to reduce greenhouse gas emissions to 1990 levels by 2010. He said at the time, "Those who wish to repeal our state's clean energy laws through postponement to some fictitious future are running up the white flag of surrender to a polluted environment."[17]

As Shultz neared his one hundredth birthday, he hosted a series of roundtable discussions about the social, economic, political, diplomatic and legal ramifications of technological advances. The sessions brought together eminent experts and produced stimulating discussions in an elegant circular conference room at the Hoover Institution. Shultz and James Timbie, a former State Department colleague, assembled the papers and presentations in 2020 in a provocative book, *A Hinge of History: Governance in an Emerging New World*. It was a classic Shultz endeavor—looking around the corner at the future implications of change, just as he had done in his mini-tutorials about the IT revolution for Gorbachev three decades earlier.

The COVID-19 pandemic in 2020 suspended George and Charlotte's peripatetic social life, which was slowing anyway as Shultz became more physically frail and, after several falls, started relying on a wheelchair to move around. The world's last glimpse of Shultz came in mid-December 2020 when the Hoover Institution and the Bohemian Club separately organized online events to mark his one hundredth birthday. The Hoover sessions featured scholarly presentations on critical global issues, reminiscences of Shultz and birthday greetings from a bipartisan pantheon of American leaders, world figures and the presidents of the four academic institutions where Shultz had studied or taught: Princeton, MIT, the University of Chicago and Stanford.

As the event came to an end on December 12, 2020, a new Zoom window opened showing George and Charlotte Shultz seated on a sofa in their Stanford living room. Shultz, nattily dressed, as he often was, in a plaid red sports jacket, a perfectly folded handkerchief perched in the jacket pocket, was clearly touched by the comments. He reminded viewers of the critically important role that trust plays in human affairs, whether personal, organizational, governmental or international. Repeating a phrase he often used over the course of his career, he said, "Trust is the coin of the realm." He had made the axiom the centerpiece of a pamphlet he authored to mark his centennial birthday, "Life and Learning after One Hundred Years."

The final lesson he bequeathed to the world was simple: "When trust was in the room, whatever room that was—the family room, the school-room, the coach's room, the office room, the government room, the military room—good things happened. When trust was not in the room, good things did not happen. Everything else is details."[18] Shultz died fifty-six days later, on February 6, 2021. Charlotte died on December 3, 2021.

When George Shultz was in the room, good things usually happened. There were exceptions, as when he was infected by the fever of distrust that crippled the Nixon presidency or when he did not trust himself enough to halt the trading of arms for hostages in the Middle East. And on occasion he trusted too much, as in his blind faith in Elizabeth Holmes and Theranos. At times, he hesitated to assert himself and genuflected timidly to his bosses and organizational routines, most evident in the years he struggled as secretary of state to overcome the cold war hawks around Reagan.

But over the course of his one hundred years on earth, Shultz was a formidable force for good and for peace. As a marine, he risked his life in defense of his nation. As an academic, he promoted civil rights, inclusivity and liberal ideals such as free speech and academic freedom. In retirement, he became a leader in acknowledging and combating climate change, and he dedicated himself to reducing nuclear threats. Across the decades, he served as a model of sensible, nonpartisan leadership, free of rancor and rage. And he sensed the importance of new information technologies and their power to reorder the world years ahead of his colleagues. He was the consummate problem solver. As Paul Volcker, the former Federal Reserve chairman, said of Shultz, "Time and again he would work with almost inhuman patience to bring a group into agreement upon a decision all could support, at time submerging his own preferences."[19]

No doubt, Reagan and Gorbachev deserve primary credit for winding down the cold war, and George H. W. Bush and Gorbachev for bringing it to a tranquil end. But it was Shultz who saw that the anti-Communist belligerence and military buildup of the Reagan administration had to be coupled with creative diplomacy. It was Shultz, through marathon negotiations with Shevardnadze and Gorbachev, who enabled Reagan to engage the Kremlin rather than just threaten it. Absent Shultz's patience and resilience, it seems unlikely that Reagan could ever have overcome the chaotic conflict within his national security team. And were it not for Shultz, it is hard to imagine how the ideological fervor of Reagan's first years as president could have given way to the pragmatic policies of his second term.

Jack Matlock, who worked closely with Reagan and Shultz, first as a White House aide and later as ambassador to the Soviet Union, said of Shultz's role: "Essential would be too mild. I cannot imagine relations with the Soviet Union developing the way they did if he had not been secretary of state."[20]

He truly devoted his life to the nation's service.

ACKNOWLEDGMENTS

GEORGE SHULTZ'S COOPERATION WAS indispensable to this book. He gave me exclusive access to his voluminous sealed archives at Stanford's Hoover Institution. He made himself available for numerous lengthy interviews, some covering uncomfortable ground about unflattering aspects of his career. He opened doors to a host of American and world leaders with whom he had worked. He encouraged his children to talk with me. And he and his wife, Charlotte, welcomed me to their California and Massachusetts homes. Throughout the project, he never asked me to tilt the book in his favor. He respected my independence as an author and never, directly or indirectly, pressed me to alter the manuscript.

This biography would not exist were it not for the generous support of John and Cynthia Gunn and Susan Ford Dorsey. They funded more than seven years of research work by a series of talented research assistants at Stanford's Center for International Security and Cooperation (CISAC), my book-writing home at the university. John, Cynthia and Susan knew and admired George Shultz for many years and offered to support the biography project from its inception, never interfering as the research and writing progressed. An author could not ask for better benefactors.

I had the good fortune to work with terrific research assistants. That line of excellence began as I was researching and drafting my last book, *The Partnership: Five Cold Warriors and Their Quest to Ban the Bomb*, which chronicled the effort of George Shultz, among others, to reduce nuclear threats. Invaluable research about Shultz for that project was handled by Gabriela Aoun, the primary research assistant, and Niko Milonopoulos and Kolby Hanson, both Stanford undergraduates at the time. Jason Saltoun-Ebin identified and collected a stream of declassified national security documents about Shultz's service as secretary of state at the Ronald Reagan Library. Jason published several collections of these documents, an invaluable resource for historians.

When I turned my attention to the Shultz biography, Kelsey Davidson, a Stanford political science major, stepped into the role of primary research assistant after she graduated in 2012. She was brilliant and indefatigable. Kelsey returned from days at the National Archives outside Washington, DC, with boxes of documents about Shultz's minor but telling role in the Watergate scandal, including reports and notes of IRS field investigators looking into the tax returns of Larry O'Brien, a Democratic Party leader. Kelsey spent weeks exploring Shultz's leading role in the desegregation of urban school systems in the South. When I had to cancel a trip to Israel at the last minute because of a family medical crisis, Kelsey gamely traveled to Tel Aviv on her own in July 2013 to interview family and friends of Josef Levy, a young Israeli whom Shultz met and admired at the University of Chicago. Levy's death during the 1967 Six-Day War left an enduring mark on Shultz. After her stint as research assistant, Kelsey went on to earn a master of arts degree from the Kennedy School at Harvard and a law degree from Harvard Law School. Pazner Garshowitz, an Israeli journalist, provided invaluable repor2ng about Josef Levy, his family and his service in the Israeli Defense Forces.

Rebecca Hecht was next, starting in 2014 after receiving a master of arts degree at Stanford in East Asian history. She was a Stanford 2012 graduate, double majoring in history and French. Rebecca joined me for interviews with Henry Kissinger in New York; Colin Powell in Alexandria, Virginia; James A. Baker III in Houston; and Shultz childhood and college friends in New Hampshire and Florida. Her extensive research work on Shultz's early life, wartime service as a marine and time as a graduate student and assistant professor at MIT, and as a professor and dean at the University of Chicago, was superb. She traveled to Jerusalem in February 2016 to chronicle Shultz's encounters with the family of Josef Levy as they commemorated Levy's death. Rebecca, a gifted writer, produced the first draft of several chapters and deftly managed a mountain of research material. She went on to enroll in rabbinical studies at Hebrew Union College. She will be a wonderful rabbi.

Katharina Hermann picked up where Rebecca left off. Kathi, an Austrian, was spending a quarter at Stanford in 2016 as a graduate student when we first met. She had done her undergraduate studies at Vienna University of Economics and Business and received a master of arts degree in advanced international studies at Diplomatic Academy Vienna. It fell to Kathi, among other duties, to assemble a comprehensive time line of Shultz's years as secretary of state, drawing on the many streams of research done by her predecessors and me. This was a monumental task that Kathi executed perfectly, in effect, producing a highly detailed outline for the book section about Shultz's critical role in winding down the cold war. Kathi is now working for the Austrian Finance Ministry.

When Kathi returned to Vienna, Gabriela Levikow took over after graduating from Stanford, where she was a political science major. I had met Gabby during her freshman year when my wife and I dined with a group of new students. Her interest in national security issues and nuclear weapons made her a great fit for the job. During her two-year stint, Gabby produced a series of deep research reports on numerous aspects of the George Shultz story, including his role in the Iran-Contra scandal that nearly brought down the Reagan presidency. She combed through dozens of declassified CIA reports about the Soviet Union and did an extraordinary job reconstructing the Reagan administration's futile efforts to retaliate militarily for deadly Islamic extremist suicide terrorist attacks in 1983 against the American embassy in Lebanon and the marine barracks there. Gabby is now enrolled at Duke Law School.

Courtney Douglas, a 2020 Stanford graduate, was next. Courtney was an English major, political science minor and editor of the *Stanford Daily*. She signed up in 2020 to work on my next project, a fresh look at Robert McNamara. Courtney skillfully handled an array of final research assignments about Shultz and gamely agreed to prepare the end notes for this book, a daunting task that she performed with meticulous care.

Early in the Shultz project, Hannah Meropol devoted the summer between her first and second years at Stanford to digging into the Reagan administration's broader effort to grapple with the rise of terrorism in the Middle East. Hannah's research report would have made a PhD candidate proud. Alexa Philippou, between newspaper jobs after graduating from Stanford, contributed helpful research about Shultz's entanglement with Theranos. As the project was winding down in 2020, Elizabeth Lindqwister, a rising Stanford senior, smartly tackled a dizzying range of research assignments, most about American-Soviet relations. Emily Schrader, a rising Stanford junior, ably fielded a number of homestretch research questions in 2022 as the book moved toward publication. Matt Kristoffersen, a 2022 Yale graduate headed to Harvard Law School in 2024, took over full-time research duties for my book projects in August 2022, skillfully tackling several last tasks on this book.

I am indebted to all the research assistants for building a formidable library of historical documents spanning Shultz's life and career and guiding me through the history with insightful research reports.

This book would also not have been possible without the sustained support of Susan Schendel, Shultz's executive assistant during the last decades of his work at Stanford. Susan died in late 2020, just weeks before Shultz's death, after stoically enduring a long battle with cancer. To the end, she did everything she could to help me locate various Shultz papers and get in touch with his many former government associates. I will never forget her last call, made from her hospital bed, as she assisted me for a final time. Susan's dedication to Shultz and his wife, Charlotte, reflected her strength of character and her great heart.

Judith Lipp and Grace Hawes, Susan's colleagues in the Shultz office suite at Hoover, were unfailingly helpful, as was David Fedor, who conveyed numerous messages between Shultz and me during the pandemic, when he was one of the few people permitted to spend time at Shultz's campus home. Before the pandemic closed the Hoover Institution archives, the archive staff always responded with alacrity and precision to my many document requests.

Jim Mattis, the former marine general who went on to serve as Donald Trump's first defense secretary, graciously assisted me while he was based at Stanford before Trump's election. Jim instructed me how to gain access to Shultz's marine records, walked me through the stages of training that Shultz received before being sent to combat zones in the Pacific and reviewed the chapter on Shultz's wartime service. Gary Roughead, former chief of naval operations, also based at Stanford, generously introduced me to the Navy History and Heritage Command and its commander, Sam Cox. Cox kindly shared with me the journal he kept as an intelligence officer aboard the USS *Eisenhower* in 1983 when the aircraft carrier was deployed in the eastern Mediterranean, ready to launch air strikes against terrorist sites in Lebanon. Multiple strikes were aborted at the last minute.

Financial support for research also came from the Hoover Institution and the Stanford Institute for Economic Policy Research (SIEPR). My thanks go to John Raisian and John Shoven, the former directors of Hoover and SIEPR, respectively, for making the support possible; and to Condoleezza Rice, the current Hoover director and former secretary of state, who shared her memories of Shultz, helped put me in touch with former senior government officials and often compared notes with me about our common interest: the Soviet Union.

I am thankful for the intellectual support of CISAC codirectors during the lifespan of this project: Scott Sagan, Sig Hecker, Amy Zegart, Mariano-Florentino Cuellar, David Relman, Colin Kahl and Rod Ewing. I benefited greatly from the historical knowledge and friendship of Stanford history professors David Holloway, David Kennedy, and Norman Naimark. The directors of Stanford's Freeman Spogli Institute for Internal Studies (FSI), of which CISAC is a component, consistently made institutional resources available. Coit Blacker started the pattern when he warmly welcomed me to FSI after I retired from the *New York Times*. His successors— Tino Cuellar, who went on to become a member of the California Supreme Court and now serves as president of the Carnegie Endowment for International Peace; Gerhard Casper, who served as Stanford president from 1992 to 2000; and Mike McFaul, the former American ambassador to Russia and Obama White House aide—extended the welcome. FSI and CISAC staff supported the project in countless ways. My thanks go to Andrea Gray, Megan Gorman and Elizabeth Gardner, who managed the hiring and employment of research assistants and many other tasks related to the book project and my association with CISAC. My life at CISAC has benefited in countless ways from the kindness and efficiency of Tracy Hines.

I am grateful for the cooperation of the Richard Nixon Presidential Library and the Ronald Reagan Presidential Library. Timothy Naftali, former director of the Nixon Library, kindly pointed me to key materials about Shultz's service during the Nixon administration. Staff members at the Library of Congress and the National Archives also were very helpful. The family of Caspar Weinberger graciously granted permission for me to review his papers at the Library of Congress. Tom Blanton and his colleagues at the National Security Archive at George Washington University were, as always, wonderfully helpful. The archive's vast collection of declassified documents is an invaluable resource for historians of the cold war.

Bechtel family members—Stephen D. Bechtel Jr., Riley Bechtel and Alan Dachs—talked at length with me about Shultz's years as a top executive at the Bechtel Group, the global engineering and construction company. I appreciate the unusual access to the privately owned and publicity-shy company.

Gerhard Casper and my brother, William Taubman, professor emeritus of political science at Amherst College and winner of the Pulitzer Prize for his biography of Nikita Khrushchev, read drafts of this book and gave me thoughtful feedback, as did readers asked by Stanford University Press to review the manuscript. I do not know their identities but am thankful for their unsparing critiques, valuable suggestions and corrections. Lawrence Goulder, professor of economics at Stanford, carved out time in his busy schedule to review several chapters that deal with Shultz's role as an economist at MIT and the University of Chicago and as labor secretary, OMB director and Treasury secretary.

Several of my former colleagues at the *New York Times* encouraged me to do this book and cheered me along at moments when the finish line seemed impossibly distant, including Tom Friedman, Maureen Dowd, Nick Kristof, David Sanger, Steve Weisman, Eric Schmitt and Jeff Gerth. Bernard Gwertzman and Leslie Gelb, who covered the Reagan administration for the *Times*, shared their memories with me.

Amanda Urban, my literary agent for four decades, was wise about this book and provided smart counsel through the course of the project. She has long been an invaluable guide to the world of book publishing and a wonderful friend.

I am grateful to Alan Harvey, director of the Stanford University Press, and his colleagues, including Marie-Catherine Pavel, for their thoughtful handling of the manuscript and publication of the book. Tim Roberts deftly managed the copyediting process and other manuscript matters. Cynthia H. Lindlof did a meticulous job of copyediting. Adam Schnitzer, marketing and sales director, enthusiastically and effectively planned for the book launch.

During the years I toiled on the book, I made a living by working part-time at Stanford as associate vice president for university affairs and secretary of the Stanford Board of Trustees. My university colleagues were understanding as I tried to balance book and university work. I am especially grateful to John Hennessy, who gave me the opportunity to work with him during his time as Stanford president, and to his successor, Marc Tessier-Lavigne, who extended the welcome. The three Board chairs with whom I worked—Leslie Hume, Steve Denning and Jeff Raikes—could not have been more supportive. So, too, have been the members of the Board, many of whom wondered if I would ever finish the book.

I have long found family support to be the irreplaceable anchor of a book project and have been blessed by patient and loving kinfolk. My brother, William, and his wife, Jane, have never wavered in their support. My sons, Michael and Greg, and Michael's wife, Gabi, have kept my spirits up, and my granddaughters, Sophia and Avery, are a source of unending joy.

Felicity Barringer, my wife, has been a patient sounding board for my book projects, a constant source of astute editing advice and my closest friend and loving companion for more than fifty years. We met as Stanford undergraduates in the late 1960s, married in 1971 and worked alongside one another as journalists for decades, Felicity as a reporter and editor at the *Washington Post* and the *New York Times*. With Felicity at my side, anything is possible!

August 31, 2022, Menlo Park, California

NOTES

PREFACE

1. Mikhail Gorbachev, interview by William Taubman, October 19, 2015.

2. The other was Elliot Richardson, who served as secretary of health, education, and welfare (January 24, 1970–January 29, 1973); secretary of defense (January 30, 1973–May 24, 1973); attorney general (May 25, 1973–October 20, 1973); and secretary of commerce (February 2, 1976–January 20, 1977).

3. "Memorandum from Secretary of State Shultz to President Reagan," in *Foreign Relations of the United States, 1981–1988*, 5:347.

4. Goodby, "The Putin Doctrine and Preventive Diplomacy," 23. Shultz made the comment in a preface to a journal article by James E. Goodby, a retired US ambassador and arms control negotiator. The article, which Shultz endorsed, described the threat presented by Putin's view, or doctrine, that lands of the former Soviet Union constituted a sphere of Kremlin strategic interest.

5. Quotation from George Shultz according to Gerhard Casper, letter to the author, April 24, 2021.

6. Garchik, "George Shultz on Trump's Talks in Finland."

7. Shultz, "On Trust."

8. Securities Exchange Commission, list of Theranos stockholders and number of shares each owned. Not a publicly available document. The author has a copy.

9. Griffith and Woo, "Elizabeth Holmes Is Found Guilty."

10. Thomas Simons, interview by the author, May 19, 2009.

11. Henry Kissinger, interview by the author and Rebecca Hecht, November 14, 2014.

12. Colin Powell, interview by the author and Rebecca Hecht, October 1, 2015.

13. Gates, *From the Shadows*, 281.

14. Eduard Shevardnadze, interview by the author, July 27, 2012.

15. Gaddis, *The Cold War* and *The United States and the End of the Cold War*, among others; Matlock, *Autopsy on an Empire*; Oberdorfer, *From the Cold War to a New Era*; Service, *The End of the Cold War*.

CHAPTER ONE

1. Shultz Family, "Shultz Family History."

2. Shultz Family, "Shultz Family History."

3. George P. Shultz, interview by the author, November 19, 2012.

4. Shultz Family, "Shultz Family History."

5. According to Margaret's birth certificate, her father was born in New York state, and her mother, in Scotland.

6. Shultz, "My Early Life," 9.

7. Shultz Family, "Shultz Family History."

8. Shultz, "My Early Life," 9. He was made All Souls' rector in 1905; prior to that he was curate of St. Michael's Church.

9. George P. Shultz, interview by the author and Kelsey Davidson, July 14, 2012.

10. Shultz, "My Early Life," 10.

11. George P. Shultz, interview by the author, September 5, 2012.

12. "Miss M. L. Pratt the Bride of B. E. Shultz," 17.

13. "Rev. George S. Pratt Is Dead," 8.

14. Shultz, "My Early Life," 10.

15. The congregation increased from 6,253 in 1900 to 17,805 in 1930.

16. The Marx Brothers' first film, *Humor Risk*, was shot in Fort Lee in 1922.

17. Bumiller, "Gentle George and the Quiet Roar at State."

18. George P. Shultz, interview by the author and Rebecca Hecht, May 15, 2015.

19. Shultz, "My Early Life," 1.

20. Shultz, "My Early Life," 1.

21. Shultz, "My Early Life," 7.

22. George P. Shultz, interview by the author, April 6, 2012.

23. George P. Shultz, interview by the author, September 5, 2012.

24. The stadium was dedicated in 1925.

25. George P. Shultz, interview by the author, April 6, 2012.

26. Shultz Family, "Shultz Family History."

27. Shultz, "My Early Life," 4; and George P. Shultz, interview by the author and Rebecca Hecht, May 15, 2015.

28. George P. Shultz, interview by the author, May 10, 2013.

29. George P. Shultz, interview by the author, September 5, 2012.

30. Shultz, "My Early Life," 1.

31. George P. Shultz, interview by the author, April 6, 2012.

32. Shultz, "My Early Life," 4.

33. George P. Shultz, interview by the author, May 10, 2013.

34. George P. Shultz, interview by the author, April 6, 2012.

35. Jim Baldwin, interview by the author and Rebecca Hecht, August 25, 2014.

36. George P. Shultz, interview by the author, April 6, 2012.

37. George P. Shultz, interview by the author, April 6, 2012.

38. Shultz, "My Early Life," 18.

39. Shultz, "My Early Life," 18.

40. Alex Shultz, interview by the author, August 12, 2012.

41. Shultz, "My Early Life," 5.

42. Shultz, "My Early Life," 5.

43. George P. Shultz, interview by the author and Rebecca Hecht, May 15, 2015.

44. Birl Shultz, letter to George P. Shultz, December 15, 1932.

45. Birl Shultz, letter to George P. Shultz, December 15, 1932.

46. Birl Shultz, letter to George P. Shultz, December 15, 1932.

47. George P. Shultz, interview by the author, May 10, 2013.

48. Freedman, *Children of the Great Depression*.

49. George P. Shultz, interview by the author, September 5, 2012.

50. George P. Shultz, interview by the author, April 6, 2012.

51. George P. Shultz, interview by the author, April 6, 2012.

52. George P. Shultz, interview by the author, May 10, 2013.

53. George P. Shultz, interview by the author, May 10, 2013.

54. George P. Shultz, interview by the author, May 10, 2013.

55. George P. Shultz, interview by the author, November 19, 2012.

56. Kennedy, *Freedom from Fear*, 252.

57. Kennedy, *Freedom from Fear*, 289.

58. Kennedy, *Freedom from Fear*, 285.

59. Cook, interview for *Turmoil and Triumph*.

60. George P. Shultz, interview by the author, April 6, 2012.

61. Shultz, "My Early Life," 13.

62. Boyden was Deerfield's headmaster during 1902–1968 and oversaw its transition from a public school into an elite private school.

63. George P. Shultz, interview by the author, April 6, 2012.

64. Shultz, "My Early Life," 8.

65. Cook, interview for *Turmoil and Triumph*.

66. Fitzgerald, *This Side of Paradise*.

67. *Princeton Alumni Weekly*, vol. 40, October 6, 1939.

68. *Princeton Alumni Weekly*, vol. 40, October 6, 1939.

69. George P. Shultz, interview by the author, April 6, 2012.

70. George P. Shultz, interview by the author, November 19, 2012.

71. George P. Shultz, interview by the author, November 19, 2012.

72. George P. Shultz, interview by the author, November 19, 2012.

73. Cook, interview for *Turmoil and Triumph.*

74. Maynard, *Princeton.*

75. Cook, interview for *Turmoil and Triumph.* John Brooks went on to become a longtime staff writer for the *New Yorker,* where he focused on financial journalism. He died in 1993.

76. Fitzgerald, *This Side of Paradise.*

77. Bob Young, interview by the author and Rebecca Hecht, August 29, 2014.

78. Jim Baldwin, interview by the author and Rebecca Hecht, August 25, 2014.

79. Jim Baldwin, interview by the author and Rebecca Hecht, August 25, 2014.

80. Cook, interview for *Turmoil and Triumph.*

81. George P. Shultz, interview by the author and Rebecca Hecht, October 15, 2015.

82. George P. Shultz, letter to Nancy Ager, August 7, 1996.

83. Bumiller, "Gentle George."

84. Jim Baldwin, interview by the author and Rebecca Hecht, August 25, 2014.

85. Bumiller, "Gentle George."

86. Cook, interview for *Turmoil and Triumph.*

87. Bob Young, interview by the author and Rebecca Hecht, August 29, 2014.

88. Bumiller, "Gentle George."

89. Bob Young, interview by the author and Rebecca Hecht, August 29, 2014.

90. George P. Shultz, interview by the author, April 6, 2012.

91. George P. Shultz, interview by the author, April 6, 2012.

92. George P. Shultz, interview by the author, April 6, 2012.

93. George P. Shultz, interview by the author, April 6, 2012.

94. George P. Shultz, interview by the author, May 10, 2013.

95. George P. Shultz, interview by the author, April 6, 2012.

96. George P. Shultz, interview by the author, November 19, 2012.

97. George P. Shultz, interview by the author, April 6, 2012.

98. Shultz, "Agricultural Program of the Tennessee Valley Authority," 3.

99. Shultz, "My Early Life," 14.

100. Shultz, "My Early Life," 14.

101. Shultz, "My Early Life," 14.

102. George P. Shultz, telephone interview by the author, March 28, 2020.

103. Arana-Ward, "George Shultz."

104. Shultz, *Turmoil and Triumph*, 25.

105. Cook, interview for *Turmoil and Triumph.*

106. Cook, interview for *Turmoil and Triumph.*

107. Cook, interview for *Turmoil and Triumph.* In later years, George Shultz was

cagey about this tattooing incident, referring to it coyly: "There was a lot of talk in my latter days as Secretary of State about an allegation that I had a tattoo of a tiger on my rear end. I was never willing to confirm or deny this story, and occasionally when people flattered me and said I ought to run for President, I said I couldn't possibly consider it because it was alleged that I had this tattoo on my rear end, and that tale would dominate the campaign and drive out the real issues. Of course, beyond that, if it ever did emerge that I had such a tattoo, the investigation of the circumstances under which I got it would surely make me ineligible to be President." Shultz, "My Early Life," 18.

108. George P. Shultz, interview by the author, April 6, 2012.

109. "George Shultz." ʼ

110. Shultz, "My Early Life," 18.

111. Shultz, "My Early Life," 18.

112. Shultz, "My Early Life," 19.

CHAPTER TWO

1. George P. Shultz, interview by the author, July 5, 2012.

2. George P. Shultz, interview by the author, September 5, 2012.

3. George P. Shultz, interview by the author, September 5, 2012.

4. George P. Shultz, interview by the author, September 5, 2012.

5. George P. Shultz, interview by the author, May 2, 2013.

6. George P. Shultz, interview by the author, May 2, 2013.

7. George P. Shultz, interview by the author, July 5, 2012.

8. Gwertzman, "The Shultz Method."

9. After-Action Report from September 7, 1943, US Marine Corps, Seventh Antiaircraft Artillery Battalion, Third Marine Brigade, written November 22, 1943, Library of the Marine Corps, Quantico, Virginia.

10. George P. Shultz, interview by the author and Rebecca Hecht, October 15, 2015.

11. George P. Shultz, interview by the author and Rebecca Hecht, October 15, 2015.

12. After-Action Report from September 7, 1943, Library of the Marine Corps.

13. George P. Shultz, interview by the author, September 2, 2009.

14. George P. Shultz, interview by the author, January 9, 2014.

15. George P. Shultz, interview by the author and Rebecca Hecht, October 15, 2015.

16. George P. Shultz, interview by the author, November 12, 2012. Marine records show that the sergeant under Shultz's command who was killed by Japanese fire that day was William H. Palat, born in Booth, Texas, on August 20, 1919. He was appointed private first class on March 20, 1942. His mother, Frances Palat, was

notified of his death in a telegram from the commandant of the Marine Corps on September 14, 1943: "Deeply regret to inform you that your son platoon seargent [*sic*] William H. Palat US Marine Corps died of wounds received in action in the performance of his duty and in the service of his country to prevent possible aid to our enemies. Please do not divulge the name of his ship or station. Present situation necessitates interment temporarily in the locality where death occurred and you will be notified accordingly. Accept my heartfelt sympathy letter follows."

17. George P. Shultz, interview by the author and Rebecca Hecht, October 15, 2015.

18. Helena Maria O'Brien, Service Record, US Army, courtesy of the Shultz family.

19. George P. Shultz, interview by the author and Rebecca Hecht, October 15, 2015.

20. George P. Shultz, letter to Norman Cook, December 4, 1944.

21. George P. Shultz, letter to Norman Cook, July 25. No year is listed on the letter, but context suggests that it was written in 1944.

22. George P. Shultz, letter to Norman Cook, July 25, likely in 1944.

23. George P. Shultz, interview by the author and Rebecca Hecht, October 15, 2015.

24. George P. Shultz, letter to Norman Cook, December 4, 1944.

25. George P. Shultz, letter to Norman Cook, December 4, 1944.

26. George P. Shultz, letter to Norman Cook, April 10, 1945.

27. George P. Shultz, letter to Norman Cook, June 3, 1945.

28. George P. Shultz, letter to Norman Cook, June 3, 1945.

29. George P. Shultz, interview by the author and Rebecca Hecht, October 15, 2015.

30. George P. Shultz, interview by the author, September 2, 2012.

31. Norman Cook Sr., letter to Norman Cook, August 26, 1945.

32. George P. Shultz, interview by the author and Kelsey Davidson, July 14, 2012.

CHAPTER THREE

1. Shultz, "My Early Life," 22.

2. Weinstein, "Paul A. Samuelson."

3. George P. Shultz, interview by the author, April 6, 2012.

4. George P. Shultz, interview by the author, May 10, 2013.

5. Douglas M. McGregor, *Ninth Annual Report of the Industrial Relations Section*, November 1, 1946, Institute Archives, Massachusetts Institute of Technology (MIT Archives).

6. George P. Shultz, interview by the author, May 10, 2013.

7. Wren, "Joseph N. Scanlon," 20–27.

8. Wren, "Joseph N. Scanlon," 20-27.

9. Daniel Wren, "Joseph Scanlon: The Man and the Plan," letter from Douglas M. McGregor to James R. Killian Jr. on the appointment of Joseph Scanlon, April 13, 1946, MIT Archives.

10. George P. Shultz, interview by the author, November 19, 2012.

11. "On Leadership," podcast.

12. Shultz, *Ideas & Action*, 20.

13. George P. Shultz, interview by the author, November 19, 2012.

14. Shultz Family, "Shultz Family History."

15. Shultz, "My Early Life," 24.

16. George P. Shultz, interview by the author and Rebecca Hecht, October 15, 2015.

17. Shultz, "My Early Life," 24.

18. Margaret Shultz, interview by the author, August 11, 2012.

19. "Awarded Degree of Doctor of Philosophy, February 1949," *Graduation Exercises Book, June 1949,* MIT Archives.

20. George P. Shultz, interview by the author, April 6, 2012.

21. Shultz, *Learning from Experience.*

22. George P. Shultz, "Pressures on Wage Decisions: A Case Study in the Shoe Industry" (PhD diss., Massachusetts Institute of Technology, 1951), MIT Archives, 4.

23. George P. Shultz, interview by the author, April 6, 2012.

24. Shultz, "My Early Life," 25.

25. Margaret Shultz, interview by the author, August 11, 2012.

26. Margaret Shultz, interview by the author, August 11, 2012.

27. Margaret Shultz, interview by the author, August 11, 2012.

28. Shultz family photo and memory book, prepared by Susan Schendel, 18.

29. According to a Stow, Massachusetts, town clerk's report of the annual town meeting from February 28, 1953, George Shultz received 295 votes for the two-year planning board.

30. Shultz, *Turmoil and Triumph*, 27.

31. Livingston, "Keyserling Faces Test," 19.

32. Milton Friedman, remarks at memorial service for Arthur Burns, July 22, 1987.

33. "Economic Council," 2.

34. "Senate-House Conferees Vote," 1.

35. Hargrove and Morley, *The President and the Council of Economic Advisers*, 98.

36. Sobel and Katz, *Biographical Directory*, 24.

37. Hargrove and Morley, *The President and the Council of Economic Advisers*, 100.

38. Shultz family photo and memory book, 21.

39. George P. Shultz, interview by the author and Rebecca Hecht, May 15, 2015.

40. Shultz, "My Early Life," 27.

41. George P. Shultz, interview by the author, November 19, 2012.

42. George P. Shultz, interview by the author, November 2, 2009.

43. John Burchard, letter to Ralph Freeman, January 29, 1957, MIT Archives.

44. George P. Shultz, interview by the author and Rebecca Hecht, October 15, 2015.

45. George P. Shultz, interview by the author, November 19, 2012.

CHAPTER FOUR

1. "On Leadership," podcast.

2. George P. Shultz, interview by the author and Rebecca Hecht, October 15, 2015.

3. George P. Shultz, interview by the author and Rebecca Hecht, October 15, 2015.

4. Margaret Shultz, interview by the author, August 11, 2012.

5. Alex Shultz, interview by the author, August 12, 2012.

6. George P. Shultz, interview by the author, November 19, 2012.

7. Silk, "Milton Friedman Nobel Laureate."

8. "A Heavyweight Champ."

9. Shultz, "The Chicago Economics Tradition."

10. George P. Shultz, Business 344 syllabus, Massachusetts Institute of Technology, fall semester 1960, MIT Archives.

11. George P. Shultz, interview by the author, November 19, 2012.

12. George P. Shultz, interview by the author, November 19, 2012.

13. George P. Shultz, interview by the author, November 19, 2012; and email correspondence with the author, June 5, 2020.

14. George P. Shultz, interview by the author, August 25, 2008.

15. George P. Shultz, email correspondence with the author, June 5, 2020.

16. "U. of C. Appoints Dean of Business College."

17. George P. Shultz, interview by the author, November 19, 2012.

18. George P. Shultz, interview by the author, May 2, 2013.

19. "The Fort Worth Project," 53–57.

20. Arnold Weber, oral history interview with Timothy Naftali, 3.

21. George P. Shultz, interview by the author, May 2, 2013.

22. George P. Shultz, interview by the author, May 2, 2013.

23. George P. Shultz, interview by the author, July 23, 2014.

24. George P. Shultz, interview by the author, July 23, 2014.

25. George P. Shultz, interview by the author, May 2, 2013.

26. "Opportunities Open to Negroes in Management."

27. George P. Shultz, interview by the author, July 23, 2014.

28. Margaret Shultz, interview by the author, August 11, 2012.

29. Gwertzman, "The Shultz Method."

30. George P. Shultz, interview by the author, August 31, 2012.

31. Shmuel Shay, interview by Kelsey Davidson, July 28, 2013.

32. Itzik Nir, interview by Kelsey Davidson, July 28, 2013.

33. George P. Shultz, interview by the author, August 31, 2012.

34. George P. Shultz, interview by the author, Kelsey Davidson and Hannah Meropol, July 10, 2013.

35. George P. Shultz, interview by the author, Kelsey Davidson and Hannah Meropol, July 10, 2013.

36. George P. Shultz, interview by the author, November 12, 2013.

37. February 6, 2016, Jerusalem, Israel. The scene was witnessed and recorded by Rebecca Hecht.

38. Shultz, *Turmoil and Triumph*, 32.

CHAPTER FIVE

1. George P. Shultz, interview by the author, May 2, 2013; and Henry Wadsworth Longfellow, "There Was a Little Girl" (1882).

2. George P. Shultz, interview by the author, January 9, 2014.

3. George P. Shultz, interview by the author, April 26, 2012.

4. Reeves, *President Nixon*, 292.

5. Raskin, "Said Nixon to George Shultz."

6. Naughton, "Shultz Quietly Builds Up Power."

7. Raines, "George Wallace."

8. George P. Shultz, interview by the author, May 2, 2013.

9. H. R. Haldeman, oral history interview with Raymond H. Geselbracht, 33–35.

10. Shultz, *Turmoil and Triumph*, 9.

11. George P. Shultz, interview by the author, May 2, 2013.

12. "Transcript of Nixon's Program on Television," 37.

13. Peter Shultz, interview by the author, December 26, 2012.

14. "Federal Government Finances and Employment," in *Statistical Abstract of the United States*, Sec. 14. The volume details the Labor Department's budget ($3.688 trillion) on page 379, figure 543, and the Labor Department's employment data (10,108 employees) on page 396, figure 570.

15. George P. Shultz, interview by the author, May 2, 2013.

16. Raskin, "Said Nixon to George Shultz."

17. George P. Shultz, interview by the author, May 2, 2013.

18. George P. Shultz, interview by the author, May 2, 2013.

19. George P. Shultz, interview by the author, May 2, 2013.

20. Shultz, *Issues on My Mind*, 21.

21. George P. Shultz, interview by the author, April 26, 2012.

22. Arnold Weber, oral history interview with Timothy Naftali, 20.

23. Arnold Weber, oral history interview with Timothy Naftali, 20.

24. George P. Shultz, interview by the author, April 26, 2012.

25. George P. Shultz, interview by the author, April 26, 2012.

26. George P. Shultz, interview by the author, April 26, 2012.

27. Levine, "Campus to Cabinet."

28. Barbara White, interview by the author, December 26, 2012.

29. Peter Shultz, interview by the author, December 26, 2012.

30. Richard Nixon, Inaugural Address, January 20, 1969, Richard Nixon Presidential Library (Nixon Library).

31. Reeves, *President Nixon*, 133.

32. Reeves, *President Nixon*, 98–99.

33. Kutler, *Abuse of Power*, 115.

34. George P. Shultz, interview by the author, August 25, 2016.

35. Comptroller General of the United States, "Review of Economic Opportunity Programs," 91st Cong., 1st Sess. (1969), 53.

36. Arnold Weber, oral history interview with Timothy Naftali, 20.

37. Pichler, "The Jobs Corps Transition," 338–339.

38. Pichler, "The Job Corps Transition," 343.

39. Arnold Weber, oral history interview with Timothy Naftali, 21.

40. "Job Corps Test Won."

41. "Jobs Corps Test Won."

42. George P. Shultz, interview by the author, April 26, 2012.

43. Levine, "Campus to Cabinet."

44. Levine, "Campus to Cabinet."

45. George P. Shultz, interview by the author, April 26, 2012.

46. Shultz, *Issues on My Mind*, 35.

47. Kotlowski, *Nixon's Civil Rights*, 116.

48. Kotlowski, *Nixon's Civil Rights*, 103.

49. Transcript of press conference with George Shultz, September 23, 1969, US Department of Labor.

50. Kotlowski, *Nixon's Civil Rights*, 99–100.

51. Kotlowski, *Nixon's Civil Rights*, 99.

52. George P. Shultz, interview by the author, September 5, 2012.

53. Transcript of press conference with George Shultz and Arthur Fletcher, December 20, 1969, White House Roosevelt Room, Office of the White House Press Secretary.

54. George P. Shultz, interview by the author, September 5, 2012.

55. George P. Shultz, interview by the author, May 2, 2013.

56. Wicker, *One of Us*, 486–487.

57. Strober and Strober, *The Nixon Presidency*.

58. Reeves, *President Nixon*, 117.

59. Reeves, *President Nixon*, 117.

60. Reeves, *President Nixon*, 117.

61. Wicker, *One of Us*, 488.

62. Reeves, *President Nixon*, 117.

63. Wicker, *One of Us*, 493.

64. In addition to Agnew, Shultz, Mitchell and Finch, the task force included Winton M. Blount, the postmaster general; Donald Rumsfeld, director of the Office of Economic Opportunity; and two counselors to President Nixon, Daniel P. Moynihan and Bryce Harlow. Cabinet Committee on Education, Record Group 220, Nixon Library.

65. George P. Shultz, interview by the author, May 2, 2013. An internal administration history of the task force, drafted by Wallace Henley, an aide to Robert Mardian, never explicitly states that Agnew disassociated himself, but Agnew all but disappears from the detailed narrative account after the initial phase of task force work.

66. George P. Shultz, interview by the author, May 2, 2013.

67. Wallace Henley, "A History: School Desegregation and the Role of the Cabinet Committee on Education," prepared at the request of George P. Shultz, under the direction of Robert C. Mardian, White House Central Files, 64–65, Nixon Library.

68. George P. Shultz, interview by the author, May 2, 2013.

69. Henley, "A History," 91.

70. Henley, "A History," 91. The history does not identify the lawmaker who spoke to Mardian.

71. Henley, "A History," 94.

72. George P. Shultz, interview by the author, May 2, 2013.

73. George P. Shultz, interview by the author, May 2, 2013.

74. George P. Shultz, interview by the author, July 23, 2014.

75. Wicker, *One of Us*, 504.

76. George P. Shultz, interview by the author, July 23, 2014.

77. George P. Shultz, interview by the author, July 23, 2014.

CHAPTER SIX

1. Reston, "A Tendency to Stay Too Long."

2. George P. Shultz, "Problems and Principles," oral history interview with Paul Burnett, 70.

3. "Architect of Nixon's New Economics."

4. Richard Nixon, "Address to the Nation on Economic Productivity and Policy," June 17, 1970, Nixon Library, June 17, 1970.

5. George P. Shultz, "Problems and Principles," oral history interview with Paul Burnett, 84.

6. Arthur Burns, Statement on the State of the Economy before the Senate Banking, Housing, and Urban Affairs Committee, March 10, 1971, Congressional Record Archive.

7. Shultz, "Prescription for Economic Policy."

8. Friedman, "Why the Freeze Is a Mistake."

9. Shultz and Taylor, *Choose Economic Freedom*, 25.

10. Shultz and Taylor, *Choose Economic Freedom*, 35.

11. Shultz, *Thinking about the Future*, 123.

12. Shultz and Dam, *Economic Policy beyond the Headlines*, 114.

13. Shultz and Taylor, "Friedman Speech at the O'Hare International Bank Executives Club, March 14, 1974," in *Choose Economic Freedom*, 37–38.

14. Garten, *Three Days at Camp David*.

15. Conversation between Richard M. Nixon, H. R. Haldeman and John Ehrlichman, May 13, 1971, University of Virginia Miller Center Archive.

16. Martin, "Johnnie M. Walters."

17. George P. Shultz, interview by the author, July 10, 2017.

18. "A Resolution Authorizing and Directing the Committee on the Judiciary to Investigate Whether Sufficient Grounds Exist for the House of Representatives to Exercise Its Constitutional Power to Impeach Richard M. Nixon," Statement of Information, Hearings before the Committee on the Judiciary, Book VIII, Internal Revenue Service, paragraphs 22–23, Congressional Record Archive.

19. George P. Shultz, interview by the author, July 10, 2017.

20. Johnnie M. Walters, "Affidavit," June 10, 1974, Hearings before the Committee on the Judiciary, House of Representatives, 93rd Cong. (Washington, DC: US Government Printing Office, 1974), 231.

21. Conversation between Richard M. Nixon and John Ehrlichman, August 3, 1972, 5:00 p.m.–5:30 p.m., Executive Office Building, University of Virginia Miller Center Archive.

22. Conversation between Richard M. Nixon and John Ehrlichman.

23. "Text of 2 Memos on I.R.S."

24. "Text of 2 Memos on I.R.S."

25. Conversation between Richard M. Nixon, Bob Haldeman and John Dean regarding George Shultz, September 15, 1972, University of Virginia Miller Center Archive.

26. Martin, "Johnnie M. Walters."

27. Lawrence F. O'Brien, oral history interview with Michael L. Gillette.

28. Lawrence O'Brien, oral history interview with Michael L. Gillette. In July

1968, during a meeting between O'Brien and Maheu in Washington, DC, Maheu gave O'Brien an envelope that Maheu said contained twenty-five thousand dollars, which Hughes wanted to donate to the vestiges of the Robert F. Kennedy presidential campaign. "December 18, 1973 Office Interview of Lawrence F. O'Brien," memorandum to Howard Hughes from Stephen E. Haberfield, January 3, 1974, National Archives, Record Group 460: Records of the Watergate Special Prosecution Force, Hughes/Rebozo Investigation, Box 97.

29. Special Agent Donald C. Skelton, "Memorandum of Interview: Re: Hughes Tool Company," August 17, 1972, National Archives, Record Group 460: Records of the Watergate Special Prosecution Force, Misuse of the IRS, Box 8.

30. "Sensitive Case Report: Hughes Tool Company," Internal Revenue Service, June 1972, National Archives, Record Group 460: Records of the Watergate Special Prosecution Force, Misuse of the IRS, Box 10.

31. Jay Horowitz, "White House Misuse of Internal Revenue Service against Lawrence F. O'Brien, Sr.," April 22, 1975, Watergate Special Prosecutor Report, National Archives, Record Group 460: Records of the Watergate Special Prosecution Force, Hughes/Rebozo Investigation, Box 111.

32. Walters, "Affidavit," June 10, 1974.

33. Walters, "Affidavit," June 10, 1974.

34. Richard Nixon, Testimony/Deposition, June 23–24, 1975, National Archives, Record Group 460: Records of the Watergate Special Prosecution Force, Nixon Grand Jury Records, Folder 9/2.

35. Skelton, "Memorandum of Interview," August 17, 1972.

36. Skelton, "Memorandum of Interview," August 17, 1972.

37. Phone call between Shultz and Walters Re: O'Brien Tax Investigation, August 29, 1972, John Ehrlichman Papers, Box 3, Hoover Institution Archive, Stanford.

38. Horowitz, "White House Misuse of Internal Revenue Service," 27.

39. Horowitz, "White House Misuse of Internal Revenue Service," 30.

40. Kutler, *Abuse of Power*, 132.

41. Kutler, *Abuse of Power*, 135.

42. Transcript of a recording of a meeting between the president, H. R. Haldeman and John Dean, Oval Office, September 15, 1972, Nixon Library.

43. Shanahan, "I.R.S. Said to Shift Plans for Rebozo."

44. George P. Shultz, interview by the author, July 10, 2017.

45. Walters, *Our Journey*, 95.

46. George P. Shultz, interview by the author, July 10, 2017.

47. George P. Shultz, interview by the author, July 10, 2017.

48. Margaret Shultz, interview by the author, August 11, 2012.

49. Henry L. Hecht, Watergate Special Prosecutor Memo, George Shultz Witness File, April 18, 1974, National Archives, Record Group 460: Records of the Watergate Special Prosecution Force, Misuse of IRS, Box 25.

50. Walters, *Our Journey*, 84–85.

51. Ferrell, *Inside the Nixon Administration*, 95.

52. George P. Shultz, interview by the author, April 26, 2012.

53. Henry Kissinger, interview by the author and Rebecca Hecht, November 14, 2014.

54. George P. Shultz, letter to Richard M. Nixon, May 8, 1974, George Shultz Papers, Box 537, Hoover Institution Archive.

55. Margaret Shultz, interview by the author, August 11, 2012.

56. Bob Young, interview by the author and Rebecca Hecht, August 29, 2014.

57. Ferrell, *Inside the Nixon Administration*, 104–105.

58. Ferrell, *Inside the Nixon Administration*, 116–117.

59. Raymond G. H. Seitz, interviews by the author and Rebecca Hecht, October 30–31, 2014.

60. George P. Shultz, "Problems and Principles," oral history interview with Paul Burnett, 98–99.

61. George P. Shultz, interview by the author, August 31, 2012.

62. George P. Shultz, interview by the author, August 31, 2012.

63. Shultz family photo and memory book, 38.

64. George P. Shultz, interview by the author and Rebecca Hecht, December 1, 2014.

65. Riley Bechtel, interview by the author, January 13, 2014.

66. George P. Shultz, interview by the author, August 31, 2012.

67. Alan Dachs, interview by the author, January 3, 2014.

CHAPTER SEVEN

1. George P. Shultz, interview by the author, May 18, 2012.

2. Haig, *Caveat*, 314.

3. Shultz, *Turmoil and Triumph*, 3–4.

4. George P. Shultz, interview by the author, May 18, 2012.

5. Reagan, *The Reagan Diaries*, June 25, 1982, 91.

6. Gwertzman, "Haig Resigns."

7. Gwertzman, "Haig Resigns."

8. Fuerbringer, "Man in the News."

9. Fuerbringer, "Man in the News."

10. Isaacson, "Shultz: Thinker and Doer," 15.

11. Goshko, "Haig Resigns at State."

12. "National Security Decision Directive 32: U.S. National Security Strategy," May 20, 1982, Ronald Reagan Presidential Library (Reagan Library), digital archive.

13. Richard Perle, interview by the author and Rebecca Hecht, November 10, 2014.

14. Raymond Seitz, interview by the author and Rebecca Hecht, October 30, 2014.

15. George P. Shultz, interview by the author and Rebecca Hecht, December 1, 2014.

16. George P. Shultz, interview by the author, May 18, 2012.

17. George P. Shultz, interview by the author, January 9, 2014.

18. Shultz, *Turmoil and Triumph*, 8.

19. Mann, *The Rebellion of Ronald Reagan*, 14. Original source: Memo to President-Elect Ronald Reagan from Richard Nixon, November 17, 1980, Nixon Library.

20. Richard M. Nixon, letter to George P. Shultz, February 25, 1982, George Shultz Papers, Box 537, Hoover Institution Archive.

21. George P. Shultz, letter to Richard M. Nixon, March 9, 1982, George Shultz Papers, Box 537, Hoover Institution Archive.

22. Schlesinger, *Journals, 1952–2000*, 553.

23. George P. Shultz, interview by the author, May 10, 2013.

24. James Baker, interview by the author and Rebecca Hecht, September 22, 2014.

25. George P. Shultz, letter to Ronald Reagan, November 1982, George Shultz Papers, Box 537, Hoover Institution Archive.

26. George P. Shultz, interview by the author, November 12, 2013.

27. At the time, the author was a member of the State Department press corps.

28. Haig, *Inner Circles*, 547.

29. Leslie H. Gelb, interview by the author and Rebecca Hecht, October 27, 2014. In the interview with the author, Gelb noted, "Haig was one of my best sources; I hated it when he was fired." At that point in Gelb's interview with Haig, Gelb stopped taking notes because, he said, if "you start taking down notes when somebody says that, they stop."

30. Allen, "When Reagan Was Shot."

31. Dowd, "Man with the President's Ear," 31.

32. Dowd, "Man with the President's Ear," 31.

33. George Elliott, letter to Caspar Weinberger, January 21, 1983, Caspar Weinberger Papers, Box 594, Library of Congress.

34. William Clark, oral history interview with Stephen F. Knott.

35. Caspar Weinberger, oral history interview with Stephen F. Knott and Russell L. Riley.

36. Caspar Weinberger, Diary, November 17, 1972, Caspar Weinberger Papers, Box 221, Library of Congress.

37. Caspar Weinberger, oral history interview with Stephen F. Knott and Russell L. Riley.

38. George P. Shultz, oral history interview with Stephen Knott.

39. Persico, *Casey*, 158–159.

40. Persico, *Casey*, 183.

41. Raymond G. H. Seitz, *Journal*, July 1982–June 1984, July 20, 1982, George Pratt Shultz Papers, Boxes 1109–1112, Hoover Institution Archive.

42. Raymond Seitz, interview by the author and Rebecca Hecht, October 30, 2014.

43. In his journal, Ray Seitz kept detailed notes about his personal conversations with Shultz and about Shultz's interactions with aides and other officials in the Reagan administration.

44. Haig, *Caveat*, 350–351.

45. Taubman, *The Partnership*, 8.

CHAPTER EIGHT

1. Reagan, *An American Life*, 115.

2. Reagan and Novak, *My Turn*, 128–129.

3. FitzGerald, *Way Out There in the Blue*, 30.

4. Ronald Reagan, "A Time for Choosing," October 27, 1964, Reagan Library.

5. Ronald Reagan, Republican National Convention Address, August 19, 1976, Reagan Library.

6. FitzGerald, *Way Out There in the Blue*, 28.

7. Schweizer, *Reagan's War*, 35–36.

8. Schweizer, *Reagan's War*, 107; Reagan, *Reagan, in His Own Hand*, 147.

9. Schweizer, *Reagan's War*, 121–122.

10. Ronald Reagan, Inaugural Address, January 20, 1981, Reagan Library.

11. Ronald Reagan, "Remarks to Members of the National Press Club on Arms Reduction and Nuclear Weapons," November 18, 1981, Reagan Library.

12. Cannon, *President Reagan*, 259.

13. Anderson and Anderson, *Reagan's Secret War*, 50.

14. Gwertzman, "Reagan Offers 4-Point Plan."

15. Ronald Reagan, "Address to Parliament on Promoting Democracy," June 8, 1982, Reagan Library.

16. Apple, "President Urges Global Crusade for Democracy."

17. George P. Shultz, interview by the author, August 12, 2019.

18. Shultz, "The Cold War."

19. Shultz, "The Cold War."

20. Shultz, *Learning from Experience*, 64.

21. Shultz, "The Cold War."

22. George P. Shultz, interview by the author, July 5, 2012.

23. George P. Shultz, interview by the author, November 12, 2013.

24. Shultz, *Turmoil and Triumph*, 119.

25. George P. Shultz, interview by the author, November 12, 2013.

26. Central Intelligence Agency, *Prospects for Accelerated Soviet Defense Effort*, August 1, 1981, Central Intelligence Agency, Freedom of Information Act Electronic Reading Room.

27. George P. Shultz, oral history interview with Stephen Knott.

28. Helmut Schmidt, interview by the author, July 22, 2013.

29. Margaret Shultz, interview by the author, August 11, 2012.

30. Alan Dachs, interview by the author, January 3, 2014.

31. Shultz, *Turmoil and Triumph*, 1133.

32. Shultz, *Learning from Experience*, xviii.

33. Raymond G. H. Seitz, interviews by the author and Rebecca Hecht, October 30–31, 2014.

34. George P. Shultz, interview by the author, April 7, 2009.

CHAPTER NINE

1. George Shultz, Statement to the Senate Foreign Relations Committee, Confirmation Hearings to be Secretary of State, 97th Cong., Congressional Record Archive, July 13, 1982.

2. Shultz, Confirmation Hearings to be Secretary of State.

3. Gwertzman, "Shultz Is Unanimously Confirmed."

4. Shultz, Confirmation Hearings to be Secretary of State.

5. Gwertzman, "Shultz Is Unanimously Confirmed."

6. George P. Shultz, interview by the author, November 12, 2013.

7. Richard M. Nixon, letter to George P. Shultz, July 27, 1982, George Shultz Papers, Box 537, Hoover Institution Archive.

8. Raymond G. II. Scitz, interviews by the author and Rebecca Hecht, October 30–31, 2014.

9. Seitz, *Journal*, July 22, 1982.

10. Seitz, *Journal*, July 24, 1982.

11. Seitz, *Journal*, July 22, 1982.

12. Seitz, *Journal*, July 22, 1982.

13. George P. Shultz, interview by the author, November 12, 2013.

14. Seitz, *Journal*, July 26, 1982.

15. Seitz, *Journal*, August 4, 1982.

16. Seitz, *Journal*, August 4, 1982.

17. Seitz, *Journal*, August 6, 1982.

18. Collier, *Political Woman*, 159.

19. Seitz, *Journal*, August 14, 1982.

20. Seitz, *Journal*, August 14, 1982.

21. Seitz, *Journal*, August 17, 1982.

22. Seitz, *Journal*, August 17, 1982.

23. Seitz, *Journal*, August 17, 1982.

24. Weinberger, *In the Arena*, 259.

25. Colin Powell, interview by the author and Rebecca Hecht, October 1, 2015.

26. George P. Shultz, interview by the author, January 9, 2014.

27. George P. Shultz, letter to Caspar Weinberger, December 1980, George Shultz Papers, Box 539, Hoover Institution Archive.

28. George P. Shultz, letter to Caspar Weinberger, August 10, 1982, George Shultz Papers, Box 539, Hoover Institution Archive.

29. Seitz, *Journal*, August 19, 1982.

30. Seitz, *Journal*, August 19, 1982.

31. George P. Shultz, oral history interview with Stephen Knott.

32. Seitz, *Journal*, August 19, 1982.

33. Seitz, *Journal*, August 26–27, 1982.

34. Gates, *From the Shadows*, 279.

35. Weinberger, *Fighting for Peace*, 157–158.

36. Powell and Persico, *My American Journey*, 303.

CHAPTER TEN

1. Helmut Schmidt, interview by the author, July 22, 2013.

2. Peter Shultz, interview by the author, December 26, 2012.

3. Peter Shultz, interview by the author, December 26, 2012.

4. William Clark, oral history interview with Stephen F. Knott.

5. William Clark, oral history interview with Stephen F. Knott.

6. Richard Perle, interview by the author and Rebecca Hecht, November 10, 2014.

7. Rozanne Ridgway, interview by the author and Rebecca Hecht, November 11, 2014.

8. Leslie Gelb, interview by the author and Rebecca Hecht, October 27, 2014.

9. Seitz, *Journal*, November 10, 1982.

10. Raymond G. H. Seitz, interviews by the author and Rebecca Hecht, October 30–31, 2014.

11. Seitz, *Journal*, September 13, 1982.

12. Richard Perle, interview by the author and Rebecca Hecht, November 10, 2014.

13. James Goodby, interview by the author, July 1, 2009.

14. "Memorandum from the President's Assistant for National Security Affairs (Clark) to President Reagan," in *Foreign Relations of the United States, 1981–1988*, 4:23.

15. Richard Perle, interview by the author and Rebecca Hecht, November 10, 2014.

16. Seitz, *Journal*, September 15, 1982.

17. Gwertzman, "Lifting of U.S. Sanctions."

18. Shultz, *Turmoil and Triumph*, 138.

19. Seitz, *Journal*, October 15, 1982.

20. Seitz, *Journal*, October 18, 1982.

21. Seitz, *Journal*, November 13, 1982.

22. Seitz, *Journal*, November 11, 1982.

23. Seitz, *Journal*, November 12, 1982.

24. Seitz, *Journal*, November 13, 1982.

25. Seitz, *Journal*, November 15, 1982.

26. Seitz, *Journal*, November 15, 1982.

27. Seitz, *Journal*, November 16, 1982.

28. "The USSR after Brezhnev," Central Intelligence Agency, Secret Analysis, November 1982, Approved for Release February 2007, 4.

29. Keenan, "Andropov."

30. Epstein, "The Andropov Hoax."

31. Seitz, *Journal*, November 23, 1982.

32. Seitz, *Journal*, November 23, 1982.

33. Shultz, *Turmoil and Triumph*, 159.

34. Shultz, *Turmoil and Triumph*, 159.

35. Seitz, *Journal*, January 7, 1983.

36. Seitz, *Journal*, January 12, 1983.

37. "Statement by Reagan on Changes."

38. Seitz, *Journal*, January 14, 1983.

39. Seitz, *Journal*, January 15, 1983.

40. Seitz, *Journal*, January 26, 1983.

41. Seitz, *Journal*, January 21, 1983.

42. Seitz, *Journal*, January 22, 1983.

43. William P. Clark, "National Security Decision Directive 75: U.S. Relations with the USSR," January 17, 1983, Ronald Reagan Library, digital archive.

44. "Memorandum from Secretary of State Shultz to President Reagan," in *Foreign Relations of the United States, 1981–1988*, 4:1.

45. Shultz, *Turmoil and Triumph*, 162.

46. Seitz, *Journal*, January 26, 1983.

47. "Memorandum from the President's Assistant for National Security Affairs (Clark) to President Reagan," in *Foreign Relations of the United States, 1981–1988*, 4:12.

48. Ronald Reagan, Address before a Joint Session of the Congress on the State of the Union, January 25, 1983, Ronald Reagan Library.

49. Seitz, *Journal*, January 28, 1983.

50. Raymond Seitz, interviews by the author and Rebecca Hecht, October 30–31, 2014.

51. Seitz, *Journal*, January 29, 1983.

52. Seitz, *Journal*, January 29, 1983.

CHAPTER ELEVEN

1. George P. Shultz, interview by the author and Rebecca Hecht, December 1, 2014.

2. George P. Shultz, interview by the author, November 12, 2013.

3. Seitz, *Journal*, February 14, 1983.

4. George P. Shultz, interview by the author, August 25, 2008.

5. Baker, *The Politics of Diplomacy*, 30.

6. Johnson, "Washington Talk."

7. Katharine Graham, toast to Shultz at a Graham dinner, December 14, 1988, George Shultz Papers, Box 534, Hoover Institution Archive.

8. Katharine Graham, letter to George Shultz, October 30, year not listed, George Shultz Papers, Box 534, Hoover Institution Archive.

9. Reagan and Novak, *My Turn*, 63.

10. Colacello, "Ronnie & Nancy."

11. Colacello, "Ronnie & Nancy."

12. Reagan and Novak, *My Turn*, 242–243.

13. Colacello, "Ronnie & Nancy."

14. George P. Shultz, interview by the author, May 18, 2012.

15. George P. Shultz, interview by the author, July 23, 2014.

16. Colin Powell, interview by the author and Rebecca Hecht, October 1, 2015.

17. Nancy Reagan, written answers to questions from the author, December 2011.

18. George P. Shultz, interview by the author, November 12, 2013.

19. Margaret Shultz, interview by the author, August 11, 2012.

20. Nancy Reagan, written answers to questions from the author, December 2011.

21. Raymond G. H. Seitz, interviews by the author and Rebecca Hecht, October 30–31, 2014.

22. Michael Deaver, oral history interview with Stephen F. Knott, James Sterling Young and Russell L. Riley, University of Virginia Miller Center, September 12, 2002.

23. Seitz, *Journal*, February 2, 1983.

24. Seitz, *Journal*, February 11, 1983.

25. Shultz, *Turmoil and Triumph*, 165.

26. Dobrynin, *In Confidence*, 517–518.

27. Shultz, *Turmoil and Triumph*, 165.

28. Whitney, "U.S. Still Giving Pentecostalists Soviet Asylum."

29. Shultz, *Turmoil and Triumph*, 165.

30. Reagan, *The Reagan Diaries*, February 15, 1983, 131.

CHAPTER TWELVE

1. Seitz, *Journal*, February 16, 1983.

2. Seitz, *Journal*, February 16, 1983.

3. Seitz, *Journal*, February 16, 1983.

4. Seitz, *Journal*, February 16, 1983.

5. Seitz, *Journal*, February 17, 1983.

6. Seitz, *Journal*, February 17, 1983.

7. Seitz, *Journal*, February 18, 1983.

8. Seitz, *Journal*, February 23, 1983.

9. Seitz, *Journal*, March 2, 1983.

10. Seitz, *Journal*, March 7, 1983.

11. Seitz, *Journal*, February 28, 1983.

12. Ronald Reagan, Speech at the Annual Convention of the National Association of Evangelicals, March 8, 1983, Reagan Library.

13. Seitz, *Journal*, March 9, 1983.

14. Seitz, *Journal*, March 10, 1983.

15. Seitz, *Journal*, March 10, 1983.

16. Seitz, *Journal*, March 11, 1983.

17. Seitz, *Journal*, March 11, 1983.

18. Seitz, *Journal*, March 12, 1983.

19. Seitz, *Journal*, March 17, 1983.

20. Shultz, *Turmoil and Triumph*, 294.

21. McGrory, "The Haigization of Shultz."

22. Oberdorfer and Goshko, "Shultz Calls for Move by Hussein."

CHAPTER THIRTEEN

1. Colin Powell, interview by the author and Rebecca Hecht, October 1, 2015.

2. Seitz, *Journal*, March 24, 1983.

3. Seitz, *Journal*, March 22, 1983.

4. Shultz, *Turmoil and Triumph*, 27.

5. Seitz, *Journal*, March 22, 1983.

6. Seitz, *Journal*, March 22, 1983.

7. Reagan, *The Reagan Diaries*, March 22, 1983, 139.

8. Seitz, *Journal*, March 23, 1983.

9. Ronald Reagan, Strategic Defense Initiative Speech, March 3, 1983, Reagan Library.

10. Weisman, "Reagan Proposes U.S. Seek New Way to Block Missiles."

11. Richard Burt, interview by the author and Rebecca Hecht, November 10, 2014.

12. Seitz, *Journal*, March 24, 1983.

13. Seitz, *Journal*, March 24, 1983.

14. Seitz, *Journal*, March 25, 1983.

15. Seitz, *Journal*, March 25, 1983.

16. Reagan, *The Reagan Diaries*, April 6, 1983.

17. Matlock, *Autopsy on an Empire*, 58.

18. Seitz, *Journal*, May 17, 1983.

CHAPTER FOURTEEN

1. Shultz, *Turmoil and Triumph*, 285.

2. Seitz, *Journal*, May 18, 1983.

3. Seitz, *Journal*, May 25, 1983.

4. Seitz, *Journal*, May 25, 1983.

5. Seitz, *Journal*, May 28, 1983.

6. Seitz, *Journal*, May 28, 1983.

7. Seitz, *Journal*, May 31, 1983.

8. Seitz, *Journal*, June 1, 1983.

9. Seitz, *Journal*, June 6, 1983.

10. Seitz, *Journal*, June 11, 1983.

11. Shultz, *Turmoil and Triumph*, 277.

12. Shultz, *Turmoil and Triumph*, 281.

13. Shultz, *Turmoil and Triumph*, 358–360.

14. Seitz, *Journal*, July 11, 1983.

15. Seitz, *Journal*, July 21, 1983.

16. Seitz, *Journal*, July 22, 1983.

17. Seitz, *Journal*, July 22, 1983.

18. Seitz, *Journal*, July 22, 1983.

19. Taubman, "Reagan Plans Rise."

20. Taubman, "Pentagon Seeking a Rise."

21. Taubman, "U.S. Seeks Increase in Covert Activity."

22. Weisman, "Reagan Denies Aim Is Bigger Presence."

23. Seitz, *Journal*, July 25, 1983.

24. Seitz, *Journal*, July 25, 1983.

25. Seitz, *Journal*, July 25, 1983.

26. George Shultz, interview by Don Oberdorfer, July 11, 1989.

27. Shultz, *Turmoil and Triumph*, 313.

28. Shultz, *Turmoil and Triumph*, 313.

29. Seitz, *Journal*, July 25, 1983.

30. Seitz, *Journal*, July 25, 1983.

31. Reagan, *The Reagan Diaries*, July 25, 1983, 169.

32. Seitz, *Journal*, July 26, 1983.

33. Seitz, *Journal*, July 28, 1983.

34. Seitz, *Journal*, July 29, 1983.

35. Seitz, *Journal*, July 29, 1983.

36. Seitz, *Journal*, July 29, 1983.

37. William Clark, oral history interview with Stephen F. Knott.

38. *Time*, cover, August 8, 1983.

39. Dowd, "Man with the President's Ear."

40. Isaacson, "Disappearing Act at Foggy Bottom."

41. Seitz, *Journal*, August 1, 1983.

42. Seitz, *Journal*, August 2, 1983.

43. Seitz, *Journal*, August 3, 1983.

44. Seitz, *Journal*, August 3, 1983.

45. Shultz, *Turmoil and Triumph*, 317. In *Turmoil and Triumph*, Shultz says that the conversation with Reagan took place on Friday, August 5, 1983. Seitz was away on Thursday, August 4, and Friday, August 5, and reported upon returning on Monday that another Shultz aide, Charles Hill, said that the conversation with President Reagan was on August 4, 1983.

46. Seitz, *Journal*, August 10, 1983.

CHAPTER FIFTEEN

1. Seitz, *Journal*, August 29, 1983.

2. The reconstruction of the final minutes of KAL 007 is based on two primary sources of information: the aircraft's flight data and cockpit recorders that were recovered by the Soviet Union shortly after the attack and secretly withheld for a decade from the International Civil Aviation Organization until Boris Yeltsin turned over the data; and recordings of Soviet defense force communications between ground controllers and pilots as the Korean flight was stalked and attacked. Cockpit Voice Recorder Database, "Korean Air 007, September 1, 1983." https://tailstrike.com/database/1-september-1983-korean-air-007/.

3. George P. Shultz, interview by the author and Rebecca Hecht, May 15, 2015.

4. Kengor and Doerner, *The Judge*, 245.

5. Reagan and Novak, *My Turn*, 260.

6. Seitz, *Journal*, September 1, 1983.

7. "Transcript of Shultz News Conference on the Korean Airliner."

8. Seitz, *Journal*, September 1, 1983.

9. Seitz, *Journal*, September 2, 1983.

10. Dobrynin, *In Confidence*, 537.

11. Seitz, *Journal*, September 1, 1983.

12. Seitz, *Journal*, September 2, 1983.

13. Seitz, *Journal*, September 3, 1983.

14. Ronald Reagan, "Address to the Nation on the Soviet Attack on a Korean Civilian Airliner and on the Observance of Labor Day," September 3, 1983, Reagan Library.

15. Gelb, "Plane Tragedy Poses Tough East-West Issues."

16. George P. Shultz, interview by the author and Rebecca Hecht, May 15, 2015.

17. Seitz, *Journal*, September 5, 1983.

18. Weisman, "Reagan, Denouncing Soviet, Bars Series of Negotiations."

19. Seitz, *Journal*, September 6, 1983.

20. Seitz, *Journal*, September 6, 1983.

21. Seitz, *Journal*, September 6, 1983.

22. Seitz, *Journal*, September 8, 1983.

23. Matlock, *Reagan and Gorbachev*, 68.

24. Seitz, *Journal*, September 8, 1983.

25. Gwertzman, "Shultz Confronts Gromyko Directly."

26. Cannon, "Justice Probe Fails to Disclose Source."

27. Baker and Glasser, *The Man Who Ran Washington*, 207–208.

28. James A. Baker III, oral history interview with James Sterling Young.

29. William Clark, oral history interview with Stephen F. Knott.

30. Seitz, *Journal*, September 15, 1983.

31. Seitz, *Journal*, September 16, 1983.

32. Seitz, *Journal*, October 13, 1983.

33. Seitz, *Journal*, October 13, 1983.

34. Seitz, *Journal*, October 13, 1983.

35. Seitz, *Journal*, October 14, 1983.

36. Seitz, *Journal*, October 14, 1983.

37. Baker and Glasser, *The Man Who Ran Washington*, 214.

38. Seitz, *Journal*, October 15, 1983.

39. Seitz, *Journal*, October 18, 1983.

40. Shultz, *Turmoil and Triumph*, 321.

41. William Clark, oral history interview with Stephen F. Knott.

CHAPTER SIXTEEN

1. Seitz, *Journal*, October 23, 1983.

2. Reagan, *The Reagan Diaries*, April 19, 1983.

3. Seitz, *Journal*, October 24, 1983.

4. Reagan, *An American Life*, 452–453.

5. Reeves, *President Reagan*, 182.

6. Naftali, *Blind Spot*, 132.

7. McFarlane and Smardz, *Special Trust*, 270.

8. Clines, "Reagan Declares Marines' Role Is 'Vital.'"

9. Ronald Reagan, "Address at Cherry Point Marine Corps Air Station on the U.S. Casualties in Lebanon and Grenada," Cherry Point, North Carolina, November 4, 1983, Reagan Library Archive.

10. Cox, "Sea Stories."

11. Cox, "Sea Stories."

12. Cox, "Sea Stories."

13. George P. Shultz, interview by the author and Rebecca Hecht, October 15, 2015.

14. George P. Shultz, interview by the author, January 9, 2014.

15. George P. Shultz, interview by the author, July 5, 2012.

16. McFarlane and Smardz, *Special Trust*, 268.

17. Caspar Weinberger, oral history interview with Stephen F. Knott and Russell L. Riley.

18. George P. Shultz, interview by the author, January 9, 2014.

19. Cox, "Sea Stories."

20. Cox, "Sea Stories."

21. Frankel, "Israeli Warplanes Bomb 2 Camps."

22. McFarlane and Smardz, *Special Trust*, 270–271.

23. National Security Planning Group 76 Document, November 12, 1983, Special Situation Group Meeting, National Security Planning Group Records, Box 91305, Reagan Library.

24. Cox, "Sea Stories."

25. McFarlane and Smardz, *Special Trust*, 270–271.

26. McFarlane and Smardz, *Special Trust*, 270–271.

27. Weinberger, *Fighting for Peace*, 161–162.

28. Reagan, *An American Life*, 463–464.

29. James Baker, interview by the author and Rebecca Hecht, September 22, 2014.

30. Colin Powell, interview by the author and Rebecca Hecht, October 1, 2015.

31. Shultz, *Turmoil and Triumph*, 646.

32. "Excerpts from Shultz's Address on International Terrorism."

33. Shultz, *Turmoil and Triumph*, 648.

34. George P. Shultz, interview by the author, July 5, 2012.

35. Shultz, *Turmoil and Triumph*, 650.

CHAPTER SEVENTEEN

1. Seitz, *Journal*, October 24, 1983.

2. Seitz, *Journal*, October 28, 1983.

3. Seitz, *Journal*, November 5, 1983.

4. Jones, *Able Archer 83*, 3; and "Editorial Note," in *Foreign Relations of the United States, 1981–1988*, 4:1420–1434.

5. George P. Shultz, oral history interview with Stephen Knott.

6. Seitz, *Journal*, November 18, 1983.

7. Seitz, *Journal*, November 30, 1983.

8. Seitz, *Journal*, December 5, 1983.

9. Seitz, *Journal*, December 9, 1983.

10. Seitz, *Journal*, December 6, 1983.

11. Seitz, *Journal*, December 13, 1983.

12. Seitz, *Journal*, December 13, 1983.

13. Seitz, *Journal*, December 15, 1983.

14. Seitz, *Journal*, December 15, 1983.

15. Seitz, *Journal*, January 10, 1984.

16. Ronald Reagan, Speech on Soviet-American Relations, January 16, 1984, Reagan Library.

17. Ronald Reagan, Speech on Soviet-American Relations, January 16, 1984, Reagan Library.

18. Smith, "Reagan's Address."

19. Gwertzman, "Shultz Vows 'Constructive Spirit.'"

20. Seitz, *Journal*, January 18, 1984.

21. Weisman, "Gromyko and Shultz Cut Tension."

22. Seitz, *Journal*, January 24, 1984.

23. Seitz, *Journal*, January 26, 1984.

24. Seitz, *Journal*, February 6, 1984.

25. Ronald Reagan, Address before a Joint Session of the Congress on the State of the Union, January 25, 1984, Reagan Library.

26. Seitz, *Journal*, February 7, 1984.

27. Seitz, *Journal*, February 8, 1984.

28. Seitz, *Journal*, February 9, 1984.

29. Mann, *The Rebellion of Ronald Reagan*, 151.

30. Seitz, *Journal*, February 10, 1984.

31. Seitz, *Journal*, February 14, 1984.

32. Seitz, *Journal*, February 22, 1984.

33. Andersen, "Hanging Tough Was Not Enough," 22.

34. Gwertzman, "Anatomy of a Resignation Rumor."

35. Seitz, *Journal*, March 21, 1984.

36. Seitz, *Journal*, March 23, 1984.

37. Seitz, *Journal*, February 22, 1984.

38. Seitz, *Journal*, February 27, 1984.

39. Seitz, *Journal*, March 2, 1984.

40. Seitz, *Journal*, March 4, 1984.

41. Seitz, *Journal*, March 6, 1984.

42. Seitz, *Journal*, March 7, 1984.

43. Seitz, *Journal*, March 7, 1984.

44. Seitz, *Journal*, March 27, 1984.

45. "Transcript of Mondale Address Accepting Party Nomination."

46. Reagan, *The Reagan Diaries*, August 11, 1984, 259.

47. Shultz, "The Cold War."

48. "Minutes of a National Security Planning Group Meeting," in *Foreign Relations of the United States, 1981–1988*, 4:978–982.

49. "Minutes of a National Security Planning Group Meeting," in *Foreign Relations of the United States, 1981–1988*, 4:978–982.

50. "Personal Note Prepared by the Deputy Secretary of State (Dam)," in *Foreign Relations of the United States, 1981–1988*, 4:986.

51. Shultz, *Turmoil and Triumph*, 482.

52. Reagan, *Reagan, in His Own Hand*, 496–498.

53. Reagan, *The Reagan Diaries*, September 28, 1984, 386–387.

54. Shultz, "The Cold War."

55. Shultz, *Turmoil and Triumph*, 485.

56. Gwertzman, "Gromyko Meetings End with Accord."

57. Clines, "Mondale Steps Up Attack on Reagan."

58. Debate between the President and Former Vice President Walter F. Mondale in Kansas City, Missouri, October 21, 1984, Reagan Library.

59. Raines, "Reagan and Mondale Clash."

60. McFarlane and Smardz, *Special Trust*, 323.

61. McFarlane and Smardz, *Special Trust*, 324.

62. McFarlane and Smardz, *Special Trust*, 286.

63. Reagan, *The Reagan Diaries*, November 14, 1984, 277.

64. Shultz, *Turmoil and Triumph*, 497.

65. Shultz, *Turmoil and Triumph*, 501.

66. "Editorial Note," in *Foreign Relations of the United States, 1981–1988*, 4:1103–1106.

67. Shultz, *Turmoil and Triumph*, 498.

68. Shultz, *Turmoil and Triumph*, 504.

69. "National Security Decision Directive 153," in *Foreign Relations of the United States, 1981–1988*, 4:1252.

70. Shultz, *Turmoil and Triumph*, 510–511.

71. Shultz, *Turmoil and Triumph*, 519.

72. Reagan, *The Reagan Diaries*, January 8, 1985, 292.

73. Reagan, *The Reagan Diaries*, January 9, 1985, 292.

74. Gwertzman, "Reagan Sees Hope."

75. Ronald Reagan, Second Inaugural Address, January 21, 1985, Reagan Library.

CHAPTER EIGHTEEN

1. Reagan, *The Reagan Diaries*, March 11, 1985, 307.

2. "Memorandum from John Lenczowski of the National Security Council staff to the President's Assistant for National Security Affairs, March 12, 1985," in *Foreign Relations of the United States, 1981–1988*, 5:4.

3. "A Leader with Style—and Impatience."

4. Ronald Reagan, letter to Mikhail Gorbachev, March 11, 1985, National Security Archive.

5. Shultz, *Turmoil and Triumph*, 530.

6. Shultz, *Turmoil and Triumph*, 531–532.

7. Shultz, *Turmoil and Triumph*, 532.

8. Oberdorfer, *From the Cold War to a New Era*, 111.

9. Thomas, "Russian Denounces Space Weapons."

10. Dobrynin, *In Confidence*, 569.

11. George P. Shultz, letter to Ronald Reagan, March 24, 1985, Jack Matlock Files, Series I Chronological File, Reagan Library.

12. Shultz, *Turmoil and Triumph*, 534.

13. Shultz, *Turmoil and Triumph*, 535.

14. Reagan, *The Reagan Diaries*, April 1, 1985, 312.

15. Shultz, *Turmoil and Triumph*, 537.

16. Shultz, *Turmoil and Triumph*, 563–564.

17. Shultz, *Turmoil and Triumph*, 565.

18. Taubman, *Gorbachev*, 257.

19. Shultz, *Turmoil and Triumph*, 566.

20. Reagan, *The Reagan Diaries*, May 17, 1985, 328.

21. "Paper Prepared in the Central Intelligence Agency," in *Foreign Relations of the United States, 1981–1988*, 5:176.

22. "Telegram from the Embassy in the Soviet Union to the Department of State," in *Foreign Relations of the United States, 1981–1988*, 5:190.

23. "Memorandum from Jack Matlock of the National Security Council Staff to the President's Assistant for National Security Affairs (McFarlane)," in *Foreign Relations of the United States, 1981–1988*, 5:192.

24. Schmemann, "Gromyko Is Named Soviet President."

25. George P. Shultz, interview by the author, July 10, 2013.

26. Shultz, *Turmoil and Triumph*, 573.

27. Eduard Shevardnadze, interview by the author, July 27, 2012.

28. Matlock, *Autopsy on an Empire*, 73.

29. Matlock, *Autopsy on an Empire*, 74.

30. "Notes of a Meeting," in *Foreign Relations of the United States, 1981–1988*, 5:333.

31. "Gorbachev's Prospective Course," in *Foreign Relations of the United States, 1981–1988*, 5:336–342.

32. Shultz, *Turmoil and Triumph*, 578–579.

33. "Memorandum from Secretary of State Shultz to President Reagan," in *Foreign Relations of the United States, 1981–1988*, 5:345.

34. "Memorandum from Secretary of State Shultz to President Reagan," in *Foreign Relations of the United States, 1981–1988*, 5:347.

35. Reagan, *The Reagan Diaries*, September 11, 1985, 352.

36. Shultz, *Turmoil and Triumph*, 576–577.

37. Shultz, *Turmoil and Triumph*, 577.

38. "Notes of a Private Meeting between Secretary of State Shultz and Soviet Foreign Minister Shevardnadze," in *Foreign Relations of the United States, 1981–1988*, 5:417.

39. "Memorandum from Secretary of State Shultz to President Reagan," in *Foreign Relations of the United States, 1981–1988*, 5:420.

40. Reagan, *The Reagan Diaries*, September 26, 1985, 355–356.

41. Shultz, *Turmoil and Triumph*, 576–577.

42. Eduard Shevardnadze, interview by the author, July 27, 2012.

43. Reagan, *The Reagan Diaries*, September 27, 1985, 356.

CHAPTER NINETEEN

1. "Memorandum from the Under Secretary of Defense for Policy (Ikle) to Secretary of Defense Weinberger," in *Foreign Relations of the United States, 1981–1988*, 5:647.

2. Shultz, *Turmoil and Triumph*, 589.

3. "Telegram from the Embassy in the Soviet Union to the Department of State: Secretary's Meeting with Gorbachev," in *Foreign Relations of the United States, 1981–1988*, 5:589.

4. Shultz, *Turmoil and Triumph*, 590.

5. Shultz, *Turmoil and Triumph*, 591.

6. Shultz, *Turmoil and Triumph*, 594.

7. Reagan, *The Reagan Diaries*, November 5, 1985, 365–366.

8. Dobrynin, *In Confidence*, 583.

9. Schmemann, "Mood in Moscow."

10. Dobrynin, *In Confidence*, 583–584.

11. Reagan, *The Reagan Diaries*, November 13, 1985, 368.

12. "Memorandum to the File: The President and Frank Carlucci," in *Foreign Relations of the United States, 1981–1988*, 6:83.

13. Schmemann, "Hectic Prelude."

14. Gwertzman, "Slim Chance Seen."

15. Gordon, "Weinberger Urges U.S. to Avoid Vow."

16. Reagan, *The Reagan Diaries*, November 17, 1985, 369.

17. Reagan, *The Reagan Diaries*, November 19, 1985, 369.

18. Gorbachev, *Memoirs*, 403.

19. James F. Kuhn, oral history interview with Stephen F. Knott and Darby Morrisroe.

20. Gorbachev, *Memoirs*, 405–406.

21. Oberdorfer, *From the Cold War to a New Era*, 143–144. The quote comes from a March 27, 1990, Oberdorfer interview with President Reagan. It is largely consistent with contemporaneous notes of the conversation between President Reagan and Mikhail Gorbachev made by the American translator in the room.

22. George P. Shultz, interview by the author, January 15, 2021.

23. "Memorandum of Conversation: Reagan-Gorbachev Meetings in Geneva, Second Private Meeting," in *Foreign Relations of the United States, 1981–1988*, 5:671.

24. Reagan, *The Reagan Diaries*, November 19, 1985, 369–370.

25. Gorbachev, *Memoirs*, 408.

26. Reagan and Novak, *My Turn*, 336–340.

27. "Memorandum of Conversation: Reagan-Gorbachev Meetings in Geneva, Dinner Hosted by the Gorbachevs," in *Foreign Relations of the United States, 1981–1988*, 5:683.

28. George P. Shultz, interview by the author, January 6, 2021.

29. Reagan, *The Reagan Diaries*, November 20, 1985, 370.

30. Shultz, *Turmoil and Triumph*, 606.

31. Cannon and Lee, "Reagan, Gorbachev Vow to Curb Arms Race."

32. Shultz, *Turmoil and Triumph*, 606.

33. Ronald Reagan, Address before a Joint Session of the Congress following the Soviet-United States Summit Meeting in Geneva, November 21, 1985, Reagan Library.

34. Cannon, "Gorbachev, Sincere, Reagan Tells Aides."

CHAPTER TWENTY

1. Shultz, *Turmoil and Triumph*, 700.

2. "Letter from President Reagan to Soviet General Secretary Gorbachev," in *Foreign Relations of the United States, 1981–1988*, 5:840.

3. "Letter from Soviet General Secretary Gorbachev to President Reagan," in *Foreign Relations of the United States, 1981–1988*, 5:886.

4. Shultz, *Turmoil and Triumph*, 709.

5. Shultz, *Turmoil and Triumph*, 706–707.

6. Shultz, *Turmoil and Triumph*, 711.

7. Shultz, *Turmoil and Triumph*, 712.

8. Schmemann, "Soviet Announces Nuclear Accident."

9. Gorbachev, *Memoirs*, 189.

10. Gorbachev, *Memoirs*, 193.

11. Shultz, *Turmoil and Triumph*, 726.

12. Shultz, *Turmoil and Triumph*, 742.

13. "Letter from President Reagan to Soviet General Secretary Gorbachev," in *Foreign Relations of the United States, 1981–1988*, 5:1098.

14. Reagan, *The Reagan Diaries*, September 7, 1986, 435.

15. Safire, "Gorbachev's Hostage."

16. "Special National Intelligence Estimate: Gorbachev's Policy toward the United States," in *Foreign Relations of the United States, 1981–1988*, 5:1116.

17. Gorbachev, *Memoirs*, 414.

18. "Memorandum from Secretary of State Shultz to President Reagan," October 2, 1986, in *Foreign Relations of the United States, 1981–1988*, 5: 1239.

19. "Dear Mr. President," Mikhail Gorbachev letter to Ronald Reagan, September 15, 1986, Reykjavik File, National Security Archive, Washington DC, NSA Electronic Briefing Book No. 203, edited by Svetlana Savranskaya and Thomas Blanton, Document 1.

20. Stephen Sestanovich, "Gorbachev's Goals and Tactics at Reykjavik," National Security Council, October 4, 1986, Reykjavik File, National Security Archive, Washington, DC, NSA Electronic Briefing Book No. 203, edited by Svetlana Savranskaya and Thomas Blanton, Document 6.

21. Gorbachev's instructions for the group preparing for Reykjavik, October 4, 1986, Reykjavik File, National Security Archive, Washington, DC, NSA Electronic Briefing Book No. 203, edited by Svetlana Savranskaya and Thomas Blanton, Document 5.

22. Matlock, *Reagan and Gorbachev*, 211. Original source: Chernyaev, *My Six Years with Gorbachev*, 81.

23. George P. Shultz, interview by the author, August 27, 2010.

24. Shultz, *Turmoil and Triumph*, 760–762.

25. Reagan, *An American Life*, 676.

26. Nitze, *From Hiroshima to Glasnost*, 429–430.

27. Shultz, *Turmoil and Triumph*, 763.

28. October 12, 1986, Entry, Charles Hill Notebooks, Charles Hill Papers, Reagan Library; and "Notes of a Conversation," in *Foreign Relations of the United States, 1981–1988*, 11:704–737.

29. Shultz, *Turmoil and Triumph*, 764.

30. Shultz, *Turmoil and Triumph*, 764–765.

31. Reagan, *An American Life*, 677.

32. This account of the summit talks is based on notes taken during the Reagan-Gorbachev meetings by American and Soviet note takers. The Soviet notes were made public by the Gorbachev Foundation in 1993 and published that year by Mirovaya Ekonomika i Mezhdunarodnye Otnosheniya. The notes were subsequently translated into English by the Foreign Broadcast Information Service and published on August 30, 1993. The State Department notes were declassified on January 14, 2000. Both sets of notes are available at the National Security Archive: Reykjavik File, National Security Archive, Washington, DC, NSA Electronic Briefing Book No. 203, edited by Svetlana Savranskaya and Thomas Blanton.

33. Notes in Reykjavik File, National Security Archive, Washington, DC, NSA Electronic Briefing Book No. 203, edited by Svetlana Savranskaya and Thomas Blanton.

34. Notes in Reykjavik File, National Security Archive, Washington, DC, NSA Electronic Briefing Book No. 203, edited by Svetlana Savranskaya and Thomas Blanton.

35. George Shultz Press Conference from Iceland, NBC, October 12, 1986; and George Shultz Press Conference from Iceland, CBS, October 12, 1986, Reagan Library.

36. George P. Shultz, interview by the author, February 3, 2010.

37. Shultz, *Turmoil and Triumph*, 775.

38. Gorbachev, *Memoirs*, 419.

39. Gwertzman, "Reagan-Gorbachev Talks End in Stalemate."

40. George P. Shultz, Address before the International House of Chicago and the Chicago Sun-Times Forum, University of Chicago, November 17, 1986, transcript produced through the US Government Printing Office.

41. George P. Shultz, interview by the author, February 3, 2010.

42. Shultz, *Turmoil and Triumph*, 780.

CHAPTER TWENTY-ONE

1. Seitz, *Journal*, April 16, 1984.

2. Seitz, *Journal*, May 3, 1984.

3. Seitz, *Journal*, May 23, 1984.

4. "Chronology: The Iran-Contra Affair: The Making of a Scandal, 1983–1988," Digital National Security Archive Collection, last updated June 16, 2015.

5. Shultz, *Turmoil and Triumph*, 793.

6. Shultz, *Turmoil and Triumph*, 794–795.

7. Shultz, *Turmoil and Triumph*, 807, 826.

8. Abraham Sofaer, interview by the author, October 12, 2020.

9. Drozdiak, "Shultz, Weinberger Dispute Tower Panel on Their Roles."

10. Walsh, *Final Report of the Independent Counsel for Iran/Contra Matters*, chap. 24, 62.

11. Walsh, *Firewall*, 334–335.

12. Walsh, *Final Report of the Independent Counsel for Iran/Contra Matters*, chaps. 24, 27.

13. Shultz, *Turmoil and Triumph*, 806.

14. Abraham Sofaer, interview by the author, October 12, 2020.

15. Shultz, *Turmoil and Triumph*, 819.

16. Shultz, *Turmoil and Triumph*, 822–823.

17. Shultz, *Turmoil and Triumph*, 837.

18. A. B. Culvahouse, oral history interview with Stephen F. Knott and Darby Morrisroe.

19. Shultz, *Turmoil and Triumph*, 838.

20. Shultz, *Turmoil and Triumph*, 841.

21. Shultz, *Turmoil and Triumph*, 853.

22. Shultz, *Turmoil and Triumph*, 863.

23. Ronald Reagan, Oval Office Address on the Iran Arms and Contra Aid Controversy, March 4, 1987, Reagan Library.

24. Ronald Reagan, Oval Office Address on the Iran Arms and Contra Aid Controversy, March 4, 1987, Reagan Library.

CHAPTER TWENTY-TWO

1. Shultz, *Turmoil and Triumph*, 870.

2. "Memorandum from the President's Assistant for National Security Affairs (Carlucci) to President Reagan," in *Foreign Relations of the United States, 1981–1988*, 6:125–126.

3. Mann, *The Rebellion of Ronald Reagan*, 53.

4. Shultz, *Turmoil and Triumph*, 884.

5. Shultz, *Turmoil and Triumph*, 870.

6. Oberdorfer, *From the Cold War to a New Era*, 219.

7. Shipler, "Shultz Visits Embassy Seder."

8. Shultz, *Turmoil and Triumph*, 887.

9. Shultz, *Turmoil and Triumph*, 891.

10. Shultz, *Turmoil and Triumph*, 893.

11. Taubman, *Gorbachev*, 395.

12. Shultz, *Turmoil and Triumph*, 895.

13. Shultz, *Turmoil and Triumph*, 897.

14. "Telegram from Secretary of State Shultz to President Reagan," in *Foreign Relations of the United States, 1981–1988*, 6:246.

15. Shipler, "Shultz Calls Pact on Mid-range Arms in Europe Possible."

16. Shultz, *Turmoil and Triumph*, 899.

17. Shultz, *Turmoil and Triumph*, 904.

18. Frank Carlucci, oral history interview with Philip Zelikow.

19. Oberdorfer, *From the Cold War to a New Era*, 235.

20. "Missile Accord; Remarks by Reagan and Shultz on Soviet Talks."

21. "Excerpts from Remarks by Yeltsin and Ligachev."

22. Shultz, *Turmoil and Triumph*, 999.

23. Shultz, *Turmoil and Triumph*, 1001.

24. "Telegram from Secretary of State Shultz to the Department of State and the White House," in *Foreign Relations of the United States, 1981–1988*, 6:207.

25. Reagan, *The Reagan Diaries*, October 25, 1987, 542.

26. Shipler, "Gorbachev, Demanding Change on 'Star Wars.'"

27. "Telegram from the Embassy in the Soviet Union to the Department of State," in *Foreign Relations of the United States, 1981–1988*, 6:486.

28. Shultz, *Turmoil and Triumph*, 1001–1002.

29. "Non-Paper Prepared by Secretary of State Shultz: How to Deal with Gorbachev," in *Foreign Relations of the United States, 1981–1988*, 6:530–531.

30. Robert Gates, "Memorandum from Director of Central Intelligence Webster to President Reagan," November 24, 1987, in *Foreign Relations of the United States, 1981–1988*, 6:592–593.

31. "Memorandum Prepared by the Deputy Director of Central Intelligence (Gates): Gorbachev's Gameplan: The Long View," in *Foreign Relations of the United States, 1981–1988*, 6:592–595.

32. Gates, *From the Shadows*, 424; and "Memorandum of Conversation: NST Experts Meeting," in *Foreign Relations of the United States, 1981–1988*, 6:595–597.

33. Gates, *From the Shadows*, 426.

34. Taubman, "The Summit."

35. "Memorandum for the Record: Secretary's Ride with Gorbachev," in *Foreign Relations of the United States, 1981–1988*, 6:608.

36. Gorbachev, *Memoirs*, 447.

37. Oberdorfer, *From the Cold War to a New Era*, 260.

38. Oberdorfer, *From the Cold War to a New Era*, 261.

39. "Memorandum of Conversation: President's Meeting with Gorbachev," in *Foreign Relations of the United States, 1981–1988*, 6:625.

40. Colin Powell, interview by the author and Rebecca Hecht, October 1, 2015.

41. Shultz, *Turmoil and Triumph*, 1011–2012. Akhromeyev committed suicide in 1991 after supporting the failed coup attempt against Gorbachev.

42. Apple, "The Summit."

43. Shultz, *Turmoil and Triumph*, 1012.

44. Gordon, "The Summit."

45. Shultz, *Turmoil and Triumph*, 1014–1015.

46. Shultz, *Turmoil and Triumph*, 1015.

47. Shultz, *Turmoil and Triumph*, 1015.

CHAPTER TWENTY-THREE

1. Kissinger, "Arms-Control Fever."

2. George P. Shultz, letter to Henry Kissinger, January 19, 1988, George Shultz Papers, Box 535, Hoover Institution Archive.

3. "Minutes of a National Security Planning Group Meeting," in *Foreign Relations of the United States, 1981–1988*, 6:910.

4. Shultz, *Turmoil and Triumph*, 1098.

5. "Memorandum from Secretary of State Shultz to President Reagan: The Moscow Summit," in *Foreign Relations of the United States, 1981–1988*, 6:1035.

6. "Minutes of a National Security Planning Group Meeting," in *Foreign Relations of the United States, 1981–1988*, 6:1038.

7. "Minutes of a National Security Planning Group Meeting," in *Foreign Relations of the United States, 1981–1988*, 6:1038.

8. Mann, *The Rebellion of Ronald Reagan*, 293.

9. Diary of Anatoly S. Chernyaev, June 19, 1988, National Security Archive.

10. Colin Powell, interview by the author and Rebecca Hecht, October 1, 2015.

11. "Memorandum of Conversation: The President's First One-on-One Meeting with General Secretary Gorbachev," in *Foreign Relations of the United States, 1981–1988*, 6:1046.

12. "Memorandum of Conversation: The President's First One-on-One Meeting with General Secretary Gorbachev," in *Foreign Relations of the United States, 1981–1988*, 6:1046.

13. "Memorandum of Conversation: The President's First One-on-One Meeting with General Secretary Gorbachev," in *Foreign Relations of the United States, 1981–1988*, 6:1046.

14. "Memorandum of Conversation: The President's First One-on-One Meeting with General Secretary Gorbachev," in *Foreign Relations of the United States, 1981–1988*, 6:1046.

15. "Memorandum of Conversation: The President's First One-on-One Meeting with General Secretary Gorbachev," in *Foreign Relations of the United States, 1981–1988*, 6:1046.

16. "Memorandum of Conversation: Organizational Questions, Summit Documents, Afghanistan," in *Foreign Relations of the United States, 1981–1988*, 6:1056.

17. Reagan, *The Reagan Diaries*, May 29, 1988, 613.

18. Reagan, *The Reagan Diaries*, May 30, 1988, 613.

19. "Memorandum of Conversation: First Plenary Meeting," in *Foreign Relations of the United States, 1981–1988*, 6:1067.

20. "Soviet Visitors in Vermont Encounter the Echo of a Dissenter."

21. Jack Matlock, cable describing the dinner, 1988 Summit Archive, May 31, 1988, National Security Archive.

22. Barringer, "Moscow Summit: Preaching to the Unconverted."

23. Taubman, "Moscow Summit."

24. Shultz, *Turmoil and Triumph*, 1103.

25. Oberdorfer, *From the Cold War to a New Era*, 298.

26. Front-page photo of Woody Lee standing beside the "football" briefcase containing the nuclear codes, *New York Times*, via Reuters, June 1, 1988.

27. Shultz, *Turmoil and Triumph*, 1104.

28. Barringer, "Moscow Summit: The Social Side."

29. Oberdorfer, *From the Cold War to a New Era*, 302.

30. Oberdorfer, *From the Cold War to a New Era*, 301–303.

31. "Memorandum of Conversation: Dinner with the Gorbachevs, Reagans, Shultzes, and Shevardnadzes," in *Foreign Relations of the United States, 1981–1988*, 6:1118–1120.

32. "Memorandum from Secretary of State Shultz to President Reagan," in *Foreign Relations of the United States, 1981–1988*, 6:1123–1124.

33. Reagan, *The Reagan Diaries*, June 1, 1988, 893–894.

34. Oberdorfer, *From the Cold War to a New Era*, 307.

35. Shultz, *Turmoil and Triumph*, 1137.

36. Shultz, *Turmoil and Triumph*, 1108.

37. Oberdorfer, *From the Cold War to a New Era*, 321.

38. Shultz, *Turmoil and Triumph*, 1108.

39. Shultz, *Turmoil and Triumph*, 1108.

40. Shultz, *Turmoil and Triumph*, 1108.

41. "The Gorbachev Era: The Implications for US strategy," American Association for the Advancement of Science Colloquium on Science, Arms Control and National Security, CIA Freedom of Information Act Electronic Reading Room Archive, October 14, 1988.

42. George P. Shultz, interview by the author, February 3, 2010.

43. Ronald Reagan, "Farewell Address to the Nation," January 11, 1989, Reagan Library.

44. Shultz, *Turmoil and Triumph*, 1135.

45. Shultz, *Turmoil and Triumph*, 1136.

46. Shultz, *Turmoil and Triumph*, 1131.

47. Altman, "Reagan's Twilight."

EPILOGUE

1. Kakutani, "Reagan Didn't Let Reality Hamper His Beliefs."

2. George P. Shultz, "Notes Taken by Mr. Shultz during Meeting with President Putin," July 13, 2007, Box 1996, Hoover Institution Archive.

3. Goodby, "The Putin Doctrine and Preventive Diplomacy," 23.

4. Barack Obama, "Remarks in Prague as Delivered," April 5, 2009, Obama White House Archive, Office of the Press Secretary.

5. The author attended the dinner described, and Kissinger made the comment to the author.

6. Background interview with a Shultz associate, by the author.

7. Carreyrou, "Hot Startup Theranos Has Struggled."

8. Tyler Shultz comments at 2022 STAT Health Tech Summit, May 24, 2022, Commonwealth Club, San Francisco, California.

9. Carreyrou, "Theranos Whistleblower Shook the Company."

10. Tyler Shultz, *Thicker than Water*, at 3:06:10.

11. Tyler Shultz, *Thicker than Water*, at 3:13:05.

12. Securities Exchange Commission, list of Theranos stockholders and number of shares each owned. Not a publicly available document. The author has a copy.

13. Carreyrou, "Tyler and George," at 37:16.

14. Dunn et al., "Ex-Theranos CEO Elizabeth Holmes Says 'I Don't Know.'"

15. Tyler Shultz, *Thicker than Water*, at 3:34:27.

16. Shultz and Baker, "A Conservative Answer to Climate Change."

17. Gordon and Caldwell, "Congress' New Chance for Clean Energy."

18. Shultz, "Life and Learning after One Hundred Years."

19. Volcker and Gyohten, *Changing Fortunes*, 118.

20. Jack Matlock, interview by the author and Rebecca Hecht, October 2, 2015.

BIBLIOGRAPHY

INTERVIEWS AND ORAL HISTORIES

With Kelsey Davidson
Itzik Nir, July 28, 2013, Tel Aviv, Israel
Shmuel Shay, July 28, 2013,Tel Aviv, Israel

With Don Orberdorfer
George P. Shultz, July 11, 1989, location unknown.

With Philip Taubman
James Baker, September 22, 2014, Houston, Texas
Riley Bechtel, January 13, 2014, San Francisco, California
Stephen D. Bechtel Jr., January 8, 2014, San Francisco, California
Lee Butler, October 1, 2010, Laguna Beach, California
Richard Combs, July 12, 2009, Three Rivers, California
Alan Dachs, January 3, 2014, San Francisco, California
Sidney Drell, February 14, 2011, Stanford, California
Susan Eisenhower, March 24, 2010, Washington, DC
Chip Farley, August 14, 2014, via telephone
Chip Farley, October 12, 2014, Santa Fe, New Mexico
James Goodby, July 1, 2009, Stanford, California
Bernard Gwertzman, October 28, 2014, New York, New York
Lord Geoffrey Howe, July 23, 2012, London
Kathy Jorgeson, August 11, 2012, Cummington, Massachusetts
Max Kampelman, March 25, 2010, Washington, DC
Sam Nunn, November 18, 2008, Atlanta, Georgia
William Perry, August 14, 2008, Stanford, California
William Perry, November 10, 2008, Stanford, California
William Perry, February 22, 2011, Stanford, California

Condoleezza Rice, April 21, 2010, Stanford, California
Helmut Schmidt, July 22, 2013, Hamburg, Germany
Eduard Shevardnadze, July 27, 2012, Tbilisi, Georgia
Alex Shultz, August 12, 2012, Cummington, Massachusetts
George P. Shultz, August 25, 2008, Stanford, California
George P. Shultz, April 7, 2009, Stanford, California
George P. Shultz, July 1, 2009, Stanford, California
George P. Shultz, September 2, 2009, Stanford, California
George P. Shultz, November 2, 2009, Stanford, California
George P. Shultz, February 3, 2010, Stanford, California
George P. Shultz, August 27, 2010, Stanford, California
George P. Shultz, April 6, 2012, Stanford, California
George P. Shultz, April 26, 2012, Stanford, California
George P. Shultz, May 18, 2012, Stanford, California
George P. Shultz, July 5, 2012, Stanford, California
George P. Shultz, August 31, 2012, Stanford, California
George P. Shultz, September 2, 2012, Stanford, California
George P. Shultz, September 5, 2012, Stanford, California
George P. Shultz, November 12, 2012, Stanford, California
George P. Shultz, November 19, 2012, Stanford, California
George P. Shultz, November 30, 2012, Stanford, California
George P. Shultz, May 2, 2013, Stanford, California
George P. Shultz, May 10, 2013, Stanford, California
George P. Shultz, November 12, 2013, Stanford, California
George P. Shultz, January 9, 2014, Stanford, California
George P. Shultz, July 23, 2014, Stanford, California
George P. Shultz, August 25, 2016, Stanford, California
George P. Shultz, July 10, 2017, Stanford, California
George P. Shultz, July 31, 2017, Stanford, California
George P. Shultz, August 12, 2019, Stanford, California
George P. Shultz, January 6, 2021, Stanford, California
George P. Shultz, January 15, 2021, Stanford, California
Margaret Shultz, August 11, 2012, Cummington, Massachusetts
Peter Shultz, December 26, 2012, Stanford, California
Tom Simons, May 19, 2009, Cambridge, Massachusetts
Abraham Sofaer, October 12, 2020, telephone interview
Barbara White, December 26, 2012, Stanford, California

With Philip Taubman and Kelsey Davidson
George P. Shultz, July 14, 2012, Stanford, California

With Philip Taubman, Kelsey Davidson and Hannah Meropol

George P. Shultz, July 10, 2013, Stanford, California

With Philip Taubman and Rebecca Hecht
James A. Baker III, September 22, 2014, Houston, Texas
Jim Baldwin, August 25, 2014, Hanover, New Hampshire
Richard Burt, November 10, 2014, Washington, DC
Leslie H. Gelb, October 27, 2014, New York, New York
Kent Hill, August 27, 2014, Washington, DC
Henry Kissinger, November 14, 2014, New York, New York
Jack Matlock, October 2, 2015, Durham, North Carolina
Richard Perle, November 10, 2014, Chevy Chase, Maryland
Colin Powell, October 1, 2015, Alexandria, Virginia
Rozanne Ridgway, November 11, 2014, Arlington, Virginia
Raymond Seitz, October 30–31, 2014, Orford, New Hampshire
George P. Shultz, December 1, 2014, Stanford, California
George P. Shultz, May 15, 2015, Stanford, California
George P. Shultz, October 15, 2015, Stanford, California
Bob Young, August 29, 2014, Vero Beach, Florida

With William Taubman
Mikhail Gorbachev, October 19, 2015, Moscow, Russia

Oral Histories and Other Interviews
James A. Baker III, oral history interview with James Sterling Young, University of
    Virginia Miller Center, June 15, 2004
Frank Carlucci, oral history interview with Philip Zelikow, University of Virginia
    Miller Center, August 28, 2001
William Clark, oral history interview with Stephen F. Knott, University of Virginia
    Miller Center, August 17, 2003
Norman Cook, interview for *Turmoil and Triumph: The George Shultz Years* (docu-
    mentary written, directed and produced by David deVries, 2010), September
    16, 2008
A. B. Culvahouse, oral history interview with Stephen F. Knott and Darby Morris-
    roe, University of Virginia Miller Center, April 1, 2004
Michael Deaver, oral history interview with Stephen F. Knott, James Sterling Young
    and Russell L. Riley, University of Virginia Miller Center, September 12, 2002
H. R. Haldeman, oral history interview with Raymond H. Geselbracht, Richard
    Nixon Presidential Library, April 13, 1988
James F. Kuhn, oral history interview with Stephen F. Knott and Darby Morrisroe,
    University of Virginia Miller Center, October 9, 2001
Lawrence F. O'Brien, oral history interview with Michael L. Gillette, Lyndon B.
    Johnson Presidential Library, July 21, 1987

George P. Shultz, oral history interview with Stephen Knott, University of Virginia Miller Center, December 18, 2002

George P. Shultz, "Problems and Principles: George P. Shultz and the Uses of Economic Thinking," oral history interview with Paul Burnett, University of California, Berkeley, 2015

Arnold Weber, oral history interview with Timothy Naftali, Richard Nixon Presidential Library, November 15, 2007

Caspar Weinberger, oral history interview with Stephen F. Knott and Russell L. Riley, University of Virginia Miller Center, November 19, 2002

ARCHIVES AND LIBRARIES

Congressional Record Archive, Washington, DC

Hoover Institution Archives, Stanford, California

Institute Archives, Massachusetts Institute of Technology, Cambridge, Massachusetts

Library of Congress, Washington, DC

Library of the Marine Corps, Quantico, Virginia

National Archives, Washington, DC

National Security Archive, George Washington University, Washington, DC

Princeton University Archives, Princeton, New Jersey

Richard Nixon Presidential Library, Yorba Linda, California

Ronald Reagan Presidential Library, Simi Valley, California

University of Virginia, Miller Center of Public Affairs, Charlottesville, Virginia

BOOKS

Anderson, Martin, and Annelise Anderson. *Reagan's Secret War: The Untold Story of His Fight to Save the World from Nuclear Disaster.* New York: Crown, 2009.

Baker, James. *The Politics of Diplomacy.* New York: G. P. Putman's Sons, 1995.

Baker, Peter, and Susan Glasser. *The Man Who Ran Washington.* New York: Penguin Random House, 2020.

Ferrell, Robert H., ed. *Inside the Nixon Administration: The Secret Diary of Arthur Burns, 1969–1974.* Lawrence: University Press of Kansas, 2010.

Cannon, Lou. *President Reagan: The Role of a Lifetime.* New York: PublicAffairs, 2008.

Chernyaev, Anatoly. *My Six Years with Gorbachev.* University Park: Pennsylvania State University Press, 2000.

Collier, Peter. *Political Woman: The Big Little Life of Jeane Kirkpatrick.* New York: Encounter, 2012.

Dobrynin, Anatoly. *In Confidence: Moscow's Ambassador to America's Six Cold War Presidents.* New York: Random House, 1995.

Fitzgerald, F. Scott. *This Side of Paradise.* New York: Scribner's, 1920.

FitzGerald, Frances. *Way Out There in the Blue: Reagan, Star Wars and the End of the Cold War*. New York: Simon and Schuster, 2001.

Freedman, Russell. *Children of the Great Depression*. New York: Clarion Books, 2005.

Gaddis, John Lewis. *The Cold War: A New History*. New York: Penguin Books, 2006.

Garten, Jeffrey E. *Three Days at Camp David: How a Secret Meeting in 1971 Transformed the Global Economy*. New York: Harper, 2021.

Gates, Bob. *From the Shadows: The Ultimate Insider's Story of Five Presidents and How They Won the Cold War*. New York: Simon and Schuster, 2007.

"George Shultz." In *The Nassau Herald: A Record of the Class of Nineteen Hundred and Forty-Two*. Princeton, NJ: Princeton University Press, 1942.

Gorbachev, Mikhail. *Memoirs*. London: Transworld Publishers, 1997.

Haig, Alexander M. *Caveat: Realism, Reagan and Foreign Policy*. New York: Scribner's, 1984.

Haig, Alexander M. *Inner Circles: How America Changed the World: A Memoir*. New York: Grand Central Publishing, 1992.

Hargrove, Erwin C., and Samuel A. Morley. *The President and the Council of Economic Advisers*. Boulder, CO: Westview Press, 1984.

Jones, Nate, ed. *Able Archer 83: The Secret History of the NATO Exercise That Almost Triggered Nuclear War*. New York: New Press, 2016.

Kengor, Paul, and Patricia Clark Doerner. *The Judge: William P. Clark, Ronald Reagan's Top Hand*. San Francisco: Ignatius Press, 2007.

Kennedy, David M. *Freedom from Fear: The American People in the Great Depression*. New York: Oxford University Press, 1999.

Kotlowski, Dean J. *Nixon's Civil Rights: Politics, Principle, and Policy*. Cambridge, MA: Harvard University Press, 2002.

Kutler, Stanley. *Abuse of Power: The New Nixon Tapes*. New York: Free Press, 1997.

Mann, James. *The Rebellion of Ronald Reagan: A History of the End of the Cold War*. New York: Viking, 2009.

Matlock, Jack F. *Autopsy on an Empire: The American Ambassador's Account of the Collapse of the Soviet Union*. New York: Random House, 1995.

Matlock, Jack F. *Reagan and Gorbachev: How the Cold War Ended*. New York: Random House, 2004.

Maynard, W. Barksdale. *Princeton: America's Campus*. University Park: Pennsylvania State University Press, 2012.

McFarlane, Robert C., and Zofia Smardz. *Special Trust*. London: Cadell and Davies, 1994.

Naftali, Timothy. *Blind Spot: The Secret History of American Counterterrorism*. New York: Basic Books, 2009.

Nitze, Paul. *From Hiroshima to Glasnost: At the Center of Decision: A Memoir*. New York: Grove/Atlantic, 1989.

Oberdorfer, Don. *From the Cold War to a New Era*. Baltimore: Johns Hopkins University Press, 1998.

Persico, Joseph E. *Casey: The Lives and Secrets of William J. Casey: From the OSS to the CIA*. New York: Viking, 1990.

Powell, Colin, and Joseph E. Persico. *My American Journey*. New York: Ballantine, 2010.

Reagan, Nancy, with William Novak. *My Turn: The Memoirs of Nancy Reagan*. New York: Random House, 1989.

Reagan, Ronald. *An American Life*. New York: Simon and Schuster, 1990.

Reagan, Ronald. *The Reagan Diaries*. Edited by Douglas Brinkley. New York: HarperCollins, 2009.

Reagan, Ronald. *Reagan, in His Own Hand: The Writings of Ronald Reagan That Reveal His Revolutionary Vision for America*. Edited by Kiron K. Skinner, Annelise Anderson and Martin Anderson. New York: Free Press, 2001.

Reeves, Richard. *President Nixon: Alone in the White House*. New York: Simon and Schuster, 2001.

Reeves, Richard. *President Reagan: The Triumph of Imagination*. New York: Simon and Schuster, 2005.

Schlesinger, Arthur M., Jr. *Journals, 1952–2000*. New York: Penguin Books, 2007.

Schweizer, Peter. *Reagan's War: The Epic Story of His Forty-Year Struggle and Final Triumph over Communism*. New York: Anchor, 2003.

Service, Robert. *The End of the Cold War*. New York: PublicAffairs, 2015.

Shultz, George P. *Ideas & Action: Featuring the 10 Commandments of Negotiation*. Erie, PA: Free to Choose Press, 2010.

Shultz, George P. *Issues on My Mind: Strategies for the Future*. Stanford, CA: Hoover Institution Press, 2013.

Shultz, George P. *Learning from Experience*. Stanford, CA: Hoover Institution Press, 2016.

Shultz, George P. *Thinking about the Future*. Stanford, CA: Hoover Institution Press, 2019.

Shultz, George P. *Turmoil and Triumph*. New York: Scribner's, 1993.

Shultz, George P., and Kenneth W. Dam. *Economic Policy beyond the Headlines*. Chicago: University of Chicago Press, 1977.

Shultz, George P., and John B. Taylor. *Choose Economic Freedom*. Stanford, CA: Hoover Institution Press, 2020.

Sobel, Robert, and Bernard S. Katz, eds. *Biographical Directory of the Council of Economic Advisers*. New York: Greenwood Press, 1988.

Strober, Deborah Hart, and Gerald Strober. *The Nixon Presidency: An Oral History of the Era*. London: Thistle Publishing, 2015.

Taubman, Philip. *The Partnership: Five Cold Warriors and Their Quest to Ban the Bomb*. New York: HarperCollins, 2012.

Taubman, William. *Gorbachev: His Life and Times*. New York: W. W. Norton, 2017.

Tumulty, Karen. *The Triumph of Nancy Reagan*. New York: Simon and Schuster, 2021.

Volcker, Paul, and Toyoo Gyohten. *Changing Fortunes: The World's Money and the Threat to American Leadership*. New York: Crown, 1992.

Walsh, Lawrence E. *Firewall: The Iran-Contra Conspiracy and Cover-Up*. New York: W. W. Norton, 1998.

Walters, Johnnie M. *Our Journey*. Macon, GA: Stroud and Hall, 2014.

Weinberger, Caspar. *Fighting for Peace: Seven Critical Years in the Pentagon*. New York: Grand Central Publishing, 1990.

Weinberger, Caspar. *In the Arena: A Memoir of the 20th Century*. New York: Regnery Publishing, 2003.

Wicker, Tom. *One of Us: Richard Nixon and the American Dream*. New York: Random House, 1991.

ARTICLES

Allen, Richard V. "When Reagan Was Shot, Who Was 'in Control' at the White House?" *Washington Post*, March 25, 2011.

Altman, Lawrence K. "Reagan's Twilight; a Special Report; a President Fades into a World Apart." *New York Times*, October 5, 1997.

Andersen, Kurt. "Hanging Tough Was Not Enough: For the Proud Secretary of State, Lebanon Is a Personal Defeat." *Time*, February 27, 1984.

Apple, R. W. "President Urges Global Crusade for Democracy." *New York Times*, June 9, 1982.

Apple, R. W. "The Summit: A Tempered Optimism; at the End of an Unlikely Journey, Reagan and Gorbachev Are Mindful of Differences." *New York Times*, December 9, 1987.

Arana-Ward, Marie. "George Shultz." *Washington Post*, March 13, 1994.

"The Architect of Nixon's New Economics." *Businessweek*, March 20, 1971.

Barringer, Felicity. "Moscow Summit: Preaching to the Unconverted; President Meets with Dissidents, and Tea and Empathy Are Served." *New York Times*, May 31, 1988.

Barringer, Felicity. "Moscow Summit: The Social Side; First Ladies' Traveling Road Show: We're Fine, Thank You Very Much." *New York Times*, May 30, 1988.

Bumiller, Elizabeth. "Gentle George and the Quiet Roar at State." *Washington Post*, December 14, 1982.

Cannon, Lou. "Gorbachev, Sincere, Reagan Tells Aides." *Washington Post*, November 23, 1985.

Cannon, Lou. "Justice Probe Fails to Disclose Source of Leaks on Mideast." *Washington Post*, December 16, 1983.

Cannon, Lou, and Gary Lee. "Reagan, Gorbachev Vow to Curb Arms Race." *Washington Post*, November 22, 1985.

Carreyrou, John. "Hot Startup Theranos Has Struggled with Its Blood-Test Technology." *Wall Street Journal*, October 16, 2015.

Carreyrou, John. "Theranos Whistleblower Shook the Company—and His Family." *Wall Street Journal*, November 18, 2016.

Carreyrou, John. "Tyler and George." *Bad Blood: The Final Chapter*. Podcast, November 11, 2021, at 37:16.

Clines, Francis X. "Mondale Steps Up Attack on Reagan." *New York Times*, October 1, 1984.

Clines, Francis X. "Reagan Declares Marines' Role Is 'Vital' to Counter Soviet in Lebanon; Toll at 192." *New York Times*, October 25, 1983.

Colacello, Bob. "Ronnie & Nancy." *Vanity Fair*, July 1998.

Dowd, Maureen. "The Man with the President's Ear." *Time*, August 8, 1983.

Drozdiak, William. "Shultz, Weinberger Dispute Tower Panel on Their Roles." *Washington Post*, March 6, 1987.

Dunn, Taylor, Victoria Thompson, Rebecca Jarvis and Ashley Louszko. "Ex-Theranos CEO Elizabeth Holmes Says 'I Don't Know' 600-Plus Times in Never-before-Broadcast Deposition Tapes." *ABC News*, January 23, 2019. https://abcnews.go.com/Business/theranos-ceo-elizabeth-holmes-600-times-broadcast-deposition/story?id=60576630.

"Economic Council: Columbia's Dr. Arthur Burns Named to President's Advisory Group." *Wall Street Journal*, March 7, 1953.

Epstein, Edward Jay. "The Andropov Hoax." *New Republic*, February 7, 1983.

"Excerpts from Remarks by Yeltsin and Ligachev." *New York Times*, July 2, 1988.

"Excerpts from Shultz's Address on International Terrorism." *New York Times*, October 26, 1984.

"The Fort Worth Project of the Armour Automation Committee." *Monthly Labor Review* 87, no. 1 (January 1964): 53–57.

Frankel, Glenn. "Israeli Warplanes Bomb 2 Camps of Moslem Radicals." *Washington Post*, November 16, 1983.

Friedman, Milton. "Why the Freeze Is a Mistake." *Newsweek*, August 30, 1971.

Fuerbringer, Jonathan. "Man in the News; a Man of Many Worlds." *New York Times*, June 26, 1982.

Garchik, Leah. "George Shultz on Trump's Talks in Finland." *San Francisco Chronicle*, July 20, 2018.

Gelb, Leslie H. "Plane Tragedy Poses Tough East-West Issues." *New York Times*, September 4, 1983.

Goodby, James. E. "The Putin Doctrine and Preventive Diplomacy." Introduction by George Shultz on "The Need for Consensus on American Goals." *Foreign Service Journal*, November 2014, 23.

Gordon, Kate, and Jake Caldwell. "Congress' New Chance for Clean Energy." *CNN*, November 9, 2010.

Gordon, Michael R. "The Summit: Avoiding the Obstacles; U.S. and Soviet Put Aside Thorniest Issues and End Summit Talks on a Positive Note." *New York Times*, December 11, 1987.

Gordon, Michael. "Weinberger Urges U.S. to Avoid Vow on 1979 Arms Pact." *New York Times*, November 16, 1985.

Goshko, John M. "Haig Resigns at State." *Washington Post*, June 26, 1982.

Griffith, Erin, and Erin Woo. "Elizabeth Holmes Is Found Guilty of Four Counts of Fraud." *New York Times*, January 3, 2022.

Gwertzman, Bernard. "Anatomy of a Resignation Rumor." *New York Times*, February 25, 1984.

Gwertzman, Bernard. "Gromyko Meetings End with Accord on Further Talks." *New York Times*, September 30, 1984.

Gwertzman, Bernard. "Haig Resigns over Foreign Policy Course, but Cites No Issues; Reagan Names Shultz." *New York Times*, June 26, 1982.

Gwertzman, Bernard. "Lifting of U.S. Sanctions." *New York Times*, November 15, 1982.

Gwertzman, Bernard. "Reagan-Gorbachev Talks End in Stalemate as U.S. Rejects Demand to Curb 'Star Wars.'" *New York Times*, October 13, 1986.

Gwertzman, Bernard. "Reagan Offers 4-Point Plan for U.S. Soviet Missile Curbs and Force Limits in Europe." *New York Times*, November 19, 1981.

Gwertzman, Bernard. "Reagan Sees Hope of 'New Dialogue' with the Russians." *New York Times*, January 10, 1985.

Gwertzman, Bernard. "Shultz Confronts Gromyko Directly on Plane Incident." *New York Times*, September 9, 1983.

Gwertzman, Bernard. "Shultz Is Unanimously Confirmed by the Senate as Secretary of State." *New York Times*, July 16, 1982.

Gwertzman, Bernard. "The Shultz Method." *New York Times*, January 2, 1983.

Gwertzman, Bernard. "Shultz Vows 'Constructive Spirit' in Stockholm Talk with Gromyko." *New York Times*, January 13, 1984.

Gwertzman, Bernard. "Slim Chance Seen for Arms Agenda at Summit Talks." *New York Times*, November 11, 1985.

"A Heavyweight Champ, at Five Foot Two: The Legacy of Milton Friedman, a Giant among Economists." *The Economist*, November 23, 2006.

Isaacson, Walter. "Disappearing Act at Foggy Bottom." *Time*, August 8, 1983.

Isaacson, Walter. "Shultz: Thinker and Doer." *Time*, July 5, 1982.

"Job Corps Test Won by Nixon in Senate." *New York Times*, via United Press International, May 14, 1969.

Johnson, Julie. "Washington Talk: The First Lady; Strong Opinions with No Apologies." *New York Times*, May 25, 1988.

Kakutani, Michiko. "Reagan Didn't Let Reality Hamper His Beliefs, Shultz Says." *New York Times*, May 4, 1993.

Keenan, George F. "Andropov." *New York Times*, November 14, 1982.

Kissinger, Henry A. "Arms-Control Fever." *Washington Post*, January 19, 1988.

"A Leader with Style—and Impatience." *New York Times*, March 12, 1985.

Levine, Richard J. "Campus to Cabinet: Shultz, an Ex-Professor, Wins General Acclaim as Secretary of Labor." *Wall Street Journal*, June 9, 1969.

Livingston, J. A. "Keyserling Faces Test: To Find Niche for Economic Advisors." *Washington Post*, May 17, 1950.

Martin, Douglas. "Johnnie M. Walters, I.R.S. Chief Who Resisted Nixon's Pressure, Dies at 94." *New York Times*, June 26, 2014.

McGrory, Mary. "The Haigization of Shultz: Mr. Calm Guy Self-Destructs." *Washington Post*, March 6, 1983.

"Miss M. L. Pratt the Bride of B. E. Shultz—Her Uncle Officiates." *New York Times*, January 23, 1916.

"Missile Accord; Remarks by Reagan and Shultz on Soviet Talks." *New York Times*, via the Associated Press, September 19, 1987.

Naughton, James M. "Shultz Quietly Builds Up Power in Domestic Field." *New York Times*, May 31, 1971.

Oberdorfer, Don, and John M. Goshko. "Shultz Calls for Move by Hussein: Jordan's Decision Sought on Joining Middle East Talks." *Washington Post*, March 13, 1983.

"On Leadership: Dr. George Shultz and Dr. William Perry." Podcast. Vice Provost for Graduate Education, Stanford, April 29, 2009. https://podcasts.apple.com/es/podcast/vice-provost-for-graduate-education/id385783323?l=en.

"Opportunities Open to Negroes in Management." *Chicago Tribune*, ProQuest Historical Newspapers database, October 25, 1965. https://www.proquest.com/docview/180044580/BF38AC61E7FE4223PQ/2?accountid=14026.

Pichler, Joseph A. "The Job Corps Transition." *Industrial and Labor Relations Review* 25, no. 3 (April 1972): 336–353.

Raines, Howell. "George Wallace, Symbol of the Fight to Maintain Segregation, Dies at 79." *New York Times*, September 15, 1998.

Raines, Howell. "Reagan and Mondale Clash on Arms Control and C.I.A. in Debate over Foreign Policy." *New York Times*, October 22, 1984.

Raskin, A. H. "Said Nixon to George Shultz: 'I Track Well with You.'" *New York Times*, August 23, 1970.

Reston, James. "A Tendency to Stay Too Long." *New York Times*, March 14, 1974.

"Rev. George S. Pratt Is Dead: Rector Emeritus of All Souls' Anthon Memorial Church." *New York Times*, July 29, 1920.

Safire, William. "Gorbachev's Hostage." *New York Times*, September 4, 1986.

Schmemann, Serge. "Gromyko Is Named Soviet President." *New York Times*, July 2, 1985.

Schmemann, Serge. "Hectic Prelude: Both Sides Anticipate Some Tough Summit Talk." *New York Times*, November 10, 1985.

Schmemann, Serge. "Mood in Moscow: Limited Summit Expectations." *New York Times*, November 8, 1985.

Schmemann, Serge. "Soviet Announces Nuclear Accident at Electric Plant." *New York Times*, April 29, 1986.

"Senate-House Conferees Vote to Wipe Out President's Council of Economic Advisers." *Washington Post*, via the United Press International, March 13, 1953.

Shanahan, Eileen. "I.R.S. Said to Shift Plans for Rebozo." *New York Times*, July 11, 1974.

Shipler, David K. "Gorbachev, Demanding Change on 'Star Wars,' Bars Summit Talk Now." *New York Times*, October 24, 1987.

Shipler, David K. "Shultz Calls Pact on Mid-range Arms in Europe Possible." *New York Times*, April 16, 1987.

Shipler, David K. "Shultz Visits Embassy Seder for Noted Soviet Dissidents." *New York Times*, April 14, 1987.

Shultz, George P. "The Agricultural Program of the Tennessee Valley Authority." Princeton University Senior Thesis, Princeton University, Department of Economics, 1942.

Shultz, George P. "The Chicago Economics Tradition." *Free to Choose Network*, n.d. https://www.freetochoosenetwork.org/programs/turmoil_triumph/explore/shultz/economics_tradition.php.

Shultz, George P. "On Trust." *Foreign Service Journal*, November 2020, 26–29.

Shultz, George P. "Prescription for Economic Policy: 'Steady as You Go.'" Address before the Economic Club of Chicago, April 22, 1971. https://web.stanford.edu/~johntayl/Shultz%20on%20Steady%20As%20You%20Go.pdf.

Shultz, George P., and James A. Baker III. "A Conservative Answer to Climate Change." *Wall Street Journal*, February 7, 2017.

Shultz, Tyler. *Thicker than Water.* Audible Originals Podcast, 2020, at 3:06:10.

Silk, Leonard. "Milton Friedman Nobel Laureate." *New York Times*, October 17, 1976.

Smith, Hendrick. "Reagan's Address: Trying a New Tactic." *New York Times*, January 17, 1984.

"Soviet Visitors in Vermont Encounter the Echo of a Dissenter." *New York Times*, via the Associated Press, May 7, 1983.

"Statement by Reagan on Changes." *New York Times*, January 13, 1983.

Taubman, Philip. "Moscow Summit: Unmaking History and Debating Rights; Reagan Presses Gorbachev on Church and Civil Rights; 'Sermonizing' Annoys Hosts." *New York Times*, May 31, 1988.

Taubman, Philip. "Pentagon Seeking a Rise in Advisors in Salvador to 125." *New York Times*, July 24, 1983.

Taubman, Philip. "Reagan Plans Rise in Military Moves in Latin America." *New York Times*, July 23, 1983.

Taubman, Philip. "The Summit: The Stakes Are Momentous; What Gorbachev Wants: Success in the Talks, Spurring Change at Home." *New York Times*, December 9, 1987.

Taubman, Philip. "U.S. Seeks Increase in Covert Activity in Latin America." *New York Times*, July 25, 1983.

"Text of 2 Memos on I.R.S." *New York Times*, June 28, 1973.

Thomas, Jo. "Russian Denounces Space Weapons." *New York Times*, December 18, 1984.

"Transcript of Mondale Address Accepting Party Nomination." *New York Times*, July 20, 1984.

"Transcript of Nixon's Program on Television Introducing His Cabinet Members." *New York Times*, December 12, 1968.

"Transcript of Shultz News Conference on the Korean Airliner." *New York Times*, September 2, 1983.

"U. of C. Appoints Dean of Business College." *Chicago Daily Tribune*, August 22, 1962.

Weinstein, Michael M. "Paul A. Samuelson, Economist, Dies at 94." *New York Times*, December 13, 2009.

Weisman, Steven R. "Gromyko and Shultz Cut Tension, Reagan Says, but Did Not Agree." *New York Times*, January 21, 1984.

Weisman, Steven R. "Reagan Denies Aim Is Bigger Presence in Latin Countries." *New York Times*, July 27, 1983.

Weisman, Steven R. "Reagan Proposes U.S. Seek New Way to Block Missiles." *New York Times*, March 24, 1983.

Weisman, Steven R. "Reagan, Denouncing Soviet, Bars Series of Negotiations; Demands It Pay for Jet Loss." *New York Times*, September 6, 1983.

Whitney, Craig R. "U.S. Still Giving Pentecostalists Soviet Asylum." *New York Times*, November 9, 1978.

Wren, Daniel. "Joseph N. Scanlon: The Man and the Plan." *Journal of Management History* 15, no. 1 (2009): 20–27.

COLLECTIONS OF GOVERNMENT DOCUMENTS

Comptroller General of the United States. "Review of Economic Opportunity Programs." 91st Cong., 1st Sess., 1969, 53.

"Federal Government Finances and Employment." *Statistical Abstract of the United States*. Sec. 14. Washington, DC: Government Printing Office, 1969.

Foreign Relations of the United States, 1981–1988. Volume IV, *Soviet Union, January 1983–March 1985*. Edited by Elizabeth C. Charles. Washington, DC: Department of State, Government Printing Office, 2021.

Foreign Relations of the United States, 1981–1988. Volume V, *Soviet Union, March 1985–October 1986.* Edited by Elizabeth C. Charles. Washington, DC: Department of State, Government Printing Office, 2020.

Foreign Relations of the United States, 1981–1988. Volume VI, *Soviet Union, October 1986–January 1989.* Edited by James Graham Wilson. Washington, DC: Department of State, Government Printing Office, 2016.

Foreign Relations of the United States, 1981–1988. Volume XI, *Soviet Union, START I.* Edited by James Graham Wilson. Washington, DC: Department of State, Government Printing Office, 2021.

Prospects for Accelerated Soviet Defense Effort. Central Intelligence Agency Freedom of Information Act Electronic Reading Room, August 1, 1981.

"A Resolution Authorizing and Directing the Committee on the Judiciary to Investigate Whether Sufficient Grounds Exist for the House of Representatives to Exercise Its Constitutional Power to Impeach Richard M. Nixon." Statement of Information, Hearings before the Committee on the Judiciary, Book VIII, para. 22–23. Internal Revenue Service.

Transcript of press conference with George Shultz. US Department of Labor, September 23, 1969.

Transcript of press conference with George Shultz and Arthur Fletcher. White House Roosevelt Room, Office of the White House Press Secretary, December 20, 1969.

"The USSR after Brezhnev," Central Intelligence Agency, Secret Analysis, November 1982, 4. Approved for release February 2007.

Walsh, Lawrence E. *Final Report of the Independent Counsel for Iran/Contra Matters.* United States Court of Appeals for the District of Columbia Circuit, Division for the Purpose of Appointing Independent Counsel, Division No. 86-6, 1993, chap. 24, 62.

Correspondence and Pamphlets

Cook, Norman Sr. Letter to Norman Cook Jr. August 26, 1945.

Cox, Samuel J. "Sea Stories: 1976–2004." Unpublished written narratives provided to the author by Cox.

Henley, Wallace. "A History: School Desegregation and the Role of the Cabinet Committee on Education." Prepared at the request of George P. Shultz, under the direction of Robert C. Mardian, White House Central Files, Nixon Presidential Library.

Shultz Family. "Shultz Family History." Family document, December 13, 2004. Provided to the author by George P. Shultz.

Shultz, Birl. Letter to George P. Shultz, December 15, 1932. Courtesy of George P. Shultz.

Shultz, George P. "The Cold War." Monograph provided to the author, June 2, 2015.

Shultz, George P. Letter to Nancy Ager, August 7, 1996. Courtesy of Nancy Ager.

Shultz, George P. Letters to Norman Cook, 1944–1945. Courtesy of the Cook family.

Shultz, George P. "Life and Learning after One Hundred Years." Personal pamphlet, Stanford, California, December 13, 2020.

Shultz, George P. "My Early Life." Personal pamphlet, Stanford, California, December 1991.

INDEX